ORGANIZATIONS AND HUMAN BEHAVIOR

A Book of Readings

Edited by
Gerald D. Bell

PRENTICE-HALL, INC., Englewood Cliffs, New Jersey

To Tina, Kathryn, and Sharon

Current printing (last digit):

10 9 8 7 6 5 4 3 2 1

Library of Congress Catalog Card No.: 67–12975
Printed in the United States of America
C

PRENTICE-HALL INTERNATIONAL, INC., *London*
PRENTICE-HALL OF AUSTRALIA, PTY. LTD., *Sydney*
PRENTICE-HALL OF CANADA, LTD., *Toronto*
PRENTICE-HALL OF INDIA (PRIVATE) LTD., *New Delhi*
PRENTICE-HALL OF JAPAN, INC., *Tokyo*

PREFACE

As teachers, we often forget about students. What are their interests? How do they learn? What excites them? These questions often get buried under our research and professional activities. We are interested in these issues but the image of "publish or perish" hanging over our heads, among other things, reduces our concern. It seemed to me that one practical way to move away from this bind was to attempt to develop classroom materials—such as reading assignments—around the students. That is, if parts of a course design were seriously formulated with student learning as the primary goal, some of our teaching pressures would be reduced and learning hopefully enhanced. These ideas, which we have outlined, were the basis for this reader.

The guiding framework used to prepare the reader was to select articles which 1) were highly interesting, 2) readable by the students, 3) had been tested in class, 4) covered the main topics within the area of behavior in organizations, and 5) were of high quality from a professional point of view.

The book is designed to be used as a basic part of the reading material for courses in industrial-organizational sociology, organizational behavior, human, personnel, and industrial relations or industrial psychology. It has been developed to be used alone or for courses which utilize texts, paperbacks, and/or selected reading assignments. It has been kept short so that it will be easily adaptable in the above types of courses.

The author's teaching experience as well as studies in the behavioral sciences suggest that students, and others, are most interested in things in which they are involved, and with which they have had experience. With these postulates in mind I have selected articles, whenever feasible, that directly pertain to student life and to things with which students have had personal experience. Articles such as "Button-down Collar Culture," and "America's Upper Class Colleges," refer directly to student life, and at the same time are excellent contributions to the topics of the sections in which they are included. Also, reading such as "The Religious Factor and Economic Behavior," "Some Effects of Close and Punitive Styles of Supervision," are examples of articles devoted to topics with which most students have had much involvement and experience.

Each of the articles included in the reader has been tested in different courses to find how it affects students. The articles included are those that have met the test of student as well as professional scrutiny, according to the guiding principles of selection mentioned above—interest, readability, coverage, and quality.

In determining the main sections to be covered in the reader, the author, during the past two years, conducted an informal survey among leading industrial sociologists and organizational behaviorists to gain their views concerning the major areas of the field. With their theories, a review of the literature in the major journals, and with the author's own perspectives the sections were determined.

I am grateful for the exciting and stimulating introduction to organizational behavior provided in seminars in industrial and organizational sociology at Yale University taught by Stanley H. Udy, Jr. and Chris Argyris. Wilbert E. Moore and Neil J. Smelser provided helpful comments on the plan of the reader. Several colleagues have provided many useful ideas which have contributed to the formulation of the book. Thanks go to Charles M. Bonjean, Christine D. Bell, Claude S. George, Elton F. Jackson, Dannie J. Moffie, Judson B. Pearson, Charles Perrow, Robert Rehder, F. J. Roethlisberger, Richard L. Simpson, and James D. Thompson.

G. D. B.

CONTRIBUTORS

CHRIS ARGYRIS
Professor of Industrial
  Administration,
Yale University

ALFRED BALK
Freelance writer,
Evanston, Illinois

ALEX BAVELAS
Institute for Defense Analysis

GERALD D. BELL
Assistant Professor, School
  of Business Administration
  and of the Institute for
  Research in Social Science;
University of North Carolina
Visiting Assistant Professor,
Harvard School of Business
  (1966–67).

PETER M. BLAU
Professor of Sociology,
University of Chicago

ALBERT A. BLUM
Assistant Professor,
  School of Labor
  and Industrial Relations,
Michigan State University

CHARLES M. BONJEAN
Assistant Professor of Sociology
University of Texas

JAMES S. DAVIE
Coordinator of Research,
  Department of
  University Health; Dean,
  Timothy Dwight College;
  Member of Department of
  Sociology;
Yale University

FRED DAVIS
Project Director,
  Nursing Careers Project,
  San Francisco Medical Center,
University of California

ROBERT C. DAY   Assistant Professor of Sociology,
Washington State University

EMILE DURKHEIM   Late French Sociologist

AMITAI ETZIONI   Associate Professor of Sociology;
Research Associate, Institute
of War and Peace Studies,
Columbia University

FRED H. GOLDNER   Assistant Professor,
Graduate School of Business,
Columbia University

CHARLES C. GORDON   Lecturer in Sociology,
University of North Carolina

DAVID GRANICK   Professor of Economics,
University of Wisconsin

ROBERT H. GUEST   Professor of Organization
and Administration,
The Tuck School,
Dartmouth College

ROBERT L. HAMBLIN   Professor of Sociology,
Washington University

A. PAUL HARE   Associate Professor and
Chairman, Department of
Sociology and Anthropology,
Haverford College

GENE R. HAWES   Consultant,
Columbia University Press

ROBERT L. HEILBRONER   Visiting Professor, Graduate
Faculty,
New School for Social Research

GERHARD LENSKI   Professor of Sociology and
Research Professor in the
Institute for Social Science,
University of North Carolina

JAMES G. MARCH

Dean, College of Letters
and Science,
University of California, Irvine

DAVID C. McCLELLAND

Professor of Psychology;
Chairman, Department of
Social Relations,
Harvard University

ROBERT K. MERTON

Giddings Professor of Sociology,
Columbia University

DELBERT C. MILLER

Professor of Sociology and
Business Administration,
Indiana University

EDNA E. RAPHAEL

Senior Research Associate,
Division of
Community Studies,
Institute for Juvenile Research,
Chicago

W. RICHARD SCOTT

Associate Professor of Sociology,
Stanford University

HERBERT A. SIMON

Associate Dean, Graduate School
of Industrial Administration,
Carnegie Institute of Technology

RICHARD L. SIMPSON

Professor of Sociology and of the
Institute for Research
in Social Science,
University of North Carolina

HARVEY L. SMITH

Professor of Sociology and
Director of Social Research
University of North Carolina

GEORGE STRAUSS

Professor, School of
Business Administration and
Institute of Industrial
Relations,
University of California,
Berkeley

CHARLES R. WALKER
Director, Yale Technology Project, Ret'd.,
Curator, Yale Technology and Society Collection

MAX WEBER
Late German Sociologist

WILLIAM H. WHYTE, JR.
Editor of *Fortune* Magazine

HAROLD L. WILENSKY
Professor of Sociology,
Research Sociologist in the Institute of Industrial Relations,
University of California, Berkeley

CONTENTS

ORGANIZATIONS AND HUMAN BEHAVIOR

Introduction*

The investigation of the life of a person on his job within large organizations is passing from its early descriptive beginnings to a more rigorous, hypothesis-testing phase. Students of industrial sociology, personnel and human relations, management, public administration, and industrial psychology have begun to approach the study of human behavior in organizations by focusing on similar problems in a systematic fashion. The major topics which we investigate are:

1. The individual—the interrelationships of his personality and work
2. The characteristics of organizations and occupations
3. The relationships of the first two factors to industrial and economic dimensions of society

The study of these three areas has been approached increasingly from a comparative point of view. For example, in our analysis of organizational behavior we examine production, research, and service firms; hospitals, prisons, universities, and secondary and elementary schools; small groups, military establishments, restaurants, and unions.[1]

This comparative approach—that is, studying similar problems in different organizations—has contributed greatly to our understanding of behavior in formal organizations. The comparative method has enabled us to begin to move from merely describing specific types of institutions as such to examining structures and processes found in all types of organizations—factors such as leadership, motivation, and communication.

Let us now turn to an analysis of the three major areas of individual, organizational, and industrial behavior. Our purpose here is to suggest a theoretical framework into which the readings included in this volume can be placed. A noted deficiency in the field of organizational behavior is the absence of a theoretical base.[2] Thus, although our attempt merely touches on many complex topics, we hope to contribute to the development of organizational theory.

The Individual— His Personality and Work

Why do people work?

Picture for a moment a classroom in a typical American university. The students are freshmen, in the latter stages of adolescence, who are in a major phase of life as far as determining their future is concerned. Undoubtedly, one of the most central questions with which they are concerned is "Why do I have to work?" Most of us could readily picture the expression on the face of a boy as he looks dreamily out the window of one of his "boring" classes; we could imagine equally well the energy that suddenly erupts when he darts from his classes at the end of the day. The gloom stems from disinterest in his work and the glee from anticipation of desired recreational and social activities. On the other hand, many students devote great effort to their studies. How do the millions of youth in our society develop their feelings about work activities? Why do individuals differ in their propensities for working hard?

Viewed in an historical perspective, the reason that men in primitive societies worked was in order to survive; to have food and shelter they had to hunt, gather, and build. But as economies developed to

---

* *Prepared especially for this volume. See notes.*

1

the stage at which individuals no longer needed to devote all their waking hours to working for survival, they did not stop working. Over a long period of time, norms evolved which stated that a respected citizen was one who worked. Consequently, when a child grew up, he worked not only for survival but also because his family, friends, and traditions taught that a good person should work.

If our hypothetical student, then, attempts to determine why he must work, he will probably first examine the influence of his family. Parents have a significant effect in two areas of an individual's occupational life. First, the type of occupation one pursues is most often related to that of his father and other close relations. Actors, physicians, plumbers, and executives come from families whose fathers have occupations closely related to acting, medical, plumbing, and executive endeavors. Second, parents are a major stimulus in the development of the ambition that an individual carries with him into his occupation. The extent to which a person wants to be "the best" in whatever he does is often a result of the degree to which his parents urge him to excel.[3]

Along with the family, the socioeconomic class in which one is raised also acts as a significant determinant of the type of occupation and the level of achievement an individual will pursue. "Son, you can go out and get a job and make as much money as I am" is often the advice of fathers in lower working classes. The middle and upper social groups view education more favorably and go to extensive means to persuade their children of the value of educational opportunities. Consequently, children from the higher social classes are more likely to achieve educational and occupational success than those from lower socioeconomic categories. Joseph Kahl's findings suggest that, among children bright enough to do well in college nine out of ten whose fathers are in major white-collar jobs expect to go to college, whereas only three out of ten

plan to do so in the group whose fathers are laborers.[4]

The per cent of students in any given high school who are from the upper, middle, or lower classes also seems to act as a channel through which social-class values are transmitted to youth. Wilson investigated the relationship between social-class composition of high schools and aspiration levels of teenagers in the San Francisco area.[5] His findings suggest that when youth from middle and upper-class families attend a high school whose student body is mostly from lower classes, their aspiration levels are significantly lowered. On the other hand, when working-class children attend high schools in which most students are from higher socioeconomic groups, their desires for educational and occupational achievements are greatly increased.[6]

An individual's religious background and affiliations also influence his desires to work and to achieve. Gerhard Lenski examined the association between religious affiliation and occupational mobility in Detroit and found that Jews tended to move up the socioeconomic ladder most often, white Protestants second, Catholics third, and nonwhite Protestants least often.[7]

The environmental stimuli given above are highly related to an individual's personality structure generally and to his motivational orientations toward work specifically. In looking at personality we assume that one's motivation, or the amount of effort he puts forth to obtain a goal, is generally determined by two factors. The first is the amount of incentive value or satisfaction he attaches to the achievement of a particular goal. The second is his perception of how likely he

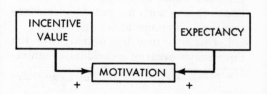

will be to attain the goal if he tries. The more that both of these factors are present, the higher is one's motivation.[8]

An individual's family, social class, school, and religious affiliations help to develop and to transmit the idea that specific levels of satisfaction are to be found in hard work. In the upper classes particularly, these reference groups aid children in attaining successes and offer rewards for achievements. In the lower socioeconomic groups, however, children's expectations of attainment of high occupational goals are not increased as much by parental intervention and encouragement. Consequently, motivation toward work and achievement is lessened when fewer satisfactions are attached to achieving work goals and when there has been little past success in attaining one's goals.

With these thoughts in mind it is important to ask, "What additional personality characteristics does an individual bring to his job?"

What an Individual Brings to the Job

"Every man is in certain respects (a) like all other men, (b) like some other men, (c) like no other man."[9]

Like all other men

Similarities among men stem from common features in their biological endowments, their physical environments, and their societies and cultures .[10] A.H. Maslow has further specified the similarities among men by developing five general types of human needs: physiological, safety, belonging, status, and self-actualization needs.[11]

Physiological needs are controlled mostly by chemical and neural conditions—the needs for food, water, oxygen, sex, and rest. Safety needs refer to the individual's tendencies to protect himself against extremes of temperature and to avoid serious injuries. Needs to belong involve desires to have satisfying relationships with others. Status needs concern a person's desires to be well thought of by his peers, to present a favorable image to his associates, and to maintain his positions in his reference groups. Finally, the need for self-actualization is a general category which refers to desires to act out or to fulfill his potential abilities and personal characteristics. We shall have more to say about this latter need shortly.

These universalities of human life produce similar patterns of personality for men of all times, places, and races;[12] however, these factors are often taken for granted and seldom commented upon.

Like some other men

Some individuals tend to have more personal traits in common than do others. Often this is a result of being socialized in comparable social groups—such as the same social class, occupation, age and sex group. One hundred individuals from the upper socioeconomic class are more similar than another hundred persons from a mixture of classes. A group of seafaring people have many similar qualities, even if they come from different communities. Professional golfers are more alike than a random sample of weekend golfers, and so forth.

Like no other men

Finally, we know that every individual is in many respects like no other man. Each person's way of behaving, of reacting to similar events, of attempting to succeed in his occupation and family life is unique. This uniqueness is caused by the fact that each person receives a different biological makeup and diverse social and cultural experiences. An identical quality, quantity, and sequence of such determining influences is never reproduced.[13]

As Clyde Kluckhohn and Henry A. Murray comment, "In personal relations, in psychotherapy, and in the arts, this uniqueness of personality usually is, and should be, accentuated."[14] But in the study of individuals and their working lives we must necessarily often look for uniformities and general categories common to many persons. In order to formulate theories and design organizations of work so that most people may find fulfillment in their jobs and organizations may meet their objectives efficiently, we are forced to trim off subtle differences in personalities and to look at similarities between them.

One attempt to examine similarities of individuals as they are related to work behavior is made by Chris Argyris.[15] He is concerned with the personal characteristics that workers bring to the job and with the extent to which they find opportunities to fulfill their needs in their occupations. In other words he is most interested in a person's self-actualization in his work.

Argyris hypothesizes that as individuals progress from childhood to adulthood they develop certain personality characteristics. They tend to :

1. Progress from being passive to being more active
2. Develop from a state of dependency upon others to one of relative independence as adults—that is, they gain ability to "stand on their own two feet"
3. Progress from being able to behave in only a few ways to behaving in many different ways
4. Move from having erratic, shallow interests to having deeper, more complex interests
5. Develop from having a short time perspective (that is, their behavior is primarily determined by their present situation) to having a longer time perspective as adults—past, present, and future
6. Progress from a lack of awareness of self to an awareness of and control over self as adults.[16]

Argyris suggests, then, that most individuals in our Western world develop personality characteristics as suggested above. He further postulates that the more an individual is able to exercise these "adult traits," the more he will be self-actualized. The question which then looms important is, "To what extent do present organizations and occupations encourage this more 'mature behavior'?" We shall examine this question in more detail in the readings in Part Five on work and personality. Let us now explore the characteristics of organizations in which individuals participate.

Organizational Behavior

What is an organization?

What do you think would be the similarities and differences between such a social gathering as a cocktail party and such a formal organization as a work department in General Motors? First we can note that, in addition to the fact that both units consist of a group of individuals who interact in ways that are meaningful to each other, both groups have the characteristics shown in Table 1.

TABLE I

Elements	Cocktail Party	Corporate Work Department
1. Goals	To have a good time and make friends and business contacts	To produce a certain product or service, make money, and establish satisfactory relations at work
2. Rules	Members know that customary rules in such a gathering limit their behavior—for example, one usually doesn't get drunk at the boss's house	Rules define one's work habits, time of arrival and departure, dress, physical movements, sick leaves, vacations, and so forth
3. Roles	Each member tends to act in a way expected of him	Each member is usually

	by other members, and he in turn expects others to act in specific ways—for example: the "funny person" is expected to tell jokes and make others laugh; the host to provide the raw materials and to allocate them among the members; the wives to keep their husbands on their feet, and so forth	given specific duties to perform, and others expect him to carry them out at given times and in given ways
4. Hierarchy of Authority	From hosts, special guests, average guests, down to the caterers	From supervisors, foremen, skilled workers, down to the unskilled employees
5. Reward System	Special attention is given to those who excel in reaching the group goals; ostracism, gossip, and negative comments are given to the deviant members of the group	Financial rewards, fringe benefits, and promotions are given to the "good" employees and withheld from the "bad" ones
6. Forms of Compliance	Members react to control attempts of leaders or to the reward system in different ways: some by complete satisfaction and cooperation, some by negative reactions and antagonism	Members react in given ways to the control structure of the organization: by forming unions, by lowering production, by absenteeism, or, in general, by being satisfied and cooperating or being dissatisfied and not cooperating
7. Coordination Activities	Each member adjusts his behavior to others; he aids others in getting drinks, finding seats— when someone spills something, others help to clean it up	Members adjust their speed of production to that of other members of the work group; if one job breaks down the other workers have to change their activities
8. Communication Patterns	Communication patterns exist, everyone is in communication with the host, and the host must try to make sure all members are engaged in communicating with each other; those highest in the hierarchy of authority tend to initiate and receive the most communication	Communication networks exist among different members of the group, depending upon need for coordination, physical proximity, and ease of communication; communication is initiated usually from the top but is often encouraged to come from lower-ranking members

While you were examining Table 1, you probably said, "Yes, both of these units seem to have the elements mentioned, but they still are not the same." It is true that a social gathering and a formal organization are not easily compared. There are several characteristics which distinguish these units. One important difference is that these groups vary considerably in the degree to which each of the elements—goals, rules, roles, hierarchy of authority, and so forth—is clearly and formally defined. In a corporation the rules are usually better specified than those of a social gathering. Similarly, the roles expected of one within his occupational pursuits are much more precisely taught than those expected of him at a party. Thus, when individuals interact in a group, their behavior will possess the major elements of organization listed in Chart I but will very greatly in the extent to which the elements are clearly specified. (Blau and Scott discuss this factor in their article in Section II.) When these elements are explicitly defined, we term the organization a formal one.

Another difference between a social gathering and a corporation or formal organization lies in the importance assigned to the major elements of organization. A social organization, be it a community, fraternity, or party, may place more emphasis upon communication among members, whereas a business establishment might stress the importance of rules. (These notions will be explored more fully in the articles in Part Two.)

Since most occupations in our society are performed within the more formalized organizations, we will concentrate on these units in this volume.

If we are to examine formal organizations, it would be helpful to place these major elements of organization in a theoretical framework. The framework we find helpful in trying to understand behavior in organizations is fourfold. That is, we define the things which go on in organizations as falling primarily into one of four general categories:

1. Technical system
2. Administrative system
3. Personal or socioemotional system
4. Cultural system[17]

Lets us first examine these *components,* then discuss their *interrelationships,* and finally place the total organization within its *societal context.*

Technical system

The technical system contains those activities which are performed in carrying out major productive tasks that enable the organization to develop a service or product. Workers on the assembly line in a production plant, most physicians and nurses in a hospital, professors and secretaries in a university are carrying out major productive tasks of their respective organizations.

Administrative system

This component of organizations encompasses activities performed by those who primarily attempt to allocate resources and people, set goals and policies, integrate and coordinate activities performed in the technical system, plan the recruitment of new members, and, finally, encourage full participation from the present membership.

Personal system

This component of organization consists of those activities which express and result from members' feelings about their jobs and work relationships. The satisfactions individuals derive from their jobs, the involvement and participation they find in their work, the emotional climate of their relationships with fellow employees have significant effects upon their behavior.

Cultural system

The cultural properties of an organization consist of its guiding traditions, values, philosophies, and goals. Those activities concerned with and symbolizing the articulation of the society's and the organization's customs also fall within this category.

Interrelationships Between the Four Components of Organization

As you have probably begun to notice, each of the above four components is highly interrelated; each category influences and is influenced by the others. We shall briefly summarize the consequences of each component for the others.

Effects of the technical system

The technical or productive activities encourage management to shape the *administrative components* in particular ways. One investigation suggests, for example, that the more unpredictable the demands of production workers' jobs are, the less inclined will management be to establish rules or close supervision.[18] In other words, the more unpredictable the work demands are, the more decentralization and flexibility there will be.

The technical activities also are highly related to the *personal system*. Many bemoan, for example, the loss of variety placed at the worker's hand.[19] Social commentators say that lack of novelty in work is producing a robot-like society.[20] And research suggests that job satisfaction and productivity suffer when variety is taken out of work.[21] In the view of an auto assembly-line employee:

My job is to see that the body fits properly, clean the steering column. After the body is dropped on the chassis, I put in four bolts; I spray rubber dough on the toe plates, I hook up a striplight wire; I clip speedometer cables in two places, place a cover shield on the steering column. That's about it in a minute and a half.... Anybody that wants to work on a moving line has got rocks in his head.... It's rough. It's too steady, too much of a pace.[22]

Dislike of routine jobs is not the exclusive preserve of skilled and unskilled workers, however, for supervisors and staff personnel also seem to be unfavorably disposed toward repetitive activities.[23] Correspondingly, Andrews reports that scientists who perform several different tasks, such as teaching and administration, along with their research tend to have higher performance rates than those who work full time only at research.[24]

In a similar vein, with the advance of automation and technology, the growing specialization of tasks is producing numerous occupations for which we have no names. Consequently, many workers' occupational titles lack social significance outside of their trade or company. As Robert K. Merton comments, "The splintering of work tasks involves *loss of public identity of the job*. Who but a chosen few, for example, can distinguish a fin sticker in an automobile plant from other radiator-core assemblers."[25]

In general then, the more routine the productive activities the less satisfied the workers. The physical distribution of jobs and the work flow also have important influences upon the interactions between workers and consequently upon their attitudes.

Finally, technical activities have an important, yet subtle, impact upon the *culture* of an organization; the goals and traditions of an institution are constantly being reshaped as technological changes of both machinery and knowledge occur. For example, as we acquire more knowledge and skill in methods of retraining criminals, many of the prisons whose goals have traditionally been only to protect society have adopted new policies for rehabilitating society's deviants. (See Donald R. Cressey's article in Part Three for a discussion of this point.)

Effects of the administrative system

The administrative component of an organization also has important effects upon the other three categories—technical, personal, and cultural. When workers are dissatisfied with their jobs, administrators often reshape the nature of productive processes. They expand workers' responsibilities, make their tasks more difficult to perform, and consequently alter the nature of *technical activities*. In turn, the very fact that administrators select the types of products and services as well as the necessary machinery indicates that they mold the technical system to a large degree.[26]

The effects of administrative activities upon the *personal adjustments* of employees are probably quite familiar to the readers. The style of leadership your professor uses in conducting his class affects your attitudes toward him. When your summer-job supervisor rewarded you by telling you that your work was very good or by giving you a raise, you undoubtedly felt highly gratified—a response which signifies the impact of administrative activities upon your personal life at work. Similarly, you probably have been in situations in which you had to wait in line for a long time or had to get "four copies of a form filled out and signed by twelve people." The anger which you may have felt at the lack of planning again demonstrates the close connection between administrative structure and personal adjustments.

The *culture characteristics* of a bureaucracy are molded by management's efforts in many, often subtle, ways. The employees of Eastman Kodak, for example, have relatively little interest in forming unions, since they are so happy with their patterns of work, communication, and reward. In other companies, however, the practicies of administrators stimulate much unrest and general union development.

Several of the early glass-manufacturing establishments formed in the 1800's in America were started by entreprenuers of European descent. The cultures of their corporations quickly took on the values of the managers: their goals were to produce quality products; their leisure time was devoted to European recreational pursuits. When mass production started to appear, these companies were often the slowest to change their patterns of activity. For example, quality and craftsmanship remained high in priority, and quantity (mass production) was of little importance. Consequently, new technological developments were not readily adopted by these firms.

Effects of the personal system

The satisfaction an individual experiences in his work, the sentiments he holds toward his supervisors, and the feelings he experiences with his co-workers are important determinants of his life within an organization. One's personal adjustment has significant effects first of all upon the *technical activities*. If a worker is highly dissatisfied with his job, for example, he may damage the machinery of production, slow down his output, or perform his tasks in a nonspecified manner.

Workers' personal sentiments also have important effects upon the *administrative activities*. Employees' feelings are expressed to administrators by various means—through union grievances, work slowdowns, subtle comments, and/or more direct communications. Managers usually desire the positive commitment of employees and invest a great amount to time, energy, and money to gain it. If employees are discontented, administrators often alter the communication networks, reward structures, styles of leadership, and so forth, in order to increase satisfaction and commitment.

Finally, the feelings and personal relationships of employees are translated over time into *cultural traditions* and policies of the organization. When new members are brought into a work group, they are taught by the older employees the history of their relationships with various supervisors, the feelings generally held about specific jobs, and so forth.

Individuals, Organizations, and Society

Thus far we have explored what an individual brings to his job regarding his personality and the characteristics of organizations in which he participates. Now we would like to ask, "How are these two topics related to the society in which the individual works?" To examine the interrelationships between the individual, organization, and society, let us break down the activities and sentiments which characterize a society into four categories similar to those we used to examine formal organizations:

1. Technology
2. Administrative activities
3. Personal factors
4. Cultural system

Technology

Every society has a technological base of skills, tools, and knowledge that the members and the formal organizations of society use to provide for their needs. Each society differs in the degree of development of technology. The United States, for example, has a more advanced level of technology in such things as space and medicine than do other countries such as Pakistan or India. Thus, the kinds of productive activities which can be carried on in space centers and hospitals will be much different in America than in India. The structure of organizations within a society, then, is highly dependent upon the levels of technology existing in that society.

As a society becomes more industrialized, the rate of technological innovation increases. Similarly, the larger organizations within a society tend to develop relatively higher levels of technological change than do the smaller units. Consequently, larger enterprises experience greater pressures for reorganization of their administrative, personal, and cultural systems.

Current developments in automation and computers symbolize the rapid rate of technological change in the Western world. Automation refers to the development of productive equipment which no longer needs to be designed to fit the physical and mental capacities of man (that is, where machines control their own operations, they correct their own errors and move products throughout the entire production cycle). Automation has created numerous changes in occupations and organizations within our society. In Esso's refinery at Fawley, England, for example, six men on any shift process 5.5 million gallons of crude oil a day.[27]

The electronic processing of information by computers has also had significant effects upon patterns of work. In the kitchens of the Sara Lee Company in Deerfield, Illinois, the computer system not only mixes and bakes twelve different kinds of cakes, but also packages them, freezes them, stores them, starts them on their way to the store, and even handles some of the bookwork. Their computers direct operations at about 15,000 points in the plant, issue 180,000 instructions every three seconds, monitor some 300 variables in the cake-baking process, and scan 200 incoming messages per second. The kinds of occupations that exist, the patterns of supervision, and worker relationships are significantly altered by these types of changes in technology.

A potential disaster which many see as a consequence of automation is unemployment. Although there is no clear evidence, the balance of arguments suggests that automation is reducing the number of jobs available in our society more rapidly than it is creating new ones. In farming, for example, in 1949 one man could produce enough food for 15 people, but in 1960 one man could produce enough for 24. Since 1945 productivity in bituminous-coal mining rose 96 per cent, but employment fell by 262,000. Railroad productivity has increased by 65 per cent, and employment has declined by 540,000.[28] Although all these changes are not due solely to automation, a large part of the decrease in number of jobs does result from the elimination of unskilled jobs by automatic machinery.

Furthermore, automation makes work physically easier, thereby permitting older people to work with automatic machinery. Such a development may be a mixed blessing, however, since unions and management are encouraging earlier retirement because of unemployment and older individuals—often the most difficult to reeducate—need to be retrained for new jobs in automation.

Automation has potentially positive

benefits, however, since it creates new jobs which require higher education and occupational skills. It frees human hands from physical labor and increases leisure time. These consequences must remain in the "potential benefits" category, however, because although there are increased demands for highly trained employees, society's ability to produce enough trained individuals lags behind the demand. Similarly, with physical labor having been taken out of most jobs, we are now confronted with problems of keeping people physically fit. And finally, even though free time for leisurely pursuits has grown, many people are unhappy with extra time on their hands. With these thoughts in mind, let us now direct our attention to the administrative components of society.

Administrative activities

The mechanisms by which (1) natural and human resources are allocated to different industries, organizations, and occupations, (2) productive and social activities of individuals are coordinated, and (3) participation in society's activities are rewarded and punished are much less clearly defined in a society than in a formal organization. Yet, in most societies, mechanisms of government or administrative control develop which attempt to handle the above types of problems.

Societies, usually in the form of governmental units, differ in the degree to which they formalize their attempts to solve problems of allocation, coordination, rewards, and so forth. Russia, for example, has an explicit, pervasive governmental apparatus, whereas certain underdeveloped countries have merely informal governmental networks. The occupations and formal organizations in Russia, correspondingly, are significantly affected by the governmental rules, whereas in the emerging nations the organizations and occupations are less intensely circumscribed.

The operations of governmental units also determine the very existence of many types of organizations and occupations. For example, as the war on poverty expands in America so does the growth of public-service agencies and occupations.

Similarly, research grants which support a large share of our universities' budgets are increasingly awarded to those conducting research on "poverty topics." Consequently, a significant share of our world of work is being molded by governmental directives.

We have mentioned ways in which a society's administrative components are related to occupations and organizations within it. Our intent is to suggest patterns in which the two are associated rather than to present a comprehensive analysis of their interrelationships. Let us now turn to an examination of the personal-social components of a society.

The personal factors

In our discussions of what motivates people to work and of what people bring to their jobs, we mentioned several dimensions of personal feelings and desires of members of a society and the relationship of these to their work lives. A few additional comments should be made about individuals' personal adjustments in their social lives and their participation in organizations.

Research suggests that the more satisfied an individual is with his family life, the more happy he is with his job. In turn, when individuals are asked how satisfied they are with life in general, their answers are closely associated with their satisfactions in family and occupational roles.[29] Thus, one's personal adjustment at work is highly related to his participation in other major societal activities.

Several investigations also suggest a close association between a person's mental health and his vocational success. J. P. LaPlace gave personality tests to forty-nine major-league baseball players (they were designated as being successful in their occupation). And he administered the tests to sixty-four minor-league players (they were labeled as being less successful). When LaPlace compared the personality profiles of the two groups, he found that the minor-league players showed a greater tendency to take personal offense, a lower ability for self-discipline, and less capacity to adjust to activities requiring initiative.[30] In another study, although the reasons for the relationships are not clear, L. G. Wispe and K. E. Lloyd found that among the forty-three insurance agents who made up a district force of a life insurance company, the salesmen who preferred a more democratic type of relationship with their supervisors had better sales records than those who preferred authoritarian relationships.[31]

The above investigations suggest the close connection between personal characteristics and adjustments on the job. Let us turn our attention now to the final dimension of society within which formal organizations exist—the cultural aspects.

Cultural system

Each society has a culture with unique patterns in which the organizations of work operate. For example, in our society the belief in democracy is carried into the plant, and employees expect to be given opportunities to participate in making decisions about work activities. And the "good" supervisor is one who controls his subordinates in a democratic fashion.

A significant contrast to these patterns is displayed in other societies, however. In Germany before World War II employees wanted their supervisors to be domineering. Leaders who sought subordinates' suggestions were disliked and thought to be weak, unfit supervisors.[32] In Japan (although this practice is currently undergoing revision) employees are hired for life and are seldom fired even if they are poor workers. In a sense, when an individual is hired he becomes a member of a large family. Pay and promotion are based upon the number of children the employee has and upon his seniority.[33] These examples illustrate the tendency of employees reared in a given culture to carry values consistent with that culture into organizations and occupations in which they participate.

Conclusions

The above general introduction and theoretical scheme will hopefully aid the reader in tying the separate articles included in this book into a meaningful, theoretical framework. Part One, "Industry and Society," is concerned with associations between the four major elements of society as they are related to organizations and occupations. In Part Two our interest turns to the study of general theories of formal organizations. In Part Three we explore patterns of organization found within different types of enterprises—hospitals, voluntary associations, prisons, unions, and colleges. The relationships between technical activities, administration, personal, and cultural patterns are the focus of attention in Part Four entitled the "Internal Dimensions of Organization." In Part Five we examine the all-important question, "What are the consequences of industry, organization, and occupation for an individual's personality?" And finally, the diversity in patterns of behavior and values associated with different types of occupations is discussed in Part Six.

* For helpful comments on several of the ideas presented herein, thanks go to Paul R. Lawrence, Jay W. Lorsch, and James D. Thompson.

[1] See Stanley H. Udy, Jr., "The Comparative Analysis of Organizations," in James G. March, ed., *Handbook of Organizations* (Chicago: Rand McNally & Co., 1965).

[2] See my forthcoming report of a survey of industrial sociologists in the United States, "Views of Industrial Sociologists."

[3] Gerald D. Bell, "Processes in the Formation of Adolescents' Aspirations," *Social Forces* (December, 1963), pp. 179–186; Richard L. Simpson, "Parental Influence and Social Mobility," *American Sociological Review, 27* (August, 1962), pp. 517–522.

[4] Joseph Kahl, "Adolescent Ambition" (unpublished doctoral dissertation, Harvard University, 1951).

[5] Alan Wilson, "Residential Segregation of Social Classes and Aspirations of High School Boys," *American Sociological Review, 24* (December, 1959).

[6] *Ibid.*

[7] Gerhard Lenski, *The Religious Factor* (Garden City, N.Y.: Doubleday & Co., Inc., 1961).

[8] Harry J. Crockett, Jr., "The Achievement Motive and Differential Occupational Mobility in the United States," *American Sociological Review, 27* (April, 1962), pp. 191–204.

[9] Clyde Kluckhohn and Henry A. Murray, *Personality in Nature, Society, and Culture* (New York: Alfred A. Knopf, Inc., 1955), p. 53.

[10] *Ibid.*

[11] A. H. Maslow, *Motivation and Personality* (New York: Harper & Row, Publishers, Inc., 1954).

[12] Kluckhohn and Murray, *op. cit.*, p. 54.

[13] *Ibid.*, p. 55.

[14] *Ibid.*

[15] Chris Argyris, *Personality and Organization* (New York: Harper & Row, Publishers, Inc., 1957).

[16] *Ibid.*

[17] These ideas were developed in Professor Stanley H. Udy's Seminar in Industrial Sociology, Yale University, 1963.

[18] Gerald D. Bell, "The Influence of Technological Components of Work Upon Management Control," *Academy of Management Journal,* 8 (June, 1965), pp. 127–133.

[19] Erich Fromm, *The Sane Society* (New York: Holt, Rinehart & Winston, Inc., 1955).

[20] George Orwell, *1984* (New York: New American Library of World Literature, Inc., 1955).

[21] Nancy C. Morse, *Satisfaction in the White-Collar Job* (Ann Arbor: Institute for Social Research, University of Michigan, 1953); Chris Argyris, *Understanding Organizational Behavior* (Homewood, Illinois: Dorsey Press, Inc., 1960); F. C. Mann and L. K. Williams, "Some Effects of the Changing Work Environment in the Office," *Journal of Social Issues,* 18 (1962), pp. 90–101.

[22] Thomas M. Lodahl, "Patterns of Job Attitudes in Two Assembly Technologies," *Administrative Science Quarterly,* 8 (March, 1964), pp. 482–520.

[23] Frank Friedlander and Eugene Walton, "Positive and Negative Motivations Toward Work," *Administrative Science Quarterly,* 9 (September, 1964), p. 206.

[24] Frank M. Andrews, "Scientific Performance and Time in Teaching or Administration," *Administrative Science Quarterly,* 9 (September, 1964), p. 193.

[25] Robert K. Merton, *Social Theory and Social Structure,* Rev. ed. (New York: Free Press of Glencoe, Inc., 1957), p. 564.

[26] Gerald D. Bell, "Formality Versus Flexibility in Complex Organizations: A Comparative Investigation Within a Hospital" (unpublished doctoral dissertation, Yale University, Department of Sociology, 1965).

[27] Arnold B. Barach, *U.S.A. and Its Economic Future* (New York: The MacMillan Company, 1964).

[28] *Ibid.*

[29] See forthcoming article by Gerald D. Bell and James Molitor.

[30] J. P. LaPlace, "Personality and Its Relationship to Success in Professional Baseball," *Research Quarterly of the American Association of Physical Education, and Recreation,* 25 (1954), pp. 313–319.

[31] L. G. Wispe and K. E. Lloyd, "Some Situational and Psychological Determinants of the Desire for Structured Interpersonal Relations," *Journal Of Abnormal and Social Psychology,* 51 (1955), pp. 57–60.

[32] Kurt Lewin, *Resolving Social Conflicts* (New York: Harper & Row, Publishers, Inc., 1948).

[33] James C. Abeglen, *The Japanese Factory* (New York: Free Press of Glencoe, Inc., 1958).

part one INDUSTRY AND SOCIETY

We are so accustomed to the presence of large industrial establishments, transportation facilities, mass communication, and education in
contemporary America that we often find it difficult to clearly understand what the preindustrial world was like. In the article, "The Making of Economic Society," Robert Heilbroner paints an exciting portrait
of how our modern economic society evolved from quite "primitive"
conditions. He considers two main questions: (1) "How does a society
organize to produce the goods and services it needs for its own perpetuation?"; and (2) "How does a society distribute the fruits of its
production among the members of society?"

We next turn to the famous theories of the German sociologist, Max
Weber, concerning the "Protestant Ethic and the Spirit of Capitalism."
Weber suggests that one of the key factors in the rapid industrialization
of Western Europe and the United States was the "Protestant Ethic"
which viewed work as a calling. Weber's work raises the question, "Are
there differences today in socioeconomic success between Protestants,
Catholics, and Jews?" The contemporary article by Gerhard Lenski
attempts to answer this classical question raised by Weber. In the
"Religious Factor and Economic Behavior," Lenski reports significant
differences in the extent of socioeconomic mobility of these religious
groups.

In viewing the relationships between industry and society, the statement has been made

> We survive in rich nations because the tasks we cannot do ourselves are
> done for us by an army of others on whom we can call for help. If we
> cannot grow food, we can buy it; if we cannot provide for our needs
> ourselves, we can hire the services of someone who can.[1]

The causes and consequences of this occupational specialization are the
interests of the French sociologist, Emile Durkheim, in his article "The
Division of Labor in Society."

Carrying the notion of the division of labor into modern society,
Harold Wilensky discusses a dilemma which results from industrialization and increased division of labor. In "Mass Society and Mass
Culture," Wilensky suggests that occupational specialization encourages
individual differences in personality and behavior among the members
of a society. On the other hand, the mass utilization of communications

---

[1] Robert L. Heilbroner, *The Making of Economic Society* (Englewood
Cliffs, N. J.: Prentice-Hall, Inc., 1962), p. 3.

13

media (TV, radio, magazines) and education are suggested to be producing similarities among members of society. Which force is most influential? Is everyone in our society becoming more alike? Or are we maintaining uniqueness because of occupational differences? Wilensky's findings suggest that mass culture is winning out and that Americans are losing a large share of their individuality. In the final selection Charles Bonjean examines the important relationships between changes in economic conditions, occupational structures and personality characteristics of our society.

1 The Making of Economic Society

ROBERT L. HEILBRONER

Man, it is repeatedly said, does not live by bread alone. Indeed, when we look back over the pageant of what is usually called "history," the humble matter of bread hardly strikes the eye at all. Power and glory, faith and fanaticism, ideas and ideologies are the aspects of the human chronicle that crowd the pages of history books. If the simple quest for bread is a moving force in human destiny, it is well concealed behind what one philosopher-historian has called "that history of international crime and mass murder which has been advertised as the history of mankind."[1]

Obviously, man cannot live without bread. Like every other living thing, as the imperious first rule of continued existence, the human being must eat. And this first prerequisite is less to be taken for granted than at first appears, for the human organism is not, in itself, a highly efficient mechanism for survival. From each one hundred calories of food it consumes, it can deliver only about twenty calories of mechanical energy. On a decent diet, man can produce just about one horsepower-hour of work daily, and with that he must replenish his exhausted body. With what is left over, he is free to build a civilization.

In many countries, the basic expectation of human continuity is far from assured. In the vast continents of Asia and Africa, in the Near East, even in some countries of South America, brute survival is the problem which stares humanity in the face. Millions of human beings have died of starvation or malnutrition in our present

era, as countless hundreds of millions have died over the long past. Whole nations are acutely aware of what it means to face hunger as a condition of ordinary life: it has been said, for example, that the Egyptian *fellah*, from the day he is born to the day he dies, never knows what it is to have a full stomach. In many of the so-called underdeveloped nations, the life span of the average person is less than half of ours. Not many years ago, an Indian demographer made the chilling calculation that of one hundred Asian and one hundred American infants, more Americans would be alive at sixty-five than Indians at *five!* The statistics, not of life, but of premature death throughout most of the world are overwhelming and crushing.

The individual and society

For most Americans, these considerations are apt to seem tragic but remote. None of us is conscious of a struggle for existence to anything resembling a life-or-death degree. That it might be possible for us to experience severe want, that we might ever know in our own bodies the pangs of hunger experienced by an Indian villager or a Bolivian peon is a thought which it is nearly impossible for us to entertain seriously.

Short of a catastrophic war, it is highly unlikely that any of us ever will know the full meaning of the struggle for existence. Nonetheless, even in our prosperous and secure society, there remains, however unnoticed, an aspect of life's precariousness, a reminder of the underlying problem of survival. *This is our helplessness as economic individuals.*

It is a curious fact that as we leave the most impoverished peoples of the world, where the human being with his too few

From Robert L. Heilbroner, The Making of Economic Society, *pp. 1–16.* © *1962. Reprinted by permission of Prentice-Hall, Inc., Englewood Cliffs, New Jersey.*

calories of energy scratches out for himself a bare subsistence, we find the economic insecurity of the individual many times multiplied. The solitary Eskimo, Bushman, Indonesian, Nigerian, left to his own devices, will survive a considerable time. Living close to the soil or to their animal prey, the peoples with the lowest standards of living in the world can sustain their own lives, at least for a while, almost single-handed. With a community numbering only a few hundred, they can live indefinitely. Indeed, a very large percentage of the human race today lives in precisely such fashion—in small, virtually self-contained peasant communities which provide for their own survival with a minimum of contact with the outside world. This large majority of mankind suffers great poverty, but it also knows a certain economic independence. If it did not, it would have been wiped out centuries ago.

When we turn to the New Yorker or the Chicagoan, on the other hand, we are struck by exactly the opposite condition, by a prevailing ease of material life, coupled at the same time by an extreme *dependence* of the individual in his search for the means of existence. In the great metropolitan areas where most Americans live, we can no longer envisage the solitary individual or the small community surviving, short of looting warehouses or stores for food and necessities. The overwhelming majority of Americans have never grown food, caught game, raised meat, ground grain into flour, or even fashioned flour into bread. Faced with the challenge of clothing themselves or building their own homes, they would be hoplessly untrained and unprepared. Even to make minor repairs in the machines which surround them, they must call on other members of the community whose business it is to fix cars, or repair plumbing, or whatever. Paradoxically, perhaps, the richer the nation, the more apparent is this inability of its average inhabitant to survive unaided and alone.

We survive in rich nations because the tasks we cannot do ourselves are done for us by an army of others on whom we can call for help. If we cannot grow food, we can buy it; if we cannot provide for our needs ourselves, we can hire the services of someone who can. This enormous *division of labor* enhances our capacity a thousandfold, for it enables us to benefit from other men's skills as well as our own.

Along with this invaluable gain comes a certain risk. It is a sobering thought, for example, that we depend on the services of only 180,000 men—fewer than one out of every three hundred people working in the nation—to provide us with that basic commodity, coal. An even smaller number of workers—less than 75,000—are responsible for running the locomotives which haul all the nation's rail freight and passenger service. A still smaller number—under 15,000—comprises our total commercial aircraft pilot and navigator crew. A failure of any one of these very small groups to perform its functions would cripple us: in the case of airplane pilots, slightly; in the case of locomotive engineers, badly; in the case of coal miners, perhaps disastrously. As we know, when from time to time we face a bad strike, our entire economic machine may falter because a strategic group ceases to perform its accustomed tasks.

Along with the abundance of material existence as we know it goes a hidden vulnerability: our abundance is assured only insofar as the organized cooperation of huge armies of people is to be counted upon. Indeed, our continuing existence as a rich nation hinges on the tacit precondition that the mechanism of social organization will continue to function effectively. *We are rich, not as individuals, but as members of a rich society, and our easy assumption of material sufficiency is actually only as reliable as the bonds which forge us into a social whole.*

Economics, scarcity, and social organization

The problem of how societies forge and maintain bonds which guarantee their material survival is the basic problem of economics.

We know very little of how those bonds may have been originally constituted. Man appears on the scroll of history as a member of a group, and as such, the beneficiary of a rudimentary division of labor. Yet it is noteworthy that even his simplest familial cooperation is not achieved instinctually as is the case with communities of insects or of animals, but must be buttressed with magic and taboo and maintained by more or less repressive laws and traditions.

Strangely enough, then, we find that man, not nature, is the source of most of our economic problems. To be sure, the economic problem itself—that is, the need to struggle for existence—derives ultimately from the scarcity of nature. If there were no scarcity, goods would be as free as air, and economics, at least in one sense of the word, would cease to exist as a social preoccupation.

And yet if the scarcity of nature sets the stage for the economic problem, it does not impose the only strictures against which men must struggle. For scarcity, as a felt condition, is not solely the fault of nature. If Americans today, for instance, were content to live at the level of Mexican peasants, all our material wants could be fully satisfied with but an hour or two of daily labor. We would experience little or no scarcity, and our economic problems would virtually disappear. Instead, we find in America—and indeed in all industrial societies—that as the ability to increase nature's yield has risen so has the reach of human wants. In fact, in societies such as ours, where relative social status is importantly connected with the possession of material goods, we often find that "scarcity" as a psychological experience and goal becomes more pronounced as we grow wealthier: Our desires to possess the fruits of nature race out ahead of our mounting ability to produce goods.

Thus the "wants" that nature must satisfy are by no means fixed—while, for that matter, nature's yield itself is not a constant, but varies over a wide range, depending on the social application of human energy and skill. Scarcity is therefore not attributable to nature alone but to "human nature" as well; and economics is ultimately concerned not merely with the stinginess of the physical environment, but equally with the appetite of the human temperament.

Hence we must begin a systematic analysis of economics by singling out the functions which social organization must perform to bring human nature into social harness. And when we turn our attention to this fundamental problem, we can quickly see that it involves the solution of two related and yet separate elemental tasks:

1. A society must organize a system for producing the goods and services it needs for its own perpetuation.
2. It must arrange a distribution of the fruits of its production among its own members, so that more production can take place.

These two tasks of economic continuity are, at first look, very simple. But it is a deceptive simplicity. Much of economic history, as we shall see, is concerned with the manner in which various societies have sought to cope with these elementary problems; and what strikes us in surveying their attempts is that most of them were partial failures. (They could not have been total failures, or society would not have survived.) Hence it behooves us to look more carefully into the two main economic tasks to see what hidden difficulties they may conceal.

The production problem

What is the difficulty which the production problem poses? What are the obstacles which a society encounters in organizing a system to produce the goods and services it needs?

Since nature is usually stingy, it would seem that the production problem must be essentially one of engineering, or technical efficiency. It would seem to revolve around the effort to economize, to avoid waste and apply social effort as efficaciously as possible.

This is indeed an important task for any society, and a great deal of formal economic thought, as the word itself suggests, is devoted to economizing. Yet this is not the core of the production problem. Long before a society can even concern itself about using its energies "economically," it must first marshall the energies to carry out the productive process itself. That is, *the basic problem of production is to devise social institutions which will mobilize human energy for productive purposes.*

This basic requirement is not always so easily accomplished. For example, in the United States in 1933, the energies of nearly thirteen million people—one quarter of our work force—were not directed into the production process. Although these unemployed men and women were eager to work, although empty factories were available for them to work in, despite the existence of pressing wants, somehow a terrible and mystifying breakdown short-circuited the production process, with the result that an entire third of our previous annual output of goods and services simply disappeared.

We are by no means the only nation which has, on occasion, failed to find work for willing workers. In the very poorest nations, where production is most desperately needed, we frequently find that unemployment is a chronic condition. The streets of the Asian cities are thronged with people who cannot find work. But this, too, is not a condition imposed by the scarcity of nature. There is, after all, an endless amount of work to be done, if only in cleaning the filthy streets or patching up the homes of the poor, building roads, or planting forests. Yet, what seems to be lacking is a social mechanism to put the unemployed to work.

Both these examples point out to us that the production problem is not solely, or perhaps even primarily, a physical and technical struggle with nature. On these "scarcity" aspects of the problem will depend the speed with which a nation may forge ahead and the level of well-being it can reach with a given effort. But the original mobilization of productive effort itself is a challenge to its social organization, and on the success or failure of that social organization will depend the volume of the human effort which can be directed to nature.

Putting men to work is only the first step in the solution of the production problem. Men must not only be put to work; they must be put to work *in the right places.* They must produce the goods and services which society needs. In addition to assuring a large enough quantity of social effort, the economic institutions of society must also assure the *proper allocation of that social effort.*

In a nation such as India or Brazil, where the great majority of the population is born in peasant villages and grows up to be peasant cultivators, the solution to this problem offers little to vex our understanding. The basic demands of society— food and fiber—are precisely the goods which its peasant population "naturally" produces. But in an industrial society, the proper allocation of effort becomes an enormously complicated task. People in the United States demand much more than bread and cotton. They need, for instance, such things as automobiles. Yet no one "naturally" produces an automobile. On the contrary, in order to produce one, an extraordinary spectrum of special tasks must be performed. Some people must make steel. Others must make rubber. Still others must coordinate the assembly process itself. And this is but a tiny sampling of the far from "natural" tasks which must be performed if an automobile is to be produced.

As with the mobilization of its total production effort, society does not always succeed in the proper allocation of its effort. It may, for instance, turn out too many cars or too few. Of greater importance, it may devote its energies to the production of luxuries while the majority of its people are starving. Or it may even court disaster by an inability to channel its productive effort into areas of critical importance. In the early 1950's, for instance, the British suffered a near economic collapse because they were unable to get enough of their workers to mine coal.

Such allocative failures may affect the production problem quite as seriously as a failure to mobilize an adequate quantity of effort, for a viable society must produce not only goods, but the *right* goods. And the allocative question alerts us to a still broader conclusion. It shows us that the act of production, in and of itself, does not fully answer the requirements for survival. Having produced enough of the right goods, society must now *distribute* those goods so that the production process can go on.

The distribution problem

Once again, in the case of the peasant who feeds himself and his family from his own crop, this requirement of adequate distribution may seem simple enough. But when we go beyond the most primitive society, the problem is not always so readily solved. In many of the poorest nations of the East and South, urban workers have often been unable to deliver their daily horsepower-hour of work because they have not been given enough of society's output to run their human engines to capacity. Worse yet, they have often languished on the job while granaries bulged with grain and the well-to-do complained of the ineradicable "laziness" of the masses. At the other side of the picture, the distribution mechanism may fail because the rewards it hands out do not succeed in persuading people to perform their necessary tasks. Shortly after the Russian Revolution some factories were organized into communes in which managers and janitors pooled their pay, and from which all drew equal allotments. The result was a rash of absenteeism on the part of the previously better-paid workers and a threatened breakdown in industrial production. Not until the old

unequal wage payments were reinstituted did production resume its former course.

As was the case with failures in the production process, distributive failures need not entail a total economic collapse. Societies can exist—and indeed, in the majority of cases, do exist—with badly distorted productive and distributive efforts. It is only rarely, as in the instances above, that maldistribution actively interferes with the actual ability of a society to staff its production posts. More frequently, an inadequate solution to the distribution problem reveals itself in social and political unrest or even in revolution.

Yet this, too, is an aspect of the total economic problem. For if society is to ensure its steady material replenishment, it must parcel out its production in a fashion that will maintain not only the capacity but the willingness to go on working. And thus again we find the focus of economic inquiry directed to the study of human institutions. For a viable economic society, we can now see, is not only one which can overcome the stringencies of nature, but one which can contain and control the intransigence of human nature.

The Three Solutions to the Economic Problem

Thus to the economist, society presents itself in an unaccustomed aspect. He sees it essentially as an elaborate mechanism for survival, a mechanism for accomplishing the complicated tasks of production and distribution necessary for social continuity.

But the economist sees something else as well, something which at first seems quite astonishing. Looking not only over the diversity of contemporary societies, but back over the sweep of all history, he sees that man has succeeded in solving the production and distribution problems in but three ways. That is, within the enormous diversity of the actual social institutions which guide and shape the economic process, the economist divines but three overarching *types* of systems which separately or in combination enable humankind to solve its economic challenge. These great systemic types can be called economies run by Tradition, economies run by Command, and economies run by the Market. Let us briefly see what is characteristic of each.

Tradition

Perhaps the oldest and, until a very few years ago, by far the most generally prevalent way of solving the economic challenge has been tradition. It has been a mode of social organization in which both production and distribution were based on procedures devised in the distant past, rigidified by a long process of historic trial and error, and maintained by heavy sanctions of law, custom, and belief.

Societies based on tradition solve the economic problems very manageably. First, they deal with the production problem—the problem of assuring that the needful tasks will be done—by assigning the jobs of fathers to their sons. Thus a hereditary chain assures that skills will be passed along and that the on-going jobs will be staffed from generation to generation. In ancient Egypt, wrote Adam Smith, the first great economist, "every man was bound by a principle of religion to follow the occupation of his father and was supposed to commit the most horrible sacrilege if he changed it for another."[2] And it was not merely in antiquity that tradition preserved a productive orderliness within society. In our own Western culture, until the fifteenth or sixteenth centuries, the hereditary allocation of tasks was also the main stabilizing force within society. Although there was some movement from country to town and from occupation to occupation, birth usually determined one's role in life. One was born to the soil or to a trade; and on the soil or within the trade, one followed in the footsteps of one's forebears.

Thus tradtion has been the stabilizing and impelling force behind a great repetitive cycle of society, assuring that society's work would be done each day very much

as it had been done in the past. Even today, among the less industrialized nations of the world, tradition continues to play this immense organizing role. In India, until very recently at least, one was born to a caste which had its own occupation. "Better thine own work is, though done with fault," preached the Bhagavad-Gita, the great philosophic moral poem of India, "than doing other's work, even excellently."

Tradition not only provides a solution to the production problem of society, but it also regulates the distribution problem. Take, for example, the Bushmen of the Kalahari Desert in South Africa who depend for their livelihood on hunting prowess. Elizabeth Marshall Thomas, a sensitive observer of these peoples, reports on the manner in which tradition solves the problem of distributing their kill.

> The gemsbok has vanished. . . . Gai owned two hind legs and a front leg, Tsetchwe had meat from the back, Ukwane had the other front leg, his wife had one of the feet and the stomach, the young boys had lengths of intestine. Twikwe had received the head and Dasina the udder.
>
> It seems very unequal when you watch Bushmen divide the kill, yet it is their system, and in the end no person eats more than any other. That day Ukwane gave Gai still another piece because Gai was his relation, Gai gave meat to Dasina because she was his wife's mother. . . . No one, of course, contested Gai's large share, because he had been the hunter and by their law that much belonged to him. No one doubted that he would share his large amount with others, and they were not wrong, of course; he did.[3]

The manner in which tradition can divide a social product may be, as the illustration shows, very subtle and ingenious. It may also be very crude and, by our standards, harsh. Tradition has often allocated to women, in nonindustrial societies, the most meager portion of the social product. But however much tradition may accord with or depart from our accustomed moral views, we must see that it is a workable method of dividing society's production.

Traditional solutions to the economic problems of production and distribution are most commonly encountered in primitive agrarian or nonindustrial societies, where in addition to serving an economic function, the unquestioning acceptance of the past provides the necessary perseverance and endurance to confront harsh destinies. Yet even in our own society, tradition continues to play a role in solving the economic problem. It plays its smallest role in determining the distribution of our own social output, although the persistence of such traditional payments as tips to waiters, allowances to minors, or bonuses based on length of service are all vestiges of old traditional ways of distributing goods, as is the differential between men's and women's pay for equal work.

More important is the place which tradition continues to hold, even in America, as a means of solving the production problem—that is, in allocating the performance of tasks. Much of the actual process of selecting an employment in our society is heavily influenced by tradition. We are all familar with families in which sons follow their fathers into a profession or a business. On a somewhat broader scale, tradition also dissuades us from certain employments. Sons of American middle-class families, for example, do not usually seek factory work, even though factory jobs may pay better than office jobs, because "bluecollar employment" is not in the middle-class tradition.

Even in our society, which is clearly not a "traditional" one, custom provides an important mechanism for solving the economic problem. But now we must note one very important consequence of the mechanism of tradition. *Its solution to production and distribution is a static one.* A society which follows the path of tradition in its regulation of economic affairs does so at the expense of large-scale rapid social and economic change.

Thus the economy of a Bedouin tribe or a Burmese village is in few essential respects changed today from what it was a hundred or even a thousand years ago. The bulk of the peoples living in tradition-bound societies repeat, in the daily patterns of their economic life, much of the routines which characterized them in the distant past. Such societies may rise and fall, wax and wane, but external events—war, climate, political adventures and misadventures—are mainly responsible for their changing fortunes. Internal, self-generated economic change is but a small factor in the history of most tradition-bound states. Tradition solves the economic problem, but it does so at the cost of economic progress.

Command

A second manner of solving the problem of economic continuity also displays an ancient lineage. This is the method of imposed authority, of economic command. It is a solution based not so much on the perpetuation of a viable system by the changeless reproduction of its ways, as on the organization of a system according to the orders of an economic commander-in-chief.

Not infrequently we find this authoritarian method of economic control superimposed upon a traditional social base. Thus the Pharaohs of Egypt exerted their economic dictates above the timeless cycle of traditional agricultural practice on which the Egyptian economy was based. By their orders, the supreme rulers of Egypt brought into being the enormous economic effort which built the pyramids, the temples, the roads. Herodotus, the Greek historian, tells us how the Pharaoh Cheops organized the task.

[He] ordered all Egyptians to work for himself. Some, accordingly, were appointed to draw stones from the quarries in the Arabian mountains down to the Nile, others he ordered to receive the stones when transported in vessels across the river.... And they worked to the number of a hundred thousand men at a time, each party during three months. The time during which the people were thus harassed by toil lasted ten years on the road which they constructed, and along which they drew the stones; a work, in my opinion, not much less than the Pyramid.[4]

The mode of authoritarian economic organization was by no means confined to ancient Egypt. We encounter it in the despotisms of medieval and classical China which produced, among other things, the colossal Great Wall or in the slave labor by which may of the great public works of ancient Rome were built. Of course, we find it today in the dictates of the communist economic authorities. In less drastic form, we find it also in our own society, for example, in the form of *taxes* —that is, in the preemption of part of our income by the public authorities for public purposes.

Economic command, like tradition, offers solutions to the twin problems of production and distribution. In times of crises, such as war or famine, it may be the only way in which a society can organize its manpower or distribute its goods effectively. Even if devastated by a great natural disaster. On such occasions we may press people into service, requisition homes, impose curbs on the use of private property such as cars, or even limit the amount of food a family may consume.

Quite aside from its obvious utility in meeting emergencies, command has a further usefulness in solving the economic problem. Unlike tradition, the exercise of command has no inherent effect of slowing down economic change. Indeed, the exercise of authority is the most powerful instrument society has for *enforcing economic change*. One example is, of course, the radical alterations in the systems of production and distribution which authority has effected in modern China or Russia. But again, even in our own society, it is sometimes necessary for economic authority to intervene into the normal flow of economic life to speed up or bring about change. The government may, for instance,

utilize its tax receipts to lay down a network of roads which brings a backwater community into the flux of active economic life. It may undertake an irrigation system which will dramatically change the economic life of a vast region. It may very considerably affect the distribution of income among social classes.

To be sure, economic command which is exercised within the framework of a democratic political process is very different from that which is exercised by strong-arm methods: There is an immense social distance between a tax system controlled by Congress and outright expropriation or labor impressment by a supreme and unchallengeable ruler. Yet whilst the means may be much milder, the *mechanism* is the same. In both cases, command diverts economic effort toward goals chosen by a higher authority. In both cases it interferes with the existing order of production and distribution, to create a new order ordained from "above."

This does not in itself serve to commend or condemn the exercise of command. The new order imposed by the authorities may offend or please our sense of social justice, just as it may improve or lessen the economic efficiency of society. Clearly, command can be an instrument of a democratic as well as of a totalitarian will. There is no implicit moral judgment to be passed on this second of the great mechanisms of economic control. Rather, it is important to note that no society—certainly no modern society—is without its elements of command, just as none is devoid of the influence of tradition. If tradition is the great brake on social and economic change, so economic command can be the great spur to change. As mechanisms for assuring the successful solution to the economic problem, both serve their purposes, both have their uses and their drawbacks. Between them, tradition and command have accounted for most of the long history of man's economic efforts to cope with his environment and with himself. The fact that human society *has* survived is testimony to their effectiveness.

The market

There is also a third solution to the economic problem—that is, a third solution to the problem of maintaining socially viable patterns of production and distribution. This is the *market organization of society,* an organization which in truly remarkable fashion, allows society to ensure its own provisioning with a minimum of recourse either to tradition or command.

Because we live in a market-run society, we are apt to take for granted the puzzling —indeed, almost paradoxical—nature of the market solution to the economic problem. But assume for a moment that we could act as economic advisers to a society which had not yet decided on its mode of economic organization. Suppose, for instance, that we were called on to act as consultants to one of the new nations emerging from the continent of Africa.

We could imagine the leaders of such a nation saying, "We have always experienced a highly tradition-bound way of life. Our men hunt and cultivate the fields and perform their tasks as they are brought up to do by the force of example and the instruction of their elders. We know, too, something of what can be done by economic command. We are prepared, if necessary, to sign an edict making it compulsory for many of our men to work on community projects for our national development. Tell us, is there any other way we can organize our society so that it will function successfully—or better yet, more successfully?"

Suppose we answered, "Yes, there is another way. Organize your society along the lines of a market economy."

"Very well," say the leaders. "What do we then tell people to do? How do we assign them to their various tasks?"

"That's the very point," we would answer. "In a market economy no one is assigned to any task. The very idea of a market society is that each person is allowed to decide for himself what to do."

There is consternation among the leaders. "You mean there is *no* assignment of some men to mining and others to cattle raising? No manner of selecting some for transportation and others for cloth weaving? You leave this to people to decide for themselves? But what happens if they do not decide correctly? What happens if no one volunteers to go into the mines, or no one offers himself as a railway engineer?"

"You may rest assured," we tell the leaders, "none of that will happen. In a market society, all the jobs will be filled because it will be to people's advantage to fill them."

Our respondents accept this with uncertain expressions. "Now look," one of them finally says, "let us suppose that we take your advice and let our people do as they please. Now let's talk about something important, like cloth production. Just how do we fix the right level of cloth output in this 'market society' of yours?"

"But you don't," we reply.

"We don't! Then how do we know there will be enough cloth produced?"

"There will be," we tell him. "The market will see to that."

"Then how do we know there won't be *too much* cloth produced?" he asks triumphantly.

"Ah, but the market will see to that too."

"But what *is* this market that will do all these wonderful things? Who runs it?"

"Oh, nobody runs the market," we answer. "It runs itself. In fact there really isn't any such *thing* as 'the market.' It's just a word we use to describe the way people behave."

"But I thought people behaved the way they wanted to!"

"And so they do," we say. "But never fear. They will want to behave the way you want them to behave."

"I am afraid," says the chief of the delegation, "that we are wasting our time. We thought you had in mind a serious proposal. But what you suggest is madness. It is inconceivable. Good day, sir," And with great dignity the delegation takes its leave.

Could we seriously suggest to such an emergent nation that it entrust itself to a market solution of the economic problem? That will be a problem to which we shall return. But the very perplexity which the market idea would rouse in the mind of someone unacquainted with it may serve to increase our own wonderment at this most sophisticated and interesting of all economic mechanisms. How *does* the market system assure us that our mines will find miners, our factories workers? How does it take care of cloth production? How does it happen that in a market-run nation each person can indeed do as he wishes and, withal, fulfill the needs which society as a whole presents?

Economics and the market system

Economics, as we commonly conceive it and as we shall study it in much of this book, is primarily concerned with these very problems. Societies which rely primarily on tradition to solve their economic problems are of less interest to the professional economist than to the cultural anthropologist or the sociologist. Societies which solve their economic problems primarily by the exercise of command present interesting economic questions, but here the study of economics is necessarily subservient to the study of politics and the exercise of power.

It is a society which solves its economic problems by the market process that presents an aspect especially interesting to the economist. For here, as we shall see, economics truly plays a unique role. Unlike the case with tradition and command, where we quickly grasp the nature of the economic mechanism of society, when we turn to a market society we are lost without a knowledge of economics. For in a market society it is not at all clear that the problems of production and distribution will be solved by the free interplay of individuals without guidance from tradition or command.

In subsequent chapters of this book we shall analyze these puzzling questions in more detail. But first there is a problem which has surely occurred to the reader. As our hypothetical interview with the leaders of an emergent nation must have suggested, the market solution appears very strange to someone brought up in the ways of tradition or command. Hence the question arises: how did the market solution itself evolve? Was it imposed, full-blown, on our society at some earlier date? Or did it arise spontaneously and without forethought? These are questions to which we must first turn, as we retrace the evolution of our own market system out of the tradition- and authority-dominated societies of the past.

Footnotes

1 Karl Popper, *The Open Society and Its Enemies,* 3rd ed. (London: Routledge & Kegan Paul, Ltd., 1957), II, 270.

2 *The Wealth of Nations* (New York: Modern Library, Inc., 1937), p. 62.

3 *The Harmless People* (New York: Alfred A. Knopf, Inc., 1959), pp. 49–50.

4 *Histories,* trans. Cary (London: 1901), Book II, p. 124.

2 The Protestant Ethic and the Spirit of Capitalism—Max Weber

edited by GERALD D. BELL

As capitalism appeared and flourished in Europe and America, Protestants gained positions of wealth, power, and prestige to a much greater extent than did Catholics. Business leaders, owners of capital, and higher grades of skilled labor were overwhelmingly Protestant. Why was this the case? Max Weber, writing during the latter part of the nineteenth and the early part of the twentieth century, devoted his attention to answering this question.

He looked for his answer in the basic doctrines of different religions. Before examining this development, however, Weber wrestles with the sticky question of whether or not the Protestants' relative success was due to factors other than their religion. He first examined an historical accident explanation. That is, he raised the question: "Were the Protestants highly successful because they happened to acquire wealth and power first and merely maintained their station in life thereafter?"

Weber initially argues that if it were an historical accident that Protestants acquired their powers and positions then there should have been few differences in the types of education which Protestants and Catholics acquired. However, Weber cites the fact that Protestants tended to emphasize technical, industrial, and commercial studies, whereas Catholics preferred the humanities. Clearly, Weber suggests, there is a basic

Edited from Max Weber, The Protestant Ethic and the Spirit of Capitalism, *trans. Talcott Parsons, by permission of the publisher, Charles Scribner's Sons. Copyright 1958. World rights granted by George Allen & Unwin, Ltd.*

value difference between people in these two religious groupings.[1]

He indicates that Catholics had a stronger tendency to remain in their crafts, whereas Protestants were attracted to a larger extent into the growing factories. Weber suggests that the explanation of the educational and occupational differences "...is undoubtedly that the mental and spiritual peculiarities acquired from the environment, here the type of education favored by the religious atmosphere of the home community and the parental home, have determined the choice of occupation, and through it the professional career."[2] It is suggested, then, by the above notions that the historical argument for Protestant-Catholic occupational differences does not sufficiently explain the Protestants' relative success.

After examining the historical question, Weber then turns to what some had mentioned as a possible explanation of the Protestants' success—political influence. National or religious minorities which are in a position of subordination to a group in power have in the past, due to their exclusion from positions of political influence, been driven into economic activity. "Their ablest members seek to satisfy the desire for recognition of their abilities in this field, since there is no opportunity in the service of the state."[3]

Catholics, however, had shown no tendency toward prominent economic development in the times when they were a persecuted group. On the contrary, Protestants had shown special tendencies toward economic growth both when they were a majority and a minority group, both as a ruled and a ruling class. Because of these factors Weber also rules out the political influence argument. He suggests, then, that "the principal explanation of this difference must be sought in the permanent intrinsic character of their religious beliefs, and not only in their temporary external historical-political situations."[4]

The Spirit of Capitalism

Before Weber begins his analysis of the basic doctrinal differences between Catholics and Protestants he takes time to explain what he calls the *spirit of capitalism*. This "spirit" refers to the beliefs and values people developed as the capitalistic economy evolved. He cites as examples of this spirit some of Benjamin Franklin's famous notions which state: "time is money"; "when one does not work he might as well be throwing money into the sea"; "one who works hard has good credit"; and "good credit is money." The unique quality of this philosophy appears to be the "...ideal of the honest man of recognized credit, and above all the idea of duty of the individual toward the increase of his capital, which is assumed as an end in itself."[5] What is expressed in these words is an all-encompassing ethic or guideline for behavior.

Weber suggests that the idea of acquisition and hard work is the most characteristic feature of capitalistic culture. The individual is suppised to feel an obligation for diligent work regardless of his type of occupation or profession. Furthermore, one does not work hard to acquire wealth and a later life of luxury; hard labor is viewed rather as an end in itself.

Before such beliefs as these which composed the spirit of capitalism could come to dominate the lives of large groups of individuals they had to originate somewhere; this is the question to which Weber turns next.

The Origins of the Spirit of Capitalism

Weber suggests that Luther's support of the idea of a calling, or a life goal of work, brought about the first stages of the Protestant Ethic and the spirit of capital-

ism. Luther suggested that "the only way of living acceptable to God was not to surpass worldly morality in a monastic asceticism, but solely through the fulfillment of the obligations imposed upon the individual by his position in the world. That was his calling."[6]

Luther looked at the Catholic monastic life as a selfish renunciation of one's duty to God. One's duty to work was an outward expression of brotherly love, because one's specialized tasks of work produced goods for other individuals and vice versa. The division of labor ensured that every individual worked for others.

In his attempt to analyze how the sociopsychological sanctions which originated in religious beliefs gave direction to practical conduct, Weber then turns to Calvinism. He points out that Calvinism was the faith which inspired great cultural and political struggles during the sixteenth and seventeenth centuries. The most characteristic feature of Calvinism at that time was the doctrine of predestination, which taught that only a small proportion of individuals were chosen for eternal grace. Some men were saved and the rest were damned. Furthermore, predestination was irrevocable. To even think that one could change his destiny was to doubt God's absolute power.

Since man was unable either by his own skills or by the aid of others (such as priests) to alter his destiny, he was forced to meet his fate alone. This complete "... elimination of salvation through the church and the sacraments...was what formed the absolutely decisive difference from Catholicism."[7]

This doctrine, according to Weber, must have created a feeling of unprecedented inner loneliness on the part of the individual. On the other hand, it formed the basis of that bleak individualism which is characteristic of countries with a Puritan past. This individualism took the form of distrust of others and a distrust of the aid of friendship. And it placed responsibility for religious matters entirely upon the individual.

If one imagines himself living during

this Reformation under the dogma of predestination, he can readily perceive that the question, "Am I one of the elect?" must have taunted the minds of the believers. Undoubtedly, people wanted to find some way to determine whether or not they were one of the blessed. In Weber's words, ". . .wherever the doctrine of predestination was held, the question could not be suppressed whether there were any infallible criteria by which membership in the *electi* could be known."[8]

In answer to the above questions two types of pastoral advice were given. First, it was suggested that it was an absolute duty to consider oneself chosen and that one should fight off all doubts since these were temptations of the devil. Lack of self-confidence was thought to result from insufficient faith. The second type of pastoral advice was that the way to acquire self-confidence was by intense worldly activity. Work and work alone was considered to disperse religious doubts and to provide the certainty of grace. Work in this sense, then, was ". . .the most suitable means of counteracting feelings of religious anxiety. . ."[9] Good works became, then, an indispensable sign of election.

A life dedicated to work and acquisition was not quite a means of purchasing salvation but a way of giving one self-confidence that he was one of the chosen. In practice this meant that God helps those who help themselves. "Thus the Calvinist, as it is sometimes put, himself creates his own salvation, or, as would be more correct, the conviction of it."[10]

With Calvinism, then, came an idea which was beautifully compatible with capitalism. This was the idea that to prove one's faith one must actively participate in worldly activities. Furthermore, the God of Calvinism required a constant, rational life of good deeds. There was no allowance for the Catholic cycle of sin, repentance, atonement, release followed by sin again. The Calvinist could not hope to atone for misdeeds by increased efforts at a later date as the Catholic could. For the Puritans life was meant to be a rational activity, where magic as a means of salvation had no place. For Catholics, however, the church could absolve the members for their imperfections. The priest ". . .dispensed atonement, hope of grace, certainty of forgiveness, and thereby granted release from that tremendous tension to which the Calvinist was doomed. . ."

By these arguments Weber suggests that the beliefs of Calvinism matched very well if not eagerly supported the values necessary for the expansion of capitalism. In a general perspective, then, Weber's work may be viewed as a contribution to the understanding of ways in which ideas become guiding forces in history.

---

[1] One may question, of course, whether or not Weber's arguments refute the historical explanation.

[2] Weber, p. 30

[3] *Ibid.*

[4] *Ibid.*, p. 40.

[5] *Ibid.*, p.51.

[6] *Ibid.*

[7] *Ibid.*, pp. 104–105.

[8] *Ibid.*, p. 110.

[9] *Ibid.*, p. 112.

[10] *Ibid.*, p. 115.

[11] *Ibid.*, p. 117.

3 Religion and Economics

by GERHARD LENSKI

Since Weber first drafted his controversial essay on the Protestant Ethic, revolutionary changes have overtaken the economies of Western nations. Though private enterprise is far from dead, these nations have clearly passed beyond the stage where capitalistic principles dominate the operation of the economy.[1] Even in the United States, which so often prides itself on being the last bastion of capitalism, capitalist institutions are hedged about with countless new arrangements designed to protect the masses of citizens against the consequences of the unchecked operation of capitalism. Nowhere are these newer arrangements more evident than in the modern metropolis.

How have these changes affected the relationship between religion and economics? What role does religion play in the new economic order? Do Protestants rise more rapidly in the economic world than Catholics, as Weber claimed was once true? What is the position of the Jewish group in our modern economy? If socioreligious group membership makes a difference, is it because of the influence of the churches or the subcommunities? What influence do devotionalism and doctrinal orthodoxy have on economic behavior? These are the questions which we shall seek to answer in this chapter.

SOCIORELIGIOUS GROUP MEMBERSHIP AND ECONOMIC BEHAVIOR

Vertical Mobility

For many years following Weber's publication of his essays on the Protestant Ethic and the spirit of capitalism, it was generally accepted that Protestants were more successful than Catholics in the competition for economic advancement. The chief question debated was whether the Protestant advantage was because of Protestantism, or in spite of it.[2]

More recently, however, several scholars have challenged the assumption that Protestants are more successful than Catholics, at least when opportunities for advancement are equal.

In the first of these studies, Mack, Murphy, and Yellin concluded that they are not.[3] Their study was based on questionnaire responses obtained from a sample of salesmen, engineers, and bank officials. These authors concluded that there were no statistically significant differences between Catholics and Protestants in their actual occupational advancement or aspirations for advencement. However, a careful analysis of their data indicates that their conclusion is not warranted so far as actual movement is concerned.[4] On the contrary, statistically significant differences did exist, demonstrating that Protestants were upwardly mobile more often than Catholics.

In a more recent discussion of the same subject, Lipset and Bendix also report finding no differences between the rates of mobility of Catholics and Protestants, using a national sample of American men interviewed in connection with the 1952 presidential election.[5] However, their analysis of these data is somewhat cursory, and therefore their conclusions cannot be accepted at face value. Especially serious is their failure to control for the size of the community in which their respondents were raised. As they later demonstrate, this has a significant effect on mobility, with those raised in larger cities being more successful economically then those raised in small towns and on the farms.[6] This is important because census data show that while less than a quarter of the white Protestants in this country live in communities of 250,000 or more, more than half of the Catholics do. Thus the Protestants in their sample competed under a severe handicap.

Findings of the 1958 survey

Our evidence from the 1958 Detroit Area Study survey is consistent with the actual findings of the Mack, Murphy, Yellin study, and indicates that white Protestant men rise further in the class system than Catholics. When white Protestants were compared with Catholics who began life at the same point in the class system, the former rose to (or stayed in) the ranks of the upper-middle class more often than the latter. At the opposite extreme, Catholics wound up in the lower half of the working class more often than Protestants three out of four times. Differences were especially marked among the sons of middle-class men and farmers.

Unfortunately, there were not enough Jewish males in our sample to permit analysis, but the heavy concentration of Jews in the middle class, and even the upper-middle class, found in all recent studies, including our own, indicates their rapid rise in the economic system. Only a generation or two ago a substantial proportion of American Jews were manual workers.

In the case of Negro Protestants, our findings were hardly surprising. The great majority were sons of either farmers or semiskilled and unskilled workers. Their sons remain concentrated in the ranks of the semi- and unskilled. Of the 19 Negro Protestants sons of farmers, only 2 had escaped from the lower half of the working

class. Among the 16 sons of lower working-class fathers, only 3 had risen.

To a considerable degree this lack of mobility is due to white hostility and resistance, though this is probably not a sufficient explanation. Other groups, such as the Japanese, Chinese, and Jews, have gotten ahead despite opposition. This suggests that we must look for other factors if we are to explain fully the economic failure of Negro Protestants in Detroit and other northern metropolitan centers.

Weller's findings

Concurrent with the present study, and related to it, Neil J. Weller carried out an intensive analysis of vertical mobility among the most urbanized and Americanized segments of the white Catholic and Protestant groups.[7] His study was based on an analysis of 1100 white, male Catholics and Protestants raised in American communities of 25,000 or more in states north of the Mason-Dixon line. These men were interviewed in Detroit Area Study surveys from 1952 to 1958.

Weller's findings, based on six separate samples, are essentially the same as those obtained in the 1958 survey. The chief differences occur among the sons of upper working-class fathers. The 1958 data suggest that Protestants with this background are more likely than Catholics to arrive at both of the extremes in the class system, while his data suggest the opposite conclusion. This is a relatively minor inconsistency when compared with the general similarity in findings.

Because of the size of his sample, Weller was able to introduce into his analysis certain controls which were not possible in the 1958 data alone. For example, he introduced an important control for ethnicity to see if it was possible that the relative lack of success of Catholics in the job world might reflect economic discrimination against persons of southern or eastern European background. Such a hypothesis seemed plausible in view of the much greater concentration of such persons in the Catholic population. Weller's analysis demonstrated clearly, however, that this was not the explanation for Catholic-Protestant differences. With both ethnicity and class origins held constant, white Protestants advanced further on the average in the job world than Catholics in all of the seven possible comparisons.

Taking advantage of the size of his sample, Weller also examined the important question of trends to see if there was any evidence that Catholic-Protestant differences are declining in magnitude. His analysis of this question was based on comparisons of the younger men (under forty) in his sample with the older. His basic finding was that differences between Catholics and Protestants were equally great in the two age categories, and, if anything, were slightly larger among the younger men. In short, Weller's data provide no support for the hypothesis that Catholic-Protestant differences in this area are declining.

On the basis of all the avilable evidence, it is reasonably safe to say that in the modern American metropolis socially significant differences exist in the rates of mobility among the four major socioreligious groups. The Jewish group seems clearly to be the most successful, with white Protestants second, Catholics third, and Negro Protestants fourth. The only evidence to the contrary is the Lipset-Bendix study, which suggests that there is no difference between the Catholic and white Protestant groups. However, as noted previously, this evidence is based on a very limited analysis of the data.

The fact that the Negro group ranks last and the Catholic group next to last suggests that success depends simply on economic opportunity, which in turn depends on the social acceptability of a group to the economically dominant white Protestants.[8] However, the marked success of the Jewish group clearly indicates that the problem is more complex, for if this hypothesis were correct, Catholics should have been far more successful than Jews. Furthermore, in countries where Catholics were originally economically dominant (as in Latin America), we would expect Catholics to be more successful on the average than Protestants, but this does not seem to have the case. In short, we are led to search for other factors if we are to develop a more adequate theory to account for these differences.

Aspirations and Ambition

In both popular and technical discussions of vertical mobility, much is made of the importance of ambition and of aspirations for advancement. In an effort to determine whether or not members of the major socioreligious groups differ in their desire for advancement we gave respondents a card listing five criteria which might be used to assess the desirability of a job. They were asked to rank these in order of their importance in a man's job. The criteria were:

1. High income
2. No danger of being fired
3. Working hours short, lots of free time
4. Chances for advancement
5. The work is important and gives a feeling of accomplishment

Jewish respondents ranked opportunities for advancement higher than any of the other groups, though differences were small. The mean score for members of the Jewish group was 2.35 (the score would have been 1.00 if all members of the group had ranked "chances for advancement" first, and 5.00 if all had ranked it last). White Protestants came second with a mean score of 2.41, Catholics third with 2.44, and Negro Protestants last with 2.56. This ordering corresponds to the ordering when the groups were ranked in terms of upward mobility, or actual advancement, but the differences here are so small that they cannot account for more than a small part of the differences in actual mobility.

When only the answers given by men were considered, the magnitude of the differences between groups increased a little, though they still remained small. Jewish males came first with a mean score of 1.95, white Protestants second with 2.29, and Catholics and Negro Protestants tied for third, both scoring 2.45.

From this evidence we can only conclude that even if there are differences in aspirations and ambition among the groups, they cannot explain more than a small part of the differentials in vertical mobility. Clearly, more than ambition is required to rise in contemporary American society. Other, less obvious, qualities are also necessary if an individual is to get ahead, and some of these are apparently even more important.

Our finding in this area coincides with an earlier finding of Lipset, Trow, and Coleman, based on their analysis of the printers' union.[9] They asked a sample of union members in New York City whether they would go into a different type of work if they could start all over again. Jewish printers were the most likely to say that they would start over in some nonmanual, higher-status occupation. Protestants ranked second in taking this view, and Catholics last, though Protestant-Catholic differences were not large. From this the authors inferred that mobility aspirations are strongest among the Jewish printers, and weakest among the Catholics.

Attitudes Toward Work

In Weber's classic essay on the Protestant Ethic, an entire chapter is devoted to a discussion of Luther's doctrine of "the calling." It was Weber's contention that this important Protestant doctrine played a major role in the formation of the spirit of modern capitalism. Luther insisted that all worthwhile occupations are equally important in the sight of God, and that God calls some men to serve Him as cobbler, farmer, and magistrate, just as He calls others to serve Him as minister or priest. In this way he reoriented his followers' thinking about work and its importance in life. For those

Protestants who took Luther's doctrine of the calling seriously, secular vocations provided a vehicle for service to God just as much as religious vocations. Work was no longer merely a means for earning the necessities of life; it was one of the major means by which men might serve God. Hence, a man did not labor as little as possible, as he might when confronted with a task that was merely difficult and unpleasant. Rather, he worked as hard as possible.

As Weber pointed out, the doctrine of the calling came to be modified in the Calvinist tradition, and subsequently underwent still further modification at the hands of Deists such as Benjamin Franklin. However, the important point is that, beginning in the sixteenth century, those in the Protestant tradition were trained to take a very different view of work from those raised in the Catholic tradition. Catholics continued to regard work primarily as a necessary evil; a consequence of Adam's fall and a penalty for sin. By contrast, Protestants came to view it as an opportunity for serving God, or, in the Deist version, for building character.

To date almost nothing has been done to explore the relevance of this doctrine for the world of work in contemporary American society. In what may be the only study with evidence on this subject, Melville Dalton found that, in one industrial plant which he studied, white Protestant machinists worked harder and produced more than Catholics in comparable jobs.[10] He found that Catholics were much more likely than Protestants to deliberately restrict output.

In our present study we have no work records such as Dalton used. Instead, we are obliged to rely on the expressions of attitudes toward work supplied by Detroiters in interviews in their homes. However, while our evidence is inferior to Dalton's in this respect, we have the advantage of a much broader and more representative sample.

In an effort to gain some insight into the influence of religion on job performance, we asked each of the men we interviewed the following question: "Some people tell us that they couldn't really be happy unless they were working at some job. But others say that they would be a lot happier if they didn't have to work and could take life easy. How do you feel about this?" (Q. 5).

We then asked: "Why is that?" (Q. 5a).

On the basis of their responses to these two questions, each of the members of our sample was placed in one of three categories. First there were those who expressed a positive attitude toward work. That is to say, they valued work for its own sake, or for the intrinsic rewards it provides. In this group also were those who rejected a life of ease because they regarded it as immoral. As a Baptist engineer expressed it: "Man must have a purpose in life and something to occupy his mind; I get great satisfaction from my work."

A Lutheran businessman put it this way: "Man wasn't made to be idle. The happiest people I know are very active. Man is happiest when he is creating something or loving something. It is an inherent trait in man to want to see something he has created."

A Jewish craftsman put the matter much more simply when he said: "I like to work."

A Negro Baptist welder told us: "It just isn't right if you're not working."

All of the men cited above said that they would not be happy unless they were working. However, there were others who gave the same answer to the first question, but in explaining why, indicated that work itself had no positive attraction for them. Rather, they found the alternatives even less attractive, or in some instances they indicated that they would go on working because they liked extrinsic rewards linked with work. These we classified as persons with a neutral attitude toward work.

The answer of a Catholic postal clerk is typical of a large number of such responses. He said that he would be unhappy not working, but when asked why this was, he said: "I wouldn't want to just loaf. I guess I'd want to do something, but it wouldn't have to be a job. [Why is that?] You'd get bored doing nothing."

Or, as a Lutheran photoengraver expressed it: "I'd rather work. It's a healthier life. Otherwise I'd always be boozing it up."

A Catholic high school science teacher said he did not care if he worked or not, providing he had enough money to take care of himself.

Some people, however, made it clear that they would quit their jobs immediately if they were financially independent. Their negative attitude toward work was highly evident. For example, a Lutheran optician said: "I feel I could take life easy if I had enough money. Traveling or gardening would be nice."

A Catholic insurance adjuster told us: "I have a certain nature which likes to lay around without doing anything—maybe its inborn laziness."

In general the findings indicate that Jewish males were the most likely to express a positive attitude toward work, and by far the least likely to express a negative attitude. Differences among the other groups were not large, except that white Protestants were somewhat more likely to express a positive attitude toward work than either Catholics or Negro Protestants.

1 See Karl Polanyi, *The Great Transformation: The Political and Economic Origins of Our Times* (New York: Holt, Rinehart & Winston, Inc., 1944).

2 See, for example, R. H. Tawney, *Religion and the Rise of Capitalism* (New York: Harcourt, Brace & World, Inc., 1926).

3 Raymond Mack, Raymon Murphy, and Seymour Yellin, "The Protestant Ethic, Level of Aspiration, and Social Mobility," *American Sociological Review,* 21 (June, 1956), pp. 295–300.

4 The authors divided their sample into six subsamples, each of which was analyzed

separately and chi square values computed. When this is done, the normal (and proper) procedure is to add the chi square values and also the degrees of freedom, since the samples involved are independent tests of the same proposition. Also, a one-tail test should be used when testing a theory which predicts not merely the existence of differences but also their direction (as with Weberian theory). Had these things been done, the chi square value for father-son mobility would have been 14.2 with 6 degrees of freedom. A one-tail test shows that the differences which they found would not occur because of sampling error more than two times in a hundred, or well below the accepted limits for rejecting the null hypothesis.

5 Lipset and Bendix, *op. cit.,* pp. 48–56.
6 *Ibid.,* pp. 204–213.
7 Neil J. Weller, *Religion and Social*

Mobility in Industrial Society (unpublished doctoral dissertation, University of Michigan, 1960).
8 For evidence of the economic dominance of the white Protestants, see C. Wright Mills, *The Power Elite* (New York: Oxford University Press, Inc., 1956), especially Chapters 5–7 in which he reviews the major relevant studies. See also Mabel Newcomer, *The Big Business Executive: The Factors That Made Him, 1900–1950* (New York: Columbia University Press, 1955), pp. 46–49.
9 Seymour M. Lipset, Martin A. Trow, and James S. Coleman, *Union Democracy* (New York: Free Press of Glencoe, Inc., 1956). See especially p. 116.
10 Melville Dalton, "Worker Response and Social Background," *The Journal of Political Economy,* 55 (July, 1947), pp. 323–332.

4   The Division of Labor—Emile Durkheim

edited by CHARLES GORDON

[Introduction]

Our work...will be divided into three principal parts:

To determine the function of the division of labor, that is to say, what social need it satisfies.

To determine...the causes and conditions on which it is dependent.

Finally...we shall try to classify the principal abnormal forms it presents, so that they will not be confused with the others.

Everybody knows that we like those who resemble us, those who think and feel as we do. But the opposite is no less true. It very often happens that we feel kindly toward those who do not resemble us, precisely because of this lack of resemblance. ... Difference, as likeness, can be a cause of mutual attraction. However, certain differences do not produce this

effect. We do not find any pleasure in those completely different from us. Spendthrifts do not seek the company of misers, nor moral and honest people that of hypocrites and pretenders; sweet and gentle spirits have no taste for sour and malevolent temperaments. Only certain kinds of differences attract each other. They are those which, instead of opposing and excluding, complement each other. As Bain says, there is a type of difference which repels, another which attracts, one which leads to rivalry, another which leads to friendship. If one of two people has what the other has not, but desires, in this fact lies the point of departure for a positive attraction. Thus it is that a theorist, a subtle and reasoning individual, often has a very special sympathy for practical men with their quick sense and rapid intuitions, the timid for the firm and resolute, the weak for the strong, and conversely. As richly endowed as we may be, we always lack something, and the best of us realize our own insufficiency. That is why we seek in our friends the qualities that we lack, since in joining with them, we participate in some measure in their nature and thus feel less incomplete. So it is that small friendly associations are formed wherein each one plays a role conformable to his character, where there is a true exchange of services. One urges on, another consoles; this one advises, that one follows the advice, and it is this apportionment of functions, or, to use the usual expression, this division of labor, which determines the relations of friendship.

We are thus led to consider the division of labor in a new light. In this instance, the economic services that it can render are picayune compared to the moral effect that it produces, and its true function is to create in two or more persons a feeling of solidarity. In whatever manner the result is obtained, its aim is to cause coherence among friends and to stamp them with its seal.

* * *

...We must especially determine in what degree the solidarity that it produces contributes to the general integration of society, for it is only then that we shall know how far necessary it is, whether it is an essential factor of social cohesion, or whether, on the contrary, it is only an accessory and secondary condition. To reply to this question, we must compare this social link [the division of labor] to others in order to measure how much credit is due to it in the total effect; and to that end, we must begin by classifying the different types of social solidarity.

But social solidarity is a completely moral phenomenon which, taken by itself, does not lend itself to exact observation nor indeed to measurement. To proceed to this classification and this comparison, we must substitute for this internal fact which escapes us an external index which symbolizes it and study the former in the light of the latter.

* * *

This visible symbol is the law.
Since law reproduces the principal forms of social solidarity, we have only to classify the different types of law to find therefrom the different types of social solidarity which correspond to it. . . .

To proceed scientifically, we must find some characteristic, which while being essential to juridical phenomena, varies as they vary. Every precept of law can be defined as a rule of sanctioned conduct. Moreover, it is evident that sanctions change with the gravity attributed to precepts, the place they hold in the public conscience, the role they play in society. It is right, then, to classify juridical rules according to the different sanctions which are attached to them.

They are of two kinds. Some consist essentially in suffering or at least a loss, inflicted on the agent. They make demands on his fortune, or on his honor, or on his life, or on his liberty, and deprive him of something he enjoys. We call them repressive. They constitute penal law. . . . As for the other type, it does not necessarily imply suffering for the agent, but consists only of *the return of things as they were*, in the reestablishment of troubled relations to their normal state, whether the incriminated act is restored by force to the type whence it deviated or is annulled, that is, deprived of all social value. We must then separate juridical rules into two great classes, accordingly as they have organized repressive sanctions or only restitutive sanctions. The first comprise all penal law; the second, civil law, commercial law, procedural law, administrative and constitutional law, after abstraction of the penal rules which may be found there.

[Mechanical Solidarity]

The link of social solidarity to which repressive law corresponds is the one whose break constitutes a crime. By this name we call every act which, in any degree whatever, invokes against its author the characteristic reaction which we term punishment. To seek the nature of this link is to inquire into the cause of punishment or, more precisely, to inquire what crime essentially consists of.

* * *

In effect, the only common characteristic of all crimes is that they consist...in acts universally disapproved of by members of each society.... Thus, the reality of the fact that we have just established is not contestable; that is, that crimes shock sentiments which, for a given social system, are found in all healthy consciences.

...the functioning of repressive justice tends to remain more or less diffuse. In every different social system, it does not function through means of a special magistracy, but the whole society participates in a large measure. In primitive societies where...law is wholly penal, it is the assembly of people which renders justice.

The totality of beliefs and sentiments common to average citizens of the same society forms a determinate system which has its own life; one may call it the *collective* or *common conscience*. No doubt, it has not a specific organ as a substratum; it is, by definition, diffuse in every reach of society. Nevertheless it has specific characteristics which make it a distinct reality. It is, in effect, independent of the particular conditions in which individuals are placed; they pass on and it remains....

We can, then, to resume the preceding analysis, say that an act is criminal when it offends strong and defined states of the collective conscience.... we must not say that an action shocks the common conscience because it is criminal, but rather that it is criminal because it shocks the common conscience. As for the social character of this reaction to offenses against the common conscience, it comes from the social nature of the offended sentiments. Because they are found in all consciences, the infraction committed arouses in those who have evidence of it or who learn of its existence the same indignation. Everybody is attacked; consequently, everybody opposes the attack.

* * *

Thus, the nature of collective sentiments accounts for punishment and, consequently, for crime. Moreover, we see anew that the power of reaction which is given over to governmental functionaries, once they have made their appearance, is only an emanation of that which has been diffuse in society since its birth. The one is only the reflex of the other.

Thus, the analysis of punishment confirms our definition of a crime. We began by establishing inductively that crime consisted essentially in an act contrary to strong and defined states of the common conscience. We have just seen that all the qualities of punishment ultimately derive from this nature of crime. That is because the rules it sanctions express the most essential social likenesses.

Thus we see what type of solidarity penal law symbolizes. Everybody knows that there is a social cohesion whose cause lies in a certain conformity of all particular consciences to a common which is none other than the psychic type of the society. In these conditions, not only are all the members of the group attracted to one another because they resemble one another, but also because they agree as to what is the condition of existence of this collective type, that is to say, to the society that they form by their union....There are in us two consciences: one contains states which are personal to each of us and which characterize us, while the states which comprehend the other are common to all society. The first represent only our individual personality and constitute it; the second represent the collective type, and consequently, society, without which it would not exist. When it is one of the elements of this latter which determines our conduct, it is not in view of our personal interest that we act, but we pursue collective ends. Although distinct, these two consciences are linked to one another, since, in sum, they are only one, having one and the same organic substratum. They are thus solidarity. From this results a solidarity *sui generis,* which, born of resemblances, directly links the individual with society.... It is this solidarity which repressive law expresses, at least whatever there is vital in it.

* * *

There exists a social solidarity which comes from a certain number of states of conscience which are common to all the members of the same society. That is what repressive law represents insofar as it is essential. The part that it plays in the general integration of society evidently depends upon the greater or lesser extent of the social life which the common conscience embraces and regulates. The greater the diversity of relations wherein the latter makes its action felt, the more it also creates links which attach the individual to the group; the more, consequently, social cohesion derives completely from this source and bears its mark.

Organic Solidarity
Due to the Division of Labor

The very nature of the restitutive sanction suffices to show that the social solidarity to which this type of law corresponds is of a totally different kind.

What distinguishes this sanction is that it is not expiatory, but consists of a simple *return in state.* Sufferance proportionate to the misdeed is not inflicted on the one who has violated the law or who disregards it; he is simply sentenced to comply with it. If certain things were done, the judge reinstates them as they would have been.

Neglect of these rules is not punished diffusely. The pleader who lost in litigation is not disgraced, his honor is not put in question.

Repressive law corresponds to the heart, the center of the common conscience; laws purely moral are a part less central; finally, restitutive law is born in very excentric regions whence it spreads further.

Since rules with restitutive sanctions are strangers to the common conscience, the relations that they determine are not those which attach themselves indistinctly everywhere. That is to say, they are established immediately, not between the individual and society, but between restricted, special parties in society whom they bind. But, since society is not absent, it must be more or less directly interested, it must feel the repercussions. Thus, according to the force with which society feels them, it intervenes more or less concomitantly and more or less actively, through the intermediary of special organs charged with representing it. These relations are, then, quite different from those which repressive law regulates, for the latter attach the particular conscience to the collective conscience directly and without meditation, that is, the individual to the society.

In short, the rules relative to real rights and to personal relations which are established in their turn form a definite system which has as its function, not to attach different parts of society to one another, but, on the contrary, to put them outside one another, to mark cleanly the barriers which separate them.

* * *

(In effect, the fights of individuals, as much in themselves as in things, can be determined only thanks to some compromise and mutual concessions, for everything which is accorded to some is necessarily abandoned by others. . . . In fact, in order that man might recognize the rights of others, not only logically, but in the practical workaday world, it was necessary that he consent to limit his rights, and, consequently, this mutual limitation could be made only in a spirit of agreement and accord.) But, if we suppose a multitude of individuals without previous links between them, what reason could there be to induce them to make these reciprocal sacrifices?

* * *

. . . In reality, for men to recognize and mutually guarantee rights, they must first of all love each other, they must, for some depend upon each other and on the same society of which they are a part.

(The relations governed by cooperative with restitutive sanctions and the solidarity which they express, result from the division of social labor. We have explained, moreover, that, in general, cooperative relations do not convey other sanctions. In fact, it is in the nature of special tasks to escape the action of the collective conscience, for in order for a thing to be the object of common sentiments, the first condition is that it be common, that is to say, that it be present in all consciences and all can represent it in one and the same manner. To be sure, insofar as functions have a certain generality, everybody can have some idea of them. But the more specialized they are, the more circumscribed the number of those cognizant of each of them. Consequently, the more marginal they are to the common conscience. The rules that determine them cannot have the superior force, the transcendant authority which, when offended, demands expiation.)

The violation of these rules reaches neither the common soul of society in its living parts nor even, at least not generally, that of special groups, and, consequently, it can determine only a very moderate reaction. All that is necessary is that functions concur in a regular manner. If this regularity is disrupted, it behooves us to reestablish it.

* * *

The first kind of solidarity can be strong only if the ideas and tendencies common to all members of the society are greater in number and intensity than those which pertain personally to each member. It is much stronger as the excess is more considerable. . . . Solidarity which comes from likenesses is at its maximum when the collective conscience completely envelopes our whole conscience and coincides with all points in it. . . . The social molecules which can be coherent in this way can act together only in the measure that they have no actions of their own, as the molecules of inorganic bodies. That is why we propose to call this type of solidarity mechanical.

It is quite otherwise with the solidarity which the division of labor produces. Whereas the previous type implies that individuals resemble each other, this type presumes their difference. The first is possible only insofar as the individual personality is absorbed into the collective personality; the second is possible only if each one has a sphere of action which is peculiar to him; that is, a personality. It is necessary, then, that the collective conscience leave open a part of the individual conscience in order that special functions may be established there, functions which it cannot regulate. The more this region is extended, the stronger is the cohesion which results from this solidarity. In effect, on the one hand, each one depends as much more strictly on society as labor is more divided; and, on the other, the activity of each is as much more personal as it is more specialized. Doubtless, as circumscribed as it is, it is never completely original. Even in the exercise of our occupation, we conform to usages, to practices which are common to our whole professional brotherhood. But, even in this instance, the yoke that we submit to is much less heavy than when society completely controls us, and it leaves much more open place for the free play of our initiative. Hence, then, the individuality of all grows at the same time as that of its parts. Society becomes capable of collective movement, at the same time that each of its elements has more freedom of movement. This solidarity resembles that observed among the higher animals. Each organ, in effect, has its special physiognomy, its autonomy. And moreover, the unity of the organism is as great as the individuation of the parts is more marked. Because of this analogy, we propose to call the solidarity which is due to the division of labor, organic.

* * *

Thus, it is an historical law that mechanical solidarity which first stands alone, or nearly so, progressively loses ground and that organic solidarity becomes, little by little, preponderant. But then the way in which men are solidary changes the structure of societies. . . . Consequently, if the preceding proposition is correct, there ought to be two social types which correspond to these two types of solidarity.

There is, then, a social structure of determined nature to which mechanical solidarity corresponds. What characterizes it is a system of segments homogeneous and similar to each other.

Quite different is the structure of societies where organic solidarity is preponderant.

They are constituted, not by a repetition of similar, homogeneous segments, not by a system of different organs each of which has a special role and which themselves are formed of differentiated parts. Not only are social elements not of the same nature, but they are not arranged the same way. They are not juxtaposed linearly as the rings of an earthworm nor entwined with one another, but coordinated and subordinated one to another around the same central organ which exercises a moderating action over the rest of the organisms.

* * *

In sum, a contract is not sufficient unto itself, but is possible only thanks to a regulation of the contract which is originally social. It is implied, first, because it has for its function much less the creation of new rules than the diversification in particular cases of preestablished rules; then, because it has and can have the power to bind only under certain conditions which it is necessary to define. If, in principle, society lends it an obligatory force, it is because, in general, the accord of particular wills suffices to assure . . . the harmonious coming together of diffuse social functions. But if it conflicts with social purposes, if it tends to trouble the regular operation of organs, if, as is said, it is not just, it is necessary, while depriving it of all social value, to strip it of all authority as well. The role of society is not, then, in any case, simply to see passively that contracts are carried out. It is

also to determine under what conditions they are executable, and if it is necessary, to restore them to their normal form. The agreement of parties cannot render a clause just which by itself is unjust, and there are rules of justice whose violation social justice prevents, even if it has been consented to by the interested parties.

The following propositions sum up the first part of our work.

Social life comes from a double source, the likeness of consciences and the division of social labor. The individual is socialized in the first because, not having any real individuality, he becomes, with those whom he resembles, part of the same collective type; in the second case, it is because, while having a physiognomy and a personal activity which distinguishes him from others, he depends upon them in the same measure that he is distinguished from them, and consequently upon the society which results from their union.

* * *

The similitude of consciences gives rise to juridical rules which, with the threat of repressive measures, impose uniform beliefs and practices upon all. The more pronounced this is, the more completely is social life confounded with religious life, and the nearer to communism are economic institutions.

The division of labor gives rise to juridical rules which determine the nature and the relations of divided functions, but whose violation calls forth only restitutive measures without any expiatory character.

* * *

Each of these bodies of juridical rules is, moreover, accompanied by a body of purely moral rules. Where penal law is very voluminous, common morality is very extensive; that is to say, there is a multitude of collective practices placed under the protection of public opinion. Where restitutive law is highly developed, there is an occupational morality for each profession. In the interior of the same group of workers, there exists an opinion, diffuse in the entire extent of this circumscribed aggregate, which, without being furnished with legal sanctions, is rendered obedience. There are usages and customs common to the same order of functionaries which one of them can break without incurring the censure of the corporation. This morality is distinguished from the preceding by differences analogous to those which separate the two corresponding types of law. It is localized in a limited region of society. Moreover, the repressive character of the sanctions attaching to it is much less accentuated. Professional misdeeds call forth reprobation much more feeble than attacks against public morality.

The rules of occupational morality and justice, however, are as imperative as the others. They force the individual to act in view of ends which are not strictly his own, to make concessions, to consent to compromises, to take into account interests higher than his own. Consequently, even where society relies most completely upon the division of labor, it does not become a jumble of juxtaposed atoms, between which it can establish only external transient contacts. Rather the members are united by ties which extend deeper and far beyond the short moments during which the exchange is made. Each of the functions that they exercise is, in a fixed way, dependent upon others and with them forms a solidary system. Accordingly, from the nature of the chosen task permanent duties arise. Because we fill some certain domestic or social function, we are involved in a complex of obligations from which we have no right to free ourselves. There is, above all, an organ upon which we are tending to depend more and more; this is the state. The points at which we are in contact with it multiply as do the occasions when it is entrusted with the duty of reminding us of the sentiment of common solidarity.

*   *   *

Thus, altruism is not destined to become, as Spencer desires, a sort of agreeable ornament to social life, but it will forever be its fundamental basis. How can we ever really dispense with it? Men cannot live together without acknowledging and, consequently, making mutual sacrifices, without tying themselves to one another with strong, durable bonds. Every society is a moral society. In certain respects this character is even more pronounced in organized societies. Because the individual is not sufficient unto himself, it is from society that he receives everything necessary to him, as it is for society that he works. Thus is formed a very strong sentiment of the state of dependence in which he finds himself. He becomes accustomed to estimating it at its just value, that is to say, in regarding himself as part of a whole, the organ of an organism. Such sentiments naturally inspire not only mundane sacrifices which assure the regular development of daily social life, but even, on occasion, acts of complete self-renunciation and wholesale abnegation. On its side, society learns to regard its members no longer as things over which it has rights, but as cooperators whom it cannot neglect and towards whom it owes duties. Thus, it is wrong to oppose a society which comes from a community of beliefs to which one has a cooperative basis, according only to the first a moral character and seeing in the latter only an economic grouping. In reality, cooperation also has its intrinsic morality. There is, however, reason to believe, as we shall see later, that in contemporary societies this morality has not yet reached the high development which would now seem necessary to it.

*   *   *

The other is strong only if the individual is not. Made up of rules which are practiced by all indistinctly, it receives from this universal, uniform practice an authority which bestows something superhuman upon it and which puts it beyond the pale of discussion. The cooperative society, on the contrary, develops in the measure that individual personality becomes stronger. As regulated as a function may be, there is a large place always left for personal initiative. A great many of the obligations thus sanctioned have their origin in a choice of the will. It is we who choose our professions and even certain of our domestic functions. Of course, once our resolution has ceased to be internal and has been externally translated by social consequences, we are tied down. Duties are imposed upon us that we have not expressly desired. It is, however, through a voluntary act that this has taken place. Finally, because these rules of conduct relate, not to the conditions of common life, but to the different forms of professional activity, they have a more temporal character, which, while lessening their obligatory force, renders them more accessible to the action of men.

There are, then, two great currents of social life to which two types of structure, not less different, correspond.

Of these currents, that which has its origin in social similitudes first runs on alone and without a rival. At this moment, it confounds itself with the very life of society; then, little by little, it canalizes, rarefies, while the second is always growing. Indeed, the segmental structure is more and more covered over by the other, but without ever completely disappearing.

* * *

The division of labor develops, therefore, as there are more individuals sufficiently in contact to be able to act and react upon one another. If we agree to call this relation and the active commerce resulting from it dynamic or moral density, we can say that the progress of the division of labor is in direct ratio to the moral or dynamic density of society.

The progressive condensation of societies in historical development is produced in three principal ways:

1. Whereas lower societies are spread over immense areas according to population, with more advanced people population always tends to concentrate.

2. The formation of cities and their development is an even more characteristic

symptom of the same phenomenon. The increase in average density may be due to the material increase of the birth rate and, consequently, can be reconciled with a very feeble concentration, a marked maintenance of the segmental type. But cities always result from the need of individuals to put themselves in very intimate contact with others.

3. Finally, there are the number and rapidity of ways of communication and transportation. By suppressing or diminishing the gaps separating social segments, they increase the density of society.

If condensation of society produces this result, it is because it multiplies intrasocial relations. But these will be still more numerous, if, in addition, the total number of members of society becomes more considerable. If it comprises more individuals at the same time as they are more intimately in contact, the effect will be necessarily reinforced. Social volume, then, has the same influence as density upon the division of labor.

* * *

We can, then, formulate the following proposition: The division of labor varies in direct ratio with the volume and density of societies, and, if it progresses in a continuous manner in the course of social development, it is because societies become regularly denser and generally more voluminous.

If work becomes more divided as societies become more voluminous and denser, it is not because external circumstances are more varied but because struggle for existence is more acute.

The division of labor is, then, a result of the struggle for existence, but it is a mellowed *denouement*. Thanks to it, opponents are not obliged to fight to the finish but can exist one beside the other. Also, in proportion to its development, it furnishes the means of maintenance and survival to a greater number of individuals who, in more homogeneous societies, would be condemned to extinction.

A corollary of all that has preceded is that the division of labor can be affected only among members of an already constituted society.

Hence, the claim sometimes advanced that in the division of labor lies the fundamental fact of all social life is wrong. Work is not divided among independent and already differentiated individuals who by uniting and associating bring together their different aptitudes; for it would be a miracle if differences thus through chance circumstance could unite so perfectly as to form a coherent whole. Far from preceding collective life, they derive from it. They can be produced only in the midst of a society and under the pressure of social sentiments and social needs. That is what makes them essentially harmonious. There is then a social life outside the whole division of labor, but which the latter presupposes. That is, indeed, what we have directly established in showing that there are societies whose cohesion is essentially due to a community of beliefs and sentiments, and it is from these societies that those whose unity is assured by the division of labor have emerged.

* * *

But the more general the common conscience becomes under the necessity of dealing with more and more kinds of phenomena, the greater the place it leaves to individual variation. When God is far from things and men, his action is no longer omnipresent, nor ubiquitous. There is nothing fixed save abstract rules, which can be freely applied in different ways. Then they no longer have the same ascendancy nor the same force of resistance to increasing individuality.

5 Mass Society and Mass Culture*

by HAROLD L WILENSKY

Several major questions about the social impact of affluence have come to dominate intellectual discussion concerning the shape of modern society. Some of them involve the nature, extent, and impact of mass culture and mass leisure. Everyone agrees that abundance everywhere brings a rise in mass communications (through radio, television, and press), the development of mass education and the concomitant spread of literacy, and, finally, mass entertainment on a grand scale. I propose to deal with these trends in the context of ideas about the "mass society." I will:

1. Analyze the interplay of high culture

Reprinted from Harold Wilensky, "Mass Society and Mass Culture," American Sociological Review, 29 (1964), pp. 173–197, by permission of the American Sociological Association and the author.

and mass culture, with special attention to the structural roots of cultural standardization and heterogeneity in rich countries

2. Present data on the quality of media exposure in a variety of occupational groups and strata in the Detroit metropolitan area—so that we may both gauge the extent of cultural uniformity and locate the sources of resistance to mass culture

My general aim is to fill in gaps in theories of the mass society and to arrive at a more valid vision of modern society.

Theories of Mass Society and the Functions of the Mass Media

Traditional theorists of "urbanism" or of the "mass society" tend to be pessimistic in ideology and macroscopic in sociology; their empirical critics tend to be optimistic—some would say fatuous—in ideology and microscopic in sociology. Both seek to interpret the impact of industrialism and urbanism on social structure and culture. Together they have given us most of the imagery with which we construct our picture of the affluent society.

From Tocqueville to Mannheim[1] the traditional theorists have been concerned with one or both of two problems:

1. The debilitation of culture-bearing elites (and of the core values they sustain) brought on by their diminishing insulation from popular pressures
2. The rise of the masses, who, for various reasons, are increasingly susceptible to demagogues and extremist movements[2]

These scholars are said to believe that the mobility, heterogeneity, and centralization of modern society destroy or weaken the ties that bind men to the common life, rendering the mass manipulatable, leaving mass organizations and the mass media in control. Although they vary in their depiction of the generating forces, they tend to accent either the atrophy of primary and informal relations or the atrophy of self-governing secondary groups and associations.[3]

Now the empirically-minded critics—a later generation studying a more industrialized society—have countered with these propositions: Primary groups survive, even flourish. Urban-industrial populations have not stopped participating in voluntary associations, which in America and perhaps in other pluralist systems, continue to multiply. Moreover, in every industrial society, whether pluralist or totalitarian, there are potent limits to the powers of the mass media, the big organizations, and the centralized state.[4]

I count myself as one of the critics,[5] but I am restive about the way the debate has progressed.[6] The parties talk past one another and ideological blinders obstruct the vision far more than in other areas of sociological investigation. Nowhere is this

more true than in the sketchy treatment of mass culture in theories of the mass society and in the almost ritualistic recital of the "two-step flow" slogan by the students of media ineffectiveness.

The main theme of the theorists is this: The *mass society* develops a *mass culture,* in which cultural and political values and beliefs tend to be *homogeneous* and *fluid.* In the middle and at the bottom—in the atomized mass—people think and feel alike; but thoughts and feelings, not being firmly anchored anywhere, are susceptible to fads and fashions. At the top, poorly organized elites, themselves mass-oriented, become political and managerial manipulators, responding to short-run pressures; they fail to maintain standards and thereby encourage the spread of populism in politics, mass tastes in culture—in short, a "sovereignty of the unqualified."[7]

The empirically minded critics of such theories are impressed by the diversity of modern life. Concerning the leveling and fluidity of culture, they point to an extraordinary variety of cultural products, assert that it is easier to prove that mass tastes have been upgraded than that such tastes have been vulgarized, and protest that high culture has not declined but merely become more widely available. Concerning the role of the mass media in politics and culture, the critics cite considerable diversity of media content as well as persistence in habits of exposure. And where diversity of *content* falls short, they argue, there is everywhere enormous diversity in *response.* While the optimists are well aware of the limits of their studies, they seem always to come to the same punch line: The burden of evidence indicates that the media are not omnipotent; they are absorbed into local cultures via the two-step flow from media to local group to person; and this absorption involves a self-selection of exposure corresponding to previous attitude.[8]

It is a pity that these students of the media who know mass communication best are not more ideologically sensitive and not more concerned with general characterizations of society; equally unfortunate is it that the theorists, at home in the world of ideologies and utopias, are not more sophisticated in the handling of data. For systematic observation and theoretical problems must be brought together if we are to understand the interplay of social structure, high culture, and mass culture.

Mass culture and high culture

For my purposes here the most useful definition that distinguishes high culture from mass culture is one that emphasizes the social context of production. "High culture" will refer to two characteristics of the product:

1. It is created by or under the supervision of a cultural elite operating within some aesthetic, literary, or scientific tradition (these elite are the top men in the sphere of education, aesthetics, and entertainment who carry the core values and standards of that sphere and serve as models for those working in it).
2. Critical standards independent of the consumer of the product are systematically applied to it.

The quality of thought or expression of the cultural object and the social milieu in which it is produced define high culture. This definition has the advantage of leaving open questions about the organization and recruitment of cultural elites, the social controls to which they are subject (e.g., pressures from patron, market, or mass), the conditions under which a high-quality product—a Shakespearian play, a Mozart symphony—can become popular, the ways in which the product is or is not absorbed into the culture of the consumer.

"Mass culture" will refer to cultural *products manufactured solely for a mass market*. Associated characteristics, not intrinsic to the definition, are *standardization* of product and *mass behavior* in its use. Mass culture tends to be standardized because it aims to please the average taste of an undifferentiated audience. Common

tastes shape mass culture; critical standards sustained by autonomous producing groups shape high culture. Another frequent but not inevitable correlate of mass culture is a high rate of mass behavior—a uniform and direct response to remote symbols.[9] It is expressed in strong attachment to and dependence on distant public objects and concerns—e.g., acts, thoughts, and feelings regarding the nation (hyperpatriotism and xenophobia), class (Marxian class consciousness), race (racism). The definition leaves open questions about the relation of mass culture to high culture, the conditions under which a product of mass culture can meet the standards of high culture, the degree to which mass culture is fluid or, like folk culture, stable (characterized by little original creation in each generation), whether traditions of expression and performance develop in it, the extent to which the impact of the mass media is mediated by audience standards and the extent to which those very standards are themselves anchored in the media.

In short, these concepts permit sociological analysis of cultural products in the social contexts in which they are created and used. They have the disadvantage of being difficult (but not impossible) to apply in empirical research.

Theoretical problem and assumptions

Our problem is the relation of the main structural trends associated with abundance to the form and content of high culture and mass culture. The main research question is, "which groupings of modern populations acquire a 'mass' character and which do not—with what net effect on culture, high and low?" More precisely, will the heterogeneity of culture rooted mainly in the division of labor give way to the homogeneity of culture rooted mainly in the centralized state, mass education, the mass media, and mass entertainment?

Five assumptions about modern society have guided my approach to this question:

1. Social differentiation persists, even increases.

2. Cultural uniformity also grows.
3. In rich countries there is more independent variation of social structure and culture than in poor ones, although some of this incongruity is due to imprecise measures of structure.
4. Developments in the aesthetic-recreational sphere as well as the political sphere may remain isolated from those in the economy and locality for some time, so that in the short run mass behavior in one sphere may not become mass behavior in another.
5. But over several generations, and as rich countries grow richer, there is a strain toward consistency between structure and culture and between behavior in one institutional sphere and that in a second.

1. *Social differentiation persists, even increases.* It is rooted first in specialization by job and occupation and by the corporate and occupational communities that develop from work. It is rooted second in society-wide age-grading systems and in individual stages of the life cycle. (As sources of alienation from work and community, for instance, age and life-cycle stage, which are fixed in both biological and social nature, are invariably more important than family income, which tends toward equalization.) Finally, differentiation is rooted in religious institutions, which everywhere mesh with kinship and friendship and often form a basis for wider but separate networks of affiliation. (The labor-leisure study shows that religion is a far stronger anchor for close friendships than occupation or workplace —as measured, for instance, by the religion, occupation, and place of employment of one's three best friends.) Of course, racial and ethnic groups do assimilate, but only slowly. If they serve as a basis for variants or religious communities, as among Catholics of diverse origin, or Jews, or for protest movements, as among Negroes, such groups maintain a tenacious hold, which is often reinforced by residential segregation. The ties of locality doubt-

less diminish, despite the evidence of occasional communities in the metropolis (again ethnic, racial, or class "neighborhoods" or at least "blocks").

There is, in short, no evidence that the bonds of economy, age, religion, and the nuclear family (with family and church often meshed with extended kin) are weakening in the rich countries, although the quality of those relationships may be changing and their influence in particular social contexts is still problematic. In much of the discussion of "mass" society or "totalitarian" society, the persistence and stability of such ties are underestimated. The masses have nowhere in any developed country been kept "atomized," "available," "unattached," "in motion."[10] Many writers, shocked by the barbarity of the Stalinist and Nazi regimes, have generalized a vocabulary appropriate to brief historical or, in the case of the Nazis, selected populations, and have thereby missed the main trend. The limits of terror have been encountered by every totalitarian elite committed to economic progress. Even the most monolithic industrial societies are forced to supplement coercion with persuasion and manipulation and to attend to problems of morale and motivation. This is especially true when they confront skilled workers at every level, including cultural elites, and is most evident when persons in these categories are in short supply. The argument is both familiar and accurate: Some tasks cannot be mastered without the development of more-or-less autonomous groups—crafts, professions, scientific disciplines, and other private enclaves. Such groups cultivate technique and celebrate it, motivate disciplined work, provide stable careers and professional conviviality. The arts and sciences that flourish in the Soviet Union are not merely those which are politically safe; they are the ones which prior to the rise of Bolshevism were characterized by a high degree of skill and organization and either an aristocratic tradition (music, the ballet) or a tradition of intellectual achievement (mathematics, linguistics).[11] In short, the necessity of mobilizing social support for the performance of complex tasks sets practical limits on the baiting of intellectuals and professionals.

While the "professionalization" of occupations is often no more than a struggle for the rewards of exclusive jurisdiction, and while there are many organizational and political threats to the autonomy of professional groups, the number of occupations that are given some freedom to organize their work seems to be increasing in every rich country. And while the freezes and thaws in the intellectual climate make it difficult to assess the persistence of cultural elites under political attack, here, too, autonomy based on social differentation persists. Groups that could be expected to carry high culture maintain considerable social insulation, which stems from their unique training and jobs (and related differences in religion and family background). The separate worlds of work multiply.

2. *Nevertheless, cultural uniformity grows.* Even without the obliteration of social differences, modern society tends toward cultural standardization—a widespread sharing of beliefs, values, and tastes, crosscutting groups and categories. The forces at work are well known: popular education and mass literacy; high rates of social and residential mobility; the emergence of national markets and a national politics, both making use of nationwide media of mass communication and entertainment. Of course rich countries vary in the level of these modern developments and none has yet experienced their full impact. Even in the richest of them all, the United States, a really mass-education system has existed for less than two generations,[12] hardly time for its cultural influence to have been felt. Nevertheless, it seems likely that on its production side, modern society displays increasing diversity of structure, and on its consumption and leisure side, increasing standardization of culture.

3. *Structure and culture change at varying rates in all societies, but their independent variation is greatest at the highest levels of modernization.* The relevance here is that "mass culture" (and its correlates, standardization and fluidity of tastes in consumption and media content) can vary independently from "mass structure" (in which the mass lack firm ties to the social order and are easily mobilized into mass movements). This follows from my first two assumptions—the simultaneous growth of structural differentiation and cultural uniformity. In fact, the closest meshing of mass society and mass culture may appear neither in modern pluralist countries nor in modern totalitarian countries but instead in the new nations of Africa and Asia, where demagogic politicians, on radio, on television, in the village square, inveigh against imperialists and colonialists, manipulating a population torn loose from traditional tribal ties. As Shils suggests, "the availability of the media of mass communication is an invitation to their demagogic use—even more pronouncedly so where the populace is illiterate and scattered in many not easily accessible villages and where there is the belief that the members of this populace must be 'mobilized' for the progress of the country."[13] Where intellectual elites have achieved only embryonic development, the prominence of modern communications also means that all culture, as it moves away from traditional patterns, becomes mass culture.

The characteristics of mass society and mass culture exist in some degree in every country undergoing rapid social change, but they are most compatible in the emerging nations, however they may blend with traditional ways of life. Because the level of economic and political development conditions the effect of "mass" structures on mass culture and high culture, we cannot assume any straight-line trend from simple, poor, and nonmassified to complex, rich, and massified.

4. Not only are structure and culture divergent in modern society as it has thus far developed, but *there is considerable independence among the separate institu-*

tional spheres. Behavior in the aesthetic-recreational sphere as well as in the political sphere may for some time remain isolated from that in the economy and the locality. In my study I assumed the independent variation of patterns of work, social participation, exposure and response to mass culture, and vulnerability to mass politics; I took as problematic the conditions under which their influence is reciprocal. My data show that a modern population can display fluid politics or high susceptibility to media manipulation, propaganda, and advertising, and yet simultaneously evidence stable patterns of social relations at work and in the community. And for some men the gap left by impoverished social relations is filled by vicarious participation in television programs, vicarious involvement with media heroes, a symbolic sharing in the national nonpolitical life which acts to constrain both apathy and mass politics. The data also demonstrate, however, that much behavior spills over from one sphere to another and therefore are consistent with my fifth assumption.

5. *There is in the long run a strain toward consistency (1) among values and beliefs in diverse institutional spheres,*[14] *(2) among behavior patterns in diverse spheres, (3) between culture and social structure.*

The congruence of values in spheres as diverse as kinship, politics, and aesthetics —e.g., "idealistic" and "authoritarian" political values and child-rearing philosophies as reflected in literature—is well illustrated in a careful, sophisticated content analysis of the 45 most popular new plays in Germany and the United States in 1927.[15] In 44 per cent of the 45 German plays and only 4 per cent of the 45 American plays, *"idealism"* was a basic theme: a central character, standing above the masses, pursues high principle and is compelled to sacrifice conventional morality (as is the case of the patriot who, for the sake of his country, murders his beloved). The level of action was 51 per cent *ideological* in Germany, 96 per cent *personal*

in America: The American hero must struggle against immoral or antisocial tendencies in himself or in others which block the achievement of personal happiness; the German hero, pursuing an ideal goal, must struggle against the normal practices of society itself. Personal ambitions and satisfactions, expressed within the bounds of conventional morality, are positively sanctioned in the American plays; such strivings are often portrayed as the root obstacle in the German plays, the "materialism" and "philistinism" against which the idealist must fight. Literature and art are not mirror images of society, but in the rare case where the data are most solid and comparative, the congruence is striking.

Concerning consistency of behavior in the diverse spheres of modern life, a nation probably cannot forever have both high rates of mass behavior in consumption and low rates in politics (Britain) or rate low on mass consumption and high on mass politics (France). I assume that mass behavior in politics, consumption, and media exposure are correlated—that voting for Ike's personality is like responding to undiscussed gasoline ads, and the two can reinforce one another. Data reported elsewhere support this notion.[16]

Similarly, with respect to the congruence of structure and culture, I assume that a modern nation cannot forever have both an elite educational system and continued growth in mass culture (as in France, where the paid circulation of the *Reader's Digest* now exceeds a million, which, in proportion to population, is almost a third of its penetration in the United States), or high rates of mobility and stable, insulated leisure styles (class subcultures in Britain, ethnic subcultures in America). And the formulation sometimes advanced by students of American culture[17] that we have made progress by moving on from a concern with "politics" to a concern with "culture" and "conformity" obscures the most interesting challenge—to discover the complex connections between them. Mr. Minow's travail suggests that cultural homogeneity is rooted in the political structure as well as the market place.[18]

Thus, we may assume that the influence of mass education, the media, and the centralized state will in the long run overcome the influences of variations in work, religion, age, and locality as sources of cultural values and leisure styles, and we can expect mass culture in both Europe and America to penetrate structures now more or less insulated from it.

Educational institutions are strategic in linking structure and culture and the diverse institutional spheres. The education system is locality bound but brings wider worlds to view; its curricula are highly differentiated, reflecting the specialized occupations for which it trains youngsters, but it is the central transmitter of core values and beliefs. Universities and colleges are the main source of what high culture there is, and to some extent they innoculate against mass culture; at the same time mass education uses the media, incorporates them into its content and technique, and helps train the next generation in a style of leisure permeated by the great din of the media.[19]

Clearly, to understand the impact of abundance on culture and the limits and possibilities of public policy in overcoming cultural uniformity, we need to contrast the cultural life of countries whose governments differ in policy regarding education and the media of mass communication.[20]

Social Structure, High Culture, and Mass Culture: An Empirical Approach

Let us apply the larger debate about modern society to the mass media and mass entertainment in America. We must first grasp the fact that the mass media are the core of American leisure and that television has become the core of media exposure. The sheer arithmetic is striking. Nine in ten American homes average five to six hours daily with the TV set on. And it is not just turned on; it is generally being watched. Eight in ten

Americans spend at least four hours a day viewing television, listening to the radio, or both.[21] Additional time goes to reading newspapers and magazines.

The trend is up. An increasing fraction of the daily routine is devoted to the products of the mass media. Mainly due to the rise of television, the media together and on the average now take up almost as much time as work; substantial minorities log more hours a year in TV viewing alone than in working.

Both cause and consequence of this trend is the development of an enormous machinery of promotion. Today, our outlays for advertising are almost equal to our current expenditures on public schools (elementary and secondary)—about 11 billion annually.[22] Additional billions go to PR and the like. The more abundance, the more activity to increase the desire for it.

So far we are on safe ground. The size of this frenzied promotion effort and the astonishing amount of exposure are well known. The *impact* on the quality of American culture, however, is difficult to judge.

In tackling the problem I have tried to be specific: in approaching the *standardization* of culture I have looked for media exposure and response crosscutting social classes, educational levels, age grades, and religious and nativity categories. In handing the *heterogeneity* of culture I have searched for variations in media exposure and response with special attention to structural facts obscured by these traditional categories of sociological analysis—e.g., the quality variations within broad levels of education; the variations in tasks, work schedules, occupational groups, workplaces, and job patterns within broad occupational strata. The picture that emerges is more complicated than the assertions and counterassertions of theorists and critics, but it is also a more realistic reflection of modern life.

I will first present findings bearing on the structural roots of cultural heterogeneity and then findings that suggest the perhaps more powerful roots of cultural uniformity. I will draw from data on the quality of media exposure among 1,354 men ranging from highly educated professors, lawyers, and engineers and executives matched for age and income, through a cross section of the lower middle and upper working classes (the "middle mass") of the Detroit area, and down through 186 men unemployed and on relief.[23] We listed all their favorite TV shows, periodicals and newspapers read regularly, and all books they could name which they had read in the last two months. We then classified each program, each magazine, and each book in three "brow" levels—high quality, trash, or neither.

In coding for quality we were tolerant. The aim was to classify according to some fixed aesthetic standard, applicable to the medium, the more-or-less best performances and the clearly worst. Thus, the bias was that of Gilbert Seldes' *Seven Lively Arts*—sympathetic to the media. The product does not have to be aggressively educative to get by as highbrow, but if it is drama, the contrast is "Playhouse 90" vs. the most stereotypical detective, western, and adventure shows; if it is a paperback mystery, the contrast is Agatha Christie or Chandler vs. Spillane.

On *television programs* our staff made an effort to keep in touch with critical opinion and pooled judgments.

On *books, periodicals,* and *newspapers,* we compiled an initial classification and checked with experts. For the book code, for instance, two English professors reputed to have opposing views about the modern novel independently agreed on 97 per cent of the 200-odd high-quality titles. (That this code, like the others, is tolerant is suggested by the reaction of a literary critic who judged that perhaps half of the highbrow books would better be labeled "middling" or "upper middle"; clearly the list would not withstand the scrutiny of a Dwight MacDonald. But by that token it has the advantage of not understating the fallout from the "cul-

tural explosion" as it appears in these samples—which, as it turned out, was scanty.)

In general these codes do *not* reflect a snobbish understatement of quality exposure, and there is less disagreement at the extremes than one would expect.[24]

Findings

Only 85 of these men were exposed to any highbrow material in three or four areas; 157 score in two areas; 305 in one; 807 men reported no quality exposure in any area. At the other extreme 138 men reported very high exposure to poor TV— 25 and 30, even 35 hours of westerns, detectives, and adventure programs a week; 524 have medium scores; 692 avoid large doses of this type of program.

Although the main story is the general scarcity of quality exposure, which I will explore in detail later, ... [other findings (in a table reported in the full text of the article)] tell us something important: with sensitive measures of social position we can go far in explaining what cultural variation we do uncover. *The 17 variables explain over 46 per cent of the total variance in the number of areas in which quality exposure is reported and 25 per cent of the variance in exposure to poor TV.*

Both the measures and samples of the larger study were designed to permit projections of social and cultural trends in the affluent society based on comparisons of vanguard and rearguard groups at the same stage of the life cycle and the same social level. Does modernization increase the level of education? Then compare college graduates of growing mass institutions with those of elite colleges, which produce a declining percentage of the educated. Does economic development bring rising levels of mass aspiration? Then compare the aspiring with the less aspiring. Does it bring the dominance of large, complex organizations? Then compare the self-employed with men in workplaces of various sizes and structures. Does it make for an uneven distribution of leisure? Then compare the long-hours men with the short. Does modernization change the social composition of elites? Then compare established Protestant elites with rising Catholic populations.

My findings underscore the importance of education and the persistence of older bases of differentiation—descent (religion and nativity), age, and work situation. When we really peg the meaning of these as indicators of social position and discover their variable effects, however, we cannot help being struck with the difficulty of predicting their future functions for the maintenance or decline of cultural diversity.

The three top predictors of quality of exposure in both "number of areas of highbrow exposure" and in amount of poor TV are: (1) an index of level and quality of formal education which I interpret as degree of exposure to the liberal arts—by far the single most important variable in both cases; (2) an index of "generation American, religion, and status of religious preference"; (3) work context (size of workplace and self-employment status). The more education (and within educational levels, the higher the quality), the higher the level of taste. Among religious-nativity categories Jews, those with no preference, and established Catholics (four grandparents born in the U.S.) stand out in taste, while the most ardent consumers of lowbrow TV are Catholics of more recent American vintage (three or fewer grandparents born in the U.S.); however, two of those same highbrow categories—established Catholics and men with no preference—also produce more than their share of enthusiasts for the Western-detective-adventure shows. Jews and established high-status Protestants tend to avoid big doses of poor TV. As for work context, the good-taste categories are salaried men employed in big organizations; the poor-taste categories are self-employed or are employed in medium-sized workplaces. Long hours, a factor measuring choice of work over leisure, ranks fourth

as a predictor of highbrow media exposure; short hours ranks eighth as a predictor of lowbrow television exposure. Men 21–29 years old (all in the middle mass) stand out in lowbrow exposure; men 30–39 stand out in highbrow exposure.

What can we make of such findings? We began with the macroscopic assumption that the division of labor, religious institutions, and age-grading systems persist as powerful sources of cultural differentiation and that mass education is a source of standardization. Now that we have pinpointed the effect of these variables, slicing things a bit finer, the picture is not so simple. Take one of our favorite sociological clues to social structure: education. Will rising education levels bring an upgrading of taste, or will mass education mean an efflorescence of *Kitsch?* In answering such questions, the distinctions I have made are crucial.

. . . [The findings (presented in the original text)] report the mean scores (for each of seven categories of education) for the number of media areas in which the respondent reports any highbrow exposure and for much exposure to poor television. To take account of the increasing diversity of higher education,[26] the colleges and universities from which degree-holders had graduated were divided into two quality levels. For professors, the top twenty graduate schools in the 1957 Keniston rating[27] were coded high quality, the rest, low. For lawyers and engineers, faculty in a position to reflect professional consensus were given the complete lists and asked to rank leading schools, second-line schools, and others. The ten leading and second-line law schools and seventeen leading and second-line engineering schools were counted as high quality; the rest were coded low.[28] The aim, again, was to capture as much of the variation in exposure to the liberal arts as possible and to explore the cultural impact of the rise of mass education.

The main findings are these:

1. For the number of media areas in which highbrow exposure is reported,

amount of education makes little difference
from grade zero through "some college;"
thereafter, both quality of education and
sheer level count heavily. The biggest
jump in mean scores is between baccalaureate level and graduate level (.462), but
the difference between men with high-
and men with low-quality undergraduate
education (.318) is greater than the differences between less than high school vs.
high school (an infinitesimal .025), high
school vs. some college (.106) or even
some college and low-quality baccalaureate degree (.313).

Ultimately the mere rise in the average
education level will do little for the culti-
vation of taste in reading and in the
broadcast media; what counts is the number who complete college and especially
the number fortunate enough to go
through a few favored colleges.

2. For the avoidance of big slugs of
poor TV, sheer level of education counts
slightly more than quality, although the
differences are tiny until we come to
college populations. Here the three largest
differences are between "some college"
and the low-quality baccalaureate (2.401),
high-quality baccalaureate and low-quality
graduate school (2.060), and low-quality
and high-quality baccalaureate (1.479).

In sum: when we conceptualize "education" even at this crude level of "exposure to the liberal arts" and devise measures to match, we can gauge the cultural
impact of abundance with more precision.
These data suggest that the rising average
level of education will protect against
enervating amounts of the very shoddiest
media content but it will not cause large
populations to break the mediocrity barrier. As for the graduates of quality institutions, they will decline as a percentage of
the educated and, as I shall show below,
their exposure to quality print has declined
and perhaps will continue to decline as a
fraction of their leisure routine.

A final demonstration of the ambiguous
effects of education and of the structural
roots of cultural heterogeneity is in Table
1, which shows the impact of the organi-

zation of work and the level and quality
of education on "leisure competence." In
modern economies, group propensity and
opportunity to work vary greatly even
among occupational groups at the same
social level; Table 1 ranges my samples
in columns according to the proportion of
the group or stratum usually working 44
hours or less a week. You will recall that
the measure of "low leisure competence"
is a factor score tapping a style best described as the compulsive absorption of
much poor TV as a time-filler.

The table shows first that a simple structural fact—group schedules of work—is a
powerful source of diversity in leisure style.
"Low" leisure competence ranges from 17
per cent in long-hours groups to 65 per
cent in short-hours groups. The underdogs
are similar to short-hours engineers and
blue-collar workers: 61 per cent score low
competence. Within various work contexts, how does the education of the individual affect his leisure competence? Exposure to the liberal arts has a heavy
effect, which increases with shorter hours.
For instance, among the short-hours
groups, a high-quality bachelor's degree
brings the low competence rate down to
25 per cent; a low-quality bachelor's degree yields 45 per cent incompetence;
some college or less yields a whopping 73
per cent. The 343 men comprising that
73 per cent are the largest group and
have the lowest rate of competence in the
table. Among men not accustomed to the
wider universe made available by demanding work, it takes a long, expensive education to avoid an impoverished life. For
students of American culture who look
forward to the leisure-oriented society, in
which we retreat from work to the more
diversified joys of evershorter hours, the
moral is that those who have most leisure
have least resources for its creative use.

Structural roots of cultural homogeneity

So far I have asked, "who in all these
samples is exposed to high culture and
who avoids the very worst of mass culture?" I have not dealt with the *extent* of

highbrow exposure, the effects of diverse *types of media,* and above all, the *interaction between high culture and mass culture.* How much do men who could be expected to have cultivated tastes expose themselves to high culture? To what extent are intellectuals insulated from mass culture? Which media of communication have most and least impact on the standards of cultural elites and educated laymen?

Not everything that is wrong with our intellectuals, as Shils reminds us, can be attributed to the media or to mass culture; high culture has always been precarious.[29] But what *is* new, unique to our time, is a thorough interpenetration of cultural levels; the good, the mediocre, and the trashy are becoming fused in one massive middle mush.

Structural trends in the organization of intellectual life are at the root of the problem; among *intellectuals* and their educated publics we see: large numbers, spatial scattering, intense professional specialization, and a loss of a sense of autonomy and intellectual community (America, with more college graduates than any other nation in the world, does not have a first-rate intellectual weekly like the *Observer* in Britain). For both *intellectuals and the general population,* as I have suggested earlier, the cultural atmosphere is permeated by the mass media.

These are all in some measure requisites or consequences of abundance. Hundreds of thousands, eventually millions, of specialized experts and intellectuals are indispensable in a complex society. And the spread of higher education to the average man is both a manpower requirement of modern economies and a great achievement in equality.

The problem is not that the taste of the masses has been debased, but rather that the creators and maintainers of high culture in the humanities, the arts, the sciences, have an increasingly difficult time doing their proper work. Intellectuals are increasingly tempted to play to mass audiences and expose themselves to mass cul-

ture, and this has the effect of reducing their versatility of taste and opinion, their subtlety of expression and feeling.

There is little doubt from my data as well as others' that educated strata—even products of graduate and professional schools—are becoming full participants in mass culture; they spend a reduced fraction of time in exposure to quality print and film. This trend extends to the professors, writers, artists, scientists—the keepers of high culture themselves—and the chief culprit, again, is TV.[30]

You will remember that media researchers emphasize the limited power of mass communications by invoking the idea that the audience sorts itself out according to predisposition. By that formula, we should find the highly educated listening to Gerry Mulligan, watching Channel 9, and reading the *Partisan Review* (or at least *Harper's*); and the less educated should be listening to Elvis Presley, watching "Gunsmoke," and reading *True Detective.* The evidence is that the educated display, on balance, a mild tendency toward more discriminating tastes.

Studies consistently demonstrate that college graduates compared to the less educated have somewhat less exposure to the broadcast media, which are more uniform in their content, and somewhat more to print, which is more diversified. They are a bit more choosey in the regular programs they watch on TV; they definitely read more quality magazines and newspapers; and they listen to more serious music.[31] . . . For instance, over two-fifths of the professors, a third of the lawyers, and a tenth of the engineers compared to one in a hundred of the middle mass and none of the underdogs read a quality newspaper. And in reading the newspaper, the professional groups are somewhat more cosmopolitan and serious; they include world and national news as sections important to them more often than do the middle mass or underdogs. Similar differences appear for quality magazines read regularly. But the differences in exposure to print among my samples, as well as those in other studies based on broader samples, are not great. . . . Even here, if we pinpoint the groups and take interest in political news as a clue to wider perspectives, the most privileged, well-educated firm lawyers have only a 10 per cent edge over the middle mass; and engineers are about the same as lower white-collar workers. In his interest in world news, the solo lawyer has only a 7 per cent edge over the younger blue-collar worker. The differences in the proportion of diverse groups who rank local news as important to them in their daily reading are similarly small.[32]

Even more uniform from group to group are media habits tapped by more subtle measures of involvement with mass culture...being a loyal rooter for sports teams, rating comics as an important daily experience, becoming deeply involved with media heroes. And when we come to television, at least in America, the constraint of structural differentiation seems doomed; uniformity of behavior and taste is the main story. Nowhere else has a "class" audience been so swiftly transformed into a "mass" audience.

A recent nationwide survey of TV-viewers, sponsored by CBS, reports that those with more than four years of college average about 3 hours a day of viewing compared to the 4.3 hours of those with only grammar school education.[33] Admitted prime-time viewing is unrelated to education. When the CBS survey asked them to name their favorite programs (those watched regularly), over half of those at the top of the educational range named light-entertainment shows, the overwhelming preference of everyone else. Comedy, variety, and action (i.e., western, adventure, crime, police, private eye)—these were only slightly less common favorites among the college educated than among the less privileged.

Unfortunately, the actual record of viewing—in diaries, for instance—reveals even fewer differences.[34] Education has a lot more to do with how people *feel* about TV than what they *do* with it. College

graduates criticize TV programming, but they choose to watch extensively, and in doing so, find themselves in Mr. Minow's wasteland, unable, because of the limited highbrow fare available, to exert much more selectivity than the general population. They clearly display more signs of guilt and uneasiness at this state of affairs, but apparently it's not so punishing that it makes them flick the dial to "off."

Perhaps the most telling data demonstrating the interpenetration of brow levels, not merely in television viewing but also in reading, come from my samples in the Detroit area. Most of those who read at least one highbrow magazine also read middle- or lowbrow magazines. Only 3 per cent of all these men read only highbrow magazines. How about books? *Among college-educated professionals, only one in four claimed to have read a highbrow book in two months.* Only about three in five of the professors and lawyers, the most highly educated, entirely avoid lowbrow TV favorites. The typical professor crosses one or two levels of TV exposure. The engineers and executives, middle mass, and the underdogs on relief are quite similar in their TV-viewing habits. Television, again, appears to be a powerful force for cultural standardization, since these groups include men making more than $100,000 and others who have been unemployed for years. The department chief at GM, his foremen, and the unemployed autoworker on relief are bound together in the common culture of Huntley-Brinkley, "Restless Gun," and Mr. Clean.

If we consider magazines, books, newspapers, and TV together, what portion of these groups are exposed to any quality product in more than two areas? The answer: a minority of each group. Forty-three per cent of the professors score high on at least one item in each of three or four areas, 13 per cent of the lawyers, 5 per cent of the engineers and executives, 1 per cent of the middle mass, none of the underdogs.

The fact that the professors did so well

TABLE 1

Short-Hours Groups and Men on Relief Are Prone to Compulsive Absorption of Much Poor Television as a Time-Filler; Groups on Long Workweeks Display Higher Leisure Competence. Quality and Level of Education Increase Leisure Competence Most Among Short-Hours Groups.

Group Propensity and Opportunity to Work:*	Long-Hours Groups			Medium-Hours Groups				Short-Hours Groups				Unemployed Underdogs on Relief			Sample Total
Level of Education:	Professional or Graduate Degree			BA or More		Some College		BA or More		Some College					
Quality of Education:	High	Low	Total	High	Low	Low or Less	Total	High	Low	Low or Less	Total	Negro	White	Total	Total
	%	%	%	%	%	%	%	%	%	%	%	%	%	%	%
Leisure Competence†															
High	89	78	83	64	55	33	42	75	55	27	34	33	43	39	47
Low	11	22	17	36	45	67	57	25	45	73	65	67	57	61	52
Total	100	100	100	100	100	100	99	100	100	100	99	100	100	100	99
N	(141)	(134)	(275)	(44)	(127)	(271)	(442)	(32)	(64)	(343)	(439)	(81)	(105)	(186)	(1342)

* Long-hours groups are "Urban U." professors and all lawyers, solo or firm; only 17 to 22 per cent work 44 or fewer hours per week. Medium-hours groups are "Church U." professors, Unico engineers, and white-collar men of the middle mass, any age; 32 to 38 per cent have short work weeks. Short-hours groups are Diversico engineers, blue-collar men of the middle mass, any age; 52 to 59 per cent have short workweeks. Men on relief provide extreme contrast.

† A factor score: 47 men scoring 20–30 on "Low Leisure Competence" and 599 scoring 40–49 were combined to form the high competence category; 89 men scoring 60–79 and 619 men scoring 50–59 comprise the low competence category. Twelve unemployed in the middle mass are excluded from this table. For details on measures, see text.

in this generally dismal picture encouraged me to carry out a special analysis of deviant cases—those who use print and television for enlightenment and stimulation and seek the quality product for entertainment.

Portrait of the media purist

Who are the media purists—men who insulate themselves fully from mass culture? We could not find one case in 1,354 who was not in some area exposed to middle- or lowbrow material. By relaxing the definition, however, we located nineteen men who make rather heroic efforts to cultivate the best in the media. They either (1) report some highbrow exposure in all four media areas (magazines, books, newspapers, TV) *and* are exclusively highbrow in one or more reading areas; or (2) have no TV set or never watch TV, have some highbrow exposure in the three reading areas, and are exclusively highbrow in one reading area.

The characteristics of the nineteen men suggest that one must be a very odd fellow in America to avoid mass culture. All but two were educated in high-quality liberal arts colleges and graduate schools or were educated abroad—a very rare pattern. In occupation, sixteen were professors (thirteen of high rank, especially in the humanities, mathematics, and physics); three were prosperous corporation lawyers. As a group, the media purists have inherited higher occupational status than their colleagues (their parents tend to be established professionals and executives)—which suggests that it may take rather close family supervision over more than a generation to inculcate a taste for high culture. In religion they are more often Jewish or have no preference or are inactive Protestants. Several are intermarried or in other ways have experienced cultural discontinuity. In origin, training, and position, then, this group is at once high status and marginal.

What constitutes the style of life of media purists? In consumption, they are almost ascetic; among the professors, their relatively high incomes are spent only minimally for luxury possessions, homes, cars, vacations, or charity. They are apartment-dwellers more often than home-owners. They tend to be ambitious, independent-minded, like to "go-it-alone." Their media exposure is not only more highbrow; it is more extensive.

Although these media purists stand outside American society ideologically, they are well integrated socially and politically. As one would expect, they are to a man highly critical of the media. They are also generally estranged from the major power centers in the United States—except for the federal courts, which they feel are doing an excellent job. In participation patterns, however, they belong to more organizations and are attached to more than their colleagues. The professors among them are almost all active, liberal Democrats; the lawyers are conventional, moderate Republicans.

In short, it takes such an unusual set of experiences in family, school, and career to produce a media purist that they are practically nonexistent.

Implications for Sociological Theory

In applying the larger debate about the shape of modern society to the mass media and mass entertainment in America, I have brought systematic survey data to bear on the problem of the interplay of social structure, mass culture, and high culture. I have tried to resolve the paradox of a simultaneous growth of structural differentiation and cultural uniformity by reexamining the structural roots of media exposure and response. These data point up the need for a merger of the main characterizations of modern society—"mass," "industrial," and "urban." Specifically, three lessons can be learned.

1. The sketchy treatment of mass culture in theories of the mass society and the very limited idea of the two-step flow of mass communications, which accents the healthy absorption of the media into local cultures, demand more sophisticated

treatment of the social structures in which the media are received. My data suggest that we need to slice up social structure in ways that capture both the persistence of older divisions (age, religion, occupation) and the emergence of newer ones (the quality and content of education) and to do it more precisely than usual. To say "white collar" or "working class" is to obscure most of what is central to the experience of the person and the structure of society. To say "professional, technical, and kindred" captures more of social life but not much more. "Lawyer" and "engineer" move us closer to social reality, for these men develop quite different styles of life, rooted in diverse professional schools, tasks, work schedules, and organizational contexts. To say "independent practitioner" is to say even more, and finally, to particularize the matter with "solo lawyer" vs. "firm lawyer" is to take account of the sharp contrasts in recruitment base (social origins, religion, quality of professional training), career pattern, and rewards which divide the two.

In general, data both here and in other studies suggest that as predictors of lifestyle variables—especially cultural tastes and ideology—sex, age, and social-economic stratum are far weaker than religion, type of education, work and career—variables that represent positions in established groups. The implication is clear: return to the study of group life.

2. Television, the most "massified" of the mass media, the one with the largest and most heterogeneous audience, has become central to the leisure routine of majorities at every level. The usual differences in media exposure and response among age, sex, and class categories—easy to exaggerate in any case—have virtually disappeared in the case of television. Even here, however, where we pinpoint social groups—an occupation supported by an occupational community, a religion buttressed by a religious community—some differences do remain. And among the printed media, where most competition prevails, the chance of such groups to stylize their uses of mass communications remains strong.

3. The paradox of the simultaneous growth of structural differentiation and cultural uniformity is thus partly a matter of our weak concepts and measures of social structure and our consequent failure to spot group-linked variations in life style. But it may also reflect the state of an affluent society in transition. In order to pin down the cultural impact of continued economic growth, we require data not now in hand. For countries at similar levels of economic development, having diverse cultural traditions and systems of education and communications, we need data on levels of mass taste, organization and self-conceptions of cultural elites, distance between educated and less educated in exposure to mass culture and high culture. Until we have such systematic comparisons, I will assume that structure and culture are congruent and massified in rapidly developing new nations and that they become increasingly *in*congruent at levels of development thus far achieved. Finally, as rich countries grow richer, homogenizing structures in politics, education, and mass communications combine with an already high level of cultural uniformity to reduce the hold of differentiating structures of age, religion, work, and locality, and bring about greater consistency of structure and culture—a new combination of "mass" society and "industrial" society, mass culture and high culture.

4. Many leads in my data point to the need for synthesis not only of ideas about industrial society and mass society but also of ideas about pluralism and totalitarianism. I can here merely indicate the direction of these findings. Briefly, what takes place in the economy and the locality—work, consumption, and participation in formal associations—forms coherent styles of life, one of which I have come to label "Happy Good Citizen-Consumer." The style includes these pluralist-industrial traits: strong attachment to the community (supporting increased school taxes,

contributing generously to churches and charity, thinking of the neighborhood as one's "real home," voting in elections); consumer enthusiasm (planning to buy or to replace many luxury possessions); optimism about national crises; a strong belief that distributive justice prevails (feeling that jobs are distributed fairly). It also involves long hours at gratifying work, little or no leisure malaise; wide-ranging, stable secondary ties and, to some extent, wide-ranging, stable primary ties—the very model of a modern pluralist citizen. But this benign pattern of work, consumption, and participation is independent of participation in and feelings about mass culture. And both happy good citizenry and the uses of the mass media are more or less independent of approaches to national politics—or at least go together in ways not anticipated in received theory. Thus, the good citizen-consumers tend to be unusually prone to personality voting (party-switching, ticket-splitting), dependent on the media for opinions on issues, susceptible to advertising and to mass behavior generally (e.g., they score high on a measure of susceptibility to manipulation by the media in politics and consumption). Men who have confidence in the major institutions of American society distrust "TV and radio networks"; men who trust the media distrust other institutions. Finally, men whose social relations are stable tend to have fluid party loyalties. *To be socially integrated in America is to accept propaganda, advertising, and speedy obsolescence in consumption.* The fact is that those who fit the image of pluralist man in the pluralist society also fit the image of mass man in the mass society. Any accurate picture of the shape of modern society must accommodate these ambiguities.

* A paper presented at the 58th Annual Meeting of the American Sociological Association, Los Angeles, August 27, 1963. It is part of "Work, Careers, and Leisure Styles: A Study of Sources of Social Integration," a program of research made possible by the generous support of the National Institute of Mental Health (M–2209, 2958–63), the Department of So-

ciology of the University of Michigan, and the Center for Advanced Study in the Behavioral Sciences. The aim of the larger study is to discover those aspects of work and leisure which bind individuals and groups to community and society and those which foster alienation and estrangement. This paper is an elaboration and test of ideas in my "Social Structure, Popular Culture, and Mass Behavior," *Studies in Public Communication,* 3 (Summer, 1961), pp. 15–22; the material, used by permission of the Free Press of Glencoe, Inc., is based on a forthcoming book. I am grateful to Guy E. Swanson and David Gold for critical readings and to John C. Scott, Michael T. Aiken, and David Reynolds for research assistance.

1 Alexis de Tocqueville, *Democracy in America* (New York: Alfred A. Knopf, Inc., 1948) 2 vols.; Karl Mannheim, *Man and Society in an Age of Reconstruction* (London: Routledge & Kegan Paul, Ltd., 1940).

2 Cf. William Kornhauser's treatment of "accessible elites" and "available masses" in *The Poiltics of Mass Society* (New York: Free Press of Glencoe, Inc., 1959).

3 Cooley, Mayo, and their students emphasize the functions of primary groups in the maintenance of social order and cite reasons for their declining functions and authority. Since the primary group is the training ground for good citizenship, its decline, they felt, would produce mass men who would produce a "mass society," "anomie," or "social disorganization." Charles H. Cooley, *Social Organization* (New York: Charles Scribner's Sons, 1927); Elton Mayo, *The Human Problems of an Industrial Civilization* (Cambridge: Harvard University Press, 1933), esp pp. 122 ff. and *The Social Problems of an Industrial Civilization* (Cambridge: Harvard University Press, 1945), Chs. 2 and 5. Tocqueville, among other nineteenth-century observers, and Lederer, Neumann, and DeGré, among modern students of totalitarianism, tend to emphasize the functions of secondary associations in the maintenance of social order or democratic political systems, or both. Alienation from work, politics, and community, and a related susceptibility to mass movements, they argue, are mainly due to the weakness of independent organizations lying between the nuclear family and the state. Tocqueville, *op. cit.*; Emil Lederer, *State of the Masses* (New York: W. W. Norton & Company, Inc., 1940); Franz L. Neumann, *Behemoth* (New York: Oxford University Press, Inc., 1942); and Gerard DeGré, "Freedom and Social Structure," *American Sociological Review,* 11 (October, 1946), pp. 529–536. Cf. Robert A. Nisbet, *The Quest for Community* (New York: Oxford University Press, Inc., 1953). Emile Durkheim was aware of the possible links of both primary and secondary groups to the level of social integration. He tended to stress the atrophy of pri-

mary-group life as a source of anomie and expressed the hope that larger secondary associations (especially the occupational group or workplace) could emerge as new bonds of solidarity, new sources of civic virtue. *The Division of Labor in Society*, trans. George Simpson (New York: Free Press of Glencoe, Inc., 1947) pp. 1–31. (In later writings, Durkheim increasingly emphasized the second point.)

4 In evidence, the critics say, look at the following studies: Fritz J. Roethlisberger and William J. Dickson, *Management and the Worker* (Cambridge: Harvard University Press, 1939); Paul F. Lazarsfeld, Bernard Berelson, and Hazel Gaudet, *The People's Choice* (New York: Columbia University Press, 1948); Morris Janowitz, *The Community Press in an Urban Setting* (New York: Free Press of Glencoe, Inc., 1952); Scott Greer, "Urbanism Reconsidered: A Comparative Study of Local Areas in a Metropolis," *American Sociological Review*, 21 (February, 1956), pp. 19–25; Marvin B. Sussman, "The Help Pattern in the Middle Class Family," *American Sociological Review*, 18 (February, 1953), pp. 22–28; J. Smith, W. H. Form, and G. P. Stone, "Local Intimacy in a Middle-Sized City," *American Journal of Sociology*, 60 (November, 1954), pp. 276–284; Charles R. Wright and Herbert H. Hyman, "Voluntary Association Memberships of American Adults: Evidence from National Sample Surveys," *American Sociological Review*, 23 (June, 1958), pp. 284–294; Daniel Miller and Guy E. Swanson, *The Changing American Parent* (New York: John Wiley & Sons, Inc., 1958); E. Katz and Paul F. Lazarsfeld, *Personal Influence* (New York: Free Press of Glencoe, Inc., 1955); Michael Young and Peter Willmott, *Family and Kinship in East London* (New York: Free Press of Glencoe, Inc., 1957); Joseph T. Klapper, *The Effects of Mass Communication* (New York: Free Press of Glencoe; Inc., 1960); etc.

5 See Harold L. Wilensky and Charles N. Lebeaux, *Industrial Society and Social Welfare* (New York: Russell Sage Foundation, 1958), Ch. 5.

6 For an assessment of the evidence on the vitality of social participation, see Harold L. Wilensky, "Life Cycle, Work Situation, and Participation in Formal Associations," in R. W. Kleemeier, ed., *Aging and Leisure* (New York: Oxford University Press, Inc., 1961), and "Social Structure...," *op. cit.*; for an empirical study of the integrative potential of various types of social relations, see Harold L. Wilensky, "Orderly Careers and Social Participation," *American Sociological Review*, 26 (August, 1961), pp. 521–539.

7 Cf. Philip Selznick, "Institutional Vulnerability in Mass Society," *American Journal of Sociology*, 56 (January, 1951), pp. 320–331; Bernard Rosenberg and David Manning White,

eds., *Mass Culture* (New York: Free Press of Glencoe, Inc., 1957); and Kornhauser, *op. cit.*

8 See e.g., Klapper, *op. cit.*, and Raymond A. and Alice H. Bauer, "America, 'Mass Society' and Mass Media," *Journal of Social Issues*, 16 (1960), pp. 3–56.

9 Following Blumer and Wirth, the "mass" is a collectivity which is big, heterogeneous (dispersed geographically and cross-cutting many groups and subcultures), and socially-unstructured (comprised of individuals who do not share norms and values relevant to the situation—individuals who are unattached for a time, not in role, and can therefore behave in a uniform, undifferentiated way.) Herbert Blumer, "Elementary Collective Behavior," in Alfred McClung Lee, ed., *New Outline of the Principles of Sociology*, (New York: Barnes & Noble, Inc., 1946), pp. 185 ff., and Louis Wirth, "Urbanism as a Way of Life," *American Journal of Sociology*, 44 (July, 1938), pp. 1–24. On the public, see also Robert E. Park, *Masse und Publikum: Eine Methodologische und Soziologische Untersuchung*. Inaugural-Dissertation der Hohenphilosophischen Fakultaet der Ruprecht-Karls-Universitaet zu Heidelberg (Bern: Lack & Grunau, 1904).

10 A major theme in Kornhauser, *op. cit.*, a creative synthesis of literature on sources of extremism, is that totalitarian control depends on the institutionalization of "high availability" of the mass (p. 62). Totalitarian regimes deliberately atomize the mass (via forced migration, purges, terror), but since mass behavior is unpredictable, they need to "keep the masses in a state of constant activity controlled by the elite" (p. 123) and so, these regimes take steps to remain with their subjects "one gigantic movement" (p. 62). Three questions about this argument may be raised. First, the implication that Bolshevik power, as a key case, depends on "massification" and the latter makes the regime vulnerable runs counter to the apparent stability of Soviet society. Second, if totalitarian nations had to keep the masses in a constant state of mobilization, we would expect them to become increasingly terror-ridden. Although the variable use of terror thus far does not provide sufficient evidence on long-run trends, much totalitarian terror has seemed to give way to other means of control. Finally, the treatment of mass "availability" is tautological. Availability is indicated by (1) a high rate of mass behavior and (2) lack of attachment to independent groups. Here the hypothetical causes of mass behavior are confused with the idea of mass behavior itself (cf. 40– 41, 61–62). I have dealt with this in my study by maintaining a distinction between mass behavior as particular acts in time and space (e.g., responding to a gasoline ad or a demogogue without reference to group norms) and persistent structures that presumably give rise to

it (e.g., a pattern of impoverished social relations).

11 Within the general framework of a policy of strenuous intervention (even in strictly philosophical matters) the Soviet regime has alternated application and relaxation of controls over intellectual life. J. M. Bochenski in A. Inkeles and K. Geiger, eds., *Soviet Society,* (Boston: Houghton Mifflin Company, 1961), pp 454 ff. Despite these ups and downs, Soviet commitment to modernization has forced some liberalization. In the short run (e.g., during the period of maximum Stalinist terror) the regime can do pretty much what it likes with particular disciplines: It can wipe out genetics by persecuting Mendelian deviationists; it can proscribe quantum mechanics as inconsistent with dialectical materialism. But over the long pull, some disciplines stand up better than others. For instance, some disciplines once purged now flourish in relative freedom (linguistics, poetics); others do not (genetics, history, literary history and criticism, economics). To demonstrate such variable resistance, however, we would need data on the degree of vulnerability to the purge in each case (number put to death, imprisoned, removed from any office, removed from top office only, merely forced to recant, etc.) and on the persistence of each group beyond the purge (men and resources devoted to the discipline, quality of output, success of efforts to maintain autonomy). To demonstrate further that resistance to state penetration is a function of the pre-existing organization and tradition of the discipline as well as the indispensability of its contribution to Soviet power would require the same systematic comparisons.

12 Richard H. Bolt in a National Science Foundation study has analyzed numbers of baccalaureate and first professional degrees expressed as a percentage of the college-graduating-age cohort (median about 22 years). The ratio increased slowly from about 1.3 per cent in 1870 to about 2 per cent in 1910 and then increased roughly logistically to nearly 20 per cent by 1960. A similar acceleration of high-school graduates had already markedly set in by 1900, and by 1960, high-school graduates exceeded 70 per cent of the relevant age cohort. Unpublished manuscript, 1963.

13 Edward A. Shils, "Demagogues and Cadres in the Political Development of the New States," in Lucien W. Pye ed., *Communications and Political Development* (Princeton, N.J.: Princeton University Press, 1963), p. 67.

14 William Graham Sumner, *Folkways* (Boston: Ginn & Company, 1906), pp. 5–6.

15 Donald V. McGranahan and Ivor Wayne, "German and American Traits Reflected in Popular Drama," *Human Relations,* 1 (1948), pp. 429–455.

16 Wilensky, "Social Structure..." *op. cit.,*

p. 21. Tabulations based on 678 interviews with a cross-section of white males in the middle mass (upper working class and lower middle class) of the Detroit area, aged 21–55, show that our indicators of susceptibility in advertising and politics are indeed correlated. We assumed that candidate switchers—Democrats who went for Ike, the (less numerous) Republicans for "Soapy" Williams—were responding to personality appeals in recent campaigns. Then we asked those who own cars and notice gas ads, if, when they hear claims made in these ads, they "ever try a tankful or so to see how true the ads are." We also asked everyone how often he had bought something because he saw it advertised and then found he'd been stuck. Among those who never completed high school (whatever their income) and among young high-school graduates with low family incomes (in this sample that means $5,000–8,000), it is the loyal party men who try a tankful; but among the vanguard populations —higher-education, higher-income men—it is the candidate-switcher or ticket-splitter who takes a flier, especially among middle-aged, upper-income, high-school graduates and young college men (whatever their income). Incidentally, these same college-educated Eisenhower Democrats report that they get stuck in the product market quite often. The link between mass behavior in consumption and politics is most visible among men of the future.

17 Winston White, *Beyond Conformity* (New York: Free Press of Glencoe, Inc., 1961), and the early writings of David Riesman.

18 If there is more independent variation of politics and culture in the United States than in other rich countries, it may stem from our greater gap between intellectuals and the government, the split that Tocqueville noted between intelligence and action. In several parts of Europe, notably Britain and Scandinavia, the media to some extent feel compelled to reflect the work of the intellectuals—the statesman, the educator, the serious artist. In the United States, the media reflect more the work of the businessman as advertiser, the artist as entertainer, the politician as damagogue; they are typically managed and staffed by anti-intellectual intellectuals. Cf. Reuel Denney, *The Astonished Muse* (Chicago: The University of Chicago Press, 1957), p. 216, and Richard Chase, *The Democratic Vista* (Garden City: Doubleday & Co., Inc., 1958), *passim.*

19 The reciprocal influence of the mass media and mass education has received little serious attention. A few of the obvious possibilities are: (1) Extensive exposure in the home accustoms the child to visual and oral communication of the simplest sort; teachers and curriculum-planners respond by using the media to make education more entertaining, using the child's television experience (e.g.,

current events) as the basis for class discussion —generally displacing time otherwise devoted to a more systematic treatment of history or geography. (2) The average college receives students unaccustomed to disciplined reading and adapts assignments and techniques accordingly. (3) In school and college alike, manners, morals, and speech are more subtly influenced—with self-display becoming a new ideal and publicity-consciousness a new set of mind. The "show and tell" sessions of our elementary schools, like the audience participation and panel shows of television, combine both. Whether the post-Sputnik spurt in "hard" subjects (a product of cold-war competition) together with the oversupply of youngsters (a product of the changing age distribution, which increases competition for college entrance) will offset the penetration of mass culture into the schools is unknown. As all these forces converge, the cultural tastes of the average college professor, like those of the schoolteacher, will weigh in the outcome.

20 For some lines of inquiry, see Pye, *op. cit.*

21 G. A. Steiner, *The People Look at Television* (New York: Alfred A. Knopf, Inc., 1963), pp. 4, 112; and citations in footnote 30 below.

22 Fritz Machlup, *The Production and Distribution of Knowledge in the United States* (Princeton N.J.: Princeton University Press, 1962), p. 104.

23 The analysis is based on detailed interviews with probability samples or universes of 6 professional groups (100 solo lawyers; 107 firm lawyers in the 19 Detroit firms with 10 or more partners and associates; 31 professors at "Church University"; 68 professors at "Urban University"; 91 engineers at "Unico" and 93 at "Diversico"—generally research and development specialists, supervisors, or executives) ; a probability sample of the middle mass ($N=678$) ; and, as a sharp contrast, two samples of "underdogs," 81 Negro and 105 white, who were severely deprived. The interviews took place in the first half of 1960. Only males who were in the labor force, 55 years old or younger and currently or previously married were interviewed. All the professionals had college degrees. The special selection criteria are described in Harold L. Wilensky, "The Uneven Distribution of Leisure: The Impact of Economic Growth on 'Free Time,' " *Social Problems,* IX (Summer, 1961), p. 38; "Orderly Careers...," *op. cit.,* pp. 529–530; and "The Moonlighter: A Product of Relative Deprivation," *Industrial Relations,* 3 (October, 1963), pp. 106–108. It is important to note that the leading colleges and universities are well represented in the backgrounds of men in the professional samples. Three-quarters of the firm lawyers, for instance, are graduates of one of five elite "national" law schools—Chicago,

Columbia, Harvard, Michigan, and Yale. Like the professors—full-time faculty in the humanities and physical sciences (including mathematics) in two arts and sciences colleges— these lawyers may be assumed to have had as much opportunity to acquire discriminating tastes as their counterparts in other cities.

24 Two independent studies, using impressionistic judgments to rank magazines, arrived at results so similar to one another (a rank order correlation coefficient of .93 for 49 magazines) that one is tempted to defend a ranking of the entire range, not merely the validity of three categories. Babette Kass, "Overlapping Magazine Reading: A New Method of Determining the Cultural Level of Magazines," in Paul F. Lazarsfeld and Frank N. Stanton, eds., *Communications Research: 1948–1949* (New York: Harper & Row, Publishers, Inc., 1949), p. 133, Table 1.

26 The most perceptive treatment is David Riesman, *Constraint and Variety in American Education* (Garden City, New York: Doubleday & Co., Inc., 1958).

27 Hayward Keniston, *Graduate Study and Research in the Arts and Sciences at the University of Pennsylvania* (Philadelphia: University of Pennsylvania Press, 1959), p. 119.

28 Respondents are coded according to the highest degree attained. The category, "baccalaureate degree, low quality," includes 121 engineers plus the 53 men of the middle mass who have a degree; the 63 men with a high-quality baccalaureate are all engineers. I assumed that the best graduates and professional schools draw from the best liberal arts colleges.

29 Edward A. Shils, "Mass Society and Its Culture," *Daedalus,* 89 (Spring, 1960), pp. 288–314.

30 Any assertion about long-term trends is inferential; we lack good base-line data. My position rests on three considerations. First, there is scattered evidence that the broadcast media in competition with print generally win out—in attraction, number of hours, perhaps persuasiveness, too. Reading, especially of books and magazines, declines. T. E. Coffin, "Television's Impact on Society," *The American Psychologist,* 10 (October, 1955), p. 633; L. Bogart, *The Age of Television,* 2d ed., New York: Frederick Ungar), 1958, pp. 133 ff.; James N. Mosel, "Communications Patterns and Political Socialization in Transitional Thailand," in Pye, *op. cit.,* pp. 184–228; and Klapper, *op. cit.,* pp. 107 ff. Second, among the educated, total exposure to broadcast media has recently increased. Before television, radio listening among set owners averaged 4.9 hours daily; evening listening averaged 2.6 hours for all, 2.4 hours for college graduates. Program preferences did not vary much by education. P. F. Lazarsfeld, *The People Look at Radio,*

(Chapel Hill, N.C.: The University of North Carolina Press, 1946), pp. 97–98, 136. Today, even excluding highbrow FM, radio listening has not declined to zero. (The typical radio family that acquired a television set cut radio listening from four or five hours to about two hours a day. Bogart, *op. cit.,* p. 114.) Meanwhile, television viewing for the average product of a graduate or professional school rose from zero to three hours daily. Steiner, *op. cit.,* p. 75. If we assume no major increase in the workweek of the educated and no change in life style that can remotely touch television in sheer hours, their exposure to undifferentiated broadcast media has risen as a portion of the daily round while their exposure to serious print has declined. And the small differences in amount and quality of television exposure reported in the text indicate that the educated are not especially discriminating. Finally, the argument about the effect of intellectuals' participation in mass culture on their standards of performance and appreciation proceeds through example and counter example without the benefit of much systematic evidence. "Raymond Aron's thought," says Edward Shils, "does not deteriorate because he occasionally writes in The *New York Times Magazine." Op. cit.,* p. 306. Unfortunately, we cannot know what the quality of Aron's thought would have been if as a young man he had been watching "situation comedies" instead of reading books. As a master of ambiguous polemic, Shils presents the best defense of the view that mass culture has little effect on high culture; but in listing the structural forces that threaten high culture, he gives inadequate weight to them and no weight at all to the major problem we confront here—central tendencies in the life styles of educated strata.

31 Cf. Paul F. Lazarsfeld, *Radio and the*

Printed Page (New York: Duell, Sloan, & Pearce, Inc., 1940); B. Berelson and M. Janowitz, *Reader in Public Opinion and Communication* (New York: Free Press of Glencoe Inc., 1953), Part 7; L. Bogart, "Newspapers in the Age of Television," *Daedalus* (Winter, 1963), pp. 116–127, and other essays in that issue; and the citations in footnote 30 above.

32 If you are inclined to use the British as a case on the other side, you will receive little support from Mark Abrams' careful study of the media habits of the sociocultural elite of Great Britain. "The Mass Media and Social Class in Great Britain," paper presented at the Fourth World Congress of Sociology, Stresa, Italy, September, 1958. The upper 1 per cent in education and occupational status (from a random sample of 13,620 adults, aged 25 and over) reported media habits so similar to those of the mass public that one is reluctant to use the label "cultural elite." More of them read the *Daily Express* and *Daily Mail* than the *Times* or *Guardian;* their movie habits—both in frequency of attendance and choice of films —are hardly differentiated from those of the rest of the population. The only real gap between mass tastes and elite tastes is the preference of the latter for no TV or BBC programs over commercial programs. A qualification is in order: while prestige dailies lag in circulation, good Sunday papers—the *Observer,* the *Times,* the *Telegraph*—show a marked increase. Further, the recent return to BBC of large television audiences once lost to commercial competition tells us that a speedy decline in mass tastes is not inevitable, although it does not challenge the proposition that the interpenetration of brow levels threatens high culture.

33 Steiner, *op. cit.,* p. 75
34 *Ibid.,* p. 161.

6 Mass, Class, and the Industrial Community

BY CHARLES M. BONJEAN

Sociologists and social philosophers have set forth two contradictory theoretical perspectives in regard to the nature of stratification in contemporary American society.

The traditional perspective, stemming from the works of Marx and Weber, suggests that an increasing division of labor associated with differential rewards (both

Paper presented at the annual meeting of the Society for the Study of Social Problems, Chicago, Illinois, August, 1965. Published in

the American Journal of Sociology (Sept., 1966). Printed by permission of the author and The University of Chicago Press.

material and nonmaterial or economic and prestige) results in different societal levels, the members of which subscribe to different values and attitudes and engage in distinctive patterns of behavior.[1] Although one may identify different types of stratification theories—for example, conservative and radical or those focusing on stability as opposed to those dealing with change— the feature shared by all is their concern with heterogeneity—different values, beliefs, attitudes, and behavior at different levels in society.[2] Some investigators have even suggested that life styles of bureaucrats (sometimes termed the "new middle class") and entrepreneurs (sometimes termed the "old middle class") differ not only from those of the "working class" but from one another.[3] The concern, then, is with status and situs *differences*.

Another theoretical perspective, somewhat less systematic, not as well grounded empirically, and in some respects contradictory to stratification theory is that known as the "mass-society" perspective. The central foci of theories classified as such are many and varied, but one common thread running through many of them is the idea that an increasing division of labor and its concomitants—industrialization, bureaucratization, and urbanization —has had a leveling effect, effacing, or at least blurring, social stratification.[4] In fact, it has been suggested that the *main* theme of these theorists is: "the *mass society* develops a *mass culture* in which cultural and political values and beliefs tend to be *homogeneous* and *fluid*...."[5] Thus, the term "middle mass" has come to be used to refer to some elements formerly described as "middle class" *and* to some formerly described as "working class."[6] It has even been suggested that the traditional indicators of social class no longer discriminate among many of the attitudes and behavior patterns of the middle mass.[7]

The purpose of this investigation was to explore the relative descriptive utility of the two perspectives in a community setting recently and rapidly having undergone those processes usually considered

the antecedents of the formation of a middle mass—urbanization, bureaucratization, and industrialization. More specifically, the research design called for a comparison of three middle-mass occupational categories—independent businessmen, corporate supervisors and managers, and hourly paid workers—on a number of socio-personality and social-participation variables, selected because they are often used in descriptions of the middle mass. In short, if the middle mass is homogeneous, we would expect it to be such in regard to those characteristics of central concern to mass-society theorists. At the same time, this sampling design permits an analysis of the relative effects of class and bureaucratic work setting on these same dependent variables. Among the possible findings and their implications would be the following:

M Significant differences between all
B three categories in the order (1)
W managers, (2) businessmen, and (3) workers (or reversed, depending upon the dependent variable), would give clear support to stratification theory and question the utility of the concept "middle mass" in the industrial-community setting, as indeed these groups (as will be shown below) rank in this order on socioeconomic characteristics.

MB Significant differences between the
W working-class sample and the two middle-class samples would also support stratification theory but would question the utility of the distinction sometimes made between bureaucrats and entrepreneurs—or the "old" and "new" middle classes, at least in the industrial-community context.

M Significant differences between
BW managers and the other two categories would suggest that the middle mass may consist of the old middle class and the working class but that bureaucratization has modified the social structure of the community by sharply differentiating the new middle class from the middle mass.

MW   Significant differences between
  B   those employed in bureaucratic
       work settings (managers and
       workers) and those self-employed
       in nonbureaucratic settings (busi-
       nessmen) would lend some support
       to the mass-society perspective in
       that it would suggest that bureau-
       cratization is a leveling agent and
       that traditional indicators of social
       class no longer discriminate among
       those characteristics under investi-
       gation, at least not in the industrial
       community.

WBM   No significant differences between
       the three categories would indeed
       justify viewing all three as a homo-
       geneous middle mass.

The Community and the Samples

Prior to 1950, Gulftown[8] was an agricultural and fishing-industries center with
a population slightly in excess of 2,000.
Since that time, two major corporations
have located plants in the Gulftown area,
changing the employment structure of the
community and boosting its population to
more than 11,000. Today, almost one-third
of the community's labor force is employed by Plant X (a nonferrous metal
producer employing 1,700, some of whom
are from nearby communities, rather than
from Gulftown) and Plant Y (a chemical
company employing 850, including some
from nearby communities). Slightly more
than one-fifth of the labor force is engaged
in wholesale and retail trade activities. In
short, the community has experienced
rapid growth as a consequence of industrialization, and the largest segment of the
community's labor force is employed as
managers or hourly paid workers in
bureaucratic organizations.

Lists of salaried managers, hourly paid
workers, and independent businessmen living in Gulftown were compiled, and a
random probability sample (and ordered
alternate list) was drawn from each.[9] A
total of 332 interviews were completed
with 104 businessmen, 108 managers, and
120 workers.[10]

Managers

Personnel departments in Plants X and
Y identified all salaried employees as members of management. Their definition was
accepted for this investigation, and the
personnel managers of each plant checked
the sample lists to verify classifications.
The management sample included both
staff and line members of both plants.
Department heads, professionals, several
levels of foremen and clerks were typical
of the occupational positions represented
in this sample. All, with the exception of
line foremen, are "white-collar" employees.
As Table 1 indicates, managers ranked
higher than either of the other two groups
on all socioeconomic characteristics investigated (items 1–5): income, education,
self-classification, and class assignment by
the Index of Social Position.[11] The managers were also compared with the other
two categories on other characteristics
(Table 1, items 6–9) that could possibly
be related to the dependent variables
selected for this analysis. Because managers
were significantly younger than businessmen, we included a significantly smaller
proportion of the Spanish-surname population and fewer Catholics, and these were
used as control variables in the data analysis to be described below.

Businessmen

The independent businessmen in the
sample possess those characteristics defined
as entrepreneurial by other investigators:
They were self-employed, gained at least
half of their income in the form of profits
or fees, or worked in an organization having only two levels of supervision.[12] They
ranged from those operating small service
businesses with no employees (e.g., beauty
shops, watch repair shops, and so forth)
to three with more than thirty employees
(e.g., the owner-manager of a chain of

TABLE 1

Characteristics of Three Occupational Categories

Characteristic	Managers N = 108	Businessmen N = 104	Workers N = 120	Significant Differences
1. Median monthly income	$800.00	$661.00	$594.00	M-W, M-B, B-W*
2. Per cent having attended college	69.5	36.5	25.9	M-W, M-B
3. Per cent having graduated from college	38.9	8.6	1.7	M-W, M-B, B-W
4. Per cent classifying themselves "middle class"	69.0	54.0	35.0	M-W, M-B, B-W
5. Median Index of Social Position class placement	2.8	3.1	4.1	M-W, M-B, B-W†
6. Per cent having lived in Gulftown less than 10 years	50.9	38.5	41.7	none
7. Mean age	40.6	45.2	39.3	M-B, B-W
8. Per cent Spanish-surname	0.9	5.8	25.0	M-W, B-W
9. Per cent Catholic	14.8	21.2	26.7	M-W

* Median income for all three samples was $670. Significantly different proportions of the three samples had incomes above this grand median.

† The median index of social-position score for all three samples was 3.28. Significantly different proportions of the three samples were found in Classes I–III.

five drive-in restaurants). The median number of employees (including the respondent) was four. As shown in Table 1 (items 1–5), businessmen ranked second on all socioeconomic characteristics.

Workers

The hourly paid employees of Plants X and Y are included in this sample—operators, mechanics, potmen, machinists, power attendants, and so forth. Workers ranked lowest on all socioeconomic status characteristics investigated (Table 1, items 1–5). They were also significantly younger than the businessmen (item 7), included significantly more Catholics than the managers (item 9), and had a significantly greater proportion of Spanish-surname respondents than either of the other two samples (item 8).

Dependent Variables and Method of Comparison

All three samples were administered a standardized twenty-three-page interview schedule consisting of 282 questions (both open-end and poll types).[13] Two types of variables, often used in describing members of "mass" societies, were selected as dependent variables for this analysis. Because of the attention given by "mass-society" theorists to "personal disorganization" and to "atomization" or a deterioration of social relationships, our concern was with sociopersonality characteristics and with various measures of social participation.

1. Sociopersonality characteristics

Each of these variables concerns some perception or feeling state of the respondent in regard to some aspect of himself or his own social position. They were selected because (1) they have been used to describe members of "mass societies,"[14] (2) they have also been related to socioeconomic status,[15] and (3) some have been used in describing employees in complex organizations (and, at least by implication, are assumed to be less characteristic or not characteristic of members of small-scale organizations).[16] The research design outlined above permits us to assess the relative descriptive utility of each of these assertions. Sociopersonality characteristics considered here include alienation (and three subscales—powerlessness, normlessness, and isolation),[17] anomia,[18] self-actualization,[19] self-esteem,[20] self-estrangement,[21] and status concern.[22]

2. Social participation and involvement

These variables were selected because (1) "mass" societies have been described as "automized" societies where "personal relations" are lacking and where "intermediate relations of community, occupation, and association are more or less inoperative,"[23] (2) different forms of social participation and social involvement are said to be characteristic of different socioeconomic strata,[24] and (3) some forms of social participation and involvement are said to be associated with bureaucratic as opposed to entrepreneurial work settings.[25] Those measures of social participation and involvement selected for this analysis include two measures of community attachment,[26] neighborhood integration,[27] participation in organized groups,[28] religious participation,[29] home visits with friends,[30] visiting with relatives,[31] political participation,[32] and a general social-participation scale.[33]

The focus here, then, is to determine whether or not three occupational categories of the middle mass differ in regard to those sociopersonality characteristics attributed to this larger category and in regard to (the absence of) personal and intermediate social relations. In short, the homogeneity or heterogeneity of mass-society characteristics will be explored within a stratification-bureaucratization context.

Similarities and differences between the three samples were assessed in one of the following ways:

1. Responses to a number of items, particularly the various scales, were ranked by scale score and divided into quarters. Then the proportions of each occupational group in the first or fourth quarter were examined to see if the differences were significant.[34]

2. In some cases it was not possible to divide response distributions into quarters because (1) some items had fewer than four response categories, and (2)

a single-scale score or response category sometimes applied to far more than one-fourth of the three samples. In such cases, either the largest response category or that category most descriptive of "personal disorganization" or lack of social participation was selected for analysis.

Because the samples differed in regard to age, ethnicity, and religious affiliation (as well as socioeconomic status), (1) the responses of those 40 and younger were compared with those over 40 within and between each category, and (2) the responses of the Spanish-surname workers were compared with those of the Anglo workers. Since nearly 80 per cent of the Spanish-surname workers were also Catholics, the ethnicity control also served as a control for religion. The effects of age and ethnicity are not reported below unless they significantly alter the original relationship found between occupation and the dependent variable in question.

Results

Sociopersonality characteristics

Table 2 shows a consistent pattern of differences among the three samples in regard to those sociopersonality characteristics sometimes used to describe members of the middle mass. In most cases the managers differ significantly from the other two categories. Although the general pattern is (1) managers, (2) businessmen, and (3) workers, the differences between the latter two groups was in most cases not of sufficient magnitude to reject the null hypothesis that these categories were a part of the same universe.

Indeed the new middle class in Gulftown fails to display the personal disorganization that allegedly accompanies bureaucratization and mass society. Managers are most likely to have strong favorable self-images (item 7) and to believe their occupational roles permit relatively full expression of their individual potential as well as opportunities to expand this potential (item 6).[35] The six measures of alienation and related phenomena (items 1-5 and 8) raise some questions in regard to the observation:

"Whether the emphasis of the writer is on estrangement from work, the normlessness of contemporary culture, or the powerless feelings of the individual in large-scale organizations, mass conditions

4. feel they are "losing effective contact with significant and supporting groups" (item 2),[40]
5. feel that they must engage in behavior in which they are compelled by social situations to do violence to their own "nature,"[41]
6. receive high scores on Dean's composite alienation scale, consisting of the sums

TABLE 2
Sociopersonality Correlates of Occupational Status

Variable	Managers N = 108	Businessmen N = 104	Workers N = 120	Significant Differences
1. Alienation—per cent scoring in first quarter (low scores)	38.9	22.1	16.7	M-W and M-B
2. Alienation: isolation subscale—per cent scoring in first quarter	37.0	22.1	19.2	M-W and M-B
3. Alienation: normlessness subscale— per cent scoring in first quarter	48.1	21.2	22.5	M-W and M-B
4. Alienation: powerlessness subscale— per cent scoring in first quarter	31.5	25.9	13.3	M-W and B-W
5. Anomia—per cent scoring low (0) on the scale	51.9	26.9	23.3	M-W and M-B
6. Self-actualization—per cent scoring in first quarter	5.6	14.4	23.3	M-W
7. Self-esteem—per cent scoring high (0–1 on six-item Guttman scale)	70.4	54.8	57.5	M-W and M-B
8. Self-estrangement—per cent scoring in first quarter	37.0	27.9	17.5	M-W
9. Status concern—per cent scoring in fourth quarter	10.2	28.8	40.8	M-W and M-B*

* Differences between all three groups were significant among those respondents 40 or younger.

are described as producing feelings of malaise and insecurity."[36] Such feelings, in fact, are less characteristic of bureaucrats of the new middle class than of the other two occupational categories. Managers are *less* likely to:

1. feel a "generalized, pervasive sense of . . . 'self-to-others' alienation" (item 5),[37]
2. feel that their goals and the means they use in pursuing these goals are determined by social entities with which they do not feel "intimately identified" or by forces which they "may be unable to recognize" (item 4),[38]
3. experience a "lack of clear norms or a conflict among norms" (item 3),[39]

of scores from the subscales listed as items two through four (item 1),[42] and
7. be concerned with status or social mobility (item 9).[43]

Businessmen ranked between the managers and workers on all but two characteristics (they experienced the greatest amount of normlessness and had the lowest self-esteem) but more closely resembled the workers than the managers. In fact, they differed significantly from the workers on only one characteristic—the powerlessness dimension of alienation.

Thus, workers *and* independent businessmen were more likely than managers to possess those sociopersonality characteristics often identified with the concept "mass": social isolation, normlessness, anomia, low self-esteem, and general alienation.

Social participation and social involvement

The patterns of differences found among the responses to the social-participation and involvement variables investigated were not as consistent as those differences outlined above. Table 3 indicates that businessmen were least likely to participate

the areas investigated, differing significantly from at least one of the other two groups on seven of these. Again, workers were more likely to resemble businessmen, but the similarity was not as marked as it was in regard to the sociopersonality characteristics. Further examination of Table 3 indicates that different types of social participation and social involvement are characteristic of the different occupational categories. That the categories may differ more in regard to type of participa-

TABLE 3

Social-Participation and Involvement Correlates of Occupational Status

Characteristic	Managers N = 108	Businessmen N = 104	Workers N = 120	Significant Differences
1. Community attachment—per cent with low scores on Wilensky's community-involvement scale	4.1	15.6	29.7	M-W, M-B, W-B‡
2. Community attachment—per cent offering "unfavorable" evaluations of Gulftown	18.5	6.8	10.3	M-B†
3. Neighborhood integration—per cent of respondents knowing two or fewer neighbors well enough to call on them	5.6	28.8	15.8	M-B, M-W, M-B§
4. Organized groups—per cent belonging to no organized groups	27.8	31.7	29.8	none
5. Religious participation—per cent with low scale scores (do not attend religious services)	28.7	40.4	28.4	none*
6. Visiting friends—per cent visiting with two or fewer friends during previous month (at respondent's home or friend's home)	12.0	26.9	16.7	M-B, W-B
7. Visiting relatives—per cent seeing no related families during previous month	26.9	14.4	10.8	M-W, M-B†
8. Political participation (a) per cent not voting in 1960 presidential election	6.5	8.7	15.8	M-W ‖
(b) per cent not voting in last school election	56.5	67.3	71.7	M-W ‖
9. General social participation— per cent scoring in first quarter (low) on Teele's scale	18.6	26.9	21.7	none

* M-B, W-B approaches significance.
† Differences are not significant among those respondents 40 and younger.
‡ Difference between workers and businessmen is not significant among those over 40.
§ Difference between workers and managers is not significant among those over 40.
‖ Differences are not significant among those over 40.

or be involved in seven of the ten characteristics investigated, and they differed significantly from at least one of the other two groups on five of these characteristics. From the opposite standpoint, managers were most likely to participate in eight of

tion as opposed to level of participation is also supported by the observation that they do not differ significantly in Teele's general measure of "voluntary social isolation" (item 9).[44]

Managers were least likely to have seen

related families during the month preceding the interview (item 7),[45] and they were the least likely to offer a favorable evaluation of Gulftown (item 2).[46] Their religious participation was almost as great as that of the workers, and they were the most likely to participate or be involved in:

1. community attachment as measured by local political participation and contributions to church and charities (item 1);[47]
2. neighborhood integration (item 3);[48]
3. organized groups (item 4);[49]
4. home visits with friends (item 6);
5. political participation at both the local and national levels (items 8a and 8b);[50] and
6. general social participation (item 9).

The "loneliness' and "isolation" allegedly characteristic of members of the "mass" do not describe members of this occupational category in which the average respondent knew seven neighbors well enough to call on them, had visited with friends at his home or their homes seven times during the month preceding the interview, had attended church three times during the month prior to that during which the field work was conducted, and belonged to and attended regularly the meetings of organized groups. In short, the participation of managers in both personal and intermediate relationships is relatively high.

Workers were more likely than managers and businessmen (although they did not differ significantly from the latter) to have seen related families during the month preceding the interview (item 7), and they were the most likely to have attended religious services (item 5), although this is probably a consequence of the relatively large number of Catholics in this category.[51] Workers ranked lowest on both measures of political participation (item 8a and 8b) and displayed less community involvement than the other two categories (item 1). They were the intermediate category in regard to neighborhood integration (item 3), participation in organized groups (item 4), community attachment (item 2), home visits with friends (item 6), and general social participation (item 9). Thus, workers display relatively high participation and involvement in personal relationship (the average worker knew five or six neighbors well enough to call on them, visited with friends almost seven times per month, attended church three times a month,[52] and saw an average of three related families per month) but were less active in "intermediate" social relationships (they were less likely to vote in local and national elections, were not likely to attend regularly the meetings of organized groups, and were the most likely to display low community involvement).

Businessmen, in general, displayed the least social participation and social involvement. Although less likely than the other two categories to offer an "unfavorable" evaluation of the community (item 2), they were less involved in the community than managers (item 1). They were least likely to display neighborhood integration (item 3), home visit with friends (item 6), attend religious services (item 5), or belong to organized groups (item 4), and they were the most likely to score low on the social-participation scale (item 9), although some of these differences were not statistically significant. In short, the businessmen ranked lower than the managers in most areas of social participation and involvement and, more often than not, ranked lower than the workers on these measures. Although social isolation may be more characteristic of businessmen than of the other two categories, the central tendencies of this sample—knowing more than six neighbors well enough to call on them, home-visiting five times per month, attending religious services once a month, occasionally attending the meetings of organized groups, and visiting with related families three times a month—seem to fall short of "isolation" and "loneliness."

Summary and Implications

This comparison of three occupational categories in a community having recently experienced those changes associated with the development of mass societies or at least the formation of a large middle mass suggests (1) that the concept "middle mass" may have limited utility in the industrial community and (2) that although urbanization, industrialization, and bureaucratization may not completely homogenize or level, they may enlarge the middle strata of the community and further modify its social structure by creating a new upper stratum.

The middle mass

Because the vast majority of those characteristics frequently used to describe members of mass societies differentiate sharply the managers from the businessmen and workers, who in turn differ only slightly from one another, the concept "middle mass" may have limited utility in describing the social structure of the middle-sized industrial community. This middle mass may include local businessmen and hourly paid workers, who indeed are more likely than managers to experience various forms of alienation, lower self-actualization, lower self-esteem, and greater status concern and at the same time are somewhat less likely to engage in various forms of social participation or display as much social involvement. That occupational roles may be the source of these differences is supported by the observation that the various forms of alienation are significantly related to self-actualization but are not related to community evaluation.[53]

The new upper stratum

Managers, or the new middle class, do not resemble the working-class–old middle mass and, in fact, display characteristics clearly at variance with the observation that "the outstanding characteristic of contemporary thought on man and society is the preoccupation with personal alienation and cultural disintegration."[54] That "the structural position of the white-collar mass is becoming more and more similar to that of the wage workers"[55] may be true in some respects, but the striking

differences found between the managers and workers in this investigation seem to indicate that formal organizations may have a different impact on those at the middle levels[56] than on those at the bottom. In fact, the findings seem to indicate that bureaucratization leads to further differentiation, rather than leveling. The differences seem to indicate that after industry moved to Gulftown, a new upper stratum was added to the community social structure. The nature of this stratum lends some support to the view that the " 'new middle class' constitutes in fact an extension of the old, capitalist or bourgeois, ruling class and is in this sense a part of the ruling class... [as their occupational positions may be differentiated from those of the businessmen and workers from the standpoint of] the exercise of delegated authority—delegated, that is, from the real seat of authority in social organizations, from, in other words, their leading positions."[57] The presence of this new authority in the community may, at least in part, account for the apparent disenchantment of the independent businessmen, for the arrival of industry in their community lowered their *relative* socioeconomic standing and probably influenced their power position as well. Since roughly 20 to 25 per cent of the employees of Plants X and Y are classified as "management," this is no small category, and its impact on the community would, of course, be noticeable.

In summary, the differences found between managers and the other two categories, but not between the other two, suggest that the middle mass in industrial communities may consist of those individuals formerly described as old middle class and working class, but that bureaucratization has more sharply differentiated the new middle class from this middle mass. Thus, the traditional indicators of social class indeed differentiate and discriminate among attitudes and behavior patterns in the industrial community, but perhaps at different levels in the status structure than was previously the case.

To suggest cautions in regard to the

conclusions and especially the theoretical implications of this report should be unnecessary. Still, the following limitations should be stressed:

1. These implications in regard to the nature of stratification in contemporary American society are based on a single community study. The limitations and fallacies associated with viewing the community as a societal microcosm have been discussed adequately elsewhere.[58] Thus, at best, these findings may be representative of communities of roughly the same size experiencing the same processses.

2. Plants X and Y may not be representative of new installations in other growing communities. The ratio of managers to workers may be higher or lower, and the workers themselves may be better educated or better paid (or the reverse) than those employed in other industries. To the degree that these characteristics may differ in similar communities, new industry would have a different impact on the stratification system. Thus, caution should be exercised in generalizing to other communities.

3. The dependent variables selected for analysis may not be representative of the universe of variables from which others could have been selected as well. Furthermore, should a different criterion for selection have been imposed, different conclusions may have been likely. In short, it should not be assumed that workers generally have more in common with businessmen than managers, but, at best, they more closely resemble businessmen than managers on those characteristics frequently used to describe members of mass societies.

This investigation was made possible by a grant from the Hogg Foundation for Mental Health, Austin, Texas. The investigator acknowledges with gratitude the assistance of Robert Hancock, Joann Hayes, Lynda Painter, and Gary Vance, and the valuable suggestions made by S. Dale McLemore of the University of Texas, Richard L. Simpson of the University of North Carolina, and Atlee L. Stroup of the College of Wooster, who read an earlier draft of the manuscript.

[1] Examples of such theories are too numerous to cite. Many are summarized and the perspective itself is made explicit in Joseph A. Kahl, *The American Class Structure* (New York: Holts Rinehart & Winstons, Inc., 1957), Leonard Reissman, *Class in American Society* (New York: Free Press of Glencoe, Inc., 1959), and in many similar sources.

[2] Seymour M. Lipset and Reinhard Bendix, *Class, Status and Power: A Reader in Social Stratification* (New York: Free Press of Glencoe, Inc., 1953), pp. 9–12.

[3] See, for example, C. Wright Mills, *White Collar: The American Middle Classes* (New York: Oxford University Press, Inc., 1956), Daniel R. Miller and Guy E. Swanson, *The Changing American Parent: A Study in the Detroit Area* (New York: John Wiley & Sons, Inc., 1958), especially pp. 30–58; and David Riesman, *The Lonely Crowd: A Study of the Changing American Character* (New Haven: Yale University Press, 1950), pp. 21 ff.

[4] See, for example, Daniel Seligman, "The New Masses," in Philip Olson, ed., *America as a Mass Society* (New York: Free Press of Glencoe, Inc., 1963), pp. 249, 254; Daniel Bell, "The Theory of Mass Society," *Commentary*, 22 (July, 1956), pp. 76–77; Emil Lederer, *State of the Masses: The Threat of the Classless Society* (New York: W. W. Norton & Company, Inc., 1940), pp. 30–31; and William Kornhauser, *The Politics of Mass Society* (New York: Free Press of Glencoe, Inc., 1959), p. 27.

[5] Harold L. Wilensky, "Mass Society and Mass Culture: Interdependence or Independence?," *American Sociological Review*, 29 (April, 1964), p. 175.

[6] See, for example, Seligman, *loc. cit.*; Harold L. Wilensky, "Orderly Careers and Social Participation: The Impact of Work History on Social Integration in the Middle Mass," *American Sociological Review*, 26 (August, 1961), p. 529; Joseph R. Gusfield, "Mass Society and Extremist Politics," *American Sociological Review*, 27 (February, 1962), p. 20; Raymond A. Bauer and Alice H. Bauer, "America, 'Mass Society' and Mass Media," *Journal of Social Issues*, 16 (1960), pp. 54–55; and Reissman, *op. cit.*, pp. 193 ff.

[7] Wilensky (1961), *op. cit.*, p. 539, and Gusfield, *op. cit.*, p. 21.

[8] A pseudonym, of course.

[9] A 1962 Gulftown city directory was brought up to date one week before the field work started by examining city water and sewage connect and disconnect slips which gave the name, address, and occupation of all individuals owning or renting homes or apartments who had moved in and out of the city since the directory data had been collected.

10 Field work was done by fourteen graduate students and the investigator in September of 1964. Response rates for the three categories were: businessmen, 84.6 per cent; managers, 83.7 per cent; and workers, 88.3 per cent.

11 August B. Hollingshead, "Two-Factor Index of Social Position" (New Haven: Privately Mimeographed, 1957).

12 Respondents possessing any one of these characteristics were classified as entrepreneurial by Miller and Swanson, *op. cit.,* pp. 68–69. All Gulftown respondents possessed at least two of these characteristics and most possessed all three.

13 Because of the length of the schedule, appointments were arranged in advance with most respondents. Interviews lasted from thirty-five minutes to two hours and forty minutes, with the mean length being one hour and nineteen minutes.

14 See, for example, most of the sources cited in footnote 4 and Gusfield, *op. cit.,* p. 21.

15 The direction of the relationship and sources will be cited in the footnotes which follow.

16 See especially Chris Argyris, *Understanding Organizational Behavior* (Homewood, Ill.: Dorsey Press, Inc., 1960), pp. 14–18.

17 The scales used were those set forth by Dwight G. Dean, "Alienation: Its Meaning and Measurement," *American Sociological Review,* 26 (October, 1961), pp. 753–777. Studies which have shown an inverse relationship between alienation and socioeconomic status include Wayne E. Thompson and John E. Horton, "Political Alienation as a Force in Political Action," *Social Forces,* 38 (March, 1960), pp. 192, 195, and Russell Middleton, "Alienation, Race and Education," *American Sociological Review,* 28 (December, 1963), p. 976.

18 The scale used was that set forth by Leo Srole, "Social Integration and Certain Corollaries," *American Sociological Review,* 21 (December, 1956), pp. 709–716. Srole found an inverse relationship between anomia and social status. . . .

19 Self-actualization is the degree to which an individual's predispositions are expressed in his work. It has been found to be negatively related to bureaucratization but positively related to one's position in the organizational hierarchy. See Argyris, *loc. cit.* Argyris has used a lengthy semistructured schedule to measure self-actualization, but his technique was found to be too time consuming for the purposes of this investigation. Thus, a structured schedule was developed by the investigator and Gary G. Vance to measure the same phenomenon. A number of pretests and validation procedures indicated the new technique was valid and probably more reliable than Argyris's method. The items are available upon request.

20 The scale used was that set forth by Morris Rosenberg, "Parental Interest and Children's Self-Conceptions," *Sociometry,* 26 (March, 1963), pp. 35–49. It has been suggested that self-esteem is negatively related to bureaucratization and positively related to socioeconomic status. See Chris Argyris, *Integrating the Individual and the Organization* (New York: John Wiley & Sons, Inc., 1964), especially pp. 26–28, 54–57, and J. Bieri and R. Lobeck, "Self-concept Differences in Relation to Identification, Religion, and Social Class," *Journal of Abnormal and Social Psychology,* 62 (January, 1961), pp. 94–98.

21 In the process of selecting alienation scales, a number of previously used scales were pretested on the same sample. Scale correlations (measured by gamma) were low, suggesting that different alienation scales may measure different phenomena. A review of much of the alienation literature seemed to indicate that self-estrangement may be the underlying dimension of all forms of alienation. Thus, the investigator and Joann S. Hayes developed a seven-item Guttman type self-estrangement scale which, indeed, when pretested with seven other alienation scales, was found to be more closely related to the seven other scale scores than any of these scales were with the other seven (including self-estrangement).

22 According to Bell, *op. cit.,* p. 75, the mass-society theorists see status concern as a consequence of spatial and social mobility in which individuals assume a multiplicity of roles and feel they must prove themselves in a succession of new situations. The status-concern scale used here is a short form of the one set forth by Walter C. Kaufman, "Status, Authoritarianism and Anti-Semitism," *American Journal of Sociology,* 52 (January, 1957), pp. 379–383. The same short form has been used by Snell Putney and Russell Middleton, "Dimensions and Correlates of Religious Ideologies," *Social Forces,* 34 (May, 1961), pp. 285–290. Inverse relationships between status concern and socioeconomic status have been suggested by W. H. Sewell and A. O. Haller, "Factors in the Relationship Between Social Status and the Personality Adjustment of the Child," *American Sociological Review,* 24 (August, 1959), p. 516, and by Jack L. Roach and Orville R. Gursslin, "The Lower Class, Status Frustration, and Social Disorganization," *Social Forces,* 43 (May, 1965), pp. 501–510.

23 Kornhauser, *op. cit.,* pp. 74, 90.

24 The direction of the relationship and sources will be cited in the footnotes which follow.

25 See, in particular, Miller and Swanson, *loc. cit.,* as well as other sources to be cited below.

26 One measure of community "attachment" was that set forth by Wilensky (1961), *op. cit.,* p. 528. The second measure was based on responses to the question, "All things considered what do you think of Gulftown as a place to live?" Coders classified responses as strongly favorable, moderately favorable (included a qualification), neutral, moderately unfavorable (included a qualification), and strongly unfavorable. Previous investigations have shown inverse relationships between community attachment and socioeconomic status. See, for example, Arthur Kornhauser, *Detroit as the People See It* (Detroit: Wayne University Press, 1952), pp. 12–13.

27 The measure used was that used by Phillip Fellin and Eugene Litwak, "Neighborhood Cohesion Under Conditions of Mobility," *American Sociological Review,* 28 (June, 1963), p. 365. This measure is the number of neighbors (defined as families within walking distance of the respondent's residence) known well enough to call on. Fellin and Litwak suggest that bureaucrats display greater neighborhood integration than entrepreneurs or manual workers, because they have been trained to deal with change and integration (p. 370).

28 Respondents were asked if they attended club, lodge, union, civic-organization, or other organizational meetings regularly, occasionally, rarely, or never. Nine studies showing a direct relationship between membership in voluntary associations and socioeconomic status are summarized by W. Kornhauser, *op. cit.,* pp. 70–72.

29 A religious-participation index was constructed from responses to three questions: (1) Are you a member of a church or other religious organization? (2) How often have you attended religious services in the past month? (3) Do you hold any elective or appointive offices in your church, such as deacon, choir member, Sunday school teacher, etc.? Index scores ranged from 0 (not a member, attended no services, and holds no office) to 6 (a member, holding an office who attended services every week during the month preceding the interview). A number of studies have shown a direct relationship between religious participation and socioeconomic status. See, for example, Bernard Lazerwitz, "Some Factors Associated with Church Attendance," *Social Forces,* 39 (May 1961), pp. 306–308.

30 Respondents were asked how often they visited with friends at friends' homes each month and how often they had friends to their homes each month. Respondents were assigned a total score that was simply the sum of the two answers. A direct relationship between socioeconomic status and this form of social participation has been demonstrated in previous research. See Leonard Reissman, "Class,

Leisure, and Social Participation," *American Sociological Review,* 19 (February, 1954), pp. 78–79.

31 Respondents were asked how many related families they had seen in the past month. It has been suggested that extended family relations may not be harmonious with the career orientation of the bureaucrat. See Talcott Parsons, "Revised Analytical Approach to the Theory of Social Stratification," in Lipset and Bendix, *op. cit.,* pp. 116ff. Others state the extended family is viable because (among other reasons) class differences are moderate or shrinking (a view consistent with the mass-society perspective). See, for example, Eugene Litwak, "Occupational Mobility and Extended Family Cohesion," *American Sociological Review,* 25 (February, 1960), pp. 9–21. Still other investigators have found family participation to be more characteristic of the working class than the middle class. See, for example, Reissman, *loc. cit.*

32 Two measures of political participation were used: The respondent was asked (1) if he voted in the 1960 presidential election and (2) when the last school election had been held and if he had voted in it. Only if the answer to the first part of the question was correct or nearly correct (within one month of the actual date) was it assumed the respondent had, in fact, voted in the election. Numerous studies have shown a direct relationship between socioeconomic status and political participation. See for example, Kahl, *op. cit.,* pp. 209–210.

33 The scale used was that set forth by James E. Teele, "Measures of Social Participation," *Social Problems,* 10 (Summer, 1962), pp. 31–39. This is a three-point, "partly cumulative" scale based on visits with friends, participation in social hobbies, and participation in voluntary associations. Previous research suggests middle-class respondents rank higher than working-class respondents in all areas of social participation (explored here) except visits to and by relatives. See Kahl, *op. cit.,* Ch. V, and Reissman, *op. cit.,* pp. 186–187.

34 When the differences between the categories are described as "significant," the .05 level of statistical significance has been employed in making the evaluation.

35 The source of this definition of self-actualization is Argyris (1964), *op. cit.,* p. 32. Age may also be an important independent variable here. Among those respondents under 40, businessmen experience no significantly different degree of self-actualization than managers. Among those over 40, managers experience significantly greater self-actualization than members of either of the other two categories. This may be explained in part by the observation that the older managers occupy positions

of higher rank in the organizations than do the younger managers.

36 Gusfield, *op. cit.,* p. 21.

37 Srole, *op. cit.,* p. 711.

38 Dwight G. Dean, "Alienation and Political Apathy," *Social Forces,* 38 (March, 1960), p. 185 (quoting Gouldner).

39 *Ibid.,* p. 186.

40 *Ibid.*

41 This definition of self-estrangement is suggested by Lewis Feuer, "What Is Alienation? The Career of a Concept," in Maurice Stein and Arthur Vidich, eds., *Sociology on Trial* (Englewood Cliffs, N. J.: Prentice-Hall, Inc., 1963), p. 143.

42 The Spanish-surname workers were significantly more likely to have high scores on the alienation scale and its three subscales than were the Anglo workers. Still, comparing only the Anglo workers with the managers, the differences remain statistically significant.

43 Status concern was more characteristic of respondents over 40 in all three samples. Among those over 40, managers were significantly less likely to display status concern than either of the other two categories. In regard to those under 40, workers were significantly more likely than businessmen, who in turn were significantly more likely than managers to score high on the status-concern scale. The Spanish-surname workers were significantly more concerned with status than were the Anglo workers. When only Anglo workers are considered, they more closely resemble the businessmen but remain significantly different from managers.

44 Teele, *op. cit.,* p. 37, has also noted there may be different types of social participation. Data he gathered from a sample of 649 former mental patients indicated that "seeing friends, visiting relatives, and going to church represent three different types of social participation."

45 This finding, at first glance, appears to support Parsons' assertion that career mobility and the extended family may be antithetical. That this may be an incorrect interpretation is suggested by the further observation that this group ranked lowest on the status-concern measure and by the fact that age complicates this relationship. Among those respondents 40 or under, there were no significant differences in the number of related families seen during the previous month, lending some support to the arguments set forth by Litwak, *loc. cit.* The significant differences between the managers and the other two groups were a consequence of a much larger difference found between the groups among those respondents over 40. Spanish-surname workers were significantly more likely to have visited relatives than Anglo workers, but comparing only the Anglo workers with the managers, the difference remains significant.

46 There were no significant differences among those 40 or younger, who in all three categories were more likely than those over 40 to offer unfavorable evaluations.

47 Attachment increased with age among the businessmen and managers, but the reverse was true among the workers. Among those over 40, there was no significant difference between the businessmen and the workers. Furthermore, Spanish-surname workers were significantly more likely than Anglo workers to score low on this involvement measure. The community involvement of Anglo workers does not differ significantly from that of the businessmen.

48 Considering only those respondents 40 or under, differences between all three occupational categories were significant. Among those over 40, the worker-manager difference was negligible. Ethnicity also accounts for part of the workers differences. Considering only Anglo workers, 17.4 per cent know two or less neighbors well enough to call on them.

49 Nonmembership in organized groups is more characteristic of those 40 or under in all three categories. Among those over 40, there is a near-significant difference between managers and the other two categories. Spanish-surname workers were more likely to belong to organized groups than Anglo workers. Considering only the Anglo workers, 36.0 per cent belong to no organized groups.

50 In all three occupational categories, the older respondents were more likely than those 40 or under to have voted in both local and national elections. In fact, the differences between the older workers, businessmen, and managers were not significant. Anglo workers were less likely to have voted in the 1960 presidential election than Spanish-surname workers. Of the Anglo workers, 22.8 per cent did not vote in the 1960 presidential election, a significantly greater proportion than the proportion of nonvoting businessmen or managers.

51 Considering the Anglo workers only, 36.0 per cent had not attended religious services during the month preceding the interview. Thus, Anglo workers more closely resembled the businessmen than the managers, but differed significantly from neither category.

52 Religious participation may be more meaningfully classified as a "personal" rather than as an "intermediate" relationship among workers. See, for example, J. Milton Yinger, *Religion, Society and the Individual* (New York: The MacMillan Company, 1957), pp. 166–173.

53 Tables are available upon request.

54 Robert A. Nisbet, *Community and Power* (formerly *The Quest for Community* (New York: Oxford University Press, Inc., 1962), p. 3.

55 Mills, *op. cit.,* p. 297.

56 Top bureaucratic positions of Companies

X and Y are not located in Gulftown. Further-more, neither of the local managers was in-cluded in this sample, which is thus primarily a middle-management and front-line super-visory sample.

[57] Ralf Dahrendorf, *Class and Class Conflict* *in Industrial Society* (Stanford: Stanford Uni-versity Press, 1959), p. 53.

[58] See, for example, Albert J. Reiss, Jr., "Some Logical and Methodological Problems in Community Research," *Social Forces,* 33 (October, 1954), p. 54.

part two

FOUNDATIONS OF MODERN BUREAUCRACY

Let's face it. We are organization men. We are born in hospitals, educated in elementary, junior high, and high schools, colleges, and universities. While being educated we join clubs, fraternity and sorority organizations—from the Boy Scouts to athletic teams. When we leave college we then usually devote a few years to the military and about forty years to a firm in order to maintain our livelihood. Throughout the years of our work life we tend to join unions, professional associations, community clubs, and societies. We spend our final days in hospitals and rest homes and then are buried by well-organized funeral establishments.

The picture is true. There is no escaping it. We live in a highly organized society. The question which then becomes important is: What do we do about it? One answer is to try to understand our organizational society and thereby gain some control over our lives in organizations. The aim of this section is to give the student some understanding of life within organizations.

Peter M. Blau and W. Richard Scott, in their article "The Concept of Formal Organization," introduce the topic of the foundations of bureaucracy by defining organizations. They discuss the similarities and differences between formal and social organization and then analyze the all-important component of informal organization. Amitai Etzioni builds upon the foundation laid by Blau and Scott in his article on "Control and Compliance" patterns within work units. Etzioni suggests that firms may be classified according to ways in which leaders attempt to control the participation of members and according to ways in which the members comply with these control attempts.

The classical work of Max Weber concerning the "Ideal Bureaucracy" is presented next. Weber notes factors such as hierarchy of authority, promotion based on seniority, and the utilization of rules and regulations as ideal elements of bureaucratic organization. The notions formulated by Weber have been highly influential in the study of organizational behavior and have been very similar to the theories and practices of early entrepreneurs in the United States.

Several imaginative studies, which suggest that rigid, mechanical plans of organization such as those developed by Weber have many unintended consequences for work activities, are reviewed by James G. March and Herbert A. Simon in their article, "Dysfunctions in Organizations." And finally, the present editor's analysis of "Formality Versus

75

Flexibility" reviews the studies which have been conducted in the area of organizations and proposes a revised model of that formulated by Weber.

7 The Concept of Formal Organization*

BY PETER M. BLAU and W. RICHARD SCOTT

Social Organization and Formal Organizations

Although a wide variety of organizations exists, when we speak of an organization it is generally quite clear what we mean and what we do not mean by this term. We may refer to the American Medical Association as an organization or to a college fraternity; to the Bureau of Internal Revenue or to a union; to General Motors or to a church; to the Daughters of the American Revolution or to an army. But we would not call a family an organization, nor would we so designate a friendship clique or a community or an economic market or the political institutions of a society. What is the specific and differentiating criterion implicit in our intuitive distinction of organizations from other kinds of social groupings or institutions? It has something to do with how human conduct becomes socially organized, but it is not, as one might first suspect, whether or not social controls order and organize the conduct of individuals, since such social controls operate in both types of circumstances.

Before specifying what is meant by formal organization, let us clarify the general concept of social organization. "Social organization" refers to the ways in which human conduct becomes socially organized, that is, to the observed regularities in the behavior of people that are due to the social conditions in which they find themselves rather than to their physiological

or psychological characteristics as individuals. The many social conditions that influence the conduct of people can be divided into two main types, which constitute the two basic aspects of social organizations: (1) the structure of social relations in a group or larger collectivity of people and (2) the shared beliefs and orientations that unite the members of the collectivity and guide their conduct.

The conception of structure or system implies that the component units stand in some relation to one another and, as the popular expression "The whole is greater than the sum of its parts" suggests, that the relations between units add new elements to the situation.[1] This aphorism, like so many others, is a half-truth. The sum of fifteen apples, for example, is no more than fifteen times one apple. But a block of ice is more than the sum of the atoms of hydrogen and oxygen that compose it. In the case of the apples, there exist no linkages or relations between the units comprising the whole. In the case of the ice, however, specific connections have been formed between H and O atoms and among H_2O molecules that distinguish ice from hydrogen and oxygen, on the one hand, and from water, on the other. Similarly, a busload of passengers does not constitute a group, since no social relations unify individuals into a common structure.[2] But a busload of club members on a Sunday outing is a group, because a network of social relations links the members into a social structure—a structure which is an emergent characteristic of the collectivity that cannot be reduced to the attributes of its individual members. In short, a network of social relations transforms an aggregate of individuals into a group (or an aggregate of groups into a larger social structure), and the group is

From Formal Organizations: A Comparative Approach, by Peter M. Blau and W. Richard Scott, published by Chandler Publishing Company, San Francisco, Copyright 1962 by Chandler Publishing Company. Reprinted by permission.

more than the sum of the individuals composing it since the structure of social relations is an emergent element that influences the conduct of individuals.

To indicate the nature of social relations, we can briefly dissect this concept. Social relations involve, first, patterns of social interaction: the frequency and duration of the contacts between people, the tendency to initiate these contacts, the direction of influence between persons, the degree of cooperation, and so forth. Second, social relations entail people's sentiments to one another, such as feelings of attraction, respect, and hostility. The differential distribution of social relations in a group, finally, defines its status structure. Each member's status in the group depends on his relations with the others—their sentiments toward and interaction with him. As a result, integrated members become differentiated from isolates, those who are widely respected from those who are not highly regarded, and leaders from followers. In addition to these relations between individuals within groups, relations also develop between groups—relations that are a source of still another aspect of social status, since the standing of the group in the larger social system becomes part of the status of any of its members. An obvious example is the significance that membership in an ethnic minority, say, Puerto Rican, has for an individual's social status.

The networks of social relations between individuals and groups, and the status structure defined by them, constitute the core of the social organization of a collectivity, but not the whole of it. The other main dimension of social organization is a system of shared beliefs and orientations, which serve as standards for human conduct. In the course of social interaction common notions arise as to how people should act and interact and what objectives are worthy of attainment. First, common values crystallize, values that govern the goals for which men strive—their ideals and their ideas of what is desirable—such as our belief in democracy or the importance financial success assumes

in our thinking. Second, social norms develop—that is, common expectations concerning how people ought to behave—and social sanctions are used to discourage violations of these norms. These socially sanctioned rules of conduct vary in significance from moral principles or mores, as Sumner calls them, to mere customs or folkways. If values define the ends of human conduct, norms distinguish behavior that is a legitimate means for achieving these ends from behavior that is illegitimate. Finally, aside from the norms to which everybody is expected to conform, differential role expectations also emerge, expectations that become associated with various social positions. Only women in our society are expected to wear skirts, for example. Or, the respected leader of a group is expected to make suggestions, and the other members will turn to him in times of difficulties, whereas group members who have not earned the respect of others are expected to refrain from making suggestions and generally to participate little in group discussions.

These two dimensions of social organization—the networks of social relations and the shared orientations—are often referred to as the social structure and the culture, respectively.[3] Every society has a complex social structure and complex culture, and every community within a society can be characterized by these two dimensions of social organization, and so can every group within a community (except that the specific term "culture" is reserved for the largest social systems). The prevailing cultural standards and the structure of social relations serve to organize human conduct in the collectivity. As people conform more or less closely to the expectations of their fellows, and as the degree of their conformity in turn influences their relations with others and their social status, and as their status in further turn affects their inclinations to adhere to social norms and their chances to achieve valued objectives, their patterns of behavior become socially organized.

In contrast to the social organization

that emerges whenever men are living together, there are organizations that have been deliberately established for a certain purpose. If the accomplishment of an objective requires collective effort, men set up an organization designed to coordinate the activities of many persons and to furnish incentives for others to join them for this purpose.[4] For example, business concerns are established in order to produce goods that can be sold for a profit, and workers organize unions in order to increase their bargaining power with employers. In these cases, the goals to be achieved, the rules the members of the organization are expected to follow, and the status structure that defines the relations between them (the organizational chart) have not spontaneously emerged in the course of social interaction but have been consciously designed *a priori* to anticipate and guide interaction and activities. Since the distinctive characteristic of these organizations is that they have been formally established for the explicit purpose of achieving certain goals, the term "formal organizations" is used to designate them. And this formal establishment for explicit purpose is the criterion that distinguishes our subject matter from the study of social organization in general.

Formal Organization and Informal Organization

The fact that an organization has been formally established, however, does not mean that all activities and interactions of its members conform strictly to the official blueprint. Regardless of the time and effort devoted by management to designing a rational organization chart and elaborate procedure manuals, this official plan can never completely determine the conduct and social relations of the organization's members.[5]

In every formal organization there arise informal organizations. The constituent groups of the organization, like all groups, develop their own practices, values, norms, and social relations as their members live and work together. The roots of these informal systems are embedded in the formal organization itself and nurtured by the very formality of its arrangements. Official rules must be general to have sufficient scope to cover the multitude of situations that may arise. But the application of these general rules to particular cases often poses problems of judgment, and informal practices tend to emerge that provide solutions for these problems. Decisions not anticipated by official regulations must frequently be made, particularly in times of change, and here again unofficial practices are likely to furnish guides for decisions long before the formal rules have been adapted to the changing circumstances. Moreover, unofficial norms are apt to develop that regulate performance and productivity. Finally, complex networks of social relations and informal status structures emerge, within groups and between them, which are influenced by many factors besides the organizational chart, for example, by the background characteristics of various persons, their abilities, their willingness to help others, and their conformity to group norms. But to say that these informal structures are not completely determined by the formal institution is not to say that they are entirely independent of it; for informal organizations develop in response to the opportunities created and the problems posed by their environment, and the formal organization constitutes the immediate environment of the groups within it.

When we speak of formal organizations in this books, we do not mean to imply that attention is confined to formally instituted patterns; quite the contrary. It is impossible to understand the nature of a formal organization without investigating the networks of informal relations and the unofficial norms as well as the formal hierarchy of authority and the official body of rules, since the formally instituted and the informally emerging patterns are inextricably intertwined. The distinction between the formal and the informal aspects of organizational life is only an analytical one and should not be reified; there is only one actual organization. Note also that one does not speak of the informal organization of a family or of a community. The term "informal organization" does not refer to all types of emergent patterns of social life but only to those that evolve within the framework of a formally established organization. Excluded from our purview are social institutions that have evolved without explicit design; included are the informally emerging, as well as the formally instituted, patterns within formally established organizations.

The decision of the members of a group to formalize their endeavors and relations by setting up a specific organization, say, a social and athletic club, is not fortuitous. If a group is small enough for all members to be in direct social contact and if it has no objectives that require coordination of activities, there is little need for explicit procedures or a formal division of labor. But the larger the group and the more complex the task it seeks to accomplish, the greater are the pressures to become explicitly organized.[6] Once a group of boys who merely used to hang around a drugstore decide to participate in the local baseball league, they must organize a team. And the complex coordination of millions of soldiers with thousands of specialized duties in a modern army requires extensive formalized procedures and a clear-cut authority structure.

Since formal organizations are often very large and complex, some authors refer to them as "large-scale" or as "complex" organizations. But we have eschewed these terms as misleading in two respects. First, organizations vary in size and complexity, and using these variables as defining criteria would result in such odd expressions as "a small large-scale organization" or "a very complex complex organization." Second, although formal organizations often become very large and complex, their size and complexity do not rival those of the social organization of a modern society, which includes such organizations and their relations with one another in addition to other nonorganizational patterns. (Perhaps the complexity of formal organizations is so much emphasized because it is man-made, whereas the complexity of social organization has slowly emerged, just as the complexity of modern computers is more impressive than that of the human brain. Complexity by design may be more conspicuous than complexity by growth or evolution.)

The term "bureaucratic organization," which also is often used, calls attention to the fact that organizations generally possess some sort of administrative machinery. In an organization that has been formally established, a specialized administrative staff usually exists that is responsible for maintaining the organization as a going concern and for coordinating the activities of its members. Large and complex organizations require an especially elaborate administrative apparatus. In a large factory, for example, there is not only an industrial work force directly engaged in production but also an administration composed of executive, supervisory, clerical, and other staff personnel. The case of a government agency is more complicated, because such an agency is part of the administrative arm of the nation. The entire personnel of, say, a law-enforcement agency is engaged in administration, but administration of different kinds; whereas operating officials administer the law and thereby help maintain social order in the society, their superiors and the auxiliary staff administer agency procedures and help maintain the organization itself.

One aspect of bureaucratization that has received much attention is the elaboration of detailed rules and regulations that the members of the organization are expected to follow faithfully. Rigid enforcement of the minutiae of extensive official procedures often impedes effective operations. Colloquially, the term "bureaucracy" connotes such rule-encumbered inefficiency. In sociology, however, the term is used neutrally to refer to the administrative aspects of organizations. If bureaucratization is defined as the amount of effort devoted to maintaining the organization rather than to directly achieving its objectives, all formal organizations have at least a minimum of bureaucracy—even if this bureaucracy involves no more than a secretary-treasurer who collects dues. But wide variations have been found in the degree of bureaucratization in organizations, as indicated by the amount of effort devoted to administrative problems, the proportion of administrative personnel, the hierarchical character of the organization, or the strict enforcement of administrative procedures and rigid compliance with them.

1 For a discussion of some of the issues raised by this assertion, see Ernest Nagel, "On the Statement 'The Whole Is More Than the Sum of Its Parts,'" Paul F. Lazarsfeld and Morris Rosenberg, eds., *The Language of Social Research* (New York: Free Press of Glencoe, Inc., 1955), pp. 519–527.

2 A purist may, concededly, point out that all individuals share the role of passenger and so are subject to certain generalized norms—courtesy for example.

3 See the recent discussion of these concepts by Kroeber and Parsons, who conclude by defining culture as "transmitted and created content and patterns of values, ideas, and other symbolic-meaningful systems" and social structure or system as "the specifically relational system of interaction among individuals and collectivities." A. L. Kroeber and Talcott Parsons, "The Concepts of Culture and of Social System," *American Sociological Review,* 23 (1958), p. 583.

4 Sumner makes this distinction, in his terms, "crescive" and "enacted" social institutions. William Graham Sumner, *Folkways* (Boston: Ginn & Company, 1907), p. 54.

5 From "John Brown's Body." Holt, Rinehart & Winston, Inc. Copyright, 1927, 1928, by Stephen Vincent Benet. Copyright renewed, 1955, 1956, by Rosemary Carr Benet.

6 For a discussion of size and its varied effects on the characteristics of social organization, see Theodore Caplow, "Organizational Size," *Administrative Science Quarterly,* 1 (1957), pp. 484–505.

8 Leaders' Control and Members' Compliance

by AMITAI ETZIONI

A Classification of Power

Power is an actor's ability to induce or influence another actor to carry out his directives or any other norms he supports.[1] Goldhamer and Shils state that "a person may be said to have power to the extent that he influences the behavior of others in accordance with his own intentions."[2] Of course, "his own intentions" might be to influence a person to follow others' "intentions" or those of a collectivity. In organizations, enforcing the collectivity norms is likely to be a condition determining the power-holder's access to the means of power.

Reprinted with permission of The Macmillan Company from Complex Organizations, *by Amitai Etzioni. Copyright* © *1961 by The Free Press of Glencoe, Inc.*

Power positions are positions whose incumbents regularly have access to means of power. Statements about power positions imply a particular group (or groups) who are subject to this power. For instance, to state that prison guards have a power position implies the subordination of inmates. In the following analysis we focus on power relations in organizations between those higher and those lower in rank. We refer to those in power positions, who are higher in rank, as *elites* or as organizational *representatives*. We refer to those in subject positions, who are lower in rank, as *lower participants*.

Power differs according to the means employed to make the subjects comply. These means may be physical, material, or symbolic.[3]

Coercive power rests on the application, or the threat of application, of physical sanctions such as infliction of pain, deformity, or death; generation of frustration through restriction of movement; or controlling through force the satisfaction of needs such as those for food, sex, comfort, and the like.

Remunerative power is based on control over material resources and rewards through allocation of salaries and wages, commissions and contributions, "fringe benefits," services, and commodities.

Normative power rests on the allocation and manipulation of symbolic rewards and deprivations through employment of leaders, manipulation of mass media, allocation of esteem and prestige symbols, administration of ritual, and influence over the distribution of "acceptance" and "positive response." (A more eloquent name for this power would be persuasive, or manipulative, or suggestive power. But all these terms have negative value connotations which we wish to avoid.)

There are two kinds of normative power. One is based on the manipulation of esteem, prestige, and ritualistic symbols (such as a flag or a benediction); the other, on allocation and manipulation of acceptance and positive response.[4] Although both powers are found both in vertical and in horizontal relationships, the first is more frequent in vertical relations, between actors who have different ranks, whereas the second is more common in horizontal relations, among actors equal in rank—in particular, in the power of an "informal" or primary group over its members. Lacking better terms, we refer to the first kind as *pure normative power* and to the second as *social power*[5]. Social power could be treated as a distinct kind of power. But since powers are here classed according to the means of control employed, and since both social and pure normative power rest on the same set of means—manipulation of symbolic rewards—we treat these two powers as belonging to the same category.

From the viewpoint of the organization, pure normative power is more useful, since it can be exercised directly down the hierarchy. Social power becomes organizational power only when the organization can influence the group's powers, as when a teacher uses the class climate to control a deviant child or a union steward agitates the members to use their informal power to bring a deviant into line.

Organizations can be ordered according to their power structure, taking into account which power is predominant, how strongly it is stressed compared with other organizations in which the same power is predominant, and which power constitutes the secondary source of control. . . .

Neutralization of Power

Most organizations employ all three kinds of power, but the degree to which they rely on each differs from organization to organization. Most organizations tend to emphasize only one means of power, relying less on the other two.[6] Evidence to this effect is presented below in the analysis of the compliance structures of various organizations. The major reason for power specialization seems to be that when two kinds of power are emphasized at the same time, over the same subject group, they tend to neutralize each other.

Applying force, for instance, usually creates such a high degree of alienation that it becomes impossible to apply normative power successfully. This is one of the reasons that rehabilitation is rarely achieved in traditional prisons, that custodial measures are considered as blocking therapy in mental hospitals, and that teachers in progressive schools tend to oppose corporal punishment.

Similarly, the application of renumerative powers makes appeal to "idealistic" (pure normative) motives less fruitful. In a study of the motive which lead to purchase of war bonds, Merton pointed out that in one particularly effective drive (the campaign of Kate Smith), all "secular" topics were omitted and the appeal was centered on patriotic, "sacred" themes. Merton asked a sample of 978 people:

"Do you think that it is a good idea to give things to people who buy bonds?"

Fifty per cent were definitely opposed in principle to premiums, bonuses, and other such inducements, and many of the remainder thought it a good idea only for "other people" who might not buy otherwise.[7]

By omitting this [secular] argument, the authors of her scripts were able to avoid the strain and incompatibility between the two main lines of motivation: unselfish, sacrificing love of country and economic motives of sound investment.[8]

It is possible to make an argument for the opposite position. It might be claimed that the larger the number of personal needs whose satisfaction the organization controls, the more power it has over the participants. For example, labor unions that cater to and have control over the social as well as the economic needs of their members have more power over those members than do unions that focus only on economic needs. There may be some tension between the two modes of control, some ambivalence and uneasy feeling among members about the combinations, but undoubtedly the total control is larger. Similarly, it is obvious that the church has more power over the priest than over the average parishioner. The parishioner is exposed to normative power, whereas the priest is controlled by both normative and remunerative powers.

The issue is complicated by the fact that the *amount* of each kind of power applied must be taken into account. If a labor union with social powers has economic power which is much greater than that of another union, this fact may explain why the first union has greater power in sum, despite some "waste" due to neutralization. A further complication follows from the fact that neutralization may also occur through application of the "wrong" power in terms of the cultural definition of what is appropriate to the particular organization and activity. For example, application of economic power in religious organizations may be less effective than in indus-

tries, not because two kinds of power are mixed, but because it is considered illegitimate to use economic pressures to attain religious goals. Finally, some organizations manage to apply two kinds of power abundantly and without much waste through neutralization, because they segregate the application of one power from that of the other. The examination below of combat armies and labor unions supplies an illustration of this point.

We have discussed some of the factors related to the tendency of organizations to specialize their power application. In conclusion, it seems that although there can be little doubt that such a tendency exists, its scope and a satisfactory explanation for it have yet to be established.

Three Kinds of Involvement: A Comparative Dimension

Involvement, commitment, and alienation

Organizations must continually recruit means if they are to realize their goals. One of the most important of these means is the positive orientation of the participants to the organizational power. *Involvement*[9] refers to the cathectic-evaluative orientation of an actor to an object, characterized in terms of intensity and direction.

The intensity of involvement ranges from high to low. The direction is either positive or negative. We refer to positive involvement as *commitment*[10] and to negative involvement as *alienation*.[11] (The advantage of having a third term, *involvement,* is that it enables us to refer to the continuum in a neutral way.[12]) Actors can accordingly be placed on an involvement continuum which ranges from a highly intense negative zone through mild negative and mild positive zones to a highly positive zone.[13]

Three kinds of involvement

We have found it helpful to name three zones of the involvement continuum, as follows: *alienative,* for the high alienation zone; *moral,* for the high commitment zone; and *calculative,* for the two mild zones. This classification of involvement can be applied to the orientations of actors in all social units and to all kinds of objects. Hence the definitions and illustrations presented below are not limited to organizations but are applicable to orientations in general.

Alienative involvement—Alienative involvement designated an intense negative orientation; it is predominant in relations among hostile foreigners. Similar orientations exist among merchants in "adventure" capitalism, where trade is built on isolated acts of exchange, each side trying to maximize immediate profit.[14] Such an orientation seems to dominate the approach of prostitutes to transient clients.[15] Some slaves seem to have held similar attitudes to their masters and to their work. Inmates in prisons, prisoners of war, people in concentration camps, enlisted men in basic training, all tend to be alienated from their respective organizations.[16]

Calculative involvement—Calculative involvement designates either a negative or a positive orientation of low intensity. Calculative orientations are predominant in relationships of merchants who have continuous business contacts. Attitudes of (and toward) permanent customers are often predominantly calculative, as are relationships among entrepreneurs in modern (rational) capitalism. Inmates in prisons who have established contact with prison authorities, such as "rats" and "peddlers," often have predominantly calculative attitudes toward those in power.[17]

Moral involvement[18]—Moral involvement designates a positive orientation of high intensity. The involvement of the parishioner in his church, the devoted member in his party, and the loyal follower in his leader are all "moral."

There are two kinds of moral involvement, pure and social. They differ in the same way pure normative power differs from social power. Both are intensive modes of commitment, but they differ in

their foci of orientation and in the structural conditions under which they develop. Pure moral commitments are based on internalization of norms and identification with authority (like Riesman's inner-directed "mode of conformity"); social commitment rests on sensitivity to pressures of primary groups and their members (Riesman's "other-directed"). Pure moral involvement tends to develop in vertical relationships, such as those between teachers and students, priests and parishioners, leaders and followers. Social involvement tends to develop in horizontal relationships like those in various types of primary groups. Both pure moral and social orientations might be found in the same relationships, but, as a rule, one orientation predominates.

Actors are means to each other in alienative and in calculative relations; but they are ends to each other in "social" relationships. In pure moral relationships the means-orientation tends to predominate; hence, for example, the willingness of devoted members of totalitarian parties or religious orders to use each other. But unlike the means-orientation of calculative relationships, the means-orientation here is expected to be geared to needs of the collectivity in serving its goals, and not to those of an individual.

1 T. Parsons, *The Social System* (New York: The Free Press of Glencoe, Inc., 1951), p. 121.

2 H. Goldhamer, & E. A. Shils, "Types of Power and Status" *American Journal of Sociology* (1939), 45: 171.

3 We suggest that this typology is exhaustive, although the only way we can demonstrate this is by pointing out that every type of power we have encountered so far can be classified as belonging to one of the categories or of a combination of them.

4 T. Parsons, *The Social System* (New York: The Free Press of Glencoe, Inc., 1951), p. 108.

5 This distinction draws on the difference between social and normative integration, referred to by T. Parsons, R. F. Bales, & E. A. Shils, *Working Papers in the Theory of Action* (New York: The Free Press of Glencoe, Inc., 1953), p. 182, as the distinction between the

"integrative" and the "latent pattern maintenance" phases. In volume in progress, Shils distinguishes between social and ideological primary groups (private communication. J. S. Coleman, "Multidimensional Scale Analysis," *American Journal of Sociology* (1957), 63: 255, has pointed to the difference between group-oriented and idea-oriented attachments.

6 In more technical language, one can say that the three continua of power constitute a three-dimensional property space. If we collapse each dimension into high, medium, and low segments, there are 27 possible combinations or cells. Our hypothesis reads that most organizations fall into cells which are high on one dimension and low or medium on the others; this excludes 18 cells (not counting three types of dual structures discussed below).

7 R. K. Merton, *Mass Persuasion: The Social Psychology of a War Bond Drive* (New York: Harper & Row, Publishers, 1946), p. 47.

8 *Ibid.*, p. 45.

9 *Involvement* has been used in a similar manner by Nancy C. Morse, *Satisfactions in the White-Collar Job* (Survey Research Center, University of Michigan, 1953), p. 76–96. The term is used in a somewhat different way by students of voting, who refer by it to the psychological investment in the outcome of an election rather than in the party, which would be parallel to Morse's usage and ours. See, for example, A. Campbell, G. Gurin, and W. E. Miller *The Voter Decides* (New York: Harper & Row, Publishers, 1954), p. 33–40.

10 Mishler defined *commitment* in a similar though more psychological way: "An individual is committed to an organization to the extent that central tensions are integrated through organizationally relevant instrumental acts." Cited by C. Argyris, *Personality and Organization* (New York: Harper & Row, Publishers 1957), p. 202.

11 We draw deliberately on the associations this term has acquired from its usage by Marx and others. For a good analysis of the idea of alienation in Marxism, and of its more recent development, see D. Bell, "The 'Rediscovery' of Alienation," Journal of Philosophy, 56 (1959), 933–52. And D. Bell, *The End of Ideology*, (New York: The Free Press of Glencoe, Inc., 1960), p. 335–68. See also D.G. Dean, "Alienation and Political Apathy, *Social forces*, 38 (1960), 185–89.

12 An example of empirical indicators which can be used translate the involvement continuum into directly observable terms is offered by E.A. Shils, and M. Janowits, "Cohesion and

Distintegration in the Wehrmacht in World War II.," *Public Opinion Quarterly*, 12 (2), (1948), 282–83. They classify "modes of social disintegration" in the armed forces as follows: desertion; active surrender; passive surrender; routine resistance; "last-ditch" resistance. In the terms used here, these measures indicate varying degrees of involvement, from highest alienation (desertion) to highest commitment (last-ditch resistance).

Nettler (1958) has developed a 17-item unidimensional scale which measures alienation from society. It seems that a similar scale could be constructed for measuring alienation from or commitment to organizational power without undue difficulties. A., Kornhauser, H. L. Sheppard, and A. J. Mayer, *When Labor Votes* (New York: University Books, 1956), p. 147–48, have developed a 6-item scale, measuring the orientation of union members to their organization, which supplies another illustration of the wide use and measurability of these concepts, which are central to our analysis.

13 Several sociologists have pointed out that the relationship between intensity and direction of involvement is a curvilinear one: the more positive or negative the orientation, the more intensely it is held. L. Guttman, "The Cornell Technique for Scale and Intensity Analysis," *Education and Psychology. Measurement* 7 (4197), 247–79.

14 H. H. Gerth, and C. W. Mills, *From Max Weber: Essays in Sociology* (New York: Oxford Univesrity Press, 1946), p. 67.

15 K. Davis, "The Sociology of Prostitution," *American Sociological Review* 2 (1937) 748–49.

16 For a description of this orientation in prisons see D. Clemmer, *The Prison Community* (New York: Holt, Rinehart & Winston, Inc., 1958), p. 152ff. Attitudes toward the police, particularly on the part of members of the lower class, are often strictly alienative. See for example, E. Banfield, *The Moral Basis of a Backward Society* (New York: The Free Press of Glencoe, Inc., 1958).

17 G. M. Sykes, *The Society of Captives* (Princeton: Princeton University Press, 1958), p. 87–95.

18 The term moral is used here and in the rest of the volume to refer to an orientation of the actor; it does not involve a value-position of the observer (see T. Parsons, and E. A. Shils, *et al. Toward a General Theory of Action* Cambridge, Mass.: Harvard University Press, 1952), pp. 170ff.

9 The Ideal Bureaucracy

by MAX WEBER

The purest type of exercise of legal authority is that which employs a bureaucratic administrative staff. Only the supreme chief of the organization occupies his position of authority by virtue of appropriation, of election, or of having been designated for the succession. But even his authority consists in a sphere of legal "competence." The whole administrative staff under the supreme authority then consists, in the purest type, of individual officials who are appointed and function according to the following criteria:

1. They are personally free and subject to authority only with respect to their impersonal official obligations.
2. They are organized in a clearly defined hierarchy of offices.
3. Each office has a clearly defined sphere of competence in the legal sense.
4. The office is filled by a free contractual relationship. Thus, in principle, there is free selection.
5. Candidates are selected on the basis of technical qualifications. In the most rational case, this is tested by examination or guaranteed by diplomas certifying technical training, or both. They are appointed, not elected.
6. They are remunerated by fixed salaries in money, for the most part with a right to pensions. Only under certain circumstances does the employing authority, especially in private organizations, have a right to terminate the appointment, but the official is always

Reprinted with permission of The Free Press from The Theory of Social and Economic Organization *by Max Weber, translated by Talcott Parsons. Copyright 1947 by Talcott Parsons.*

free to resign. The salary scale is primarily graded according to rank in the hierarchy; but in addition to this criterion, the responsibility of the position and the requirements of the incumbent's social status may be taken into account.
7. The office is treated as the sole, or at least the primary, occupation of the incumbent.
8. It constitutes a career. There is a system of "promotion" according to seniority or to achievement, or both. Promotion is dependent on the judgment of superiors.
9. The official works entirely separated from ownership of the means of administration and without appropriation of his position.
10. He is subject to strict and systematic discipline and control in the conduct of the office.

This type of organization is in principle applicable with equal facility to a wide variety of different fields. It may be applied in profit-making business or in charitable organizations, or in any number of other types of private enterprises serving ideal or material ends. It is equally applicable to political and to religious organizations. With varying degrees of approximation to a pure type, its historical existence can be demonstrated in all these fields.

1. For example, this type of bureaucracy is found in private clinics as well as in endowed hospitals or the hospitals maintained by religious orders. Bureaucratic organization has played a major role in the Catholic Church. It is well illustrated by the administrative role of the priesthood in the modern church, which has expropriated almost all the old church

benefices which were in former days to a large extent subject to private appropriation. It is also illustrated by the conception of the universal Episcopate, which is thought of as formally constituting a universal legal competence in religious matters. Similarly, the doctrine of papal infallibility is thought of as in fact involving a universal competence, but only one which functions *ex cathedra* in the sphere of the office, thus implying the typical distinction between the sphere of office and that of the private affairs of the incumbent. The same phenomena are found in the large-scale capitalistic enterprise; and the larger it is, the greater their role. And this is not less true of political parties, which will be discussed separately. Finally, the modern army is essentially a bureaucratic organization administered by that peculiar type of military functionary, the "officer."

2. Bureaucratic authority is carried out in its purest form where it is most clearly dominated by the principle of appointment. There is no such thing as a hierarchy of elected officials in the same sense as there is a hierarchical organization of appointed officials. In the first place, election makes it impossible to attain a stringency of discipline even approaching that in the appointed type; for it is open to a subordinate official to compete for elective honors on the same terms as his superiors, and his prospects are not dependent on the superior's judgment.

3. Appointment by free contract, which makes free selection possible, is essential to modern bureaucracy. Where there is a hierarchical organization with impersonal spheres of competence but occupied by unfree officials—like slaves or dependents, who, however, function in a formally bureaucratic manner—the term "patrimonial bureaucracy" will be used.

4. The role of technical qualifications in bureaucratic organizations is continually increasing. Even an official in a party or a trade-union organization is in need of specialized knowledge, though it is usually of an empirical character, developed by experience rather than by formal training. In the modern state, the only "offices" for which no technical qualifications are required are those of ministers and presidents. This only goes to prove that they are "officials" only in a formal sense and not substantively, as is true of the managing director or president of a large business corporation. Thus at the top of a bureaucratic organization, there is necessarily an element which is at least not purely bureaucratic. The category of bureaucracy is one applying only to the exercise of control by means of a particular kind of administrative staff.

5. The bureaucratic official normally receives a fixed salary. By contrast, sources of income which are privately appropriated will be called "benefices." Bureaucratic salaries are also normally paid in money. Though this is not essential to the concept of bureaucracy, it is the arrangement which best fits the pure type. Payments in kind are apt to have the character of benefices, and the receipt of a benefice normally implies the appropriation of opportunities for earnings and of positions. There are, however, gradual transitions in this field with many intermediate types. Appropriation by virtue of leasing or sale of offices or the pledge of income from office are phenomena foreign to the pure type of bureaucracy.

6. "Offices" which do not constitute the incumbent's principal occupation, in particular "honorary" offices, belong in other categories. The typical "bureaucratic" official occupies the office as his principal occupation.

7. With respect to the separation of the official from ownership of the means of administration, the situation is essentially the same in the field of public administration and in private bureaucratic organizations, such as the large-scale capitalistic enterprise.

8. Collegial bodies are rapidly decreasing in importance in favor of types of organization which are in fact, and for the most part formally as well, subject to the authority of a single head. For ex-

ample, the collegial "governments" in Prussia have long since given way to the monocratic "district president." The decisive factor in this development has been the need for rapid, clear decisions, free of the necessity of compromise between different opinions and also free of shifting majorities.

9. The modern army officer is a type of appointed official who is clearly marked off by certain class distinctions. In this respect such officers differ radically from elected military leaders, from charismatic condottieri, from the type of officers who recruit and lead mercenary armies as a capitalistic enterprise, and, finally, from the incumbents of commissions which have been purchased. There may be gradual transitions between these types. The patrimonial "retainer," who is separated from the means of carrying out his function and the proprietor of a mercenary army for capitalistic purposes have, along with the private capitalistic entrepreneur, been pioneers in the organization of the modern type of bureaucracy.

The Monocratic Type of Bureaucratic Administration

Experience tends universally to show that the purely bureaucratic type of administrative organization—that is, the monocratic variety of bureaucracy—is, from a purely technical point of view, capable of attaining the highest degree of efficiency and is in this sense formally the most rational known means of carrying out imperative control over human beings. It is superior to any other form in precision, in stability, in the stringency of its discipline, and in its reliability. It thus makes possible a particularly high degree of calculability of results for the heads of the organization and for those acting in relation to it. It is finally superior both in intensive efficiency and in the scope of its operations and is formally capable of application to all kinds of administrative tasks.

The development of the modern form of the organization of corporate groups in all fields is nothing less than identical with the development and continual spread of bureaucratic administration. This is true of church and state, of armies, political parties, economic enterprises, organizations to promote all kinds of causes, private associations, clubs, and many others. Its development is, to take the most striking case, the most crucial phenomenon of the modern Western state. However many forms there may be which do not appear to fit this pattern—such as collegial representative bodies, parliamentary committees, soviets, honorary officers, lay judges, and what not—and however much people may complain about the "evils of bureaucracy," it would be sheer illusion to think for a moment that continuous administrative work could be carried out in any field except by means of officials working in offices. The whole pattern of everyday life is cut to fit this framework. For bureaucratic administration is, other things being equal, always, from a formal, technical point of view, the most rational type. For the needs of mass administration today, it is completely indispensable. The choice is only that between bureaucracy and dilletantism in the field of administration.

The primary source of the superiority of bureaucratic administration lies in the role of technical knowledge which, through the development of modern technology and business methods in the production of goods, has become completely indispensable. In this respect, it makes no difference whether the economic system is organized on a capitalistic or a socialistic basis. Inded, if in the latter case a comparable level of technical efficiency were to be achieved, it would mean a tremendous increase in the importance of specialized bureaucracy.

When those subject to bureaucratic control seek to escape the influence of the existing bureaucratic apparatus, this is normally possible only by creating an organization of their own which is equally subject to the process of bureaucratization.

Similarly the existing bureaucratic apparatus is driven to continue functioning by the most powerful interests which are material and objective, but also ideal in character. Without it, a society like our own—with a separation of officials, employees, and workers from ownership of the means of administration, dependent on discipline and on technical training—could no longer function. The only exception would be those groups, such as the peasantry, who are still in possession of their own means of subsistence. Even in case of revolution by force or of occupation by an enemy, the bureaucratic machinery will normally continue to function just as it had for the previous legal government.

The question is always who controls the existing bureaucratic machinery. And such control is possible only to a very limited degree for persons who are not technical specialists. Generally speaking, in the long run the trained permanent official is more likely to get his way than his nominal superior, the Cabinet minister, who is not a specialist.

Though by no means alone, the capitalistic system has undeniably played a major role in the development of bureaucracy. Indeed, without it capitalistic production could not continue, and any rational type of socialism would have simply to take it over and increase its importance. Its development, largely under capitalistic auspices, has created an urgent need for stable, strict, intensive, and calculable administration. It is this need which gives bureaucracy a crucial role in our society as the central element in any kind of large-scale administration. Only by reversion in every field—political, religious, economic, and so forth—to small-scale organization would it be possible to any considerable extent to escape its influence. On the one hand, capitalism in its modern stages of development strongly tends to foster the development of bureaucracy, although both capitalism and bureaucracy have arisen from many different historical sources. Conversely, capitalism is the most

rational economic basis for bureaucratic administration and enables it to develop in the most rational form, especially because, from a fiscal point of view, it supplies the necessary money resources.

Along with these fiscal conditions of efficient bureaucratic administration, there are certain extremely important conditions in the field of communication and transportation. The precision of its functioning requires the services of the railway, the telegraph, and the telephone and becomes increasingly dependent on them. A socialistic form of organization would not alter this fact. It would be a question whether in a socialistic system it would be possible to provide conditions for carrying out as stringent bureaucratic organization as has been possible in a capitalistic order. For socialism would, in fact, require a still higher degree of formal bureaucratization than capitalism. If this should prove not to be possible, it would demonstrate the existence of another of those fundamental elements of irrationality in social systems —a conflict between formal and substantive rationality of the sort which sociology so often encounters.

Bureaucratic administration means fundamentally the exercise of control on the basis of knowledge. This is the feature of it which makes it specifically rational. This consists on the one hand in technical knowledge which, by itself, is sufficient to ensure it a position of extraordinary power. But in addition to this, bureaucratic organizations, or the holders of power who make use of them, have the tendency to increase their power still further by the knowledge growing out of experience in the service; for they acquire through the conduct of office a special knowledge of facts and have available a store of documentary material peculiar to themselves. While not peculiar to bureaucratic organizations, the concept of "official secrets" is certainly typical of them. It stands in relation to technical knowledge in somewhat the same position as commercial secrets do to technological training. It is a product of the striving for power.

Bureaucracy is superior in knowledge, including both technical knowledge and knowledge of the concrete fact within its own sphere of interest, which is usually confined to the interests of a private business—a capitalistic enterprise. The capitalistic entrepreneur is, in our society, the only type who has been able to maintain at least relative immunity from subjection to the control of rational bureaucratic knowledge. All the rest of the population have tended to be organized in large-scale corporate groups which are inevitably subject to bureaucratic control. This is as inevitable as the dominance of precision machinery in the mass production of goods.

The following are the principal more general social consequences of bureaucratic control:

1. The tendency to "leveling" in the interest of the broadest possible basis of recruitment in terms of technical competence.
2. The tendency to plutocracy growing out of the interest in the greatest possible length of technical training. Today this often lasts up to the age of thirty.
3. The dominance of a spirit of formalistic impersonality, without hatred or passion, and hence without affection or enthusiasm. The dominant norms are concepts of straightforward duty without regard for personal considerations. Everyone is subject to formal equality of treatment—that is, everyone in the same empirical situation. This is the spirit in which the ideal official conducts his office.

The development of bureaucracy greatly favors the leveling of social classes, and this can be shown historically to be the normal tendency. Conversely, every process of social leveling creates a favorable situation for the development of bureaucracy; for it tends to eliminate class privileges, which include the appropriation of means of administration and the appropriation of authority as well as the occupation of offices on an honorary basis or as an avocation by virtue of wealth. This combination everywhere inevitably foreshadows the development of mass democracy.

The "spirit" of rational bureaucracy normally has the following general characteristics:

1. Formalism, which is promoted by all the interests which are concerned with the security of their own personal situation, whatever this may consist in. Otherwise the door would be open to arbitrariness, and hence formalism is the line of least resistance.
2. There is another tendency, which is apparently in contradiction to the above —a contradiction which is in part genuine. It is the tendency of officials to treat their official function from what is substantively a utilitarian point of view in the interest of the welfare of those under their authority. But this utilitarian tendency is generally expressed in the enactment of corresponding regulatory measures which themselves have a formal character and tend to be treated in a formalistic spirit. This tendency to substantive rationality is supported by all those subject to authority who are not included in the class mentioned above as interested in the security of advantages already controlled. The problems which open up at this point belong in the theory of "democracy."

10 Dysfunctions in Organizations

by JAMES G. MARCH AND HERBERT A. SIMON

When we turn from Weber to the more recent students of bureaucracy we find them paying increasing attention to the "unanticipated" responses of the organization members. Without denying Weber's essential proposition that bureaucracies are more efficient (with respect to the goals of the formal hierarchy) than are alternative forms of organization, the research and analyses of Merton (1940), Selznick (1949), and Gouldner (1954) have suggested important dysfunctional consequences of bureaucratic organization. In addition—explicitly in the case of Gouldner and implicitly in the other two authors—they have hypothesized that the unintended consequences of treating individuals as machines actually encourage a continued use of the "machine" model.

The general structure of the theoretical systems of all three writers is remarkably similar. They use as the basic independent variable some form of organizational procedure designed to control the activities of the organization members. These procedures are based primarily on what we have called the "machine" model of human behavior. They are shown to have the consequences anticipated by the organizational leaders but also to have other, unanticipated, consequences. In turn, these consequences reinforce the tendency to use the control device.

The several systems examined here posit different sets of variables and theoretical relations; however, their structures are sufficiently similar to suggest that these

studies in "bureaucracy" belong to a single class of theories.

The Merton Model

Merton (1940) is concerned with dysfunctional organizational learning; organization members generalize a response from situations where the response is appropriate to similar situations where it results in consequences unanticipated and undesired by the organization. Merton asserts that changes in the personality of individual members of the organization stem from factors in the organizational structure. Here personality refers to any fairly reliable connection between certain stimuli and the characteristic responses to them. The label "personality" is attached to such a response pattern when the pattern does not change easily or rapidly.

Merton's system of propositions begins with a *demand for control*...made on the organization by the top hierarchy. This demand takes the form of an increased *emphasis on the reliability of behavior*... within the organization. ... From the point of view of the top hierarchy, this represents a need for accountability and predictability of behavior. The techniques used to secure reliability draw upon what has been called here the "machine" model of human behavior. Standard operating procedures are instituted, and control consists largely in checking to ensure that these procedures are, in fact, followed.

Three consequences follow from this emphasis on reliability in behavior and the techniques used to install it:

1. There is a reduction in the *amount of personalized relationships*.... The bureaucracy is a set of relationships between offices, or roles. The official

Reprinted from Organizations, *pp. 36–47, by permission of the authors and the publisher, John Wiley & Sons, Inc. Copyright* © *1958.*

reacts to other members of the organization not as more or less unique individuals but as representatives of positions that have specified rights and duties. Competition within the organization occurs within closely defined limits; evaluation and promotion are relatively independent of individual achievement (for example, promotion by seniority).

2. *Internalization of the rules of the organization*...by the participants is increased.... Rules originally devised to achieve organizational goals assume a positive value that is independent of the organizational goals.

3. There is increased *use of categorization as a decision-making technique*. ...To be sure, categorizing is a basic part of thinking in any situation. The special feature involved here is a tendency to restrict the categories used to a relatively small number and to enforce the first formally applicable category rather than search for the possible categories that might be applied and choose among them. An increase in the use of categorization for decision-making decreases the *amount of search for alternative*. ...

The reduction in personalized relationships, the increased internalization of rules, and the decreased search for alternatives combine to make the behavior of members of the organization highly predictable— that is, they result in an increase in the *rigidity of behavior*...of participants. ... At the same time, the reduction in personalized relationships (particularly with respect to internal competition) facilitates the development of an *esprit de corps*— that is, increases the *extent to which goals are perceived as shared among members of the group*. Such a sense of commonness of purpose, interests, and character increases the *propensity of organization members to defend each other against outside pressures*. This, in turn, solidifies the tendency toward rigid behavior. ...

The rigidity of behavior has three major consequences. First, it substantially satisfies the original demands for reliability. ... Thus, it meets an important maintenance need of the system. Further needs of this sort are met by strengthening in-group identification, as previously mentioned. ... Second, it increases the *defensibility of individual action*. ...Simple categories rigorously applied to individual cases without regard for personal features can only be challenged at a higher level of the hierarchy. Third, the rigidity of behavior increases the *amount of difficulty with clients*...of the organization...and complicates the achievement of client satisfaction—a near-universal organizational goal. Difficulty with clients is further increased by an increase in the *extent of use of trappings of authority*...by subordinates in organization...a procedure that is encouraged by the in-group's defensiveness. ...

The maintenance of part of the system by the techniques previously outlined produces a continuing pressure to maintain these techniques, as would be anticipated. It is somewhat more difficult to explain why the organization would continue to apply the same techniques in the face of client dissatisfaction. Why do organizational members fail to behave in each case in a manner appropriate to the situation? For the answer one must extend Merton's explicit statements by providing at least one, and perhaps two, additional feedback loops in the system. (It is not enough to say that such behavior becomes a part of the "personality." One must offer some explanation of why this apparently maladaptive learning takes place.)

The second major consequence of rigidity in behavior mentioned above (increased defensibility of individual action) is a deterrent to discrimination that reinforces the emphasis on reliability of behavior. ... In addition, client dissatisfaction may in itself reinforce rigidity. On the one hand, client pressure at lower levels in the hierarchy tends to increase the *felt need for the defensibility of individual action*. ... On the other hand,

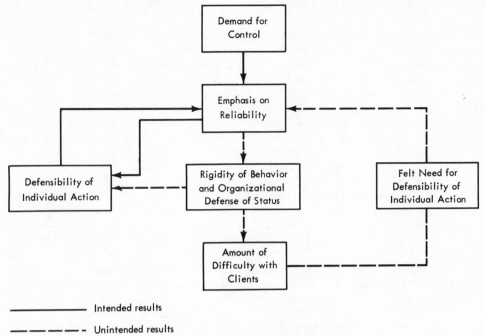

```
                    ┌──────────────┐
                    │  Demand for  │
                    │   Control    │
                    └──────┬───────┘
                           ↓
                    ┌──────────────┐
        ┌──────────→│ Emphasis on  │←─────────────┐
        │           │ Reliability  │              │
        │           └──────┬───────┘              │
        │                  ┆                       │
┌───────┴──────┐   ┌───────┴──────────┐   ┌───────┴──────┐
│Defensibility │   │Rigidity of Behavior│ │Felt Need for │
│     of       │←─ │and Organizational│   │Defensibility │
│Individual    │   │ Defense of Status│   │     of       │
│   Action     │   └───────┬──────────┘   │Individual    │
└──────────────┘           ┆              │   Action     │
                           ┆              └──────────────┘
                    ┌──────┴───────┐              ┆
                    │  Amount of   │              ┆
                    │Difficulty with│┄┄┄┄┄┄┄┄┄┄┄┄┄┘
                    │   Clients    │
                    └──────────────┘
```

──────────── Intended results

┄ ┄ ┄ ┄ ┄ Unintended results

The Simplified Merton Model

remedial action demanded by clients from higher officials in the hierachy may be misdirected. To the extent to which clients perceive themselves as being victims of discrimination (a perception that is facilitated in American culture by the importance attached to "equal treatment"), the proposals of clients or of the officials to whom they complain will probably strengthen the emphasis on reliability of behavior. This conflict between "service" and "impartiality" as goals for public organizations seems to lie behind a good deal of the literature on public bureaucracies.

We see that Merton's model is a rather complex set of relations among a relatively large number of variables. A simplified version of the model, designed to illustrate its major features, is provided in the following figure.

The Selznick Model

Where Merton emphasizes rules as a response to the demand for control, Selznick (1949) emphasizes the delegation of authority. Like Merton, however,

Selznick wishes to show how the use of a control technique (that is, delegation) brings about a series of unanticipated consequences. Also, like Merton, Selznick shows how these consequences stem from the problems of maintaining highly interrelated systems of interpersonal relations.

Selznick's model starts with the demand for control made by the top hierarchy. As a result of this demand, an increased *delegation of authority*. . .is instituted. . . .

Delegation, however, has several immediate consequences. As intended, it increases the *amount of training in specialized competences*. . . . Restriction of attention to a relatively small number of problems increases experience within these limited areas and improves the employee's ability to deal with these problems. Operating through this mechanism, delegation tends to decrease the *difference between organizational goals and achievement*. . . and thus to stimulate more delegation. . . . At the same time, however, delegation results in departmentalization and an increase in the *bifurcation of interests*. . . among the subunits in the organization. . . . The maintenance needs of the subunits dictate a commitment to the subunit goals over and above their contribution to the total organizational program. Many individual needs depend on the continued success and even expansion of the subunit. As in the previous example, the activities originally evaluated in terms of the organization goals are seen to have additional important ramifications for the subunits.

Bifurcation of interests is also stimulated by the specialized training that delegation (intendedly) produces. Training results in increased competence and, therefore, in increased *costs of changing personnel...* and this results, in turn, in further differentiation of subunit goals....

The bifurcation within the organization leads to increased *conflict among organizational subunits....* As a consequence, the *content of decisions...* made within the organization depends increasingly upon considerations of internal strategy, particularly if there is little *internalization of organizational goals by participants....* As a result there is an increase in the difference between organizational goals and achievement... and this results in an increase in delegation....

This effect on daily decisions is accentuated by two other mechanisms in Selznick's system. The struggle for internal control not only affects directly the content of decisions but also causes greater *elaboration of subunit ideologies....* Each subunit seeks success by fitting its policy into the official doctrine of the large organization to legitimize its demands. Such a tactic increases the *internalization of subgoals by participants...* within subunits....

At the same time, the internalization of subgoals is reinforced by a feedback from the daily decisions it influences. The necessity for making daily decisions creates a system of precedents. Decisions depend primarily on the operational criteria provided by the organization, and, among these criteria, subunit goals are of considerable importance.... Precedents tend to become habitual responses to the situations for which they are defined as relevant and thus to reinforce the internalization of

subunit goals.... Obviously, internalization of subgoals is partially dependent on the *operationality of organizational goals.* ...By operationality of goals, we mean the extent to which it is possible to observe and test how well goals are being achieved. Variations in the operationality of organizational goals affect the content of daily decisions... and thus the extent of subunit goal internalization.

From this it is clear that delegation has both functional and dysfunctional consequences for the achievement of organizational goals. It contributes both to their realization and to their deflection. Surprisingly, the theory postulates that both increases and decreases in goal achievement cause an increase in delegation. Why does not normal learning occur here? The answer seems to be that when goals are not achieved, delegation is— within the framework of the "machine" model—the correct response, and the model does not consider alternatives to simple delegation. On the other hand, the model offers explicitly at least two "dampers" that limit the operation of the dysfunctional mechanisms. As indicated in the next figure, where the skeleton of the Selznick model is outlined, there are two (not entirely independent) variables treated as independent but potentially amenable to organizational control, each of which restrains the runaway features of daily decision-making. By suitable changes in the extent to which organizational goals are operational or in the internalization of organizational goals by participants, some of the dysfunctional effects of delegation can be reduced.

The Gouldner Model

In terms of number of variables and relations, Gouldner's model (1954) is the simplest of the three presented here; but it exhibits the major features of the two previous systems. Like Merton, Gouldner is concerned with the consequences of bureaucratic rules for the maintenance of organization structure. Like both Mer-

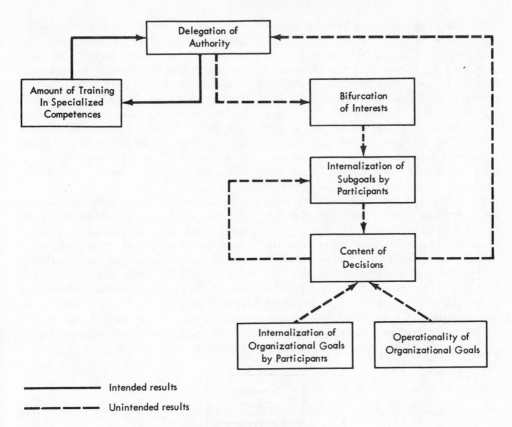

| ──────── | Intended results |
| ─ ─ ─ ─ ─ | Unintended results |

The Simplified Selznick Model

ton and Selznick, he attempts to show how a control technique designed to maintain the equilibrium of a subsystem disturbs the equilibrium of a larger system, with a subsequent feedback on the subsystem.

In Gouldner's system, the *use of general and impersonal rules*...regulating work procedures is part of the response to the demand for control from the top hierarchy.

One consequence of such rules is to decrease the *visibility of power relations*... within the group.... The visibility of authority differences within the work group interacts with the *extent to which equality norms are held*...to affect the *legitimacy of the supervisory role*.... This, in turn, affects the level of interpersonal tension...in the work group.... In the American culture of egalitarian norms, decreases in power visibility increase the

legitimacy of the supervisory position and therefore decrease tension within the group.

Gouldner argues that these anticipated consequences of rule-making do occur, that the survival of the work group as an operating unit is substantially furthered by the creation of general rules, and that consequently the use of such rules is reinforced....

At the same time, however, work rules provide cues for organizational members beyond those intended by the authority figures in the organization. Specifically, by defining unacceptable behavior, they increase *knowledge about minimum acceptable behavior*.... In conjunction with a low level of internalization of organizational goals, specifying a minimum level of permissible behavior increases the disparity between organization goals and achievement by depressing behavior to the minimum level. . . .

Performance at the minimum level is perceived by hierarchical superiors as a failure. In short, the internal stabilizing effects of the rules are matched by the unbalance they produce in the larger organization. The response to the unbalance is an increase in the *closeness of supervision* . . . over the work group. . . . This response is based on the "machine" model of human behavior: Low performance indicates a need for more detailed inspection and control over the operation of the "machine."

In turn, however, close supervision increases the visibility of power relations within the organization . . . raises the tension level in the work group, and thereby upsets the equilibrium originally based on the institution of rules. The broad outline of the model is shown in the next figure.

Gouldner's model leaves some puzzles unexplained. In particular, why is increased supervision the supervisory response to low performance? It seems reasonable that the tendency to make such a response is affected both by role perceptions and by a third equilibrating process in the system—the individual needs of the supervisors. Thus, the intensity of supervision is a function of the *authoritarianism* of supervisors . . . and a function of the *punitivity of supervisory role perception*. . . .

As in the Selznick model, the existence of "dampers" on the system poses the question of their treatment as external variables. Appropriate manipulation of equality norms, perceived commonality of interest, and the needs of supervisors will restrict the operation of the dysfunctional features of the system. The failure of top management to use such techniques of control suggests that the system may be incompletely defined.

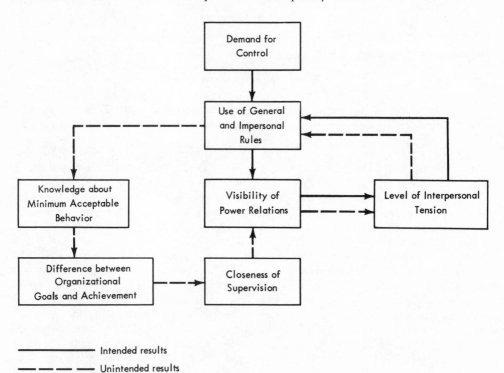

The Simplified Gouldner Model

11 Formality Versus Flexibility in Complex Organizations*

by GERALD D. BELL

Although there has been much research on organization in the past decade, for the most part it is segmented and loosely interrelated. There is an absence of theoretical formulations which tie current findings into a systematic framework. The stage has been attained, therefore, at which a middle-range theory might be beneficial in gaining a perspective on where our findings have brought us and in which direction we might aim.[1] As Robert V. Presthus comments, "An explicit sythesis between conceptual theory and empirical field research" is required at the present time in the study of organizations.[2]

We attempt here to formulate strategic, interrelated sets of hypotheses based on current research. Our attention is directed toward one, if not the most, significant topic with which recent investigations have been concerned. This is the problem of formal versus flexible patterns of organization.

We will analyze why contemporary research suggests that flexible, loosely structured enterprises are more efficient for given situations than more formally arranged systems. We first review early "formalistic investigations" to ascertain productive factors which are assumed to cause efficiency in work performance. Then, we compare these causal assumptions to those reported in recent "flexible studies." Following this analysis we attempt to trace consequences of these productive variables upon specific aspects of organization.

Formalized structures and processes refer to the degree to which role expectations and behavior are explicitly established and regulated by the administrative apparatus. An organization is formally structured when there is extensive regulation and control of behavior. Flexible structures and processes characterize those institutions in which the majority of tasks are not governed by explicitly stated regulations and policies and in which employees are not strictly governed by a rigid, clearly specified authority structure.

Theoretical foundations

Early research viewed industrial research and service enterprises as formally and rationally structured units. Production activities were assumed to be clearly defined, well coordinated, and performed in a rigid, impersonal manner.[3] The "formalized theories" were given their most elaborate development, of course, in Max Weber's organizational precepts.[4]

We find evidence of widespread influence of these doctrines in the fact that much research in the past several decades has clustered around three problems arising from formal theories. First, the "human-relations school" attacked assumptions of formalized theories concerning workers' psychological dispositions and motivational orientations.[5] Second, researchers have been concerned with dysfunctional aspects of formalized modes of

Prepared especially for this volume.

* The author is greatly indebted to Stanley H. Udy, Jr., Elton F. Jackson, and Richard L. Simpson who throughout the formulation of the investigation provided keen analytical critiques of the notions presented in this paper. Part of the research is based on the author's dissertation, Gerald D. Bell, "Formality Versus Flexibility in Complex Organizations: A Comparative Investigation within a Hospital" (Unpublished doctoral disseration, Yale University, Department of Sociology, 1964).

organization.[6] Finally, and of most significance for the present study, recent investigations have been in the direction of "structural alterations or qualifications" of the formalistic model.[7] For the most part these efforts, which we have tentatively labeled the "flexible school," suggest that in many cases organizations with structures opposite to those prescribed by Weber exist and are conducive to a high degree of efficiency.

Examples of "flexible studies" are Alvin Gouldner's research on the subsurface division of a Gypsum plant,[8] Morris Janowitz's investigation of the changing structures of the military,[9] James Thompson and Arthur Tuden's analysis of formal and flexible tendencies which result from the extent of agreement that exists on decisions concerning both causative issues and preferences among alternatives,[10] Arthur Stinchcombe's formulations on "craft bureaucracies,"[11] and, finally, in Eugene Litwak's research on "human-relations" types of organization.[12] In general, these investigations suggest that authority structures are at a minimum, interaction is on a personal basis, and there is little rule usage.

Although the points of departure and variables considered are somewhat different, the flexible studies have proposed quite divergent patterns of organization than those expounded in the formalistic design; however, the causes for these differences are by no means clear. Let us attempt to explain, then, the causal assumptions upon which these two divergent theories stand.

Lack of discretion in the formal theories

The causal notions of formalistic theorists—as exemplified by F. W. Taylor, Luther Gulick, and Max Weber—are revealed in their special emphasis upon subdivision of tasks, strict delimitation of duties, and reliability and calculability of behavior. These notions imply that duties to be performed by an individual are susceptible to easy specification and preplanning. They hold the idea, furthermore, that work demands performed in the productive system are highly predictable and repetitive. And finally, they make the all-important assumption that workers carry out their tasks by exercising only a small degree of discretion or decision-making effort.

Presence of discretion in the flexible theories

Flexible investigations have been based upon notions quite contrary to the causal assumptions of formal theorists. Flexible studies have assumed, although somewhat implicitly, that the work environment is relatively nonpredictable and encourages much discretion on the part of the workers. And, a careful analysis of the assumptions implied in the "flexible theories" suggests that the amount of discretion workers exercise is a key feature which is causally related to the degree of formality of organizational structures. It is not, as is suggested in the flexible studies, improvisation, lack of rule usage, lack of close supervision, variation in work load, professionalization, or social skills *per se* which directly cause differences in organizatonal design. More precisely (1) we hypothesize that several of these variables are *important causes of the discretion a worker exercises in performing his tasks*, and (2) *discretion, in turn, has a significant influence on the flexibility of formalistic tendencies of organizational structure.* We will now direct our attention to these two postulates in their respective order.

Discretion

For each task a worker performs he is confronted with the opportunity or sometimes the necessity to exert a certain degree of discretion—that is, judgment, choice, or selection among alternatives in order to carry out his tasks. Furthermore, the total amount of discretion he exercises is directed toward one or some combinations of three main aspects of task performance —(1) *which tasks* he performs during a given period of time, (2) *how or by which methods,* and (3) *in which sequence he* performs his tasks.

Determinants of Discretion

Discretion on the part of the employee is brought into play when the character of the work itself and the routines governing how the work is done do not automatically determine for the employee doing the job the best way to do it in every respect. Discretion and judgment are necessary when there are more ways than one to go about doing a task. When causes of a problem are not clearly defined and when the solution is lacking acceptable alternatives, the final answer must rely on judgment.[13] And when there are many such situations, it is likely that an individual will learn to exercise his discretion, since there is a certain point at which it is uneconomical for the supervisor to make decisions for him. Beyond this point, the supervisor might as well be doing the job himself. An analysis of the flexible studies previously mentioned suggests that discretion taken as the dependent variable is caused by the following independent variables: (a) predictability of work demands, (b) management control, and (c) professionalization.

Predictability

Predictability of work demands refers to the extent to which unexpected events confront an individual while he is performing his job. Stinchcombe's "unstable work situations,"[14] Litwak's "nonuniform tasks,"[15] and Janowitz's "changing elements of battle technology"[16] all seem to cluster around the predictability category.

When situational demands are unpredictable, they present the worker with novel events toward which he has the opportunity to utilize his judgment in completing his tasks. When a surgeon, for example, opens a patient's stomach and finds an unexpected object inside he will be encouraged, presumably, to alter his activities (or to utilize his discretion) to meet the exigencies of the situation. In the same manner if a stockbroker meets a new customer and begins his sales talk by presenting a "front region" of an intellectual and then perceives that he is presenting the wrong front because the customer sympathizes with anti-intellectuals, he will be encouraged to change his behavior, that is, to use his judgment in order to come up with a new "self" which will enable him to carry out his tasks more effectively. This assumes, of course, that the worker is motivated to perform his tasks adequately.[17]

In addition to the direct effect of predictability upon discretion, predictability also indirectly influences discretion via two intervening variables. These are the degree of closeness of supervision and, in turn, rule usage, both taken as components of management control.

Management control and discretion

Management has the opportunity and ability to determine the exact degree of discretion a worker exercises regardless of the extent of predictability of job demands. For example, a supervisor of a research department (a fairly unpredictable unit) might normally expect that he would have much opportunity to exert his judgment in completing his tasks; however, if management decided, for whatever reason, to establish a very rigid, encompassing set of rules for this supervisor to follow, then he would not exert high discretion even though he still was faced with many unpredictable events on his job. New problems would continue to arise, new solutions would appear; however, the supervisor would not exert his judgment in meeting these unexpected events, rather he would follow management's directives.

The point to be made here is that even though predictability might significantly affect discretion, discretion can also be influenced by management's control. But we hypothesize that management will perceive that if they control very tightly the tasks of workers who are faced with unpredictable work situations, then the rate of efficiency will be decreased. Consequently, we expect management to encourage workers who have unpredictable jobs to utilize their discretion.[18] Hence, in this case predictability is an independent variable influencing management control, and management control is an intervening variable causally related to workers' discretion.

Professionalization

Professionalization here means that workers have received a technical training to achieve a recognized occupational competence. The more professional training an employee has acquired, the more he will possess and demand skills which require discretion. In Stinchcombe's terms, craft administration differs from mass-production administration "...by substituting professional training of manual workers for detailed centralized planning of work."[19] In a similar light, Thompson and F. L. Bates rehearse the idea that the university must allow its personnel to exercise much discretion, since "knowledge" is given recognition as the basis of authority.[20] Simon Marcson also suggests that discretion and flexibility are important aspects of professional ranks of scientific research firms.[21]

Professional training improves technical competence; in a sense it creates technical and discretionary skills and at the same time produces expectations of freedom from supervisory control in the work setting. We hypothesize, than, that the higher the professional training, the higher the discretion. Correspondingly, professionalization indirectly affects discretion through the intervening variable of management control. In this latter instance the higher the professional training, the lower will be the degree of management control over a worker's behavior, and thus the higher will be an individual's discretion.

In summary, predictability, management control, and professionalization act as important determinants of employees' discretion.

Problem in past assumptions

There are several problems associated with past theories which state that some of the above variables which we assume to affect discretion act independently to cause flexible or formalistic characteristics of work arrangement.

For example, in one of the first illuminating approaches to the general flexibility-formalistic dilemma, Litwak offered a provacative first step in attempting to explain why organizations had quite varying structures. He concluded, following Weber, that jobs (1) which stress uniform situations, that is,"...the task to be dealt with is recurrent (in time as well as among many people) and important, exemplified in such occupations as that of research scientist or developmental engineer, as opposed to supervisor of an assembly line;"[22] and (2) which stress traditional areas of knowledge, such as knowledge of engineering, chemistry, economics, law, company rules, and the like, are those which bring about a rational, Weberian type of organization. On the other hand nonuniform jobs and those which require social skills tend to create organizations which stress primary relations and organizational goals.[23]

Litwak, indeed, has made a major contribution to the solution of the dilemma of formalistic-flexibilistic work patterns; however, we must carry his analysis further, and this necessitates some modifications in his causal assumptions. It is possible, for example, that such categories as social skills and traditional areas of knowledge can be somewhat misleading if, as has been proposed in this paper, the degree of discretion initiated by the worker is one of the key dimensions producing varying patterns of organization; for it is possible that jobs which require social skills (Litwak suggests jobs such as salesmen's, psychiatric social workers', and politicians') due to various cirmustances may in fact allow the job incumbent only a small degree of discretion and, therefore, tend to produce a formalistic work structure, which is opposite to that expected in Litwak's interpretation. Similarly, jobs which stress traditional areas of knowledge (economics, law), contrary to what is implied by Litwak, might be nonpredictable and require a very high degree of discretion. Again, in this latter case, we would have quite different consequences for traditional, yet high-discretion, jobs than are proposed by Litwak. Work would tend toward flexible patterns of organization rather than toward the Weberian model as Litwak proposed.

Furthermore, Litwak's concept of uniform work tasks evidently refers to the activities *actually performed* by the employee, whereas predictability as developed here refers to the *work demands* which confront an individual. These are two distinct variables. A worker might be confronted by many unique and unexpected situations while carrying out his job; however, he might meet these unique events by performing tasks in a very repetitive, routine, or—in Litwak's terms—uniform way. In this situation unexpected events would continue to occur, but the worker would in a sense ignore these situational

demands and perform his tasks in a routine manner. And in this case he would be making few decisions in performing his job. Consequently, his job would fit rather easily into a formalistic work structure.

It would appear that the general categories mentioned by Litwak and others might profitably be modified by considering predictability of work demands and discretion. What Litwak and several of the other "flexible theorists" were exploring, in essence, was something similar to these two variables, but their causal assumptions were too broad to be able to generalize to precise causal relationships concerning organizational structure. Let us view now how discretion influences organizational design.

The Discretionary Model of Organization

It is hypothesized that the relationships portrayed in the following chart will pre-

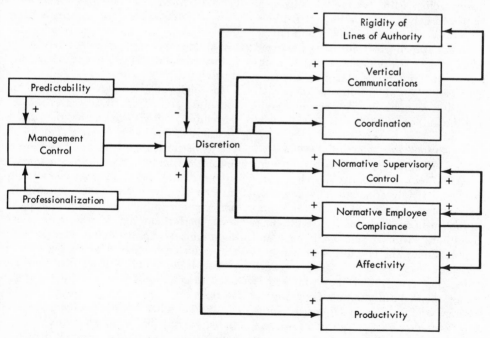

The Discretionary Model of Organization*

* The arrowed lines in the chart indicate the assumed causal direction of the relationships; and the plus and minus signs represent positive and negative associations, respectively. For example, when predictability is high, discretion is low.

vail in organizations in which the productive systems are high on discretion, If these hypotheses are valid, then high discretion units may be characterized as having more flexible structures and processes. On the other hand, in the less discretionary units the direction of each of the hypotheses will be reversed, and, therefore, there firms will be more formal and rigid in their patterns of work arrangement. In other words, the more predictable the work demands and the fewer the decisions which must be made in the productive process to attain organization goals, the more formalized will be the patterns of administrative activities, communication, and coordination; and more flexible patterns of organization will result from unpredictable and highly discretionary productive processes.

The following set of hypotheses is in no way purported to be exhaustive, rather it is a first attempt to build organizational theory from existing research. Limits must be placed upon each of these propositions, since there are many factors in addition to discretion which enter into the predicted relationships. The notation of "other things being equal" should be placed behind each hypothesis. We will begin our analysis by discussing relationships between discretion and the authority structure.

Discretion and the authority structure

We are concerned here with the extent to which lines of authority are clearly defined and rigidly adhered to. When tasks are unpredictable and encourage employees to make decisions frequently, lines of authority will be very ambiguous and flexible. Subordinates will not be expected to report to a specific superior for each action they take, rather they will tend to scatter their consultations among several different combinations of supervisors. Similarly, since demands placed upon workers' efforts are assumed to encourage them to utilize their abilities in solving work problems and to call forth fairly unique solutons to their tasks, it would not appear likely that a rigid, carefully delineated

authority system would be created in unpredictable, high-discretion systems.

On the contrary, in low-judgmental units employees' tasks will be easily specified and controlled, since work demands are highly predictable and require little decision-making effort. Correspondingly, superiors will be able to plan for and to establish rigid lines of authority more easily, and the predictability of situational demands will enable subordinate-superior relationships to be handled adequately through formalized channels. As Thompson and Bates have said, since standardization is high, deviations can be measured readily and thus responsibility accurately assigned to specific individuals.[24]

Vertical communication

A survey of literature relevant to this variable suggests a rather interesting pattern between predictability, discretion, and vertical communications. There appears to be a positive relationship between vertical communications (any verbal, written, or symbolic exchange of information between members of different levels of authority) and discretion and, thus, predictability.[25]

In high-predictability—low discretion organizations, administrators are able to determine fairly accurately the tasks, methods, and sequence in which employees are to perform their tasks, and employees make few decisions. This enables managers to coordinate and train employees easily in their routine decision-making activities and consequently requires less control of their performance.[26] Furthermore, since communication and training partially substitute for each other, the better trained a person is for a job, the less becomes the need to communicate with him about his work.[27]

On the other hand, in high-discretion units, there will be much vertical communication. But instead of work demands being so predictable and involving so few decisions that close supervision and training are facilitated, work demands are unpredictable, and employees are highly skilled and competent...exercising much discretion. These factors encourage supervisors and subordinates to communicate frequently about work-related problems. The uniqueness and complexities involved in unpredictable and high-discretion demanding activities create a great need for exchange of ideas and information between workers and superiors concerning the solution of unique events.[28] The content of supervision in the latter case will be more on an equal "give-and-take" basis than on one in which supervisors closely regulate subordinates' activities. It would be a two-way, rather than merely a downward, communication as in the former case. Topics of exchange would in both cases probably be concerned with work activities—the solution of task-related problems, grievances, and so forth. However, the type of communication in the latter case might differ in being somewhat more complex, unique, and abstract than in the former.

Coordination of activities

There is less need to coordinate activities between departments which involve unpredictable demands and high discretion than between those with high predictability and low discretion. Departments in which decision-making ability has been decentralized appear to be more self-contained than are less discretionary units. For instance, one might compare the amount of coordination which takes place between two divisions on an assembly line in an automated production plant with two departments, such as history and sociology, in the relatively discretionary organization—the university. The reason for differences in coordination is that high-discretion units are arranged in parallel department specialization, whereas low-discretion units are more functionally interdependent in Peter M. Blau and W. Richard Scott's terms.[29] In parallel specialization, work activities of one department are different from but not highly dependent on actions of others. In contrast, interdependent specialization exists when the activities of one unit are depend-

ent upon the performance of tasks in other departments. The latter case makes coordination a fundamental managerial problem.

Why are nonpredictable, high-discretion departments specialized in a parallel manner, and why are predictable, low-discretion units interdependently specialized? The answer appears to be that when work demands are predictable and routine they can be subdivided and controlled fairly easily. Thus, more specialization can be obtained. And the more that tasks can be subdivided, the more they can be effectively planned for and coordinated by management's efforts. And thus, the more likely it is that they will be interdependently specialized.

Normative supervisory control

When an employee's superior attempts to motivate him to work by appealing to service norms and professional ideologies as opposed to such monetary rewards as pay, bonuses, or promotions, the supervisor, in Etzioni's terms, is using normative control attempts.[30] In departments in which tasks, methods, and sequence of performance are not clearly specified, and thus in which responsibility for the performance of each task is not clearly definable, administrators cannot easily direct the completion of each task. Correspondingly, rewards and responsibility cannot easily be assigned to tasks which are nonpredictable and which involve a high degree of discretion.

In these cases normative control attempts will provide incentives for members to perform necessary tasks on their own, since manipulation of pay does not lead to internationalization of values but produces only superficial, expedient, and overt commitment.[31] In this connection Marcson points out that in large scientific organizations there is a necessity for a shift to less arbitrary, less direct, and less dominating control practices. In research organizations the utilization of direct and calculative control not only evokes resentment but also resistance to such control attempts.[32] Thus, we theorize that when work demands are nonpredictable and involve much discretion, normative and/or somewhat more informal constraints will appear.

Employee compliance structure

Employees meet and adjust to control attempts by management in particular patterns and intensities of compliance. Job incumbents in high-discretion and unpredictable organizations will be oriented toward administrative control more in terms of normative and ideological commitment to work than by monetary or calculative involvement. Employees will make many decisions, have a relatively high degree of self-investment and responsibility, and consequently will be highly involved in their work. When an individual exercises his judgment and initiative in solving problems, he invests a good portion of his "self" in their outcome. Research scientists, for example, often indicate a need for an authority system based on persuasion and normative encouragements.[33]

Furthermore, the coterminous presence of professionalization of jobs and normative control attempts by supervisors directed toward discretionary jobs exerts important pressures toward a congruent normative control-normative compliance structure. The internalization by workers of professional ideologies and codes of conduct partially eliminates administrators' needs to motivate and to control employees. Professional-technical socialization acts as an arm of management in the sense that it "builds" motivation into workers and at the same time acts as a continuing motivational reference group for them.

In predictable, low-discretion jobs, however, a worker invests little of his "self" in the outcome of his productive efforts. In fact, he seldom sees how his activities contribute to the final product on which he is working. Similarly, responsibilities and rewards can be more clearly assigned. Therefore, managers can revert more easily to monetary and manipulative control attempts. In turn, employees will possess a calculative orientation toward their work and the organization.

Donald I. Warren has reported tentative evidence which indirectly supports these notions. He also introduces another dimension into the relationship between predictability, discretion, and normative involvement. He points out, following Rose Coser, that when visibility of formal authority agents is low (as is presumably the case in nonpredictable, high-discretion units) then attitudinal commitment to one's work and informal constraints are more likely to be conducive to effectiveness.[34]

Affectivity in interpersonal relations

In high-discretion and unpredictable organizations workers are considered to not only have a high degree of responsibility and investment of "self" in their work, but they also are thought to have more freedom in expressing their opinions and beliefs. They are given more leeway and encouragement to display their emotions, and thus there is a high degree of affectivity in the relationships between workers in these organizations. In his pioneering study of the operating room (a high-discretion unit) in the hospital setting, Wilson reports that doctors and nurses frequently maintain close personal relationships and share many experiences.[35] Similarly, Blau suggests that in a government unemployment agency the counseling role which employees performed was often carried out with highly affective personal relationships.[36]

Productivity

Finally, in enterprises which entail highly discretionary productive units if the above variables take on the directions predicted, we assume they will obtain optimum levels of efficiency. That is, if departments in which jobs are unpredictable and involve much discretion on the part of workers are (1) left relatively unattended by members in authority, (2) entail high vertical communications, (3) have a low degree of coordination with other departments, (4) are sanctioned and rewarded by normative control attempts, (5) and, correspondingly, normatively committed to on the part of the employees, and (6) are associated with affectivity in interpersonal work relationships, then we expect this type of flexible work arrangement to be conducive to an (7) optimum level of efficiency.

Similarly, if the hypotheses are reversed for nondiscretionary firms, efficiency will also be at a high level. In other words, we are maintaining that efficiency can best be reached by two separate patterns of organization for the two ideal extremes of the discretionary predictability productive systems. On the one extreme, Weber's rational model appears to be efficient for those enterprises which encompass nondiscretionary productive tasks. On the opposite pole, more flexible patterns of work arrangement are considered to be most conducive to efficiency when productive tasks are nonpredictable and high on discretion demands.

Summary and conclusions

We have attempted to formulate tentative hypotheses which partially explain why contemporary research has reported quite varying findings from Weber's early formulations. It is assumed that in organizations in which employees exert a high degree of discretion there will be: (1) less rigid lines of authority, (2) high vertical communications, (3) low coordination, (4) high normative control by supervisors, (5) high normative commitment by employees, (6) high affectivity in interpersonal relationships, and, finally (7) relatively high productivity.

It is further theorized that discretion is determined by predictability, management control, and extent of professionalization of jobs. These postulates are tentative and, of course, assume that "other things are held equal." Hopefully, this "discretionary model" will offer suggestions to some of the provocative questions concerning formal and flexible patterns of work arrangement raised in recent works and will suggest new avenues of research.

[1] Alvin Gouldner, "Organizational Analysis," in *Sociology Today*, Robert Merton *et. al.*, eds. (New York: Basic Books, Inc., Publishers, 1959), p. 404; James D. Thompson *et. al.*, *Comparative Studies in Administration* (Pittsburgh: University of Pittsburgh Press, 1959), p. 200; Amitai Etzioni, *A Comparative Analysis of Complex Organizations* (New York: Free Press of Glencoe, Inc., 1960), p. xiii; Simon Marcson, *The Scientist in American Industry* (Princeton, N. J.: Princeton University Press, 1960), p. 122; M. D. Field, "Information and Authority: The Structure of Military Organization, *"American Sociological Review*, 24 (February, 1959), p. 17; Stanley H. Udy, Jr., *Organization of Work* (New Haven, Connecticut: Human Relations Area Files Press), 1959.

[2] Robert V. Presthus, "Behavior and Bureaucracy in Many Cultures," *Public Administration Review*, 19 (1959), p. 25; See also, James March and Herbert Simon, *Organizations* (New York: John Wiley & Sons, Inc., 1958), p. 17–26, especially their discussion of Merton, Selznick, and Gouldner; Chris Argyris, "The Fusion of an Individual with the Organization." *American Sociological Review*, 14 (June, 1954), p. 272; Peter M. Blau and W. Richard Scott, *Formal Organizations* (San Francisco: Chandler Publishing Company, 1962), p. 35.

[3] March and Simon, *op. cit.*, p. 13. The flexible model, it should be pointed out, is rational in the sense that ends are related to the means in possibly the most appropriate method available. F. W. Taylor, *Shop Management* (New York: Harper & Row, Publishers, Inc., 1912); Luther Gulick and L. Urwick, eds. *Papers on the Science of Administration* (New York: Institute of Public Administration, 1937).

[4] Hans Gerth and C. Wright Mills, trans. and eds., *From Max Weber: Essays in Sociology* (New York: Oxford University Press, Inc., 1946), p. 214.

[5] See William F. Whyte, *Man and Organization: Three Problems in Human Relations in Industry* (Homewood, Illinois: Richard D. Irwin, Inc., 1959).

[6] For an excellent review of these studies see March and Simon, *op. cit.*, pp. 26–47.

[7] We are using "model" to refer to a general theory. Included in this category are Gouldner, *op. cit.*; Arthur Stinchombe, "Bureaucratic and Craft Administration of Production: A Comparative Study," *Administrative Science Quarterly* 4 (September, 1959); Morris Janowitz, "Changing Patterns of Organizational Authority: The Military Establishment," *Administrative Science Quarterly*, 3

(March, 1959), pp. 473–493; Eugene Litwak, "Models of Bureaucracy Which Permit Conflict," *American Journal of Sociology*, 67 (September, 1961), pp. 177–184.

8 Gouldner, *op. cit.*; James D. Thompson and F. L. Bates, "Technology, Organization and Administration," *Administrative Science Quarterly*, 11 (December, 1957), pp. 325–343.

9 Janowitz, *op. cit.*, p. 481.

10 James D. Thompson and Arthur Tudan, "Strategies, Structures, and Processes of Organizational Decision," in James D. Thompson *et al., op. cit.*, pp. 195–213.

11 Stinchcombe, *op. cit.*

12 Litwak, *op. cit.*, pp. 177–184.

13 Elliot, Jaques, *The Measurement of Responsibility* (Cambridge: Harvard University Press, 1956), p. 86; Thompson and Tuden, *op. cit.*, p. 199.

14 Stinchcombe, *op. cit.*

15 Litwak, *op. cit.*

16 Janowitz, *op. cit.*

17 Finally, there is a fascinating sidelight which should be mentioned in this connection. This is the fact that if unpredictable situational demands take the form of a threat to the organization, it is possible that the hypothesized association between predictability and discretion will be reversed. Several studies have indicated that outside threats tend to cause centralization of decision-making. (Janowitz, *op. cit.*)

18 It should also be pointed out here that it is possible that management's control might, in turn, affect the degree of predictability of an employee's job.

19 Stinchcombe, *op. cit.*, p. 175.

20 Thompson and Bates, *op. cit.*, p. 333.

21 Marcson, *op. cit.*, p. 44.

22 Litwak, *op. cit.*, p. 178.

23 *Ibid.*, p. 170. Social skills refer to the actual capacity to communicate with others, to motivate them to work, to cooperate with others, and to internalize the values of the organization.

24 Thompson and Bates, *op. cit.*, p. 334.

25 On this point see Richard L. Simpson, "Vertical and Horizontal Communication in Formal Organizations," *Administrative Science Quarterly*, 4 (September, 1959), p. 196. Although the predicted directions differ from those reviewed in Simpson's research, it does not appear that the problem lies in the theory as much as it does in the difficulty of ascertaining what actually is a high level of discretion, or mechanization. This appears to be an important point for scholars of administration to consider in future research.

26 Edward Gross, "Some Functional Consequences of Primary Controls," *American Sociological Review*," 18 (August, 1953), p. 379.

27 Etzioni, *op. cit.*, p. 138.

28 When specific vertical communication exchange networks are used repeatedly and therefore become relatively patterned and accepted paths for exchange of information, communication channels are said to exist. In high-discretion organizations, since there will be many and varied decisions which must be made at a variety of times and in numerous situations, it is possible that there will be less opportunity for vertical communications to become patterned, and workers will presumably be required to consult with many different supervisors in inconsistent and sporadic patterns. Stinchcombe's analysis of communication files is consistent with this notion. (Stinchcombe, *op. cit.*)

29 Blau and Scott, *op. cit.*, p. 183.

30 Etzioni, *op. cit.*, p. xv.

31 *Ibid.*; see also Andrew F. Henry and Edgar Borgatta, "A Comparison of Attitudes of Enlisted and Commissioned Air Force Personnel," *American Sociological Review*, 18 (December, 1953), p. 670.

32 Marcson, *op. cit.*

33 *Ibid.*

34 Donald I. Warren, "The Role of Professional Peer Relations in a Formal Organization Seeting: Some Correlates of Administrative Style" (unpublished paper presented at the Annual Meeting of the American Sociological Association, Montreal, Canada, September, 1964).

35 Robert N. Wilson, "Teamwork in the Operating Room," *Human Organization*, 12 (1954).

36 Blau and Scott, *op. cit.*

part three COMPARATIVE STUDIES OF ORGANIZATION

To gain a meaningful understanding of behavior in work organizations, it is essential to study activities performed in a wide variety of enterprises. We can increase our comprehension of organization of work by transferring insights gained in one type of firm to our analyses of behavior in a different kind of unit. Thus, in this section we view patterns of work activity as they are carried out in hospitals, voluntary associations, prisons, colleges, and universities. Since the major emphasis of the book is on industrial enterprises, we will not discuss this type of unit in this section.

In the first paper, "The Hospital's Dual Status System," Harvey Smith describes the subtle, yet powerful, strains which exist in modern hospitals. Conflicts between physicians and hospital administrators create unique problems of organization. Similarly, the blocked occupational mobility of employees and conflicts in values over service versus monetary goals must be understood if we are to explain and improve the arrangement of work activities in these institutions.

A fascinating analysis is provided in Edna E. Raphael's "Power Structures in Unions." She examines the political organization of local unions as they are influenced by the spatial distribution of members and the size of membership. It is interesting to ask how these later factors might influence the organizational patterns of business and service enterprises.

A more familar work unit to the reader, the university, is the subject of the remaining two papers in this section. The first article, "Colleges of America's Upper Class," by Gene Hawes, explores the causes and consequences of upper-class participation in the university. In the final paper of this section, "Button-Down Collar Culture," James Davie and A. P. Hare discuss the informal guidelines which direct the activities of members of a university. The subtle, yet forceful, impact of the "organizational culture" is vividly portrayed. One can easily transfer the analysis presented of an academic institution to an industrial, service, or other type of enterprise. When the newly hired employee enters a firm he, just as a college freshman, is immediately confronted by a unique culture which will help to mold his behavior.

12 Two Lines of Authority: The Hospital's Dilemma

by Harvey L. Smith

Certain organizational problems distinctive to hospitals become apparent when they are viewed alongside other complex human organizations. These distinctive features provide a set of constantly recurring problems to which people working in hospitals must adapt. It is proposed here to analyze the bases of such organizational problems and to indicate the dilemmas they entail for the administration of both lay and professional hospital personnel.

George Washington once reported, after a hospital inspection, that he had found no principal director and no subordination among the surgeons. He expressed his belief that this led to disputes which would continue until the hospital was reduced to some system. This might still be considered a valid capsule criticism of many modern hospitals.

Understanding the details which underlie such criticism requires study of the human (social) matrix of hospital administraton. As a sociologist, I have undertaken such study over a period of years in a variety of hospitals in several regions of the United States. I have had, in addition, several years of military service in hospital administration. Research and some practical experience, therefore, underlie this sociological report on hospitals.

Analysis of Hospital Structure

Basically, a hospital may be viewed as an organization at cross-purposes with it-

Reprinted by permission from the author and The Modern Hospital, *Vol. 84, No. 3, March, 1955.* © *Copyright 1955 by McGraw-Hill, Inc. All rights reserved.*

self. It is the kind of human institution about which people constantly complain that they are caught "in the middle." What they are caught in the middle of is a direct function of what we shall call the basic duality of hospitals.

A clue to the nature of this duality is provided by the statement that one frequently hears in hospitals—"The big thing here is the difference between what they say we do and what we actually do." A closer look at this difference brings us closer to the operating problems of hospital administration.

Let us start with the system of controls, the hierarchy of authority, through which a hospital operates. Here are found very great differences between what the hospital says it does and what it actually does.

Take, for example, the formal organization charts which many hospitals believe reflect a true picture of their pattern of operation. A comparison of the patterns indicated on such charts with the observed relationships among people actually working in the hospital reveals that usually the hospital organization chart portrays a complex system of administrative controls over lay people. Thus, there is the hierarchy from board trustees to hospital administrator to department heads to various categories of hospital workers. Hospitals vary in the degree to which the authority and responsibility at each level, and the channels of communication among them, are explicitly developed. But a closer look at an operating hospital reveals that this is far too simple a portrayal of its actual organization for work. The primary difference involves the role of professional persons—especially the physicians. There is almost no administrative routine established in hospitals which cannot be (and frequently is) abrogated or countermanded by a physician claiming medical emergency—or by anyone acting for the physician and similarly claiming medical necessity. Upon close observation it is found that the actual authority of the medical man in the hospital is very great indeed. Although the conventional organization chart portrays the position of the medical staff as outside the line of authority, we observed physicians to be exerting power throughout the hospital structure at all levels—upon nurses, ward personnel, upon patients, and even (where physicians were trustees) directly upon administrators themselves.

Thus, two main lines of authority—lay and professional—exist in the hospital. And there are sectors of the hospital which may not clearly be assigned to either and in which the authority of both may overlap. We have called these the "hybrid areas"—typically represented by pharmacy, pathology, x-ray, admissions, and medical records. These are mixtures of lay and professional competence and authority.

Authority May Overlap

This duality of controls is a product of the complexity of hospital organization—a complexity shared by other human structures (i.e., universities) where professional competence is exercised in a matrix of lay administration. In essence, it involves the attempt to handle two different principles of authority within one institution. The work of Max Weber[1] provides us with ideas for analyzing and understanding such complexity. The authority vested in (exercised by) lay administration is of a type familiar to us all. It is close to what Weber has classically described as bureaucratic authority, functioning in a clearly defined hierarchy with "packets" of authority and prestige prescribed for each level. But the problem for the hospital is that the authority of the

bureaucrat confronts that of the medical professional, who represents what Weber has called charismatic authority. This sociological term, borrowed from theology and meaning literally "gift of grace," represents the kind of authority which a person exercises by reason of having a set of followers who attribute special powers to him. By virtue of these special powers attributed to him he is held somewhat in awe. Weber recognized that the physician was a charismatic person.[2] One of the primary characteristics of charisma is that it is defiant of administrative regulation. Possessors of charisma resist being encompassed in bureaucratic organization. It is, in these terms, the special problem of the hospital that it is an administrative structure which must contain and regulate charismatic professional persons who are defiant of lay regulation. Thus, both administrators and physicians are authoritative figures, but for different (and basically conflicting) reasons. This provides, so to speak, a built-in conflict situation for hospital administration.

Conflict Between Systems

This problem may be seen in another way—as a conflict between two systems of status in the hospital. The ideas of Chester Barnard[3] are useful in understanding this. Barnard has noted that two kinds of status may be found in human organizations. One of these he calls "scalar" status—or the status inherent in a position within some hierarchical system. High rank in an organization and high status thus coincide. The other form of status he calls "functional." Such status inheres in certain kinds of work, regardless of the position of the worker in a ranked system. Thus, in the hospital, administration represents a system of scalar status, and the physicians carry high functional status. Orders normally come from those whose status is higher than the recipient of the orders. Hospital personnel find themselves receiving orders from carriers of both forms of status—

from the administrative side whose "right" to "boss" them is explicitly recognized and from the physicians whose "right" to "boss" them is not so clearly recognized but is just as keenly experienced. Such orders often reflect the conflicts which inhere in the dual-status system.

A dual system of values, expressing these conflicts, pervades the hospital. A hospital is, of course, many things: a place where the sick are cared for and treated, a place to which physicians bring their patients, a hotel, a laundry, a healing institution, a business organization. These many "purposes" of a hospital are rarely subsumed under any single "master symbol"; rather these many activities tend to be justified, by persons working within hospitals, in terms of two dominant values or symbols: "money" and "service." And frequently these are expressed as considerations of money *versus* service (or vice versa). This means, in brief, that a hospital is not quite sure of the kind of organization that it is, or should be. Is it a service institution or a business institution? Or something of each? Hospitals are faced with the need to come as close to balancing their budgets as possible while being sensitively aware of their task of serving the health needs of a public which includes those who cannot or will not pay for their care.

In the main, administration is forced to focus upon the contingencies of fiscal survival, and the physician more often appears as the person dedicated to the service aspect of hospitals. The fact that administrators and physicians often switch sides tends to point up the reality of this dichotomy of values. The employees of the hospital who have to mediate between the often conflicting demands of "money" or "service" are again confronted with a conflict situation which is built into the hospital.

All of this makes the hospital a peculiar form of power structure. Its distinctive aspects may readily be seen if we compare an "idealized" picture of the power structure of an industrial plant with a similarly idealized picture of the "flow" of power within a hospital.

Consider industry. Here, in a nonunionized plant, we find the flow of authority from management to the worker. Where a union is present in the plant the workers are able to exert counterpressures upon management. Staff members ordinarily act in an advisory capacity to top management, although in a functionally organized plant they may exert specific authority over particular segments of the plant organization. The crucially important productive work is performed at the worker level, low in the status hierarchy. Characteristically, conflict in such an organization appears as worker resistance to management.

Crucial differences appear when we consider the power structure of a hospital. We have the similar "line" of authority from management to the worker, with little union-organization resistance in hospitals. But, at the staff level, the physicians do not act merely in a passive advisory capacity. They intervene actively and powerfully throughout the structure, exerting power upon hospital operating personnel, defiant of administrative regulation, and, where they are members of boards of trustees, are able directly to control "top management" itself. Furthermore, it is at the staff level—the high-status level of the physicians—that the crucially important productive work of this institution is performed. And it is here, characteristically, in hospitals that we find the important resistances to management (administration) generated. This distinctive aspect of the hospital power structure highlights the problems of hospital administration.

Illustrative Cases

Such basic problems appear in many guises and in many parts of the hospital. They represent a complex interweaving of the controls, status systems, and values which have been described.

The kinds of crucial problems which

may arise between lay and professional people in hospitals are illustrated by the following case. A medical director readily admitted that he was so discontented with his job that he was prepared to resign. In fact, he showed us his letter of resignation which he kept on hand in his desk. He gave as the main reason for his discontent in the hospital the fact that he, a medical director who was a physician, was under the immediate supervision of a hospital administrator who was a layman. It was the opinion of this medical director that laymen simply did not know enough about the basic things which were involved in hospitals to do such a job adequately. As he said, "You cannot put a layman over a doctor in a hospital and have it work." He stated that not only he but other physicians in the hospital felt that this was an unworkable relationship. Furthermore, he quite explicitly indicated the belief that his job involved him in something of a status dilemma. He felt himself caught between the requirements of administration and his role as a physician and said that he no longer knew for certain whether he was a physician or an administrator. This case quite clearly reveals the dilemmas which may be experienced by those charged with mediating between these two systems—the administrative and the professional.

Physicians Break Rules

In another case, an elevator man reported a hospital rule stating that there should be no smoking in the elevator. When some physicians had entered the elevator while smoking he informed them of this rule. These physicians had been extremely angry and had reported him to the director of the hospital. He had been summoned to the director's office and reprimanded for trying to give orders to the physicians. Here is a case where the charismatic person of the physician was somewhat inviolate in the face of fairly legitimate lay regulations.

The medical-record librarian reveals another kind of dilemma-situation along another kind of axis. This lay person, who is charged with approval of the contents and format of medical records, often has to use what we have called a system of indirect sanctions to effect her job. This is a kind of adaptive behavior which works more or less as follows: Instead of giving physicians a direct order concerning the charts, she tells them that unless they do thus and so the reputation of the hospital will suffer, especially at the next inspection.

This use of indirect sanctions by appealing, not to the rules and regulations which give one the right to give the order but to the value system of the dominant person (here the physician), is also clearly revealed in the case of a laundryman. He said that he never had any trouble in the hospital. Whenever he needed something he simply told the person from whom he wanted it that he was asking for what the patients needed. Thus, no direct order is given; rather there is an attempt to motivate the person to cooperate in terms of his own value system.

Or, take the case of an old pharmacist who made explicit and expert use of the dual conflict of authority within hospitals at a time when his pharmacy was to be moved to a new place in the hospital. What he had done was simply to play both sides against each other by going and saying to one side, "Don't you think it would be splendid if my pharmacy were in such-and-such a place?" Upon receiving a noncommital "Yes" he would immediately go to the other side and say, "I have been told by Doctor So-and-So that my pharmacy should be in such-and-such a place." He then interpreted demurrers by the hospital administration as wanton disregard of professional opinion and wisdom.

It is pertinent to add that this pharmacist actually sewed up the entire system by appealing directly to members of the board of trustees in this fashion. He would visit their homes, bringing medicine for them or their children and solicit their approval for the place he wanted for his pharmacy. He would then tell members of both the medical staff and hospital administration that the board of trustees, the ultimate source of authority in the hospital, had suggested a good place for his pharmacy. This old-timer, with forty-odd years of hospital pharmacy experience, revealed a very acute manner of exploiting the divided authority system of the hospital to achieve precisely what he wanted. The result of two bosses for him was independence.

Another problem was reported by the chief of a pathology service who said that every physician in the hospital was a boss for his technicians. They claimed to know what the lab reports were supposed to contain, how much time analyses of various sorts would require, and which methods of analysis should be used. The girls were constantly badgered to be quicker and more accurate. He felt that every physician in the hospital was a competing expert for his job as chief of the pathology service. Here is a point where lay and professional competence overlap to the confusion of the working personnel.

In still another case we talked with the registrar of a Veterans Administration hospital. He also reported himself as being "in the middle" and went on to add that he was really caught between the demands of the physicians in the hospital and the administrative requirements of operating the hospital. He was, in fact, caught in the classical conflict between lay and professional contingencies in the hospital, especially over the matter of the availability of beds. Administration wanted to adhere to the directives concerning criteria and categories of admission and discharge. Physicians wanted beds occupied by cases that were medically and professionally interesting. Here again there was a clear-cut conflict between the demands of the administrative and professional components of the system, and this registrar, mediating between the two, stated the classical dilemma quite clearly of being "caught in the middle."

"Money" Versus "Service"

The problems of admissions offices reveal the confusions caused by the hospital's duality of values. Here, the demands of "money" and "service" are often in conflict for operating personnel and plainly reveal the ambivalence of the hospital as to whether it is a "service" or a "business" institution. This is certainly the case where the hospital is involved in the collection of money. Hospitals are urgent, yet apologetic, about the question of collections. The "front office" (the admissions office) is often caught in the cross fire of these feelings of urgency and apology. For example, an admitting officer in one of the hospitals told us of her problem of assigning a private room to a man of uncertain means who was moribund. She said that almost against her better judgment she had assigned him a private room. He died soon after and she was very glad that she had done so. But just the same, she said, she was immensely relieved when his wife came in and paid the hospital bill immediately after his death. Here again we see clearly the dilemma of a person who is weighing equally important humanitarian and fiscal considerations against each other. It is perhaps necessary to point out that there may be no ideal solutions to this kind of problem. This may be a kind of recurrent conflict which is, so to speak, endemic to the hospital as a human organization. Administrators who understand this are better equipped to deal with the strains of their organizations.

This conflict between fiscal and humanitarian demands, as they were interpreted by two different persons in positions of authority, made for a constant duel in one hospital that was observed. They were both persons high in administration—one with training as a nurse, the other with training in business administration. Neither was clearly assigned a position superior to the other. Each constantly berated the other. The administrator with training as a nurse stressed the cold, heartless inhumanity of the business manager, who, she said, tried to screen patients entirely in terms of whether or not they could pay. The business manager complained of the idle, welfare orientation of the nurse, saying that if she had her way she would have the hospital filled with local indigents (a Skid Row was quite near), and they would have to close their doors in bankruptcy. The conflict between these two for the position of authority was so great that there did exist in fact two organization charts. One, which was more or less publicly distributed, showed the nursing administrator as chief of the hospital. The other, privately distributed but adhered to by the trustees of the hospital, showed the business manager as the "boss" of the hospital.

There are many other problems which seem to be rooted in the peculiarities of hospital organization. Certainly many of the personnel problems faced by hospital administration appear to be more acutely difficult than those faced by administrators of other kinds of organizations. For example, certain hospitals which we observed could have been characterized as "weeping organizations." As a kind of bitter jest we could have established a "weeping index" in which the copiousness of tears shed by members (usually women) of the hospital was some measure of the effectiveness of its organization.

There are several important reasons for this, all of which the hospital must realize, as it must also realize that none of these is susceptible to magic solution. One of these, for example, is that the hospital is a structure of what we have called "blocked mobility": that is, the skills which are developed in one small component of the hospital, for example x-ray or pathology or housekeeping or admissions, are not readily transferrable to other departments. When the question of promotion to another department comes up, persons within the hospital who merit consideration often do not actually possess the skills needed to occupy the new posi-

tion. In addition, their skills continue to be required in their old department, and very often department heads who have trained their personnel may resist their transfer to other parts of the hospital. This problem of "blocked mobility" is a constant source of frustration for hospital employees. Frequently, the only way to rise in the hospital structure is to leave the hospital, secure outside training, and then return at a higher level of status and competence. This means that a hospital cannot offer many of the same incentives of continuous promotion to its employees as can other institutions.

There is, of course, upward mobility available within the hospital. But some of it is of a peculiar kind and involves particularly difficult problems of interprofessional competition. For example, if we look at a hospital as a total number of a certain set of functions or operations, some of which have high prestige and others low, we find very often that professional (or subprofessional) groups within the hospital try to improve their status by taking on some of the functions of the occupation above them in the prestige scale, at the same time trying to drop off operations that are lowest in their own perstige scale. This has been true, for example, of the relationships among nurses' aides, nurses and physicians. The professionalization of nurses has included their taking over functions which previously were the physician's prerogative alone—for example, the emphasis upon the role of the nurse on the therapeutic team. In their turn the nurses' aides have attempted to focus upon basic nursing operations—some of which the nurses have been only too happy to relinquish as they themselves moved upward.

We have here a kind of dynamic relationship among members of various professions (or occupations) within the hospital which involves basic competition regarding the use of their skills and of certain functions which are assigned to them. This particular kind of competition is, of course, often disrupting to organizational stability. Frequently we find that the reapportioning of functions does not solve the conflict but simply changes its place. For example, the Veterans Administration in one hospital met the demands of the nurses by assigning some of their lower-level functions to the attendants in the hospital. Within a short time, however, the conflict had shifted from the nurses to the attendants who were trying to drop some of their lower-level functions into the hands of the janitors. In consequence, we frequently have within hospitals a kind of dynamic balance involving the functions of physicians, nurses, practical nurses, aides, maids, and janitors in which the symbolic bedpan gets passed from one to the other. Removing odious functions from one occupation assuages it temporarily. We soon find, however, that another occupation is trying to get rid of the invidious task.

This pattern is often complicated by the explicit efforts to "improve" the lower echelons through training, pay raises, raising standards of selection and performance, and so forth. Such efforts tend to hasten and augment the upward drive of subordinate groups. The superiors who set about to improve their "help" may find themselves facing competitors. Thus, a successful program of recruitment and training of psychiatric aides may frighten nurses into formal reiterations that psychiatric aides perform nursing functions and should be controlled by nurses. These are some of the problems entailed in the peculiar nature of hospital upward mobility.

Professionalization

All of this points up the fact that a hospital is a seedbed of professionalization. This makes for special kinds of motivation and provides peculiar personnel problems. It is of help to hospitals that some persons who find satisfaction in the role and prestige of being professionals may be less concerned with the salaries of their jobs. Laboratory technicians, aides, medical-record librarians,

nurses are all striving toward recognition as professionals—striving for secure organization around special sets of skills, recognition by other occupations of their changed status and increased prestige. It is important that the significant organizations of workers in hospitals are not unions demanding higher pay but protoprofessional organizations asking for changes in status and recognition. This development tends to reinforce the "service" value in hospitals rather than the "money" value.

But general problems for hospitals are also entailed by this drive toward professionalization. Each such group carries with it the beginnings of the charismatic behavior which we noted for the physicians. Each wants to become its own "boss" and is sensitive to the interference of (which may mean administration by) other groups. Again, the general authority of the hospital confronts groups of specialists, secure in the unique possession of their skills, who can say, and perhaps make it stick, "They've got to do it my way. Otherwise I'll quit—and just let them try to do it without me." Thus the nascent professions in hospitals may provide a set of motivations which aid the work of the hospital, at the same time that they complicate the organization needed for such work.

Labor-Market Competition

Hospitals also, for many categories of workers, come off second best in the labor-market competition. The higher pay scales and larger benefits in other kinds of enterprises remove hospital work from the consideration of many workers. These same advantages tend to draw many good people out of hospital work toward more lucrative jobs. In many hospitals this leads to what has been called "seniority by default"—the good people get out and entrenched mediocrity prevails. Also, the continuous nature of hospital work, which doesn't respect nights, weekends, holidays, or family responsibilities, may be responsible for mobilizing a certain proportion of "queer people" into hospital work. This may in some respects be an asset—many of these "queer people" may devote their entire lives to the hospital, literally almost never leaving it. Their usefulness is attested to by the remark of an administrator that if he only had enough "queer people" to handle the long hours and dirty work he could obtain an excellent office force. However, it is often the case with such isolated people that they present "personality problems" which are disruptive to hospital organization. This becomes crucial in those hospitals which represent a "closed community" of many people living-in twenty-four hours a day. Family-like interpersonal pathologies and mutually hostile cliques readily develop. Certain types of "queer people" can devastate such a situation. Since it does not operate purely according to the logic of profit, a hospital may have greater tolerance for such deviants than does business, for example. But they represent a recurrent problem of hospital administration nevertheless.

The particular functions which a hospital performs for its medical staff also set the stage for administrative problems. It would take us too far afield to do more than sketch this out. Briefly, one can indicate that, for physicians, a hospital affiliation may include the following functions; Provide prestige among colleagues and within professional associations; condition the size and type of practice; permit the advancement of career by extending treatment claims and obligations among fellow physicians, through which practices may be established or maintained or specialties developed; may even provide office space for them in clinics where private patients are seen. The hospital, then, is an arena for medical professional development. Administration needs to understand how its hospital is involved in this, since crucial matters such as size and type of case load and applications for staff and house-office positions may be importantly affected.

Recent research has stressed another dimension of hospital organization—its functions as a milieu of therapy. Studies, particularly in psychiatric hospitals, have shown that disturbances in the social field (social environment) of the patient, and these include interprofessional conflicts, are directly related to the course of patients' illnesses. Thus disturbances arise, and therapy may be hindered or implemented, because of factors in the hospital organization. The task of administration thus takes on hitherto unsuspected dimensions of therapeutic relevance.

This is probably particularly complicated in psychiatric hospitals. In these the task of the therapist often involves considerable individuation of patient treatment. Hospital administration, whose task includes that of establishing organizational patterns, is seen as the enemy of this therapeutic practice. Now, however, with our growing awareness of the relationship between a patient's milieu and his illness and recovery, there is good reason to believe that the establishment of proper organizational patterns by administration may very well conduce to patient health. Thus the dimensions of a new research problem emerge: the study of the relationships between the needs of individuation and organization in hospitals as these affect the health of the patients.

One of the things that emerges from the material presented is the clear need for further research to provide needed knowledge. This is true of the problem areas already addressed as well as of areas of hospital organization not yet explored.

In the latter category, for example, studies are needed of the community relationships of hospitals. What are the most effective means of community support and how may these be mobilized? What are the crucial relationships between different kinds of hospitals (i.e., by size, specialty, and so on) and different forms of community (i.e., by size, region)? What are the real communities served by hospitals and how are these related to the localities in which they operate? Who are served from these communities, who not, and why? What are the community expectations of hospital service and functions, and how closely do these coincide with the survival contingencies of the particular hospital?

What about the recruitment of operating personnel? Do small-town hospitals need small-town people to operate them? Should they be local people or strangers, and for which kind of jobs? Do local people get caught in a web of kinship obligations that make it difficult for them to perform professionally? Can a stranger more easily be professional? Is he, however, so excluded from local community understanding as to made less effective? Who, in a community, are best selected as trustees? These are part of a host of community problems involved in the administration of hospitals. Knowledge in these areas could greatly help administrators.

Administrators' Functions

And, finally, study of the growing profession of hospital administration itself would be greatly rewarding. What are the observed functions of hospital administrators in different sizes and kinds of hospitals? How close are these to what administrators say they do and think they do?

What are the intrinsic operating problems of hospital administrators? We have cited some of them—much more needs to be developed in this area. How close together are the expectations developed in professional training and the realities of this work? What is the image of this profession in the minds of other professions and of patients and the public? Is this a satisfying self-image for the hospital administrator, and if not, why? What and why are the relative advantages of being a physician or a layman in this job? The former feels guilty about not practicing medicine. The latter is denied intimate participation in many of the central interests of the institution. Is the professionalization of hospital administration tending to reduce this dilemma? Surely much new knowledge is needed here.

---

1 An eminent German social scientist who died in 1920.

2 A nursing Sister to whom this term was explained said, "Oh yes, I know what you mean. We call it the Jehovah complex!"

3 Barnard has combined a successful career as an industrial executive with insightful analyses of industrial organization.

13 Power Structure and Membership Dispersion in Unions

by Edna E. Raphael

This paper reports a study of factors that determine the form taken by the political organization of local labor unions.* In this study, it was found that the spatial distribution of members largely supersedes other explanations of the form taken by political organization. With almost unvarying regularity local unions with members sufficiently spatially concentrated to permit informal communications were found to be "democratic" organizations, whereas those with members so dispersed as to impair such communications were found to be "oligarchic." Although size of membership also influences form of political organization, its effect is obscured by an inverse correlation with spatial concentration of members. Other processes, such as age of the organization and uniformity of occupations, perhaps act through rather than independently of the spatial distribution of members to determine the form of political organization.

In the present study the data consist of

* *Reprinted with permission of The University of Chicago Press from* American Journal of Sociology, *71:3 (November, 1965), pp. 274–84.*

factual materials representing each of a random weighted sample of sixty-five local unions with widely varying national affiliations but with headquarters in Chicago and Cook County, Illinois. The data were gathered through structured interviews with at least one high-ranking official of each organization.

Although the spatial distribution of members, as it affects communications, has been considered relevant for political outcomes, often it has received casual rather than systematic attention,[1] or it has been completely ignored whereas the effects of other conditions have been studied. Instead, it is the historical process of bureaucratization in such mutual-benefit associations as labor unions that has been widely evaluated as having central importance for an understanding of the forms taken by political organization.[2] But this natural-history or bureaucratization model of the life of the local union imposes some strain up on existing data of reported studies. Some local unions appear to elude such a theoretical mold but fall easily into another. There, the presence of "democratic" or "oligarchic" forms of political organization seems to be closely dependent upon the extent to which there exist informal face-to-face communications which accompany work settings that facilitate social interaction among members.

Some exploration of the association between the bureaucratization and social-interaction models, considered simultaneously with the form taken by the political organization, is pertinent. Within the limits imposed by cross-sectional data on a sample of sixty-five local union organizations, the following sections of this paper attempt just such an examination of the issues posed by the literature. Three independent variables derived from the bureaucratization or historical model are considered: age of the organization, uniformity of members' occupations, and size of the membership. The independent variable introduced to represent the social-interaction model is the spatial distribution of members. The dependent variable, the form of political organization, is a measure of the distribution of power between high- and low-ranking local officials in each local union organization. The assumptions underlying the introduction of this "power-distribution score" as an indicator of form of political organization require some preliminary discussion.

If one were to assume as the criterion for the presence of "democratic" forms "one set of political leaders in office: and . . .one or more sets of recognized leaders attempting to gain office,"[3] then with few exceptions local unions in this study did not have "democratic" political organizations. It is largely because of the absence of institutionalized oppositions, which contend for control of elective offices, that labor unions are referred to as "oligarchic" organizations. Kerr has suggested that "if organizations where the supreme power is retained by the members and which are reasonably responsive to membership desires may be called 'democratic,' then unions may be and many are democratic."[4] It seemed that Kerr's less stringent definition might appropriately be applied to measure the presence of "democratic" or "oligarchic" organization.

Responsiveness might be inferred from the distribution of influence over day-to-day decision-making among levels of official local-union leadership. If low-ranking officials, such as committeemen and stewards who were in close daily contact with the members, had the larger share of influence over day-to-day decision-making, the probability that decisions reached represented membership desires would be high. Then unions could be considered as probably "democratic" in form of political organization. On the other hand, if influence over day-to-day decision-making resided entirely with top-ranking officials, such as executive officers who had less daily contact with the members, the probability that decisions reached represented membership desires would be low. These unions could be considered as probably "oligarchic" in form of political organization.

The power-distribution score serves as an indicator of the responsiveness to membership's expressed interest and, thereby, of the form of political organization. Among eight task areas it measures the mean level of local official leadership at which day-to-day decisions are made. The eight task areas are: (1) management's discipline of workers for poor work quality, (2) management's discipline of workers for infringement of work rules, (3) insurance inquiries, (4) personal problems of members which interfere with the work-role performances, (5) health and safety on the job, (6) personal problems of members which are not job-connected, (7) consumer problems such as wage assignments and garnishments, and (8) grievances.

In the interviews, for each task area respondents were asked, "Who does most of the work?" The replies to this question provided the raw data from which the power-distribution score was computed. Where a reply indicated that responsibility rested entirely with top-level officials (executive-level officers) a task area was given a score of 1; where responsibility was shared between top- and lower-level officials (committeemen, stewards, and so forth) the assigned score was 2; and where responsibility rested entirely within lower-level official ranks the score was 3.[5] Within each of the sixty-five unions the task scores were summed and a mean was computed. The resulting mean official level of influence over day-to-day decision-making could be considered an index of form of political organization.

Since a work setting where members are spatially widely dispersed requires some delegation of authority for making decisions to high-ranking officials, the power-distribution score might be tautological, a measure of membership dispersion rather than the intended indicator of form of political organization. The validity of the score as an index of form of political organization thus required some investigation. According to Michels,[6] "democratic" organization is associated with a more rapid turnover of persons in high-level elected offices than is "oligarchic" organization. The correlation between the power-distribution score and years of tenure in

office of the interviewed respondents, all of whom were high-ranking local-union officials, was significant although not high ($r = -.313$, $P < .05$). Thus, the power-distribution score could reasonably be employed as an indicator of form of political organization in local unions. High scores could be taken as evidence of the presence of "democratic" forms, and low scores could indicate the presence of "oligarchic" forms. With the distribution dichotomized at the mean, twenty-seven of the local unions in the sample had scores within the "democratic" range (over 1.56), and the remaining thirty-eight organizations had scores within the "oligarchic" range (under 1.56).

Findings

Three independent variables derived from the natural-history model of bureaucratization were considered: age of the organization, uniformity of members' occupations, and size of the membership. Before presenting the findings, a hypothesis is introduced for each of these variables, predicting the direction of its association with form of political organization. The observed association follows, first without and then with, the spatial distribution of members—a condition of the social-interaction model—held constant.

Age of the Organization

In generalized accounts of the history of labor unions it is held that during early periods wide membership participation, little differentiation of officers' roles from those of members, and a rapid turnover of persons in elected offices assure the presence of more "democratic" forms of political organization. But during later periods when institutionalization and bureaucratizaton take hold, membership interest and participation decline, elected officials begin to perpetuate themselves in office, and the union begins to assume a more "oligarchic" form of political organization. Stated in the form of hypothesis, the older the age of a local union is, the more "oligarchic" is its political organization. At issue is the question, "Does the association between older age and the presence of 'oligarchic' forms of political organization hold equally among unions where there is ample opportunity for wide membership participation in daily face-to-face communications and among unons where the opportunity to participate in such communication is limited?"

Variables

For the independent variable, age of the organization, the local unions in the sample were classified as established during the *early* period (those chartered or recognized prior to 1930), the *middle* period (those first recognized as official collective-bargaining agents by management between 1930 and the end of World War II), or the *late* period (those officially recognized as collective-bargaining agents by management subsequent to World War II). The three age classes roughly coincide with three major periods in the history of the American labor movement.

The second independent variable, the spatial distribution of members, is an index of the extent to which the work setting can be expected to facilitate face-to-face interaction, or the emergence of informal communications networks that involve most of the members. Thus, presence of interaction or of communications networks is not measured directly but is inferred from the spatial distribution of the members. This variable may be described as forming a continuum. At the spatially concentrated extreme are organizations with members employed in one-plant industrial settings; at the spatially dispersed extreme are organizations whose members are employed in industries so structured that most of the workers must rotate fairly continuously among shops, jobs, and employers within a geographical space of at least several square miles. Whereas the concentrated cases at least potentially represent the presence of collectivities, the dispersed ones essentially represent aggregates of persons. For purposes of the present paper,

the local unions in the sample have been assigned to one of two classes: those with spatially *concentrated* members (one- to five-plant organizations) and those with spatially *dispersed* members (ten or more plants through organizations consisting of scattered individual members engaged in rotational types of employments).[7]

Findings

In the total sample the older the organization is the more "oligarchic" is its political organization (Table 1). But when

TABLE 1

Variation in Power-Distribution Scores by Age of Organization and Spatial Distribution of Members

Spatial Distribution of Members	Age of Organization		
	Early Period	Middle Period	Late Period
Dispersed:			
Mean score	1.33	1.41	1.27
N	(20)	(7)	(2)
Concentrated:			
Mean score	1.80	1.79	1.77
N	(1)	(17)	(18)
Total:			
Mean score	1.26	1.68	1.72
N	(21)	(24)	(20)

Rows*		
Dispersed	$H = 1.86$, d.f. 2, $P > .05$	
Concentrated	$H = 0.00$, d.f. 2, $P > .05$	
Total	$H = 10.93$, d.f. 2, $P < .05$	

Columns†		
Early	$T = 9.0$	$P < .05$
Middle	$T = 43.5$	$P < .01$
Late	Not tested	

$\chi^2 = 33.6$, d.f. 2, $P < .01$, $\tau = .72$

* Wallis and Kruskal's analysis of variance test, which depends upon a comparison of ranks. See Helen M. Walker and Joseph Lev, *Statistical Inference* (New York: Holt, Rinehart & Winston, Inc., 1953), pp. 436–438.

† T is the value for entering the tables to determine level of significance in White's sum of ranks test employed here when the number of cases for either of the two treatments was less than eight. Colin White, "The Use of Ranks in a Test of Significanec Comparing Two Treatments," *Biometrics, 8* (1952), pp. 33–44.

the spatial distribution of members is held constant the association between age and form of political organization disappears: Neither among unions with spatially dispersed members nor among those with spatially concentrated members does the power-distribution score vary with the age of the organization.

These data on the relationship between the age of the local union and the form of its political organization cast some doubt upon the plausibility of the hypothesis that the presence of "oligarchic" forms is directly a function of the age of the organization. Instead, and more directly, the form taken by the political organization appears to be a function of the extent to which the work setting facilitates the emergence of informal communications networks that involve most of the members.

Cook County, Illinois, from which the sample of local unions was drawn, is an old one in the history of the American labor movement. During the early period of this history, labor unions here and elsewhere were established predominantly among persons in spatially dispersed employments. Only later were unions maintained among workers in spatially concentrated settings (Table 1). At least for Cook County, and perhaps more generally, the appearance of "oligarchic" forms of political organization has been incorrectly attributed directly to bureaucratization through age of the organization. The common occurrence of "oligarchic" political organization in the old local unions is perhaps better attributed directly to their spatially dispersed memberships and perhaps only indirectly to bureaucratization through age of the organization.

Uniformity of Members' Occupations

It is widely held that unions of workers organized on a craft basis (with members in relatively uniform occupations at one skill level) frequently exhibit more "oligarchic" forms of political organization than those organized on an industrial basis (with members in diversified jobs and occupations at varying levels of skill). The common occurrence of "oligarchic" forms of political organization in craft unions

has been considered an outcome of a more intensive bureaucratization than is found among industrial unions.[8]

The work of some students suggests a possible alternative explanation of the form of political organization in craft unions. According to their reported research findings, the form of political organization may vary, independently of bureaucratization in craft unions, with the extent to which the setting facilitates the possibilty of informal communications among the members. For example, among workers in building-trades unions, Strauss has observed more "democratic" forms of political organization when the work setting is a relatively small city.[9] Informal communications during leisure hours counter the effect of the dispersed work setting which prevents communications during working hours. In a similar vein, Lipset, Coleman, and Trow stressed, for the form taken by the political organization, the differential consequences of both the way in which the organization of the work enhances or restricts opportunities for day-to-day informal communications among members and the association among members during leisure time.[10]

At issue, then, is the question, "Does the association between craft organization and the presence of 'oligarchic' forms of political organization hold equally among unions where there is widespread membership participation in daily informal communications and among unions where membership participation in such communications is limited?" If the social-interaction model provides the more proximate explanation for the form taken by a local union's political organization, then among unions organized on a craft basis those with spatially dispersed members will have "oligarchic" forms of political organization, whereas those with spatially concentrated members will have "democratic" forms.

Variables

One additional independent variable, the unioformity of the members' occupations, is introduced here. Local unions that represent "workers performing a single, specified kind of job"[11] and/or specialties thereof are referred to as occupationally *uniform*. Those that represent workers "in a majority of the industrially related jobs found in a given area of production"[12] are referred to as occupationally *diverse*. Use of the terms "occupationally uniform" and "diverse" implies the presence of a continuum of wider variability than is associated with the use of the dichotomous designations "craft" and "industrial." Twenty-five of the local unions could be designated as occupationally uniform. The remaining forty organizations were occupationally diverse.

Findings

In the total sample, local unions with members in uniform occupations are more likely to have "oligarchic" forms of political organization than those with members in diverse occupations (Table 2). When the spatial distribution of members is held constant within each occupational class, uniform or diverse, there is little variation either in the spatial distribution of members or in the power-distribution scores. Uniform occupation of members is notably associated with the spatial dispersion of these members, whereas diversity of occupation is closely associated with spatially concentrated members. Among unions with members in uniform occupations, the power-distribution score does not vary significantly between spatial-distribution classes; however, the mean score for unions with members in uniform occupations and spatially concentrated, two- to five-plant settings (1.67), lies within the "democratic" range. Among unions with members in diverse occupations, again there is little variation in power-distribution scores between spatial-distribution classes, but in this latter case all the means lie within the "democratic" range.

The data do suggest that with spatially concentrated members both craft and industrially organized local unions tend to remain "democratic." Within any given

spatial-distribution class, however, the form of political organization is more "democratic" among unions organized on an industrial basis.

The findings on the relationship between the uniformity of the occupations of the members and their spatial distribution, for the form taken by the political organiza-

TABLE 2

Variation in Power-Distribution Scores by Uniformity of Occupations and Spatial Distribution of Members

Spatial Distribution of Members*	Uniformity of Occupations	
	Uniform	Diverse
Dispersed		
Scattered:		
Mean score	1.13	1.75
N	(13)	(1)
Ten or more plants:		
Mean score	1.24	1.57
N	(9)	(6)
Concentrated		
Two to five plants:		
Mean score	1.67	1.91
N	(3)	(11)
One plant:		
Mean score		1.73
N		(22)
Total:		
Mean score ...	1.24	1.76
N	(25)	(40)
Rows		
Scattered	Not tested	
Ten or more plants	$T = 55$	$P < .05$
Two to five plants	$T = 19$	$P < .05$
One plant	Not tested	
Total†	$z = 6.29, P < .01$	
Columns		
Uniform	$H = 2.34, P > .05$	
Diverse	$H = 1.94, P > .05$	
	$\chi^2 = 35.88$, d.f. 3, $P < .01$, $\tau = .74$.	

* To demonstrate the extreme association between uniformity of occupations and spatial distribution of members, the latter variable was expanded to four classes.
† Mann-Whitney sum of ranks test employed here when N_1 and N_2 each consists of eight or more cases. Walker and Lev, *op. cit.* (cited in Table 1), pp. 434–435.

tion, do not provide unequivocal support for either the bureaucratization or the social-interaction explanation of form of political organization. Another possible explanation, discussed briefly in the Summary and Discussion of this paper, refers to the differential professionalization of work roles, as between members of craft- and industrially organized unions.

Size of Membership

It has been held that unions with large memberships tend to be more "oligarchic" in their form of political organization than those with smaller memberships. According to this proposition large memberships (much as spatially dispersed ones) limit the chances for communications among members and between members and officers. With communications impaired, officers become separated from the membership and gain control of the organization. Seidman has claimed that it is the middle-sized one-plant organizations, those with not more than a few hundred members where the level of communications between members and officers is high and the stake in office of elected officials is low, that assume the most "democratic" forms of political organization.[13]

Faunce recently reported that he found democracy to be associated with large memberships numbering thousands of persons, rather than with middle-sized memberships.[14] It is notable that Seidman[15] introduced with middle-sized memberships the presence of one-plant (spatially concentrated members) work settings. On the other hand, Faunce did not consider the spatial distribution of members among unions with large memberships. Kovner and Lahne, who focused their attention directly upon the effect of that spatial distribution of members found with one-plant settings, did not introduce the size of the membership.[16] At issue here, then, is the question, "Does size of the membership act independently or with the spatial distribution of members to influence the form taken by the political organization of local unions?"

Variables.

The new independent variable introduced here is the size of the membership.

By number of dues-paying members, the unions in the sample were classified as either *small* (250 or fewer members), *medium* (251—1,000 members), or *large* (over 1,000 members). There were thirty-two small, fifteen medium, and eighteen large organizations in the sample.

Findings.

In the total sample of organizations, the form of political organization does not vary with size of membership (Table 3). When the spatial distribution of members is held constant within each of the three size classes, the mean power-distribution score lies within the "democratic" range when members are spatially concentrated but within the "oligarchic" range when members are spatially dispersed.

Each of the two variables, size of membership and the spatial distribution of members, appears to be independently and directly associated with variation in the power-distribution score. Thus, within both spatial-distribution classes, concentrated and dispersed, the power-distribution scores increase directly with size of membership. However, within the spatially dispersed member class, the mean scores for the three size classes remain within the "oligarchic" range. Within the spatially concentrated member class the means for the same size classes lie within the "democratic" range.

A direct correlation between size of membership and spatial dispersion of members obscures a direct correlation between size of membership and "democracy." Both larger size and spatial concentration appear to promote democracy, but since the two are inversely related, their influences tend to neutralize one another. Hence, Faunce's observation of a direct association between large memberships and the presence of "democratic" forms of political organization in local unions holds only if dispersion is controlled. Contrary to Seidman's observation, moreover, once spatial concentration is controlled, unions with large memberships are likely to have even more "democratic" forms of political organization than those with middle-sized memberships.

Summary and Discussion

With data from a random-weighted sample of local union organizations, this study attempted a consideration of the relative merits of a number of propositions about social forces that shape the form taken by the political organization of local unions. These propositions were derived from two theoretical models of explanation, the natural-history or bureaucratization model and the social-interaction or informal-communications model. Three propositions drawn from the natural-history model were examined: (1) the older the age of a local union, the more "oligarchic" is the form taken by its political organization; (2) the more uniform the occupations of the members of a local union, the more "oli-

TABLE 3
Variation in Power-Distribution Scores by
Size of Membership and Spatial
Distribution of Members

	Size of Membership		
Spatial Distribution of Members	Small (Under 251)	Medium (251– 1,000)	Large (Over 1,000)
Dispersed:			
Mean score	1.18	1.11	1.40
N	(7)	(7)	(15)
Concentrated:			
Mean score	1.67	1.88	2.41
N	(25)	(8)	(3)
Total:			
Mean score	1.57	1.52	1.57
N	(32)	(15)	(18)
Rows			
Dispersed	$H = 7.96$, d.f. 2, $P < .05$		
Concentrated	$H = 5.74$, d.f. 2, $P < .05$		
Total	$H = 0.70$, d.f. 2, $P > .05$		
Columns			
Small	$z = 25.88\ P < .01$		
Medium	$z = 3.87\ P < .01$		
Large	$z = 17.93\ P < .01$		
	$\chi^2 = 17.8$, d.f. 2, $P < .01$, $\tau = .52$		

garchic" its political organization; and (3) the larger the size of the membership of a local union, the more "oligarchic" its polit-

ical organization. An alternative proposition, drawn from the social-interaction model of explanation, stated that the form taken by the political organization in a local union varies with the extent to which the work setting permits face-face interaction or the emergence of an informal communications network that involves most of the members.

For each of the propositions drawn from the natural-history model, the direction and extent of association between corresponding operationalized independent variables (age of the organization, uniformity of members' occupations, and size of membership) and the dependent variable (form of political organization) were examined directly. Then an index that represented the extent to which the work setting facilitated the formation of informal communications networks—the spatial distribution of members—was introduced as an alternative independent variable and held constant. With this procedure it was possible separately and then simultaneously to examine the relative merits of the two models of explanation of the form taken by the local union's political organization.

The indicator employed to represent the dependent variable, the form of political organization, was termed the "power-distribution score." It was assumed that organizations with larger increments of available power concentrated in the hands of low-ranking officials who are in close daily contact with members are more responsive to membership's expressed interest, and therefore are more "democratic," than organizations where power is concentrated in the hands of a few high-ranking officials who are at some remove from the members.

As a measure of the form of political organization, the power-distribution score may appear to be tautological. In organizations with widely dispersed members, the locus of decision-making about many day-to-day union tasks, from which the score is derived, may have to be relegated to a few high-ranking officials. Or, if the members have been organized on a craft basis, some day-to-day problems may be resolved by the members themselves, through professionalization of the work role.[17] The power-distribution score does not take into account the extent to which union tasks may have been incorporated into the occupational roles of the members. In such cases, power might well be distributed between individual members and high-ranking officials, rather than within the intermediary range among lower-ranking official representatives of the members such as committeemen and stewards. The power-distribution score assumes that labor unions are more likely to have "democratic" forms of political organization if power is concentrated among intermediary officials. Thus, professionalization of work roles, with power distributed between members and top-level officials rather than at the intermediary range, may well account for the observation in this study that within any spatial-distribution class craft unions have lower power-distribution scores than industrial unions. Despite these and possibly other qualifications, the power-distribution score correlated inversely with tenure in office of high-ranking officials, by definition a measure of "oligarchic" form of political organization. It thus seemed reasonable to assume some validity for its capacity to indicate form of political organization.

Findings of the study strongly suggest that the social-interaction model provides the more proximate explanation of the form taken by the political organization in local unions. Whether young or old organizations, or with members in uniform or diverse occupations, or with small or large memberships, local unions with spatially concentrated members are more likely to have "democratic" than "oligarchic" forms of political organization. Given the same conditions but with spatially dispersed members, local unions are more likely to have "oligarchic" than "democratic" forms of political organization.

In unions with spatially concentrated members the chances for the formation of an informal communications network that involves most of the members are enhanced. Through the presence of a communications network, observability is high. High observability constrains role performances[18] of members and officers to conformity with normative prescriptions of contracts and constitutions. Where such conformity is high, a local union tends to remain "democratic" with respect to form of political organization.

In unions with spatially dispersed members the chances for the formation of an informal communications network that involves most of the members and officers are severely impaired. With the absence of communications networks observability is low. Low observability reduces the constraint upon members and officers to conform with normative prescriptions of contracts and constitutions. Deviation from prescribed role behavior then is widespread. Administrative responsibilities are assumed by a relegated, by default, to high-ranking officials whose activities in large measure remain unknown to the members, just as those of the members remain largely unknown to the officers. Where conformity with normative prescriptions of contracts and constitutions is low, a local union tends to assume an "oligarchic" form of political organization.

Two effects suggest, possibly, why bureaucratization has been so widely held an explanation of "oligarchic" political organization. There is, first of all, the complex relationship between the spatial distribution of members, uniformity of their occupations, age of the organization, and form of political organization. In the Chicago and Cook County universe from which the study sample was drawn, most unions with spatially dispersed members, as well as those organized on a craft basis, were established during early periods in the history of the American labor movement (prior to 1930). Also, organization on a craft basis is closely associated with spatially dispersed members. Hence, the common appearance of "oligarchic" forms of political organization has been attributed to bureaucratization through either organizational age or craft-union structure. But findings of the present study indicate that the association between "oligarchic" form and either age or a craft basis of organization is only indirect, through the spatial dispersion of the members of these older and craft unions and without extensive bureaucratization.

Perhaps widespread adherence to the notion that bureaucratization and "oligarchic" control in unions are related may be attributed to the negative relationsship between size of membership and spatial concentration. Large size of membership and spatial concentration of members both promote "democracy." But in the universe these two variables are inversely related to each other. Because of this inverse relation, in the universe their influences tend to neutralize one another and thus obscure their direct associations with "democracy."

* Revision of a paper read at the annual meeting of the American Sociological Association, August, 1963. Through the generosity of Peter M. Blau the field work for this study was supported by a Ford Foundation Fellowship in Business Problems. I wish to express my warm appreciation for the critical assistance and counsel of Peter M. Blau, Peter H. Rossi, Arthur L. Stinchcombe, and Henry D. McKay. Joel Seidman rovided valuable guidance during initial phases of the study, orienting me to the literature and through the maze of problems inherent in any attempt to study labor unions.

1 Joseph Kovner and Herbert J. Lahne, "Shop Society and the Union," *Industrial and Labor Relations Review,* 7 (October, 1953), pp. 3–14; Joel Seidman, Jack London, Bernard Karsh, and Daisy L. Tagliacozzo, *The Worker Views His Union* (Chicago: University of Chicago Press, 1958), pp. 195, 207; Seymour M. Lipset, Martin A. Trow, and James S. Coleman, *Union Democracy* (New York: Free Press of Glencoe, Inc., 1956); Leonard R. Sayles and George Strauss, *The Local Union* (New York: Harper & Row, Publishers, Inc., 1953); George Strauss, "Control by Membership in the Building Trades," in *Unions and Union Leadership,* Jack Barbash, ed. (New York: Harper & Row, Publishers, Inc., 1959), pp. 176–192.

2 See, for example Robert Michels, *Political Parties* (New York: Free Press of Glencoe, Inc., 1949); Lipset *et al., op. cit.*; Will Herberg, "Bureaucracy and Democracy in Local Unions," *Antioch Review,* 3 (Summer, 1943), pp. 405–

417; Joseph Shister, "Trade-Union Government: A Formal Analysis," *Quarterly Journal of Economics,* 60 (November, 1945), pp. 78–112; Seymour M. Lipset, "The Political Process in Trade Unions: A Theoretical Statement," in *Freedom and Control in Modern Society,* Monroe Berger, Theodore Abel, and Charles H. Page, eds. (Princeton, N.J.: D. Van Nostrand Co., Inc., 1954), pp. 82–124; Irving Howe and B. J. Widick, *The UAW and Walter Reuther* (New York: Random House, Inc., 1949); Sayles and Strauss, *op. cit.* The more general and now classical formulation is, of course, that of Max Weber as found in H. H. Gerth and C. Wright Mills, eds., *From Max Weber: Essays in Sociology* (New York: Oxford University Press, Inc., 1946), especially pp. 214–215.

3 Seymour Martin Lipset, *Political Man* (Garden City, N.Y.: Doubleday & Co., Inc., 1960), p. 45.

4 Clark Kerr, *Unions and Union Leaders of Their Own Choosing* (New York: Fund for the Republic, 1957), p. 18.

5 The task areas were equally weighted. The organizations in the sample were not equally engaged, either in intensity or kind, with activity in all eight of the task areas, and the computaton of the power-distribution score does not take these sources of variation into consideration. These sources of variation are discussed in some detail in my "Welfare Activity in the Local Union" (unpublished doctoral dissertation, University of Chicago, 1962).

6 Michels, *op. cit.,* pp. 401–402.

7 There were no local unions in the sample with members distributed among six to nine plants.

8 Howe and Widick, *op. cit.,* p. 244.

9 Strauss, *op. cit.*

10 Lipset *et al., op. cit.*

11 Scott Greer, *Last Man In* (New York: Free Press, of Glencoe, Inc., 1959), p. 24.

12 *Ibid.*

13 Joel Seidman, "Democracy in Labor Unions," *Journal of Political Economy,* 61 (June, 1953), pp. 221–231.

14 William Faunce, "Size of Locals and Union Democracy," *American Journal of Sociology,* 68 (November, 1962), pp. 291–298. Lipset *et al., op. cit.,* pp. 364–390, noted that the larger the membership, the greater was the interest in national-level union politics.

15 Seidman, *op. cit.*

16 Kovner and Lahne, *op. cit.*

17 Arthur L. Stinchcombe, "Bureaucratic and Craft Administration of Production: A Comparative Study," *Administrative Science Quarterly,* 4 (September, 1959), pp. 168–187.

18 Suggested by Rose Laub Coser's discussion of "Insulation from Obeservability and Types of Social Conformity," *American Sociological Review,* 26 (February, 1961), pp. 28–39.

14 The Colleges of America's Upper Class

By GENE R. HAWES

Social class, like sex and religion, is something that no truly tactful person discusses in ordinary conversation. To bring it up except as a joke is a breach of egalitarian manners, but privately it matters a great deal to many Americans.

Whether admitted or not, it is a subject of particular concern to many persons connected with American colleges. Administrators who are responsible for their college's finances must maintain ties with circles of wealth and influence to ensure the college's continued improvement. Alumni, who are asked to support their college, to befriend its recent graduates, and to send their children back to alma mater, are understandably interested in its social prestige as well as its academic reputation. Students, who unavoidably trade subtle condescensions in meeting friends, relatives, and potential employers, become increasingly aware of the status ascribed to their college. And parents who seek the "right college" for their children often act on impressions of social as well as academic rectitude, a fact that has created the largest admissions jams at the small number of colleges thought to be most desirable.

In view of such special connections between college and social standing, we might well ask what kind of relation exists between the colleges and America's highest social class. Do students from upper-class homes go to many colleges or tend to converge on a few? Has their choice of colleges changed over the years? Is it shift-

Reprinted from "America's Upper-Class Colleges," pp. 68–71, by permission of the author, the publisher, Columbia College Today *(Fall, 1963), and* Saturday Review.

ing now? Is the attitude of the colleges changing toward them?

First, let us define "upper class." This cannot be done in any absolute sense, because American society is exceptionally fluid and diverse. In both popular and scholarly convention, though, the American upper class consists of the families of long-established social prominence and large inherited wealth. Its members are descendants of highly successful individuals of at least one, but usually two or more, generations back. Since their wealth has been gained and maintained chiefly by business enterprise, America's upper class is largely a business aristocracy. Most of the families in this class follow a distinctive style of life, attending the same schools, living in the same areas in or outside large cities, frequenting the same resorts, marrying among themselves, and manifesting a loose group solidarity.

The best index to the upper class is the *Social Register.* Published annually since 1888, the *Register* has twelve current editions that list the families deemed highest in social standing in as many major urban regions of America. The *Register* reflects certain ethnic biases—for instance, relatively few of the most prominent Jewish families are included—but its biases follow those of the upper class itself. It also doubtless suffers from some mistaken judgments and important omissions. Still, its heavy use as a standard reference by the upper class itself testifies to its general reliability as an index of upper-class status. It should not be confused with *Who's Who in America,* which is a much larger index that includes persons distinguished by significant individual accomplishment.

A study of the *Social Register* discloses

that the alumni listed in it have tended to enroll at three colleges in particular: Harvard, Yale, and Princeton. Leading families in the different cities have different preferences within this trinity: New Yorkers prefer Yale, then Harvard and Princeton; Bostonians prefer Harvard, then Yale and Princeton; and Philadelphians (according to E. Digby Baltzell's *Philadelphia Gentlemen: The Making of a National Upper Class*) prefer Harvard, then Princeton and Yale. But virtually every metropolitan edition shows a concentration at these three institutions. The three are undeniably America's most popular undergraduate institutions for men of the upper class.

Despite this heavy concentration at three colleges, scrutiny of the various editions of the *Register* discloses that there is a strikingly wide dispersion of upper-class men at more than one hundred other colleges (see Table 1). The high concentration may surprise many Americans, but the wide dispersion would positively amaze, say the British, whose upper class almost to a man has attended only Oxford and Cambridge.

Hence, America does have upper-class colleges—three identified with the upper class to a marked extent and about a dozen to a moderate extent—but the nation also has many other colleges that frequently have had a handful of socially prominent young men among their students.

One other fact emerges from a study of the *Social Register*. Two universities stand out far beyond the rest among those preferred by the upper class for graduate and professional study: Harvard and Columbia (see Table 1, bottom). The fact takes on an obvious special interest in the light of Columbia's past, as we shall see.

This list of colleges with upper-class affiliation has not been an entirely stable one during the past century. There have been noteworthy shifts in upper-class representation, many of which resulted from two great changes in upper-class allegiances. The first change, which can be observed in earlier editions of the *Social*

Register, and the letters, diaries, and other writings of upper-class family members, took place between the end of the Civil War and World War I.

Before the Civil War, a venerable college could be found in almost every eastern state: the Universities of Georgia, North Carolina, South Carolina, and Virginia; William and Mary, also in Virginia; Pennsylvania, Princeton in New Jersey, Columbia in New York, Yale in Connecticut, Brown in Rhode Island, Harvard in Massachusetts, the University of Vermont, and Bowdoin in Maine. The affluent and powerful families of those states generally sent their sons to the old colleges nearby. Traveling far away to college was not only difficult but pointless, for very few students who were not from "the best families" went to college in those years. True, some families sent their sons, for reasons of health, discipline, or religion, away to such rural seats as Union College in upstate New York, Williams or Amherst in western Massachusetts, or Dartmouth in New Hampshire. But, for the most part, before the Civil War upper-class loyalties were attached to the colleges of their regions.

After the Civil War, the biggest American businesses became national in scope as great industrial and financial combines were organized. Many of the large old family fortunes multiplied enormously; many new ones were created. The American upper class became a national one and the old local aristocracies formed many new ties with each other, in business at first and shortly after in social life. It needed a Register, and one was forthcoming. The new national upper class warily recognized new members, centered its work and its homes more and more in New York, grew well accustomed to travel by rail, and started sending its sons away to college.

It was in this era of immense business growth that some colleges—especially Harvard, Yale, and Princeton—increasingly became the colleges of the national upper class then in formation. Growing concentrations of both the old and the new rich at these three colleges enjoyed campus days marked by big-time football, rowing regattas, fraternities and clubs, riots, and good parties. University clubs were even built in New York so that college ties could be sustained in gentlemanly quarters after graduation.

This change can be aptly illustrated from Columbia's past. On the eve of the Civil War, George Templeton Strong, Class of 1838, could still call Columbia College "a day school for the sons of New York's leading families." But after the 1880's, and especially after the turn of the century, young New Yorkers began to go out of town in greater numbers.

The Fish family serves as a good example. The prominent New Yorker Nicholas Fish was a friend of Alexander Hamilton,

Columbia Class of 1778, and was chairman of the college's trustees. His son, Hamilton Fish, Class of 1827, was also chairman of the trustees, both before and after his distinguished service as Secretary of State in the otherwise lackluster Grant administration. Hamilton Fish's three sons were Columbia men of the Classes of 1867, 1869, and 1871. (Typically for that era, the youngest, Stuyvesant, captained Columbia's first football team and built the Illinois Central Railroad into a large system as its president.) However, Hamilton Fish III went to Harvard, where he became a football hero before graduating in 1910.

By 1914, Frederick Paul Keppel, Class of 1898, who was one of Columbia's most astute deans, could write, "While doubtless the old New York stock will always be

TABLE 1

Alma Maters of Men Listed in the 1963 New York Social Register.*†

College	No. of Men	College	No. of Men
Yale	2234	Stanford	29
Harvard	1746	Union	28
Princeton	1422	Johns Hopkins	24
Williams	325	Michigan	24
Columbia	311	Bowdoin	23
Virginia	160	Lehigh	23
Cornell	144	Oxford (England)	22
Dartmouth	115	Wisconsin	22
Amherst	94	Stevens Institute	21
M.I.T.	85	Cambridge (England)	20
Trinity	82	Hobart	18
Pennsylvania	79	Duke	17
Brown	76	Rutgers	16
Annapolis	75	Washington & Lee	15
West Point	53	Haverford	13
N.Y.U.	41	Middlebury	13
California (Berkeley)	36	St. Lawrence	13
Georgetown	35	Chicago	12
Colgate	34	Davidson	12
North Carolina	33	Fordham	12
Hamilton	32	Vanderbilt	10
Wesleyan	31	Vermont	10

Leading Graduate and Professional Schools Attended by Men in the
1963 *New York Social Register*†

Harvard	478
Columbia	475
Yale	92

* Colleges attended by fewer than 10 men are omitted.
† Universities attended by fewer than 50 men are omitted.

represented, Columbia is not likely ever again to be a fashionable college *per se,*" that is, a college patronized largely by upper-class sons.

Why did a large portion of Columbia College's upper-class following go elsewhere? Why, when it was located in the center of American upper-class society, did Columbia not become one of the new group of fashionable colleges?

One factor was that New York continued as a great immigration center. This brought a kind of student to Columbia College with whom upper-class gentlemen could not be at ease. These immigrant sons were predominantly Jewish, Irish, and Italian. Aggressive and lacking knowledge or appreciation of America's genteel college traditions, they seemed not only deficient in money, manners, and cultural interests, but excessively prone to taking academic work seriously. An example in the 1880's was one penniless lad from

Hungary who spoke broken English, Michale Idvorsky Pupin '83, who went on to become the great inventor, author, and Columbia professor for whom the present Pupin Hall is named. The presence of these immigrant classmates at Columbia prompted some young socialites to consider seeking their education among more agreeable companions at colleges that were less ready to admit talented youngsters without consideration of their background.

Perhaps the most important factor in the decrease in the College's upper-class following, however, is suggested by the quip of some nameless observer, "While Eliot was building houses at Harvard, Butler was building schools at Columbia." It was precisely through the period of rapid change in the composition, outlook, and collegiate ties of the upper class that Columbia strained every resource to transform itself from an old classical college into a great modern university. In doing

TABLE 2
Colleges Enrolling Sons Listed in the 1963 *New York Social Register.**

College	No. of Sons	College	No. of Sons
Yale	171	Arizona	4
Harvard	123	California (Berkeley)	4
Princeton	76	Duke	4
Pennsylvania	44	Lake Forest	4
Trinity	22	Annapolis	3
Middlebury	20	Bowdoin	3
Virginia	19	Citadel	3
Stanford	15	Clarkson	3
Williams	13	Colorado	3
Hobart	12	Denver	3
North Carolina	12	Lawrence	3
Boston U.	11	Northwestern	3
Dartmouth	10	St. Lawrence	3
Columbia	9	Union	3
Brown	8	Wesleyan	3
Colby	8	Denison	2
Cornell	7	Dickinson	2
Rollins	7	Kenyon	2
Amherst	6	Lafayette	2
Rutgers	6	M.I.T.	2
Georgetown	5	Michigan	2
Hamilton	5	New Hampshire	2
Lehigh	5	Oberlin	2
Syracuse	5	Vanderbilt	2
Washington & Lee	5	Wisconsin	2

* Colleges being attended by fewer than two sons are omitted.

so, it broke its tangible and traditional links with the past and did not provide the facilities and atmosphere then expected in college by young men of social position and wealth.

By the end of World War I, Columbia had realized its goal. It was the largest and perhaps the greatest American university. But the majority of sons from upper-class homes, who at that time preferred fun and congeniality to intellectual development, were not attracted by the increased seriousness at Morningside Heights and Columbia's departure from tradition.

President Nicholas Murray Butler, who so successfully continued the work of his predecessors, Presidents Barnard and Low, in transforming the old college into a renowned university, ironically never reconciled himself to the loss of the boys from many leading families. According to Frank Bowles '28, admissions director at Columbia from 1934 to 1948 and later president of the College Entrance Examination Board, Dr. Butler asked him repeatedly in the 1930's to try to get more of these boys back into the habit of attending Columbia.

But the time was not ripe for all but a handful of upper-class families whose sons continued to become Columbia men. Years before, Dean Keppel had more accurately seen the social consequences of Columbia's academic pioneering during America's gilded age. The future of Columbia College, he wrote, lay with young men "who were willing to ask frankly the question: What does one pay for the luxury of country-club existence, men who have no desire to prepare themselves for a career of being amused, and who wish to begin to test their capacity with rivals of like mind, not in professional or graduate school, but in college?"

The drift of the upper class from the old regional colleges to Harvard, Yale, and Princeton continued through the 1920's and 1930's, reaching its peak perhaps just before World War II. Through these years, in continuation of a trend that had begun after the Civil War,

scions of the upper class were joined in college by more than equal numbers of young men from the middle class and even some numbers of the lower-class sons who possessed great skill in athletics.

After World War II, the second great change in upper-class allegiance began. All respected colleges found themselves inundated with admissions applications from returning veterans in addition to the normal crop of secondary-school graduates. At the most sought-after colleges, three and four times as many academically qualified applicants appeared as could be accommodated. Suddenly faculty admissions committees had to decide upon priorities. Who gets admitted—the extremely gifted son of a mechanic in Missouri with his G.I. Bill benefits or the gentlemanly "C" student from a prominent family and a noted prep school? The choice lay between professed commitment to develop intellect and long and rich association with the upper class.

Intellect won, though not easily or decisively, even today. Gradually, painfully, the upper-class colleges severed as amicably as possible their links with the least qualified members of the prominent families. And as the number of talented applicants has continued to mount, the average academic ability of the students at the leading social colleges has climbed to a point within the top ten per cent intellectually among all college students in the nation.

Upper-class applicants who could not meet the academic demands have had to go elsewhere to college. And, some of those applicants who could meet them *preferred* to go elsewhere. Wilbur J. Bender, Harvard's former admissions chief, recently noted:

There is no evidence that poverty and genius go together or that the rich are necessarily stupid. There is a real possibility, however, that an academically elite college would lose its appeal for the ablest boys from upper-income families who might perfer a college with a different kind of atmosphere.

A perceptive observer, it might be noted, could well have made a similar observation about Columbia College a few generations ago.

This development has not led Harvard, Yale, and Princeton to experience any marked decrease in attendance by upper-class sons, although there have been important changes in the academic atmosphere at each of these schools, especially Harvard. Upper-class undergraduates at these colleges can still associate with each other by being accepted into Harvard's Porcellian, A.D., Fly, and Spee—the upper-class clubs; or into Yale's Fence Club, D.K.E., Zeta Psi, and St. Anthony Hall; or into such eating clubs at Princeton as Ivy, Cap and Gown, Cottage, Colonial, and Tiger Inn.

Two noteworthy social consequences have resulted from the aggregate admissions decisions of the most socially desirable colleges. One is a new dispersion of upper-class sons (as indicated in Table 2). As a very rough measure of the increased dispersion the *New York Social Register* discloses that less than 45 per cent of the socially prominent boys now in college are concentrated at Harvard, Yale, and Princeton, while more than 55 per cent are dispersed among the forty-eight colleges listed in Table 2 and another thirty or forty colleges not listed here. It seems warranted to conclude that, whereas nearly two-thirds of all upper-class sons attended three particular colleges during the first half of this century, less than one-half do so at present. (A similar dispersion seems to be taking place among the upper-class daughters [see Table 3].) The dispersion of upper-class sons and daughters is generating a new set of socially desirable colleges that have some of the flavor of the old upper-class institutions.

The other, and far more important, consequence is the one that the admissions competition has had on the upper

TABLE 3
Colleges Enrolling Daughters Listed in the 1963 New York Social Register.*

College	No. of Daughters	College	No. of Daughters
Smith	48	Garland Jr.	4
Vassar	37	Goucher	4
Radcliffe	32	Manhattanville	4
Wellesley	31	North Carolina	4
Wheaton	30	Rollins	4
Bryn Mawr	28	Skidmore	4
Sarah Lawrence	25	Syracuse	4
Bradford Jr.	22	Centenary Jr.	3
Bennett Jr.	19	Colby	3
Briarcliff Jr.	18	Marymount	3
Hollins	17	Pembroke	3
Connecticut College	13	Arizona	2
Mt. Holyoke	13	Boston U.	2
Wells	10	Lake Erie	2
Barnard	6	Lake Forest	2
Colorado	6	Knox	2
Colby Jr.	6	Middlebury	2
Sweet Briar	6	Mills	2
Endicott Jr.	5	Northwestern	2
Finch Jr.	5	R. I. School of Design	2
Pine Manor Jr.	5	Scripps	2
Stanford	5	Sorbonne	2
Wheelock	5	Vermont	2
Bennington	4	Wm. Smith	2

* Colleges being attended by fewer than two daughters are omitted.

class itself. It could not be said of any period up through the 1940's that most young members of the upper class had to pursue rigorous intellectual training before they could take responsible stations in life; however, this is all too true today. It seems just as well, in view of the world in which they come to power.

America's upper-class colleges would have found it difficult to pursue the course they have taken since the late 1940's unless great needs existed within our advanced industrial society for more leaders equipped with distinguished intellectual training. Such needs do exist, and most upper-class colleges are responding to the vital requirements of national life—now beset by urgent demands from within and determined threats from without.

In part because of these needs, a new kind of American upper class is slowly being forged. Large-scale organizations, government taxation, and explosive growth in the development and application of knowledge are working to reduce the potency of enormous hereditary wealth and power. As Stimson Bullitt suggests in his excellent chapter "Class Patterns" in *To Be A Politician,* "money's close connection with power, education, and refinement has ceased." The new upper class that is forming is one of socially valuable talent and learning, not unlike Thomas Jefferson's concept of a "natural aristocracy of talents and virtues." It is assuming much of the power but not necessarily the great wealth—and cer-

tainly not the leisure—of the old upper class. The colleges with upper-class affiliations, with their spectacular increase in the amounts of scholarship aid and levels of academic standards, are helping to produce this new aristocracy of the able. They are compounding it of the best of the old upper class and the most talented of the lower and middle classes.

In contributing to this new kind of upper class, the foremost American upper-class colleges are displaying a new style of learning. It stems primarily from the large, high-quality universities that dominate American higher education today. At most of the colleges attended by upper-class sons, undergraduate education is still committed to the liberal arts tradition. However, the undergraduate program is increasingly inspired by the advanced scholarly disciplines for which the universities exist.

The new alignment of "haves" and "have-nots" according to highly developed talents rather than accumulated wealth and social position may have fundamental consequences for American democracy. Already we hear outcries against the growing "meritocracy." However, to run our complex economy, to prevent nuclear disaster, to extend freedom, and to try to make life more humane and beautiful in our increasingly bureaucratic and mechanized world, we require leaders of the very highest intellect, imagination, sensibility, and wisdom. To help develop them is more than ever the urgent task of our leading colleges.

15 Button-Down Collar Culture

By JAMES S. DAVIE AND A. PAUL HARE*

Every group existing through time comes to develop its own way of life or culture. Its members tend to do the same things in similar ways and to think similarly about what they and others do. The term "culture patterns" refers to such consensus of opinion and behavior. Because of such consensus, the individual not only comes to know how to behave in different situations and how to expect others to behave in those situations, but also is afforded a standard against which to measure his own behavior. If his behavior is in accordance with the behavior of others, he is secure in his status as a group member, and the group solidarity is correspondingly strengthened, since, in this instance, the group is not faced with the problem of deviancy which must be resolved somehow so as not to disrupt its normal life. In short, a system of rewards and punishments is built into the way of life of the group. The culture functions as a "rule book" which defines the situation for the individual in terms of how he is expected to behave. Those who conform to group norms are rewarded. Those who do not are punished. The norms of the group are not absolute,

in the sense that each individual must do exactly the same thing in exactly the same way in the same situation. Rather, they include a certain range of permissible variation. As the individual begins to deviate too sharply, he is regarded as "different." Those whose behavior and/or ideas deviate even more from accepted group practices and beliefs are regarded as "quite different," perhaps labeled as "queer" or "odd," and are regarded as being definitely detrimental to group welfare.

When one looks at the undergraduate body of a university from the general viewpoint sketched above, one begins to understand better the whys and wherefores of student behavior. The undergraduate body as a group may be observed to exhibit certain cultural patterns in every major area of its life. The present paper is concerned in general with undergraduate life at Ivy, a contemporary American college for men, and specifically with the areas of recreation and of intellectual activity as parts of the total way of undergraduate life at Ivy. It presents a shorthand description of some of the more salient aspects of Ivy culture to which the student must effect some sort of adjustment.

Reprinted from "Button-down Collar Culture," pp. 13–20 by permission of the authors, the publisher, Human Organization, Vol. 14 (1956), and the Society of Applied Anthropology.

* The authors are indebted to Professor Frederick F. Stephan, the director of a five-year study of student life of which the present research formed a part, and to Barbara Southerland-Brown, Josephine Mead, Mary Louise Graham, and Dorothy Smith, members of the research team, for their help in collecting and analyzing the data for the research.

Method

The data on which the description is based were collected in a series of group and individual interviews with a stratified sample of eight upperclassmen, following a procedure which has been described in detail in a previous publication.[1] The group to be interviewed was chosen to be representative of the student body with respect to five variables: type of secondary school attended, home state (by section of the country), financial status (scholarship, etc.), area of major subject (humanities, social science, natural science, engineering), and academic record (high, middle, low). Each member of the group was thus regarded as representative of several types of students and as an informant about these types as well as about himself. The sample was limited to juniors and seniors on the assumption that they were more familiar with campus customs. Two group interviews of two hours duration and one individual interview were held on each of the areas reported in this paper. In additional interviews the panel members described other aspects of campus life. The discussion in each interview in each area centered around such questions as: What do most students do? Are there any groups on campus whose behavior is markedly different from that of the majority? How do most students treat the student who does not do what they do? What changes occur in students during their undergraduate years? To what can one attribute these changes? In brief, the discussion attempted to delineate in a tentative way the dominant culture-patterns of the campus, the presence or absence of distinct subcultures, the reward-punishment system of the group, and the part played by the culture in changing student behavior during the college years.

After each group meeting a transcript was prepared from stenographic notes and tape recordings, and a copy was given to each group member at the next meeting to be checked for accuracy. Wherever possible, hypotheses suggested by the data were checked by means of participant observation by the investigators and by reference to external sources such as student theses, chaplain's records, the campus police blotter, dean's reports, dormitory office files, and other official college records. The group members also wrote a

brief description of their particular friendship groups on campus following a standardized outline which was adapted from Hartshorne.[2]

The findings reported here are necessarily tentative. They are to be seen more as hypotheses than as tested conclusions. From the outset, the study has been seen as a pilot study—one which has been exploratory in nature. All findings and impressions should be subjected to systematic empirical testing, even though the panel evinced a considerable amount of internal consistency with respect to their judgment of the role of culture in the development of other students and their reports on the part it has played in their own experience. In brief, the authors feel that the data gathered from the panel have a high degree of validity but that this feeling does not in any way reduce the desirability of widening the basis of study and of documenting empirically the conclusions which have been drawn.

Patterns of Recreational Activity

Any discussion of culture can include the description of two aspects of culture: the material culture, the things that are used, and the nonmaterial culture, the ways of doing things and thinking about things—ways that are learned by each succeeding generation. At Ivy much of the material culture may be summarized under the heading of "Residential College"—particularly a small, upper-class, men's college. The general theme of the nonmaterial aspects of undergraduate Ivy culture is that the patterns converge to produce and endorse the "well-rounded" man.

The undergraduate recreational patterns were found to cluster around different points in time. They can be conveniently identified by season of the year, since differences exist between the seasons with respect to the type of athletic contests played. Within any season the patterns may be divided into midweek activity which is predominantly male and weekend activity which is predominantly co-ed. There is also a cluster of patterns around such special events as the rushing period when the sophomores receive bids to the Ivy fraternities and the spring fraternity weekend. For some undergraduates there is evidence that recreational activities during vacation time are also patterned as a result of being "an Ivy man." Spring vacation in Bermuda, the summer jaunt through Europe, and attendance at debutante balls at Christmastime are appropriate examples of this. Perhaps the greatest division of recreational activities on the Ivy campus occurs between the first two and the last two college years. The prime factors creating such a division are the presence of a fraternity system to which almost all upperclassmen belong and the absence of university dining halls for upperclassmen.

A football weekend

The typical football weekend is an example of the difference in pattern brought about by fraternity membership. Because the undergraduates are not allowed to have cars, the weekend's activities take place on campus; and because there are no co-eds nor women's colleges close by, the majority of the women are imported. A few local girls are available, but these are generally relegated to weekday dates for the relatively small group of men who have them. The underclassman's date arrives Friday afternoon by train and is taken to a rooming house in town where she will spend the weekend. Both the room and the usual taxi cost money. After the date has checked in, the couple goes to a dorm cocktail party given by a group of friends. The party ends at seven or shortly after because of the formal college rule that there is to be no "sex-after-seven" in the dorms. The couple then goes over to Center Street to eat, choosing from a limited number of eating places. Men do not generally take their dates to the college dining halls unless as a "lark" or if the date is a "dud."

Dining halls are not viewed as an acceptable place because they are not glamorous enough—too rowdy and the food not good enough. After dinner the couple may go to a dance in the gym, go to the movies, drink beer at the local taverns, or, occasionally, go by bus or train into a nearby city. The dances in the gym have low status and few attend regularly. If a man does not have a date, his activities center about his dormitory room or he may try "bird-dogging," that is, trying to pick up the date of some other undergraduate who has had too many drinks to mind. The underclassmen generally limit themselves to one to three dates during the football season because of the high cost and because there is little to do. The panel estimates that it costs almost twice as much for an underclassman to bring a date to college for a weekend as it does an upperclassman. The dates are generally girls known from pre-college days.

By contrast, the upperclassman's weekend follows a more definite pattern centered about his fraternity. His date arrives by train or car on Friday and is taken to the fraternity where she will stay. From four to seven-thirty they attend a cocktail party at the fraternity, the drinks and the hors d'oeuvres are "free," having already been paid for under a party assessment. Men who drank little before coming to college may drink on this occasion because they have to pay for it anyway. The dinner hour is postponed until 7:30 to accommodate dates who arrive on late trains. The couple eats at the fraternity where there is only one extra charge for the date, since the man's dinner has already been paid for in his membership dues. Friday night the fraternity has a party or open house. Saturday after the game there is another party in the fraternity and the evening is spent "fraternity hopping," i.e. moving up and down fraternity row, drink in hand, to visit or dance in other fraternities. The fraternities are open to all fraternity men, grads, and visitors, but if an underclassman is seen on the street he may be blackballed and never allowed to join a fraternity.

Rate of change from freshman to senior year

The changes in pattern between underclass and upperclass years indicated above occur rather abruptly when the sophomores join the fraternities in the latter part of their sophomore year. Other definite turning points during the four years of college can also be identified. The individual's recreational behavior changes rapidly when he first arrives on campus in his efforts to conform to the college way of life. The pattern then remains about the same until the rushing period in the second half of the sophomore year. With the beginning of junior year, men eat in the fraternities, migrate to dormitories closer to fraternity row, and take on the upperclass pattern which continues for the last two years, with the exception of a noticeable drop in activity during their senior year while the senior thesis is being prepared.

Midweek recreational patterns

For most undergraduates the midweek recreation is more important than that of the weekend, particularly the intramural athletics for upperclassmen. As a result of the fact that Ivy is a male residential college with abundant athletic facilities and fraternities and is located in a small isolated town, midweek recreation for the majority is confined to four major areas within a few hundred yards of each other. Each day the undergraduate makes the rounds of fraternity, playing field or gym, Center Street, and his room. The activities other than intramurals which round out the pattern include bull sessions, fraternity life, card playing, social drinking at the taverns, movies, music, and reading newspapers and magazines.

On a typical weekday the undergraduate goes to classes in the morning or, if he has no classes, catches up on his sleep. Engineers or men in the sciences may have labs in the afternoon until four, while AB's (liberal arts majors) are free to participate in extracurricular activities or play cards. From four to six the men go out for intramural or team sports. After dinner there is time for a few hands of cards at the fraternity or an early show if one is a member of the "flick team." The movies are out at eleven in the evening and the taverns close at twelve. By midnight the men are returning to their rooms. Bull sessions, which play an important part in dormitory life, may begin at any time and continue until the early hours of the morning.

Subcultures in the area of recreation

The panel feels that the student body is essentially homogeneous with respect to its recreational patterns with no sharp line of differentiation into subcultures. Several groups can be identified, however, based on distinctions of degree rather than of kind. These groups can be arranged on a continuum according to the extent to which they follow the pattern of the majority. Using the majority who follow the pattern as a base point, men who exaggerate the pattern are identified as "goof-offs." At the other extreme are men who consciously do not follow the pattern and who are aware that they are a group apart; these are the "individualists." Between the majority and the individualists are three groups who also deviate from the pattern, but to a small degree. The most acceptable group is that of the "jocks" (athletes), who are asked by their coaches not to smoke or drink during training and to get to bed early. Next in order of acceptability of motive would be the men whose interest in extracurricular activities or work for student employment prohibit full participation in the pattern of recreation. Press Club men, for example, find it difficult to have a date down for a weekend and still cover their assignments; men who work nights cannot go to the movies. Finally, the "grinds" have the least acceptable motive for not participating.

They consciously choose to study rather than to go along with the gang and thereby operate against the norms of study by "wrecking the curve" by their excessive "eagerness." There is probably a considerable degree of overlapping between the population of "grinds" and that of "individualists."

Since the theme of "well-roundedness" supports a recreational pattern which includes a variety of activities, any group who emphasizes one activity or interest must necessarily deviate from the pattern. The dates coming to Ivy from the women's colleges must also be "well-rounded" if they are to participate in all the activities of the weekend. The pattern was seen as functional for upper-class social life in the larger society, since the "well-rounded" man is at an advantage among the country-club set. It is also viewed as functional for the future success in business where golf, bridge, etc. are some of the unofficial prerequisites for successful execution of the executive function.

Recreation and student development

Defining development sociologically as a change in behavior and/or ideas or values, one may examine the area of recreation from the viewpoint of what changes occur in students during the undergraduate years. Each individual on entering college may be seen as possessing a repertoire of recreational habits and interests which have been shaped by his previous experience. On exposure to undergraduate life, these may change in different ways. Some new behavior may be added, such as learning how to play squash or bridge. Some old behavior may drop out, such as playing on the football team. Former behavior may also be modified in other ways. Sometimes old practices and interests are continued but on a decreased level of frequency and intensity, such as the man who played on his secondary-school tennis team but plays tennis only informally and infrequently at college. Sometimes they are maintained

on approximately the same level, such as the man who was on his secondary-school hockey team and is now on the college hockey team. Sometimes they are accentuated sharply, such as the man who has played little or no bridge and becomes "addicted" to it at college or the man who in secondary-school days drank very little but in college drinks considerably (comparatively speaking). In discussing changes in recreational patterns with the panel, one reaches the conclusion that, all in all, there is little new behavior added. What changes do occur seem to be changes in degree rather than in kind. Perhaps the major new aspect is the time element in recreation, where the student is freer than formerly to indulge in recreational activity at hitherto unusual times. Weekday recreation seems important in this respect. Also of seeming importance is the change in the way in which weekend dating is executed. Girls are imported, which often involves considerable planning, or there are excursions from one community to another for the purpose of dating.

Of those things which are dropped at Ivy, lengthy recreational reading (particularly of novels, because of pressure of assignments), the use of cars for dating, and participation in family activities seem to stand out most. Also, there is some evidence that recreation is now confined more exclusively to the peer-group, recreational participation with younger and older people having been dropped. Parties and bull sessions appear to be the items that have been increased the most. Considerable mention is made of the more intimate contact the student now has with his peers, of which the bull session is the primary example.

Those items which have been maintained at about the same level seem to run the gamut of possibilities. At first glance, there is an apparent lack of uniformity among individual students with respect to their recreational characteristics and the changes that occur in such characteristics between entrance and graduation. At second glance, however, most individuals seem to be changing in the same general direction of an increasing conformity to the practices and beliefs of Ivy culture. This does not mean that any individual coming to Ivy must learn how to play, say, squash or billiards. The cultural norm is not that specific in dictating details. What the norm does prescribe is that the individual be "well-rounded," which means he must have a well-balanced repertoire of skills and interests which may or may not include any one specific item such as squash. The individual is judged by his versatility of behavior and interests rather than by his proficiency along one line. As one student has put the whole matter, "You can't be just a junior Phi Bete and nothing else to be a good guy. You should participate in sports, be in one extracurricular activity or more, be able to get along easily with others, drink, etc." In brief, the apparent effect of Ivy culture on the individual student's development in the area of recreation is to enlarge his repertoire of skills, increase his interests, and define the importance of recreation in relation to other areas of undergraduate life.

Patterns of Intellectual Activity

Lecture and class attendance

During the course of the average week the intellectual activity of the student is centered around study and attendance at classes, seminars, and occasional outside lectures and concerts. Most members of the panel report they attend lectures and concerts if they are interested in the particular lecture subject or musical selections. Because patterns in class attendance could be identified from official records, little time was spent with the panel on this subject. It was felt that it would be more profitable to discuss study habits and related topics about which information can seldom be gathered from official college sources. However, from the data available, it is quite apparent that the average student does not attend all his scheduled classes and seminars. The reasons most mentioned for this are: the pressure of outside activities, such as the student newspaper or annual variety show or the fraternity rushing period, which absorb considerable portions of the students' time; the pressure of assignments in some courses which necessitates cutting other courses to complete them; pressure of meeting deadlines for long-term projects, such as junior papers and senior theses, which necessitates neglect of other courses; leaving early and/or returning late from vacations and/or weekends; and occasionally oversleeping from staying up too late the night before.

Study habits

With respect to study habits, the panel identified in very broad outlines two types of students: those who study regularly and manage to keep up with all their assignments and those who leave their assignments until the last minute. In personal interviews half the panel reported they tended to let things slide and half that they kept up with their assignments fairly well. The panel felt that, as a general principle, study habits were to be accounted for on an individual basis and that men with similar study habits did not necessarily or consistently have any other characteristics in common beyond the similarity with which they handled their assignments. However, from remarks made by the panel in group discussions and personal interviews we may infer the presence of certain factors and conditions which operate to produce differences in study habits.

A. *Attitude Toward Intellectual Activities.* First, the student's attitude toward intellectual activities influences his study habits. When the panel members were asked to describe the purpose of a college education, no member limited the purpose solely to acquiring either general knowledge or vocational skills. All of the members were "sold on" the liberal arts approach but gave different reasons for liking it. Men who are going to graduate school want a broad training because they will specialize later, and men who are not going on want the same training to help them in their associations after graduation. They expect to live a fuller life as a result of their college experience, and to them the "full life" is defined as that of the "well-rounded" man.

When asked whether they thought an interest in and appreciation of scholarly and intellectual activities would be of any value for their post-college occupational success, the majority agreed that such an interest would be very important for future success. Each of the men also mentioned something else that he felt was *more* important, however, such as living and working with people, getting to know more people, learning things in extracurricular activities, becoming more tolerant, making new friendships, and being independent.

When asked to describe a scholar and then an intellectual, the panel indicated clearly the value they attached to intellectual activities. The panel felt that scholar was a term applied to men older than themselves who devoted their lives to the pursuit of knowledge, usually in some highly specialized field. Whereas they saw the term "scholar" as a vocational label, they saw the term "intellectual" as describing a psychic quality, a way of looking at life in general. It could be applied to anyone, regardless of age. In the words of the panel, the intellectual was variously described as "a creep," "a skinny little guy with glasses," and "a mental snob." When asked which they would like to have for a friend, the panel showed a general preference for the scholar over the intellectual but had considerable reservations about each. The usual answer took the form of "it depends on..." various other qualities the scholar possessed such as "being a gentleman" (very likely this stems from the phrase "gentleman and scholar"—a phrase suggesting definite personality characteristics); "not lording it over you"; "more all-round person"; "one of the boys";

"not just with a book all the time", etc. In brief, those who thought they would like the scholar for a friend tended to attribute these extra qualities to the scholar, and those who expressed reservations did so in terms of whether or not the scholar had these qualities. If he did, then they felt they would be likely to want him as a friend.

Whether or not they would like the intellectual as a friend depended again on what other qualities or attributes the intellectual possessed beyond his intellectuality. The panel identified two kinds of intellectuals: those who were just intellectual and those who were intellectual and "well rounded." When speaking of their own generation, they expressed the feeling that a "good guy can be an intellectual but if he's just an intellectual he's not a good guy."

When told of an Ivy professor's comment in a recent issue of the campus paper to the effect that anti-intellectualism and the fear of "apple-polishing" were not noticeably on the wane on the Ivy campus, the panel agreed that there was a natural fear of "apple-polishing" and that anti-intellectualism did exist. It is important to note that they saw anti-intellectualism as a term which was not necessarily derogative. They felt that what one found on campus was a value placed not only on intellectual activities but *on other things as well*. What they objected to were those men who studied and did nothing else and "who always had their nose in a book" and "knew their courses backwards and forwards." As one student commented, "I don't know anyone who would prefer to stay in his room and study rather than go out and play a little tennis or go down to the tavern and drink." In brief, the panel felt that anti-intellectualism was a perfectly acceptable attitude if the term referred to the relative emphasis placed on intellectual activities as opposed to other sorts of activities.

When asked about the value placed on grades, the panel felt that a B or C average is acceptable but went on to distinguish between the overall average and the grades in major subjects. The overall average should be high enough to keep one in college with the grades in major subjects generally being one grade higher than those in electives. For example, a B for the major and a C for the electives would be adequate. When emphasis on higher grades occurs, it tends to be connected with an expectation of postgraduate work. One factor that makes the C acceptable is the general feeling that a C at Ivy is equal to an A in most other colleges.

The Ivy student's intellectual idea was described as interest in and enjoyment of a number of fields. However, ability to do a variety of things is not enough. One should not be deceived by the false "well-rounded" man: one who appears to have broad interests but somehow does not "follow through." The "real article" is one who is able to say, "I get 60 seconds out of every minute." Ideally, it is not necessary for the intellectual who is also "well rounded" to "double clutch" at examination time. He should be able to take it as "cool" as did Mr. Goodman whose approach to examinations was recorded in the college paper:

POPULAR STIMULANTS NET GOODMAN
A PLUS

Charles Goodman, an English major, felt uncomfortable in his Sociology 209 course final exam.

After the first 45 minutes, he had completed all of the questions on the three-hour examination, but other students were still busily working. So he left his paper and ventured down to a local bar, where he quaffed numerous beers for 45 more minutes. Then he returned and was second man to turn in his paper.

Yesterday, with deep concern, he looked at the bulletin board. His grade: an A plus.

B. *The Nature of College Work.* A second factor prominently associated with study habits is the nature of the assignments imposed upon the student by the official culture. The panel suggests that AB's tend to study in fits and starts and are more likely to "double clutch" when exam time arrives than are engineers. Even those members of the panel who reported they kept up with assignments did so on a rather indefinite schedule. They studied for no specific number of hours each day, such as two, or three, or four hours a day. Nor did they have specific periods during the day which were designated for study purposes, such as evenings from nine to eleven, or afternoons from three to four. Rather, the general tendency was to work when they "could" or "felt like it" or "had to" and somehow get their work done when it was due. The culture did not specifically define when one should study, aside from the general area of "when you can," but it was more or less explicit about when one should *not* study: for example, weekday evenings after midnight and Saturdays. It was suggested that such a pattern of study is made possible by the nature of the work in liberal arts courses. Where one has long-term assignments, one can either work on them at regular intervals or delay until shortly before they are due. Also, the nature of the content is such that one can put off weekly assignments and make them up later, whereas courses in engineering and the sciences often necessitate the faithful execution of daily assignments. In the latter departments one assignment builds upon the previous one and cannot be mastered unless the previous one has been mastered. Thus, at the end of a term it is considerably easier for a student to read several novels in English or a textbook in history than it is for a science or engineering major to begin seriously studying the work in his courses.

That engineers and science majors should traditionally have the reputation of being "the hardest workers" or at least the "most worked" students on campus can partially be accounted for on the basis that the nature of their work necessitates it. Thus, whereas liberal arts students are more often seen relaxing at bull sessions, cards, or the movies, engineers and science majors are more often seen on their way to or from the laboratories and working on daily assignments. It should be pointed out, however, that the amount of time spent on schoolwork by these men is often inversely proportional to their mathematical ability, since so much of their work depends on a knowledge of mathematics. A student who is good in mathematics can often do his work in less time than a liberal arts student, particularly if the latter is given long assignments and if the emphasis is not on problem solution, formula memorization, and the mastering of fairly specific facts but on interpretation and the subtleties of esthetic appreciation. Although all men report they work hard around exam times, panel discussions suggest that the task of preparing for exams is easier for the engineer than for the liberal arts major. The nature of the work in conjunction with the AB and BS or BE degrees thus favors the adoption of essentially different patterns of studying.

C. *Institutionalized Delay.* A third factor contributing to the existence of different study-habits is what we may refer to as "institutionalized delay." This occurs particularly in the Department of Architecture where students traditionally leave their work until the last few hours before the final deadline.

D. *Lack of Supervision.* The fact that the completion of assignments is left almost entirely to the student's discretion gives the student great freedom with respect to how he handles his academic requirements. Little direct supervision of a continuing nature (such as the compulsory study halls of prep-school life and the daily quizzes and assignments of most secondary schools) is in evidence. To survive in college society one must do a certain minimum of work to meet official requirements for passing and graduation, to be sure, but beyond this subsistence level the official culture pays little systematic and explicit attention to the way in which the student organizes his intellectual life. Occasionally students experi-

ence inward pressures to exceed the subsistence level, and these pressures arise from felt needs to "keep the scholarship" or "get accepted in graduate or medical school" or from a general desire to excel. For the most part, there is little in the student culture to encourage intensive efforts to excel with respect to grades. Rather, the theme of "well-roundedness" exerts pressure on the student to spend his time on other than intellectual activities once his continued existence has been assured by the meeting of minimal requirements. As one student observed, "I'd rather see a man participate in extracurricular activities and sacrifice his average than be a Phi Bete or honor student and do nothing else." And as another observed, "If you're going to be an average guy you have to participate. You can't get along if you're just a student and nothing else." Hence, it is only the student with exceptional ability who can simultaneously receive the best marks and meet the demands of "well-roundedness" which the culture imposes. Every student is faced with the problem of what to do with a limited amount of time, and this problem usually takes the form of reconciling his own interests and needs with the demands of the official and student cultures.

E. *Contacts with Authority Figures.* The nature of the contacts the student has with older authority-figures may influence his academic behavior. The panel reports that there is comparatively little faculty-student contact. When contact does occur it is usually on the formal level of the classroom situation where there is a clearly structured teacher-pupil relationship. There are, however, some differences by year and by department. In general, there is more informal contact with faculty in upperclass years than in lowerclass years, especially in connection with junior independent work and the senior thesis. There the students report they experience closer and more meaningful interpersonal communication and get to know at least one member of the faculty on more intimate terms than the classroom or even the seminar situation would permit. In some departments, particularly the smaller ones, faculty-student relations tend to be more informal and meaningful than in other departments.

A similar situation arises with respect to the parent-son relationship. The panel members report that their parents exert little pressure on them to excel academically. The typical parental concern is that the son meet the college survival standards and eventually graduate. The parents tend to be relatively uninformed about different aspects of the college's curriculum and about the courses their sons are taking. They give little advice in this connection, apparently regarding this as the proper function of the college. It may well be that the parents can do no more than this because of difference in age and outlook, physical isolation from the campus, and general unfamiliarity with the changing nature of university education. In any event, the important point is that the students do not draw on their parents for advice nor do they seem to draw heavily on the official culture, either teaching or advisory personnel, except when required to do so. One can only assume then that the students rely on their own judgment or that of their peers. In either event, one would expect the same result: a reinforcement of student culture.

It is interesting to note that the most meaningful and sustained contacts some students have with college authority-figures are with the athletic personnel. The typical coach-player relationship is described as much more informal and close than the typical teacher-student relationship. By definition, the coach primarily exemplifies and is concerned with values and activities which are other than intellectual. Thus, for some students, one has the situation of nonintellectual values being reinforced by some college authority-figures (the athletic personnel) and intellectual values not being reinforced to an equal extent by other college authority-figures (the teaching personnel). Given a

person who is a product of American culture, in which the professional athlete is for the most part more prestigeful than the professional intellect, and introducing that person to the college scene, it is not surprising that his tendency toward anti-intellectualism does not disappear or often not even noticeably diminish.

Intellectual activity and student development

The panel reported that the transition from secondary school to college tended to be a difficult one and that the degree of difficulty experienced varied with the individual in terms of his abilities and background. Nevertheless, every student faced two types of academic problems. The first, as indicated earlier, was the nature of the work at college. Panel members reported that at college less work was done for them by the teacher, in the sense of extensive organization of course material. The lecture system was new to many. Assignments were given over a longer period of time and their length often was such that the student had to be selective in determining what was important in his assignments. There also tended to be a decrease in the amount of direct supervision of study and a corresponding increase in the necessity for learning how to organize one's time. In short, the students had to assume a greater degree of responsibility for their own work.

One of the most striking changes experienced was that of moving from the secondary-school situation where although examinations were closely supervised cheating existed to the Ivy situation where an honor system functioned in place of faculty supervision and where cheating was viewed as a taboo activity by the peer culture. As one student said of his high school, "an honest man has to cheat to get through." Another man, recalling his prep-school days, said that he always used to cheat because he felt it unfair to be asked to read the daily assignment; however, he does not cheat at college because of the honor system, adding that it was quite an adjustment to make. The change in behavior with regard to cheating occurs rather suddenly in the freshman year. First, incoming men have to sign a paper saying that they will abide by the honor system. Then, even though there might remain a tendency to cheat, they soon notice that no one else is doing so and abide by the rule. By the end of four years the honor system has become so accepted that a senior is able to make the statement, "Our guys are shocked by guys from other universities who cheat."

The second type of problem faced by each student was learning the standards of the new environment and then living up to them. In learning the new standards the student was often handicapped by a conception of himself as a student with a particular amount of ability–a conception which had been formed in his secondary-school years. High-school boys particularly reported that they entered college thinking they were "A" students on the basis of the marks they had received in secondary school and were often shocked to learn that it took considerably more ability and work to get equivalent grades in college. Prep-school students generally had experienced a more realistic grading process and had had more intensive training in their subjects and thus found the transition somewhat easier, but they too still faced the initial problem of learning "what was required of them" by the new environment. One standard they had to learn which was not directly related to course work and formal academic requirements was the attitude the student body had toward intellectual activity. The panel felt, on the whole, that the student culture supported more intellectual activity and a greater interest in serious ideas than did the secondary-school culture. A student could be interested in serious ideas and engage in intellectual activity to an extent which in secondary school would be likely to earn him the label of "pansy." However, while learning that one could

engage in more intellectual activity than before, the student also had to learn the upper limits of such activity which were permissible to the student body. He could not "go all out" for such activity *unless* he was simultaneously devoting himself to other areas of college life. In summary, the student entering college had to adjust to the different nature of college work and learn the standards of the new environment, which ranged from formal standards of grades and the honor system to informal standards of permissible amounts of work which the student's peers endorsed. The latter process is known to the students as "getting on to the system." The picture of the initial transition one forms from the panel is that of students spending their first few months trying to discover "where they stand" as individuals in relation to the formal standards of the college. Once they feel secure in this respect, one finds increasing concern for the informal standards of the peer group. Thus, by sophomore year one finds more mention of "the system" and of "curve-wreckers." This implies that there is a general tendency for the student to have learned what the formal standards are and exactly what amount of work is necessary to get certain grades. As one student remarked, "Freshmen usually work harder than sophomores because they feel they have to know everything while the sophomore knows you can get by with less."

Once the initial transition is successfully experienced there is little change in the student's intellectual patterns until his upperclass years, where, as previously mentioned, he comes in closer contact with the faculty through his department and particularly through his junior independent work and senior thesis. There is some evidence that in senior year the emphasis again shifts from the peer group to the individual. Although there seems to be a general pattern of delaying the commencement of thesis work until the last minute (particularly because of time absorbed by fraternity life and football season), students tend to think more about themselves as they prepare for life after graduation. Students particularly concerned with their grades are those who are applying for some graduate or professional school, acceptance to which often depends on the student's academic performance in his senior year. Other students are concerned with finding a job in their chosen field of interest.

In general the undergraduates are conscious of the change in their behavior. They recognize that the freshman usually works harder than the sophomore and suggest that the average upperclassman's work is inspired by interest, in contrast with that of the underclassman who is not as interested in his work. This difference probably results from the fact that seniors do the bulk of their work in their major or in electives which have been chosen for their interest value.

In summary, the panel reports that with the exception of cheating little past behavior is dropped. The most important aspects of past behavior which are intensified at college or of behavior newly learned by the individual are: the adjustment to an honor system, the acceptance of responsibility for doing the work on time, the learning of methods of note-taking in lectures, the selection of the important parts of reading assignments which are often too long to be read in their entirety, and the writing of essay exams.

From the viewpoint of the student, the net effect of the college intellectual experience was to "broaden and sharpen" him. Specifically he learned to "appreciate a book a lot more," to "understand opera," to "think better," etc. From the viewpoint of the outside observer, the college culture supported more intellectual activity than was probably condoned by the peer culture of secondary school, thus facilitating the attainment of the above benefits. However, at the same time, the student culture operated to limit the amount of intellectual activity through the equal value it placed on other activities in its emphasis on the "well-rounded" man.

Summary and Conclusions

The preceding pages have attempted to picture selected aspects of the undergraduate life of a college as that life is seen through the eyes of a panel of upperclassmen. The undergraduate body has been conceptualized not as a mere collection of individual undergraduates but as a group exhibiting shared patterns of thought and behavior—in brief, as a group with its own distinctive culture. The culture has been viewed as one of many aspects of the college environment to which the student must adjust himself during the four years of his college education. Since the evidence from the panel suggests that for the average undergraduate there is less continuous contact with other aspects of the college environment such as the faculty and coaches, and with noncollege aspects such as family and girl friends, than with the peer culture, it would appear that the culture is the most important single external factor in the student's experience. Most of his time is spent with his peers. The small size and relatively homogeneous nature of the student body tend to promote conformity and group solidarity, and this tendency is reinforced by situational factors such as the geographical location of Ivy, the absence of cars, the presence of a fraternity system, and the fact that all students must live in university dormitories on campus.

In attempting to describe the major cultural patterns in two areas of undergraduate life, the authors have emphasized the "average"—what most undergraduates do and think in these areas. In so doing, the students who represent extremes in deviation from the main patterns have been largely neglected. This is not regarded as a serious shortcoming of the study; for in presenting the culture as one aspect of the student's environment to which he must adjust, it is more important to stress what the majority do, as the patterns of the majority are those with which the student is most likely to come in contact, of which he is most likely to be aware, and to which he must make some sort of response whether positive or negative. Moreover, evidence from the panel seems to indicate that, aside from the under- and upperclass cultures, there are no clearly definable subcultures within the undergraduate society. On an individual level, the typical student sees his fellow student not just as an athlete or as an outing clubber or as a junior Phi Bete, but as an Ivy man who is *also* on the varsity hockey team, who is a history major, who has a C average, who is a member of a fraternity, who is on the staff of the college paper, who is a "good guy" and gets along with everyone, who dates, smokes, drinks, etc. In brief, the individual student presents a configurational stimulus to other students, and it is the nature of the configuration which determines the response other students will make to him. He is accepted as an Ivy man because of his enrollment at Ivy and his presence on campus, but how "good" an Ivy man he is and how well he is accepted by other students depends on "other attributes." The student who presents a configuration which represents a variety of interests and abilities in many areas of life is judged to be "well rounded" and is more readily accepted than one who presents a configuration which is "lopsided" in some respect. The configuration which may be described in terms of "well-roundedness" is the one which the undergraduate value system most highly endorses and rewards.

The pressure directed toward the molding of the "well-rounded man" seems to have the effect of reducing extremes in the student body and, correspondingly, of increasing the homogeneity of the student body. The "naturally shy and reticent" are "brought out"; the "overly studious" are "broadened" to the point where other things besides books and intellectual matters become of importance; the "Christ-smitten" are mellowed into a less moralistic and more social or democratic frame of mind, and so forth. In brief, the student's scope of interests and range of activities is broadened and balanced.

The panel interviews and the descriptions of cliques by the panel members seem to indicate that the system operates with considerable ease. As deviants from the "well-rounded" ideal are molded to fit the ideal, it becomes increasingly easier to perpetuate that ideal; for the more people in the group who are "well rounded," the more models the newcomer has to imitate. The psychic rewards of "belonging" are such that one finds it "uncomfortable" to deviate too far from the ideal. Social pressures, of a largely informal yet overt nature, are applied by the individual's clique to the point where he must conform in most respects to the clique's norms if he is to "belong." Since cliques are apparently loosely organized on campus, and since most cliques exhibit essentially similar behavior, it makes little difference to what clique one belongs. The individual chooses his friends for similarity of interests, but other cliques are not strikingly different. However, those individuals who deviate from the main norms on campus are aware of their deviation, and the only sense of "belonging" they can achieve, if they are not to conform to the ideal, is to clique with others who are "different from the average guy."

Thus it would seem that there are two major alternative paths of development open to the student at Ivy. He can be subjected to the molding process and be richly rewarded, or he can join an "outgrouper" clique whereby his interests are not appreciably changed. In this situation he may achieve the same sense of belonging to a group, but he is simultaneously aware that he does not belong to the larger group and is not sharing its rewards.

The relative importance of culture as an external factor for the development of any particular individual depends on the presence or absence of other external factors and on the strength of those factors. For some, the most influential aspect of their experience during the college years may be a possessive mother or an overbearing father. For others it may be one or two professors who succeed in stimulating a deep intellectual interest within the student. In brief, the development of any individual is a function of many factors of which undergraduate culture is one. The present study has attempted to describe some aspects of the Ivy culture which is viewed as one factor in the student's experience to which he must adjust, one way or another.

Looking Back*

It has been some fourteen years since the article on Student Culture at Ivy was written, and during this period changes have naturally occurred on the American college scene. While I cannot comment on the specific changes at Ivy, I can hazard some general observations about the nature of changes and the present usefulness of the point of view expressed in the original article. These observations are a distillation of personal experience as a dean, researcher, and counselor at institutions similar to Ivy and of impressions garnered from the formal and informal reports of others involved and interested in the college scene. Although they refer primarily to Ivy-type institutions, I believe they have relevance to the American college scene in general.

It appears to me that today's students are a more serious and less "collegiate" group than are their counterparts in the early fifties and that student cultures inevitably reflect this. There is less emphasis on the "fun" aspects of the college years and more concern with issues of significance in the world at large—social service, civil rights, foreign policy, and

---

* Prepared by James S. Davie especially for this volume.

the like. The amount of support for intellectuality provided by student cultures has certainly increased dramatically. Such changes appear to reflect both changes in the broader society (and the kind of citizens produced by general social conditions) and changes in policies, practices, and philosophies in the educational segment of society.

Because of improvement in the quality of secondary-school instruction and the greater availability of financial support as well as the sheer pressure of numbers, competition for admission to college has become progressively stiffer, and the colleges have in turn been able to raise admissions standards and to demand more of the students who are selected. The specifics of draft laws and the "pressure from above" to gain eventual admission to graduate and professional schools have served to make students more concerned with the academic part of their college experience, sometimes to the point of emphasizing grades over content. The increased support of intellectual pursuits by both the official and student cultures is further reinforced by the increasing recognition in the society at large of the crucial importance of a highly trained citizenry to a technological society.

Despite such pervasive changes there is still a great part of the college experience which is nonacademic and developmental in nature. During this period of their lives students need to do considerable experimentation and exploration if they are to develop a social role or personal identity that is both meaningful to them and functional for the adult world. These special social and psychological needs of the age group are recognized and supported by student cultures, though the manner in which they may be satisfied will vary from campus to campus.

In general, I would say that the overall viewpoint expressed in the original article is as useful today as it was before but that the content of student culture has changed. In terms of cultural themes it would appear that, although there is still a basic concern with the "well-rounded" man or with the individual as a total person, there has been increasing emphasis on specific skills of the individual in terms of their potential contribution to the highly specialized adult society of which the individual student will soon become an important part.

---

[1] A. P. Hare and J. S. Davie, "The Group Interview: Its Use in the Study of Undergraduate Culture," *Sociology and Social Research,* 39 (1954), pp. 81–87. Two studies using other methods which treat the seminar system and extracurricular activities at the same college are: F. F. Stephan and E. G. Mishler, "The Distribution of Participation in Small Groups: An Exponential Approximation," *American Sociological Review,* 17 (1952), pp. 598–608; A. P. Hare, "An Evaluation of Extra curriculum Activities," *School Review,* 63 (1955), pp. 164–168.

[2] E. Y. Hartshorne, "Undergraduate Society and College Culture," *American Sociological Review,* 8 (1943), pp. 321–322.

part four INTERNAL DIMENSIONS OF ADMINISTRATION

In Part Four we begin a more intensive analysis of some of the complex patterns of behavior which take place within organizations of work. The significant areas of administration—leadership, morale, communication, managerial change, and training—are discussed here.

In "Group Dynamics and Intergroup Relations" Alex Bavelas and George Strauss review a live production situation which is confronted by an abundance of morale problems. The fascinating result of management's efforts to alleviate these problems is that the improvements made at first later failed because they succeeded too well. From these results we gain valuable insights into workers' desires to participate in making decisions relevant to their tasks.

Richard L. Simpson analyzes the relationships between mechanization and vertical and horizontal communication patterns between supervisors. He concludes that too much emphasis has been placed on upward and downward information flow and too little concern has been given to the importance of horizontal communication.

Executive succession is the topic of the third article. Robert Guest compares an earlier study by Alvin Gouldner with his own investigation concerning changes in managerial personnel. Supervisors often feel that by replacing subordinates they can improve the conditions of a work unit.

Fred Goldner analyzes problems which might arise when employees are demoted. Several methods by which organizations solve possible disruptive consequences of demotion cluster around ambiguity in lines of authority. If workers find it difficult to define an authority hierarchy, then it is difficult for them to determine whether or not someone who changes jobs is promoted or demoted.

Robert C. Day and Robert L. Hamblin, the authors of "Some Effects of Close and Punitive Styles of Supervision," examine consequences of close versus distant supervision upon subordinates' behavior. They answer questions such as: Are more aggressive feelings produced by close or distant leadership? Is the aggression of subordinates directed only toward the leader or also toward fellow workers? What are the consequences of punitive or hostile versus nonpunitive supervision?

149

16 Group Dynamics and Intergroup Relations

By ALEX BAVELAS AND GEORGE STRAUSS*

This is the story of an experiment that failed because it succeeded too well.

The Hovey and Beard Company manufactured wooden toys of various kinds: wooden animals, pull toys, and the like. One part of the manufacturing process involved spraying paint on the partially assembled toys and hanging them on moving hooks which carried them through a drying oven. This operation, staffed entirely by girls, was plagued by absenteeism, turnover, and low morale.

A consultant, working with the foreman in charge, "solved" the problem. But the changes that were made in order to solve it had such repercussions in other parts of the plant that the company abandoned the new procedures, despite their obvious benefits to production in that local area.

The Problem

Let us look briefly at the painting operation in which the problem occurred.

The toys were cut, sanded, and partially assembled in the wood room. Then they were dipped into shellac, following which they were painted. The toys were predominantly two-colored; a few were made in more than two colors. Each color required an additional trip through the paint room.

Shortly before the troubles began, the painting operation had been re-engineered so that the eight girls who did the painting sat in a line by an endless chain of hooks. These hooks were in continuous motion, past the line of girls and into a long horizontal oven. Each girl sat at her own painting booth so designed as to carry away fumes and to backstop excess paint. The girl would take a toy from the tray beside her, position it in a jig inside the painting cubicle, spray on the color according to a pattern, then release the toy and hang it on the hook passing by. The rate at which the hooks moved had been calculated by the engineers so that each girl, when fully trained, would be able to hang a painted toy on each hook before it passed beyond her reach.

The girls working in the paint room were on a group-bonus plan. Since the operation was new to them, they were receiving a learning bonus which decreased by regular amounts each month. The learning bonus was scheduled to vanish in six months, by which time it was expected that they would be on their own—that is, able to meet the standard and to earn a group bonus when they exceeded it.

By the second month of the training period trouble had developed. The girls learned more slowly than had been anticipated, and it began to look as though their production would stabilize far below what had been planned for. Many of the hooks were going by empty. The girls complained that they were going by too fast and that the time-study man had set the rates wrong. A few girls quit and had to be replaced with new girls, which further aggravated the learning problem. The team spirit that the management had expected to develop automatically through the group bonus was not in evidence except as an expression of what the engineers called "resistance." One girl whom the group regarded as its leader (and the management regarded as the ringleader) was outspoken in making the various complaints of the group known to the foreman. The complaints had all the variety customary in such instances of generalized frustration: the job was a messy one, the hooks moved too fast, the incentive pay was not being correctly calculated, and anyway, it was too hot working so close to the drying oven.

Introducing the New Approach

The consultant who was brought into this picture worked entirely with and through the foreman. After many conversations with him, the foreman felt that the first step should be to get the girls together for a general discussion of the working conditions—something, incidentally, which was far from his mind originally and which in his own words would only have been "begging for trouble." He took this step with some hesitation, but he took it on his own volition.

The first meeting, held immediately after the shift was over at four o'clock in the afternoon, was attended by all eight girls. They voiced the same complaints again. The hooks went by too fast, the job was too dirty, the room was hot and poorly ventilated. For some reason it was this last item that they complained of most. The foreman promised to discuss the problem of ventilation and temperature with the engineers, and he scheduled a second meeting to report back to the girls. In the next few days the foreman had several talks with the engineers, and it seemed that the girls' cynical predictions about what the engineers would say were going to be borne out. They and the superintendent felt that this was really a trumped-up complaint and that the expense of any effec-

tive corrective measure would be prohibitively high. (They were thinking of some form of air conditioning.)

The foreman came to the second meeting with some apprehensions. The girls, however, did not seem to be much put out, perhaps because they had a proposal of their own to make. They felt that if several large fans were set up to circulate the air around their feet, they would be much more comfortable. After some discussion the foreman agreed that the idea might be tried out. (Immediately after the meeting, he confided to the consultant that he probably should not have committed himself to this expense on his own initiative; also, he felt that the fans would not help much anyway.) The foreman and the consultant discussed the question of the fans with the superintendent, and three large propeller-type fans were purchased. The decision was reached without much difficulty, since it seemed that the fans could be used elsewhere after their expected failure to provide relief in the paint room.

The fans were brought in. The girls were jubilant. For several days the fans were moved about in various positions until they were placed to the satisfaction of the group. Whatever the actual efficiently of these fans, one thing was clear: The girls were completely satisfied with the results, and relations between them and the foreman improved visibly.

The foreman, after this encouraging episode, decided that further meetings might also be profitable. He asked the girls if they would like to meet and discuss other aspects of the work situation. The girls were eager to do this.[1] The meeting was held, and the discussion quickly centered on the speed of the hooks. The girls maintained that the time-study men had set them at an unreasonably fast speed and that they would never be able to reach the goal of filling enough of them to make a bonus.

The turning point of the discussion came when the group's leader frankly explained that the point was not that they could not work fast enough to keep up with the hooks, but that they could not work at that pace all day long. The foreman explored the point. The girls were unanimous in their opinion that they could keep up with the belt for short periods if they wanted to. But they did not want to, because if they showed that they could do this for short periods they would be expected to do it all day long. The meeting ended with an unprecedented request: "Let us adjust the speed of the belt faster or slower depending on how we feel." The foreman, understandably startled, agreed to discuss this with the superintendent and the engineers.

The engineers' reaction naturally was that the girls' suggestion was heresy. Only after several meetings was it granted grudgingly that there was in reality some latitude within which variations in the speed of the hooks would not affect the finished product. After considerable argument and many dire prophecies by the engineers, it was agreed to try out the girls' idea.

With great misgivings, the foreman had a control with a dial marked "low, medium, fast" installed at the booth of the group leader; she could now adjust the speed of the belt anywhere between the lower and upper limits that the engineers had set. The girls were delighted and spent many lunch hours deciding how the speed of the belt should be varied from hour to hour throughout the day.

Within a week the pattern had settled down to one in which the first half hour of the shift was run on what the girls called medium speed (a dial setting slightly above the point marked "medium"). The next two and one-half hours were run at high speed; the half hour before lunch and the half hour after lunch were run at low speed. The rest of the afternoon was run at high speed with the exception of the last forty-five minutes of the shift, which was run at medium.

In view of the girls' reports of satisfac-

tion and ease in their work, it is interesting to note that the constant speed at which the engineers had originally set the belt was slightly below medium on the dial of the control that had been given the girls. The average speed at which the girls were running the belt was on the high side of the dial. Few if any empty hooks entered the oven, and inspection showed no increase of rejects from the paint room.

Production increased, and within three weeks (some two months before the scheduled ending of the learning bonus) the girls were operating at 30 to 50 per cent above the level that had been expected under the original arrangement. Naturally the girls' earnings were correspondingly higher than anticipated. They were collecting their base pay, a considerable piece-rate bonus, and the learning bonus which, it will be remembered, had been set to decrease with time and not as a function of current productivity. (This arrangement, which had been selected by the management in order to prevent being taken advantage of by the girls during the learning period, now became a real embarrassment.)

The girls were earning more now than many skilled workers in other parts of the plant. Management was besieged by demands that this inequity be taken care of. With growing irritation between superintendent and foreman, engineers and foreman, superintendent and engineers, the situation came to a head when the superintendent without consultation arbitrarily revoked the learning bonus and returned the painting operation to its original status: The hooks moved again at their constant, time-studied designated speed, production dropped again, and within a month all but two of the eight girls had quit. The foreman himself stayed on for several months, but, feeling aggrieved, then left for another job.

Analysis of Success and Failure

It is not difficult to understand why installing the fans and permitting the speed of the hooks to be controlled by them should have affected the girls the way it did. No normal person is happy in a situation which he cannot control to some extent. The fans may not have actually changed the heat or the humidity, but they were a visible and daily reminder that worker ideas were given consideration.

About the speed of the hooks an additional observation may be made. The idea that efficient work results from proceeding at a constant rate derives certainly from the operations of machines and not from the characteristic operation of human beings. If anything is clear about human performance it is that it is characterized by changes of pace. Some production operations by their nature permit little variation in this respect, but even when the possibility exists it is not readily perceived by many engineers as a source of increased efficiency. From the operator's point of view, to be paced unvaryingly by a machine which he may not even shut down with impunity may be psychologically uncomfortable. In such a situation the only avenue left for the expression of any independence is that of complaint: The machine or its master, the engineer, must be shown to be wrong. Also, there appear to be inherent and unconscious defensive mechanisms which operate against the threat of being "stretched out."

Control over the speed of the hooks in this situation not only allowed changes of pace which were in themselves restful and refreshing, but also allowed the operator the natural enjoyment of operating at top speed without fear that he might be compelled to stay there. Of course, the manner in which the change was instituted was significant. The opportunity to exercise initiative, the gratification of being listened to seriously, helped to bring about changes in the emotional overtones of the situation which were in themselves favorable to increased effort.

In the light of all this it is not surprising that the situation fell apart so com-

pletely when the management retrogressed. And the management's action, although it may not have been wise, was certainly an understandable response to what had become an uncomfortable situation. Along with the improved production in the paint room had come a host of embarrassments. The extra production in the paint room had created a pile-up in front and a vacuum behind, and both results were unwelcome to the adjoining departments. The wage structure of the plant had been shaken. The prestige of the engineers had suffered, and some of the prerogatives of management were apparently being taken over by employees.

It is clear from this instance that *local* improvements can often be obtained by the methods described here; but it is also clear that they may not lead to benefits for the enterprise as a whole. Changes in one part of an integrated organization may require widespread changes elsewhere, and the cost of such readjustments may far outbalance the benefits received in the local situation.

The changes made in the paint room implied overall managerial attitude and philosophy that were not in fact present. This being the case, there was no conceptual or philosophic resource for dealing with the eventual implications of what had been done in the paint room. The management neither expected nor was ready to make the kind of changes that seemed necessary. It would have been far better if the consultant had done with the relevant management group what he had done with the foreman in the initial discussions, so that there would have been some shared understanding of the long-range implications of the moves. In a real sense, the superintendent was justified in feeling that the foreman and the consultant between them had put him on the spot. True, his assent to the changes had been secured, but the consultant had not been sufficiently concerned with his genuine understanding of the possible consequences.

The factory is a social system, made up

of mutually dependent parts. A drastic change in one part of the system—even a change that is viewed as highly successful within that part—may give rise to conflict reactions from other parts of the system. It may then be dangerous for management to try a new approach in one small part of the system unless it is prepared to extend this approach to the whole organization.

Can the group methods that have been so successfully applied in small groups and single departments be applied on a factory-wide scale? We shall seek to answer that question in subsequent chapters.

----

* This chapter was written by George Strauss, based upon information furnished him by the consultant in the story, Alex Bavelas. The consultant also reviewed and revised the chapter.

[1] These subsequent meetings were effective largely because of the reduced tension and the goodwill engendered by the original discussions.

17 Vertical and Horizontal Communication in Formal Organizations*

By RICHARD L. SIMPSON

* * *

Writings on formal organization have stressed communication up and down the line of authority. Instructions move down, information moves up. When two men on the same level communicate, they are supposed to do it indirectly. If Supervisor A must communicate with Supervisor B, the communication goes up one chain from A, then down another to B, with their common superior linking the two chains at the top. According to this view, there is little direct communication between equals, except small talk which is not related directly to work problems.

This process is admittedly cumbersome, but advantages are claimed for it. As Miller and Form explain:

Although communication between departments on the same level occurs, theoretically it is not supposed to be direct. Reports, desires for services, or criticisms that one department has of another are supposed to be sent up the line until they reach an executive who heads the organizations involved. They are then held, revised, or sent directly down the line to the appropriate officials and departments. The reason for this ciruitous route is to inform higher officials of things occurring below them.[1]

From the literature, one infers that most communications not only should be, but are, vertical rather than horizontal,[2] but this appears to have been assumed, not demonstrated. If we examine the forerunners of modern writings on industry and bureaucracy, it is easy to see how such a belief has arisen. Among the main forerunners are Max Weber's work on bureaucracy[3] and writings on military organization, public administration, and personnel management.[4] These sources embody much the same viewpoint in that they are concerned with control, accountability, and authority. Bureaucracy, to them, is efficient because it specifies who is responsible to whom, for precisely what activities. From this implicit perspective it is easy to assume that the great advantage of bureaucracy—and the great desid-

Reprinted from "Vertical and Horizontal Communication in Formal Organizations," by permission of the author and publisher, Administrative Science Quarterly, 4 (September, 1959), pp. 188–96.

eratum in managing one—is the centralization of control so that those on top know exactly what is going on beneath them. This control is best achieved, it might seem, if everyone adheres strictly to the chain of command. It is understandable if writers steeped in this orientation adopt it as their own and assume further that what ought to be, is.

In this paper we shall explore this assumption. The procedure followed will be, first, to test the hypothesis that work-related communications between officials are more often vertical than horizontal; second, to venture an explanation of the results of the test; and, third, to resolve a seeming contradiction in recent research on industrial communications, proposing a new hypothesis concerning mechanization and automation as determinants of supervisory communication patterns.

Research Setting

Interviews were conducted with supervisors in the spinning department of a

defects, and transport the full bobbins to the textile department for final touches.

The supervisors who were studied are listed below, with a description of their responsibilities. Each position is designated by a letter corresponding to its level in the hierarchy. The plant operated continuously, with three shifts working each day, so that some positions were occupied by more than one man, one for each shift. A chain-of-command chart of spinning supervisors is shown in the following figure.

Positions and duties in the spinning department

Level A

A. *General foreman,* in charge of the spinning department. Each day he posted brief written instructions covering the work of the entire department. In addition, he was the immediate superior or B–1, B–2, and C–5— the man to whom they felt responsible and to whom they came if they needed authoritative advice. A worked the day shift only, Monday through Friday.

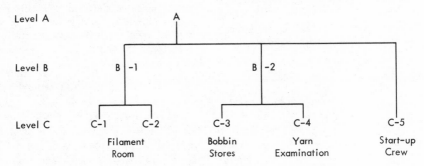

Organization Chart of Spinning Department Supervisors

synthetic textile mill. Spinning was one of three production departments in the mill: chemical, spinning, and textile. The chemical department prepared a liquid which passed through jets, cooled into solid thread, and finally wound onto whirling bobbins in the spinning department. The spinning department's job was to remove these yarn-filled bobbins from the machines, replace the full bobbins with empty ones, inspect the yarn for

Level B

B–1. *Shift foreman,* in charge of the filament room, where bobbins filled with yarn were removed from the machines and replaced with empty bobbins. Under his direct command were two first-line supervisors in the filament room, C–1 and C–2. Position B–1 was occupied by four men, one for each shift. The shifts rotated on a schedule so that during a 24-day period each group of shift workers worked six days in the daytime, then six days in the evening, then six days on the graveyard shift, then were off duty six days.

B–2. *Yarn examination and bobbin stores supervisor.* In salary classification, B–2 was one level below B–1, but in the hierarchy of command he was of the same rank, intermediate between the general foreman and the first-line supervisors. Under his direct supervision were C–3, foreman in charge of bobbin stores, and C–4, foreman in charge of yarn examination. B–2 worked the daylight hours only, Monday through Friday. At the close of each day the left written instructions for the night shifts.

Level C

C–1 and C–2. *Filament foremen.* These were first-line supervisors, each supervising the work of about 20 women in the filament room. Their immediate superior was B–1. They were shift workers; therefore there were four men holding each position, one on each shift.

C–3. *Bobbin-stores foreman.* This first-line supervisor was in charge of the group which maintained a supply of bobbins in good condition and sent bobbins to the filament room as needed. There was one foreman per shift, four in all. The immediate supervise for C–3 was B–2.

C–4. *Yarn-examination foreman.* This first-line foreman supervised the women who examined yarn for quality as it passed from the filament room to the textile department. There was one C–4 per shift. The immediate superior for C–4 was B–2.

C–5. *Start-up crew foreman.* C–5 supervised eight men who shut down and started the filament machines whenever a change was made in the type of yarn being produced. These machine changes were always made in the daytime; therefore C–5 worked the daylight hours only, Monday through Friday, and was responsible directly to A.

Research Procedure

Each supervisor was asked how many *work-related contacts* he had with every other supervisor. The question was: "About how often do you talk with ——— on business? Don't include times when you just say hello or pass the time of day; just the contacts needed to get

your work done. . . . What kinds of things do you talk about with him?" Shift workers were told that the question referred only to times when they were on the daylight shift, so as to equalize the times available for contacts between all positions. All interviewing was done in the daytime. If the answer given was indefinite, such as "often" or "hardly ever," the interviewee was asked to estimate a *specific number* for his average daily or weekly contacts. In this way information was obtained on the frequency and purpose of contacts between every pair of supervisors.

Findings and Interpretation

Table 1 shows the numbers of vertical and horizontal work-related contacts of each supervisor, the proportion of these contacts which were vertical, and the "expected" proportion which would have been vertical if each man had distributed his contacts equally among the other men. Our hypothesis that communication between officials is more often vertical than horizontal cannot be rejected; but neither can it be accepted without qualification.

The contacts of the three men at the higher levels—A, B–1, and B–2—were overwhelmingly vertical; but they could hardly have been otherwise. A, being the only man at his level, could not possibly have any horizontal contacts.[5] B–1 and B–2 could communicate horizontally only with each other, but they could communicate downward with several foremen and upward with A. They seldom had to communicate with each other, since the work relations between their sections were coordinated mainly through horizontal contacts between their subordinates, as we shall see later.

On the C-foreman level most contacts were horizontal except those of C–3, the bobbin-stores foreman. Three of these five foremen—C–1, C–2, and C–5—had markedly fewer vertical and more horizontal contacts than would have occurred on the chance expectation that every man communicates equally with every other man. The contacts of C–4 were mainly horizontal, in about the same proportion as would be expected on the basis of chance. (Our calculation of expected ratio of vertical to total contacts is based on a purely statistical notion of probability and has no necessary relation to the logic of administration. Empirically, no one would really expect to find all supervisors communicating equally often with all other supervisors.)

The preponderance of horizontal communications reported by four of the five first-line foremen (level C) is understandable if we examine the content of the communications they reported. Very few communications involved the issuing of commands or the reporting of results— the standard types of vertical communications. Most contacts of men at level C involved either (1) joint problem-solving or (2) coordination of work flow between sections. These were mainly horizontal communications.

Joint problem-solving communication was described by C–1, a filament foreman,

in explaining his contacts with C–2, the other filament foreman:

> We get together on a lot of problems. If a machine is acting up, or labor is short and we have to make sure all the machines are properly covered, we talk things over. Things are coming up all the time that we have to work out together.

It is noteworthy that they worked out these problems without consulting or informing their superior.

Coordination of work flow between sections often required horizontal contacts. The yarn-examination foreman (C–4) might notify a filament foreman (C–1 or C–2) that he was about to run out of yarn for examination. A filament foreman might ask the bobbin-stores foreman (C–3) when he could expect to receive a supply of cleaned bobbins. The start-up crew foreman (C–5) and a filament foreman might discuss the next start-up of a filament-spinning machine.

Thus contacts of men at the upper levels were mainly vertical, whereas contacts of men at the lower level were

TABLE 1
Estimated contact frequencies of spinning-department supervisors

Position	Total contacts per week	Vertical contacts per week	Horizontal contacts per week	Proportion of contacts vertical	Expected proportion vertical†
A	12.8	12.8	0	1.000	1.000
B–1	40.0	37.0	3.0	.925	.857
B–2	22.0	19.0	3.0	.864	.857
C–1	30.5	10.0	22.5	.330	.429
C–2	32.6	11.1	21.5	.341	.429
C–3	27.6	15.6	12.0	.565	.429
C–4	20.6	8.6	12.0	.417	.429
C–5	12.5	3.0	9.5	.240	.429
Total	198.6	117.1	81.5	.590	.607

* Estimated contact frequencies for each pair of supervisors were obtained by averaging the estimates made by each man; i.e., by adding the two men's estimates and dividing by two. The estimates of the two men in each reciprocal relationship were in most cases slightly discrepant, but no man in any pair claimed more than twice as many contacts between the two as the other claimed. In the case of "shift" positions occupied by more than one man, the different men's estimates were substantially alike; therefore the figures are felt to be reasonably accurate, though not precise.

† Based on the expectation that every supervisor will communicate an equal amount and divide his communication equally among all other supervisors.

mainly horizontal. There remains one exception. C–3, a first-line supervisor, had more vertical than horizontal contacts. Apparently this was because of his position in the work flow. The bobbin-stores section of C–3 was often under pressure to furnish bobbins to the filament-spinning section, but C–3 could not control the number of bobbins he received from the textile department for cleaning. Therefore, bobbin stores at times became a bottleneck. When this happened, C–3 sought help from his superior, B–2, who could contact the textile department and try to speed up the flow of bobbins. Problems requiring the attention of B–2 rarely arose in yarn examination, the section supervised by his other subordinate, C–4. The flow of work into yarn examination was set by filament spinning alone and was fairly steady, unlike the flow of work into bobbin stores, which was irregular and required coordination with both the textile department and the filament-spinning section. For these reasons B–2 had more downward contacts with one of his subordinates than with the other, and C–3 had more upward contacts than anyone else on his level.

Discussion

Our thesis has been that writers on formal organization have overemphasized vertical communication, in which instructions are given and reports are made, while underemphasizing horizontal communication, in which problems are ironed out and work-flow processes are coordinated. In the case we have described, communications of first-line foremen were mainly horizontal because of the mechanized nature of the work. In the spinning department, few instructions were necessary. Each day the general foreman (A) wrote instructions for the entire supervisory force. These instructions actually consisted of information, stating which machines were to produce what kinds of yarn. This brief information told each filament foreman and the start-up crew foreman what to do for the whole day.

Beyond that, instructions were seldom needed. The machines set the pace in filament spinning and yarn examination. Only in bobbin stores, where the work depended on coordination with another department, were frequent contacts between the foreman and his superior crucial.

This case helps to clear up an apparent contradiction between recent findings by Blau[6] and Faunce.[7] Blau states that in assembly-line work, in contrast to relatively unmechanized work, the machine sets the pace so that the foreman's command function is minimized and he becomes primarily an expediter and joint problem-solver. This situation parallels the one observed in the spinning department. Faunce, on the other hand, finds that in highly automated automobile factories there is more direct supervision than in nonautomated (but assembly-line) auto factories. Thus an increase in mechanization results in less supervision according to Blau, but in more supervision according to Faunce.

That the contradiction is more apparent than real becomes evident if we examine the data adduced by Blau, Faunce, and the present writer carefully. Blau and the author find that when there is extensive mechanization, such as that in a traditional auto assembly line or a modern synthetic textile mill, the machine sets the pace so that the need for direct supervision is at a minimum. Faunce is not denying this; he is actually discussing something different. He finds that automation—i.e., mechanization beyond the degree found in the traditional assembly line—increases the frequency and seriousness of machine breakdowns, since the machines are more complex and more interdependent than in old-style assembly-line plants. The machine breakdowns require vertical supervisory communication. Since Blau and Faunce are dealing with different degrees of mechanization, it is not surprising that they find different supervisory patterns in their different industrial settings.

This discussion suggests the following hypothesis: Mechanization reduces the need for close supervision (vertical communication), since instead of the foreman the machines set the work pace; but automation (i.e., extreme mechanization) increases the need for vertical communication, to deal with the frequent and serious machine breakdowns. This hypothesis might be stated as a typology: (a) low mechanization, high vertical communication rate; (b) medium mechanization (e.g., the traditional assembly line or the spinning department described above), low vertical communication; (c) high mechanization (i.e., automation), high vertical communication. Comparative research would be needed to test the validity of this typology and discover the precise conditions under which it holds.

---

* Revision of a paper presented to the American Sociological Society, Seattle, August 28, 1958. The data used here were gathered for a doctoral dissertation, "A Study of Supervisory Reorganization in a Factory Production Department" (University of North Carolina, 1956), under the direction of E. William Noland, to whom the author is indebted as well as to Jack L. Dyer and Ida Harper Simpson for helpful suggestions and criticisms.

1 Delbert C. Miller and William H. Form, *Industrial Sociology* (New York: Harper & Row, Publishers, 1950), p. 158.

2 *Ibid.*, see also Burleigh B. Gardner and

David G. Moore, *Human Relations in Industry* (Chicago: Richard D. Irwin, Inc., 1950), p. 43; and Wilbert E. Moore, *Industrial Relations and the Social Order* (New York: The Macmillan Company, 1951), p. 94.

3 See Max Weber, "Bureaucracy," in *From Max Weber: Essays in Sociology,* trans. H. H. Gerth and C. Wright Mills (New York: Oxford University Press 1946).

4 For examples of traditional thinking about line organization from these fields, see John Robert Beishline, *Military Management for National Defense* (New York: McGraw-Hill Book Company, 1950); Luther Gulick, "Notes on the Theory of Organization," in Luther Gulick and L. Urwick, eds., *Papers in the Science of Administration* (New York: Institute of Public Administration, 1937); and Walter Dill Scott and Robert C. Clothier, *Personnel Management* (New York: McGraw-Hill Book Company, 1926).

5 He had horizontal contacts with the chemical- and textile-department general foremen, but this analysis concerns only within-department contacts. Our impression is that most cross-department contacts at all levels were horizontal. In addition, A had vertical contacts with his superior as did all men at level C with the operatives they supervised.

6 Peter M. Blau, "Formal Organization: Dimensions of Analysis," *American Journal of Sociology,* 62 (July, 1957), pp. 58–59.

7 William A. Faunce, "Automation in the Automobile Industry," *American Sociological Review,* 23 (1958), pp. 401–407. William H. Form, in discussion from the floor at the convention where an earlier version of this paper was presented, pointed out the relevance of Faunce's study. His comments led us to revise our original conclusions, but he is in no sense to be held responsible for our analysis.

18 Demotion in Industrial Management*

by Fred H. Goldner

* * *

Organizations, like societies, face a problem of maintaining standards of behavior without destroying motivation or causing alienation. They must balance the

Reprinted with permission from the American Sociological Review, *30:5 (October, 1965) 714–25.*

inducement[1] offered by the promise of successs through upward mobility against the fear of failure invoked by the threat of downward mobility. Discussions of mobility in society have treated success and failure as separate issues, emphasizing on the one hand the functions of stratification systems in motivating people to fill important roles,[2] and, on the other, the role of downward mobility, uncertainty of success, and failure to reach culturally defined goals in producing deviant behavior.[3]

But in analyzing organizations, if not societies,[4] success and failure cannot be treated separately. The narrower boundaries of organizations and the precariousness of their existence make more crucial the problem of maintaining standards of behavior without alienating participants or destroying their motivation. One organizational incumbent frequently succeeds at the expense of another.[5] And to maintain standards of performance organizations occasionally must eliminate incompetent incumbents through such mechanisms as discharge and demotion.[6]

Unless organizations can legitimize failure, then, or at least a significant proportion of it, they risk deviant acts or withdrawal on the part of the participants. My purpose in this paper is to explore some of the ways in which organizations make demotion socially acceptable. The materials are drawn from a case study of the management of a large, rapidly growing industrial organization (currently over 50,000 employees) with facilities throughout the country in manufacturing, research, and sales. The firm manufactures many different but related products, and consequently, like similar companies, it is characterized by somewhat vague and overlapping lines of authority.

The data come largely from interviews conducted with seventy managers and executives and from unhindered observations of these men and other management personnel in their day-to-day activities over a period of fourteen months. The seventy managers and executives were located in two divisions of the company. They include the operating head of each division and the executives on two levels directly below him at headquarters. In one of the divisions men on the next two lower levels of management, both located in the field, were included.[7] The lowest

level of management represented by the respondents was classified by the company as second-line managerial. Salesmen report directly to them, and at least one first-line service manager also reports to them. At a later point, the field work was supplemented by a questionnaire administered to a sample of 343 executives and managers in *all* the divisions and functional areas of the company.[8]

Opposing Pressures

To meet competition, organizations must establish standards of performance. And the pursuit of excellence tends to create an intense internal competition in which each manager and executive must continually compete for his position with those below him. Under this system, merely adequate performance is insufficient. As one executive[9] put it: "We have a problem with people who are adequate, when you have others who could do an outstanding job." Carried to an extreme such a system results in insecurity and high turnover.

The pressure toward intense competition among the members of the organization produces a counter-pressure—the need for stability and security—which increases with the average age and length of service of managers and executives.[10] Management generally, and in this firm in particular, is inclined to take care of those who have contributed so much to the organization in the past. Given some minimal degree of efficiency, this pressure tends to produce a situation in which managers are permitted to remain as long as they perform adequately. Typical is one manager's comment about another below him:

I've worked with him a year to save him. Some guys you bust your butt to help— maybe to the point of hurting the business instead of being hard-hearted. Plus, when you get to be a business this big, just because our business changes we don't take a guy and put him in something he can't do.

A harder line is taken by those starting

out in management and by those at the top, who are under heavy pressure to maintain specific profit levels.[11] Those on the way up soon become dissatisfied with low rates of demotion, as one such manager indicates:

> The main complaint I have with the division at the branch and district-manager level is we have less adequate management than we could have. You have to lay the blame on headquarters. In the other division they cut throats as fast as they turn around. This is the way it's going to have to be in this division.

Perhaps the classic example of the open and continuously competitive type of system to which this man refers is in professional athletics. The boxer must meet all challengers. The football player's job is threatened by each new crop of recruits. But even here, mechanisms are developed to protect the incumbents. The champion boxer may be able to stall for such long periods of time that boxing associations find it necessary to issue ultimata. Veteran football players devise ways to put rookies "in their place."

Movement in the direction of relying solely on criteria of excellence creates a number of problems for the organization. The harder line adds a burden of personal risk and pressure to higher positions that must be compensated for in some manner, to enhance managers' willingness to assume the responsibilities of certain positions. Perhaps the greatest threat to organizational effectiveness in this type of structure is that it will create an atmosphere of fear, leading decision makers to prefer conservative alternatives.

Movement toward accepting "adequate" performance at the expense of excellence also creates problems for the organization. Not only is efficiency apt to decline, but dissatisfaction may spread among those in the lower echelons who resent the lack of opportunities to move up, especially when those above are thought to be inferior. As one executive put it:

If there is someone in management who isn't pulling his weight, then it is unfair to the multitude of people. There are so many people vying for so few jobs.

In the context of these opposing pressures—one favoring a competitive system based on the norm of excellence and the other favoring criteria of adequate performance—the organization must cope with failure and the task of maintaining efficiency.

This company rarely exerts its right to discharge management personnel, relying instead on the less severe mechanism of demotion. Not one of our respondents ever indicated a fear of being discharged from the company, although many were concerned about their positions within it. Demotion, in turn, is made more tolerable because a second company practice is to promote from within. These managers and executives had already performed satisfactorily, or better, at a lower level in the organization. One executive offered: "Having been successful enough to get the job, I wouldn't feel I was an utter disgrace for having failed on the job." A manager summed up a more general feeling:

> No one is getting fired if his intent is right. This is damn important. We are all stockholders and all of us have chosen this company as a career company and some of us have passed a point of no return. If we get fired, where do we go?

I have no firm evidence, but comments like these suggest that extreme anxiety is alleviated by combining employment security with uncertainty of position, while at the same time personnel are motivated to produce, to remain flexible, and to innovate. If employment security were at stake the pressure would be to work hard but also to "play it safe," and security of both employment and position would weaken incentives to produce and innovate.

The point of balance between security and efficiency required in this kind of profit-seeking industrial firm is different from that required in other kinds of organizations or even in some of the professional units within this organization. For example, universities explicitly provide tenure and do not have a complex series of offices within which to move faculty members. Since personnel are expected to "produce" innovative and challenging research, which may threaten the status quo, the balance point must be such as to provide as much security as possible to the incumbents. Thus, having proved his competence a man does not have to compete with these below. Without this security, researchers, teachers, and scholars might find it difficult to hold ideas at odds with those currently fashionable or to develop new ones.[12]

Accepting demotion

One of the most important findings in this study was that these management employees accept the real possibility of a demotion in their career. They saw demotion as a normal part of their future. They envisaged a fairly standard mobility curve that ascended, leveled off for a while, and then descended slightly. One statement by a manager illustrates this view:

In I don't move up I will eventually move backward. There is no standing still. Someplace along the line the curve is going to start downward—of effort and productivity on my part. If I am here ten years from now, I would be better off out of here in something else before they give me a fast slip on a banana peel. I'm not criticizing the company. It is the type of organization that enables us to earn as much as we do and peak out. The average industrial climate in America has a peak earning *after* 55.

Those in sales management, still compensated by some form of commission plan, are in an especially difficult situation. Their earnings curve may decline sharply at its end, since commission earnings generally exceed the straight salary earnings of others in management.[13]

Most importantly, the culture of the

TABLE 1

Views of their Chances of Demotion Expressed by 70 Executives and Managers in Interviews (in percentages)

Chances of Demotion	Headquarters Executives	District Managers	Local Managers
Good Chance	63	64	59
No Chance	8	7	3
Uncertain, or demotion not discussed	29	29	38
Total	100	100	100
(N)	(24)	(14)	(32)

organization encompasses a belief in the normality, almost the inevitability, of demotion. Sixty-three per cent of the executives who were interviewed at headquarters foresaw the possibility. (See Table 1.) Their attitude is best expressed by the one who reported:

In my circumstances, you have to be stupid not to look to the future and not to have a philosophy about it. For a man to be in it and not develop a philosophy about moving up or down—he would be a nut.

The view of headquarters from the field reinforces this image. Witness this observation by a field manager:

I like this job and realize it isn't a lifetime one and I will have to go either up or down. From what I gather in looking at [headquarters'] assignments, you have every opportunity to peak out at forty-five to fifty. You have every opportunity to fall on your head. Realistically for 99 per cent it does peak out.

The survey of 343 managers and executives also indicates that demotion is considered a normal phenomenon. The respondents were asked to indicate the probability of their being demoted sometime in their career on an 11-point scale ranging from zero (no chance at all) to ten (extremely good chance). Forty-seven per cent of them see at least a pretty good chance for their own demotion, responding in the 5-to-10 point range. (See Table 2.)

Even managers who are certain they

will continue to move up become strangely ambivalent over the possibility of going the other way:

> Your replacement is always around the corner. You can't just sit back but have to stay on the stick. I've never thought of going downward. I certainly realize the possibility

[the company] and has no money saved develops into the greatest "yes" man in the business. He can't afford to step on toes or to be canned.

Somewhat surprisingly, the questionnaire data indicate no clear relation between perceived chances of promotion

TABLE 2
Chances of Demotion as Seen by Survey Respondents (N = 343)

What are the chances
that sometime in your
career in [this company]
you might be demoted?

No chance at all:						Extremely good chance:	
			Scale				
0	1–2	3–4	5	6–7	8–9	10	Total
			Percentage				
8	23	22	25	10	8	4	100

always exists but I have no intention of going in that direction.

or:

> Leveling off hasn't entered my mind. I don't feel I have reached the limits of my abilities or desires. It will be reached some day but not necessarily. Our corporation is not famous for letting people grow old in their job.

The interviewees also point out that a belief in the possibility of demotion makes individuals within the organization more flexible and consequently more inclined to take risks:

> If you have this attitude you're a better manager and you're not afraid of the future. A guy who at fifty is solely dependent on

and those of demotion. Individuals who see no chance of being demoted and individuals who see a good chance of being demoted do not differ in the chances they see for a promotion in the near future. (See Table 3.) The absence of an inverse relation between perceived chances of promotion and demotion is further evidence that acceptance of demotion is culturally supported, making it possible to entertain simultaneously the possibilities of future success and failure.

Acceptance of demotion is due largely to mobility patterns throughout the organization, and these patterns, in turn, arise from a number of organizational and personal conditions. Some may be unique to this organization or at least to

TABLE 3
Chances of Promotion According to Chances of Demotion (in percentages)

	Chances of Promotion within Next Two Years							
Chances of Future Demotion	No Chance at all: 0	1–2	3–4	5	6–7	Extremely Good Chance: 8–9	10	Total(N)
None at all (0 on scale)	16	4	8	20	8	24	20	100 (25)
Some Chance (1–5 on scale)	2	15	12	24	18	21	9	101 (244)
Good Chance (6–10 on scale)	1	18	15	7	21	22	16	100 (73)

its present situation. I shall deal with these conditions in the remainder of this paper.

Organizational Adaptations

Mechanisms for obscuring demotions.

One of the chief devices by which the organization copes with the potential strains of demotion is to cloak the demotion in a good deal of ambiguity. By reducing the visibility of demotions the organization softens their potentially disruptive features.[14] Contributing to this ambiguity is constant movement through positions (especially lateral movement) which prevents individuals from clearly identifying a move as a demotion.

That expectations of lateral movement are part of the organizational culture can be seen in Table 4. These data show that managers and executives are just as prone to expect lateral movement as promotion. Guessing whether a move was a demotion, a promotion, or a lateral is one of the common forms of gossip in this company. A move that caused a great deal of discussion involved a high executive who was replaced, given a temporary assignment, and a few months later assigned to a position that reported directly to his successor. The discussion centered upon the novelty of such an obvious demotion, and the con-

jecture among discussants was that the individual must have requested the move. "The company wouldn't force such a thing."

Some moves are so ambiguous that observers mistakenly interpret them as demotions, or the "demoted" man may fail to recognize his loss of status or that others define his move as a demotion. This ambiguity was vividly demonstrated during a discussion between myself and a company executive. The executive received a phone call from a recently demoted friend who sought advice. After closing the call he turned in astonishment: The caller had said he was asking for advice because he knew the executive had been through a demotion. The executive then recounted all his moves, maintaining that none of them was a demotion as far as he was concerned.

Organizational participants recognize this pattern of ambiguity. In the words of one manager who was afraid he might soon be demoted:

If it broke over [a particular issue] they would demote me and I would take it and go along with it. I wouldn't like it. It would be a bitter pill, wouldn't it? I'll say one thing. There is no set pattern [of demotion] in this company. That is for sure. I think this is good. I think it is real flexible.

The ambibuity of moves is in part due

TABLE 4
Chances of Promotion and of Laterals (N=342)

			Scale				
No chance at all:						Extremely good chance:	
0	1–2	3–4	5	6–7	8–9	10	Total
			What are the chances that you will be promoted within the next two years?				
			Percentage				
3	14	12	20	18	21	11	99
			What are the chances that you will make a lateral move sometime in the future?				
			Percentage				
3	10	9	19	17	27	15	100

to the changing structure of large American industrial corporations generally. In many organizations clear-cut lines of authority no longer exist, nor are positions arranged in a clear hierarchial line that leaves no doubt of the status of each one. Boundaries of responsibility overlap and are in a constant state of flux.[15]

Ambiguity is fostered not only by diversification but also by company growth resulting in the creation of many new jobs and positions, and in most divisions of this company growth has been considerable. In divisions that have not grown, managers feel more insecure about their future. One manager posed the problem in referring to the opportunities in another division:

> No one has told *me* what will happen [in my future] just like I can't tell the salesman. We don't have the laterals the other division has.

Growth may be encouraged in the first place by attempts to deal with demotion. Organizational expansion occurs not only to meet production or profit goals but also to meet personnel "needs." Providing for employees' ambitions and cushioning the failure of those demoted leads to the creation of new positions in the organization. An executive brought this out in discussing the reasons for the search for new products:

> In broadening the base there will be places for men who can no longer run as salesmen or manager but who have something to contribute. There are many branch managers in the other division who moved into staff jobs. They are paid fine salaries but not the pressure of a branch office. Now in our division we don't have this.

Organizational expansion in response to the motivational needs of personnel might be called personnel-directed growth, or better still—*organizational "Lebensraum"*—as distinct from market directed growth produced by increased demand for the organization's goods and services and from diversification prompted by financial stability.

If the number of available positions ceases to grow, alternative mechanisms for creating ambiguity about moves are still available. Moving managers who are obviously "on the way up" into the same jobs as persons who are thought to be on the way down increases ambiguity. As a result the job itself offers no cue to onlookers as to the incumbent's true status.

One division of the company had utilized one of its geographical locations to "retire" men who could no longer meet the standards of excellence, only to run into trouble when it became known as a "dumping ground." The effectiveness of that operation was essentially destroyed until the organization started to send men on the way up to the same location, mixing them in with those who had been demoted.[16] An old-timer who is sent there now may recognize this as a demotion, but at least it is an effective operation, not one where everyone has given up. Thus, filling similar positions with both successes and failures creates an intermediary level and cushions the shock of demotion. It provides a substitute for the special positions that might be available in a growing and complex organization.

Other techniques have also been used to create ambiguity.[17] Actions typically seen as rewards for success are also sometimes used to compensate for demotion, e.g. a "trip to Europe." Managers sent for training outside the company included those being prepared for greater responsibilities and those who required a period away from the company to adjust to disappointment. Money is also used: "Some people are doing just as well in money, so it [their demotion] is not so bad."

Another major technique used to create an atmosphere of ambiguity and uncertainty might be called "zig-zag" mobility. This is the combination of a demotion with a subsequent promotion.[18] The possibility of subsequent promotions makes the adaptation process much easier for a demoted individual. Belief in the "zig-zag" pattern and acceptance of it has become part of the organizational value structure: Over half (51 per cent) of the managers and executives surveyed saw more than a fair chance (5 to 10 on the 0–10 scale) of moving back up for someone in their position who had been demoted. More important, this pattern helps set the climate for risk-taking. A manager who had undergone this kind of mobility related his experience:

> I never agreed it [my demotion] was a fair thing to begin with. I defended myself too strongly perhaps. The thing that bothered me was there was no good reason. It was quite a decision to stay in the company. I pushed it all aside and five years later made District Manager.

This "zig-zag" mobility is a natural phenomenon in a widely dispersed, diversified organization that contains many lines of "skill" and authority as well as a social acceptance of demotion.[19]

Acceptance of decline as inevitable may be conditioned by the presence or absence of a base to which the incumbent can return. As Max Weber pointed out, it is easier for a lawyer to risk defeat in politics than it is for a large-scale entrepreneur.[20] It is to this lack of a base that a group of managers, discussing demotion, referred when they mentioned the insecurity felt by specialists who go into general management. With the rapid advances being made in most fields today, a prolonged stay in general management leaves the ex-professional at a severe disadvantage if he must return to his specialty.

The vagueness of criteria for advancement.

The various mechanisms that obscure demotions, and so cushion their shock, also contribute to the vagueness of criteria for promotion. The absence of firm guides to advancement has both negative and positive consequences for the organization. One demoted executive, looking back on his demotion, commented on this vagueness:

> The problem with him [the boss] was learning what he wanted. Personally, I don't look

at this as a failure. I am learning how big business operates at this level [said sarcastically]. If I had it to do over, I would not have been so free with information. Each time I gave them some information it gave them the opportunity to ask another question and put you on the defensive. *Now I give them nothing unless I have to.*

Thus the uncertainty generated in a subordinate can have the negative consequence of motivating him to create ambiguity for those above. Withholding information from superiors certainly is a dysfunctional consequence of the ambiguity surrounding criteria of advancement.

Criteria for advancement became increasingly vague the higher the position in the organization.[21] And at the same time, the possibility of demotion increases. According to one high executive:

> The fellows right below this level recognize the possibilities of slipping [and know it when it happens. But] at this level and above you can stub your toe without being aware of it.

Those who are demoted or who are forced to anticipate it want to know why. As one executive said:

> They [should] recognize that when we get to this level we are big boys now and can take it. They should level and say why—we are prepared for it.

But offering reasons for demotions when the criteria are vague poses a difficult problem for those above. Some executives in the organization have raised the question of whether individuals should be informed of all the reasons for their demotion. This led to an interest in, as one executive put it: "The art of managerial control without heartbreak or ruin to the individual."[22] Management wanted to avoid forcing a superior to defend his judgment by using all the ammunition available to justify his decision. As Goffman describes the process in a mental institution, the man's record is searched for errors that will justify the action taken against him: "This dossier is apparently not regularly used, however, to record occasions when the patient showed capacity to cope honorably and effectively with difficult life-situations. Nor is the case record typically used to provide a rough average or sampling of his past conduct."[28] In a mental institution, however, the authorities want the patient to accept not only his confinement but also his "sickness," whereas industrial managers want a demoted individual to accept his demotion without resenting it to a degree that would reduce his effectiveness in another position. To cite only negative incidents from a man's record would undermine this objective.

Additional considerations inhibit disclosure of all the reasons for demotion. As Barnard has noted, the criteria for executive performance may refer primarily to ability to "fit in" with other executives.[24] Trying to make "fitting in" explicit is not only difficult but can also be embarrassing. So vague a criterion also increases the possibility of error, for the lack of fit may not be the individual's fault, or the present composition of the executive group may change.[25] *An organizational structure that permits zig-zag mobility has more opportunity to rectify such "mistakes."*

Personal Adaptations

Up to this point I have been discussing organizational arrangements that exist independently of particular individuals. A number of them make it easier for the "demoteds" to protect their pride and maintain their commitment to the organization. Regardless of what the organization does, however, many adaptations are worked out by individuals for themselves.[26]

The key to a demoted individual's ability to maintain his personal effectiveness lies in the process of self-redefinition —an adaptation that may occur in anticipating demotion as well as after the event.[27] An important prior adaptation is to emphasize the long hours and pressures

required as one goes up the ladder. Although most are willing to pay this price, they constantly refer to it. As one manager put it:

> Afetr having been exposed to the constant turmoil and problems connected to a growth business as rapid as ours is growing, I think there is a little more to life than what you have to give up to go into that echelon.

A higher management executive expressed his attitude even more specifically:

> I'd be an SOB if I would want to be general manager. It is the worst job I have ever seen in my life. It's unbelievable. He is twisted and torn and works from 8:00 A.M. to 11:00 P.M. all the time. Imagine having a job where your job is on the line on a problem and you have no time to think about it because you are on another problem.

Making comments on the "price" one must pay for moving up the career ladder makes it much easier to accept lack of mobility or demotion.

Anticipatory adaptations may be triggered by the demotion of an acquaintance:

> [He] had thought it never could happen to him. He wasn't mentally prepared. So I said I should [be]. If it happens what are you going to do? So every city I go to I make sure I make some friends and nice business contacts.

These prior or anticipatory adaptations will obviously be utilized by many in the organization who will never be demoted. The more such behavior takes place the greater the danger of a self-fulfilling prophecy. And as individuals stop exerting themselves to succeed or begin refusing to take risks, the organization loses some of its power. Such possibilities enhance the importance of the organizational mechanisms discussed above.

A common method of adaptation used by the respondents was to shift their attention to another "self." A man engages in a number of activities, of which his work may be only one. To compensate for a defeat in any one of these spheres of activity he may increase his investment in another sphere.[28] This is one of the chief reasons why many managers consider the West Coast and other "desirable" geographical assignments as ideal places to go after being demoted. Such locations afford special opportunities to shift attention to family and leisure activities.

One manager described the reaction of a subordinate manager he had demoted:

> There are a lot of ramifications in a demotion. [Before his demotion he] was critical of two other men who had been demoted with salary reductions and when they moved had bought more expensive homes— and yet he also did it. It was sort of an appeasement to the wife.

A shift of attention often requires a joint adaptation by the individual and his family. One executive said that he had to bring his wife into his plans only when he got to a higher management position, where the future was uncertain:

> All our wives are given this philosophy and share it. I never brought my wife into the business until I got this job. At [the previous job] I didn't have the responsibility. She knows the good things about it—that I like it and the prestige and I work for the family's future. The money, and pressures, and time away are not her ideas of the good things about it.

A similar adaptation is to shift one's interest to community activities. Sales managers, for example, not only shifted their interests to the community but also argued that other managers should do the same thing and that the company ought to supply more of the funds necessary to belong to community organizations. This proposition was usually couched in terms of increasing sales, but the men who offered it were those who were not going anywhere in the company.

The most difficult part of an individual's adaptation has to do with the people he must face. As one manager said about a demoted colleague who was scheduled to take a company-sponsored trip with a group of managers: "If I were him I wouldn't go. Everybody was ducking him."[29] Bystanders are frequently embarrassed in the presence of an acquaintance after his demotion and unsure of how to approach him. One present manager who had been demoted[30] recognized this embarrassment on the part of others, even though he was satisfied with the demotion:

> The only thing that bothered me is that when I left none of the people called me in to talk to me. I had the feeling it was a hush-hush thing, [and it was as if they were saying] quote: He is leaving headquarters and don't say anything, unquote. I don't want anybody to feel sorry for me but glad, because I certainly was.[31]

The organization is large enough to be able to move demoted individuals to other parts of the country. This facilitated adaptation by permitting demoted individuals to avoid encounters with those who had known them in their former capacity. This post-demotion adaptation, however, conflicts with one form of prior adaptation, for an individual who anticipates demotion and shifts his attention to the community faces the additional problem of withdrawing if he is subsequently demoted and sent elsewhere.

Summary

Patterns of mobility within an organization, including demotion, are a crucial part of its structure. I have described some aspects of the relations between demotion and the organizational need to maintain standards of competence as well as individual commitment in one large business firm. The willingness of managers and executives to accept demotion has enabled this organization to move them around to suit its productive needs without destroying individual commitment to the organization.

The potential dysfunctions of demotion tend to be minimized by organizational arrangements that make personnel movement ambiguous, by new positions created largely to fulfill the "ego needs" of personnel, and by the pattern I have identified as "zig-zag" mobility. Ambiguity regarding the meaning of moves has been enhanced by an absence of clear lines of authority which is characteristic of contemporary industrial organizations.

In addition to these structural arrangements for softening the blow of failure, various individual adaptations permit the demoted person to save face. One personal adaptation is, paradoxically, provided by the strong competition for higher management positions. This competition makes it necessary to spend so much energy and time on the job that an individual may find it relatively easy to forego the rewards offered at such a high price and thereby satisfy another culturally-endorsed value—spending time with one's family.

The possibility that alternative goal systems are commonly developed and substituted for the conventional goal of occupational success needs investigation, as does the evolution of conventional definitions of success and failure.[32] If all societies—and organizations—require some system of stratification, to place and motivate individuals, then consideration of the dysfunctions produced by stratification may suggest that alternative *unstratified* systems are also necessary. Perhaps all social systems necessarily include areas of endeavor that are unstratified, thus providing alternatives for those who cannot or do not wish to succeed in the stratified areas, yet must be kept within the system.

---

* I am indebted to David Caplovitz for invaluable suggestions and demands. I also wish to thank R. R. Ritti and Thomas Scheff for comments on an earlier version. This is a revised version of a paper presented at the annual meetings of the American Sociological Association, August, 1963.

1 For a discussion of such inducements, see James G. March and Herbert A. Simon, *Organizations* (New York: John Wiley & Sons, Inc., 1958), p. 99.

2 Kingsley Davis and Wilbert E. Moore, "Some Principles of Stratification," *American Sociological Review,* 10 (1945), pp. 242–249.

For later versions of this argument see Wilbert E. Moore, "But Some are More Equal Than Others," *American Sociological Review,* 28 (1963), pp. 13–18; and Melvin Tumin, "On Inequality," *American Sociological Review,* 28 (1963), pp. 19–26.

3 Robert K. Merton describes the deviance produced by failure to reach culturally defined goals in *Social Theory and Social Structure* (New York: Free Press of Glencoe, Inc., 1957), Ch. 4. For discussions of the relation between politically deviant behavior and downward mobility or uncertainty of success, see Daniel Bell, (ed.), *The Radical Right* (Garden City, N.Y.: Doubleday & Co., Inc., 1964), Chs. 1–4, 13, 14. Bruno Bettelheim and Morris Janowitz relate downward mobility to other types of deviant behavior in *Social Change and Prejudice* (New York: Free Press of Glencoe, Inc., 1964), pp. 29–34.

4 For example, people are assigned responsibility for managing systems of stratification in organizations but not in societies.

5 The bulk of the work previously devoted to career mobility within organizations has dealt with problems of turnover or succession and not with patterns of mobility or associated organizational adaptations. Among the exceptional attempts to deal with career mobility rather than succession are: Bernard Levenson, "Bureaucratic Succession" (despite its title), in Amitai Etzioni, ed., *Complex Organizations* (New York: Holt, Rinehart & Winston, Inc., 1961), pp. 362–395; and Norman H. Martin and Anselm L. Strauss, "Patterns of Mobility Within Industrial Organizations," in W. Lloyd Warner and Norman H. Martin, eds., *Industrial Man* (New York: Harper & Row, Publishers, Inc., 1959), pp. 85–101. Examples of studies of succession include: Alvin W. Gouldner, *Patterns of Industrial Bureaucracy* (New York: Free Press of Glencoe, Inc., 1954); Oscar Grusky, "Corporate Size, Bureaucratization, and Managerial Succession," *American Journal of Sociology,* 67 (1961), pp. 261–269; and Robert H. Guest, "Managerial Succession," *American Journal of Sociology,* 68 (1962), pp. 47–54.

Space limitations preclude consideration here of the important issues pertaining to strivers vs. nonstrivers. See, for example, Charles H. Coates and Roland J. Pellegrin, "Executives and Supervisors: Contrasting Definitions of Career Success," *Administrative Science Quarterly,* 1 (1957), pp. 506–517.

6 For a list of various kinds of demotion, see Douglas M. More, "Demotion," *Social Problems,* 9 (1962), pp. 213–221. Levenson, *op. cit.,* also deals with this issue. Demotion has received little attention, although most case studies that deal with management include references to demotion. Gouldner, *op. cit.,* p. 61, discusses the demotion of Bill Day. See also Melville Dalton, *Men Who Manage* (New

York: John Wiley & Sons, Inc., 1959), pp. 65, 170–172. Evidence of demotion in Russian industry is provided by Joseph S. Berliner, *Factory and Manager in the USSR* (Cambridge: Harvard University Press, 1957), p. 48; and Theodore Caplow and Reece J. McGee discuss it in a non-industrial setting in *The Academic Marketplace* (New York: Science Editions, 1961), pp. 51–52.

7 In one division all the men on the three top levels were interviewed; in the other, five of the top seventeen executives were omitted because of scheduling difficulties. Among the field group, all those reporting directly to headquarters were interviewed. On the next lower level interviews were carried out with a random sample of thirty-two from a total of 180, stratified by geographical location and numbers of employees.

8 The 343 respondents who returned the questionnaire represented 90 per cent of a 10 per cent random sample of this universe, which included the same levels of management that were included in the interviews.

9 I shall use the terms "executive" to refer to those at headquarters operations involved in the devision-making process as it affects large segments of the organization and "manager" to refer to those located in the field.

10 The organization is a relatively new one that has grown rapidly. Only recently have older men become a significant portion of management.

11 A similar conflict is taking place in the society at large, between the need for a higher economic growth rate, which requires acceptance of all technological innovations, and the consequent displacement of employees. Technological innovations seem to have been given priority, so that dissension is primarily between the private and public sectors of the economy with respect to responsibility for retraining and reallocating the displaced workers.

12 For a fictional account of the results of a system where professors, to hold their positions, must periodically meet any challenger from below in a competitive examination see George J. Stigler, "An Academic Episode," *AAUP Bulletin*, 33 (1947), pp. 661–665.

13 Careers with early peak earnings are also exemplified by professional athletes who must enter another field before forty and thereafter seldom equal their earnings as athletes. A crucial difference between sports and business, however, is that athletes expect their earnings to peak out early. In addition, when an athlete enters a new field his reference group changes. No stigma is attached to the loss of a physical ability through age.

14 For a discussion of functionally optimum degrees of visability see Merton, *op. cit.*, pp. 341–353.

15 Seventy per cent of the survey respondents responded in the 6–10 range on a 0–10 (ex-tremely false to extremely true) scale to the statement, "There is much overlapping responsibility in the company." An account of these conditions as encountered in the study of one particular management function is presented in Fred H. Goldner, "Industrial Relations and the Organization of Management" (unpublished doctoral dissertation, University of California, Berkeley, 1961), pp. 13–51.

16 Although this operating division of the company was growing in size it still was less complex than other divisions and had no opportunity to create special positions. The location in question lent itself to experimentation because its market characteristics distinguished it from the others. Highly competent employees shunned it until it was made a distinct step toward promotion. Here the ambiguity was a function of executive decision and not inherent in the nature of the work involved.

17 Some writers have taken strong issue with the presence of ambiguity in promotional systems. For a list of recommendations to reduce ambiguity in academic mobility, see Caplow and McGee, *op. cit.*, Ch. 11.

18 Professional baseball offers a clear example of zig-zag mobility. Even though the teams are in constant contact with one another, it is not unusual for a player to fail on one team and succeed on another. Players may also shift back and forth between the major and minor leagues. The position of team manager is most comparable to those in this study. A team manager released from one club is seen as a likely candidate for other teams, even those who finished higher in the standings.

19 March and Simon, *op. cit.*, p. 99, cover one aspect of this point in their proposition that "the larger the organization, the greater the perceived possibility of interorganizational transfer, and therefore, the less the perceived desirability of leaving the organization." They conclude by claiming that "a substantial amount of what would be called turnover in smaller firms is classified as 'interdepartmental transfer' in larger firms."

20 Max Weber, *From Max Weber; Essays in Sociology*, trans. and ed. by Hans H. Gerth and C. Wright Mills (New York: Oxford University Press, Inc., 1946), p. 85. The attempts of defeated union leaders to avoid the decline in status implied by such a defeat are treated by Seymour Martin Lipset, "The Political Process in Trade Unions: A Theoretical Statement," in Monroe Berger, Theodore Abel, and Charles H. Page, eds., *Freedom and Control in Modern Society* (Princeton, N. J.: D. Van Nostrand Co., Inc., 1954), pp. 82–124.

21 For one account of the kind of criteria used at the top of an organization see Chester I. Barnard, *The Functions of the Executive* (Cambridge: Harvard University Press, 1938), p. 224.

22 This conception is strikingly similar to

Erving Goffman's use of the term "cooling out" in "On Cooling the Mark Out: Some Adaptations to Failure," *Psychiatry,* 15 (1952), pp. 451–463. Clark used the same concept in a slightly different way, dealing with the function of an institution in the cooling-out process. The analogous process in the present study involves the large number of career paths that may be sought and achieved, including that of professionalization within the organization. Burton R. Clark, "The 'Cooling Out' Function in Higher Education," *American Journal of Sociology* 65 (1960), pp. 569–576.

23 Erving Goffman, *Asylums* (Garden City, N. Y.: Anchor Books, 1961, p. 155.

24 Barnard, *op. cit.*

25 An attempt to handle the notion of "fitting in" is made by the development of a concept of "person-set" in David Caplovitz, "Student-Faculty Relations in Medical School: A Study of Professional Socialization" (unpublished doctoral dissertation, Columbia University, 1961), Appendix F.

26 One conception of forms of individual adaptation to the similar phenomenon of blocked mobility in society is developed by Merton, *op. cit.,* Ch. 4. For accounts of personal adaptations to blocked mobility in organizations see Levinson, *op. cit.,* and Goldner, *op. cit.,* pp. 203–212.

27 See Goffman, "On Cooling the Mark Out," *op. cit.*

28 For an account of some of the shifts between work and other alternatives see Harold L. Wilensky, "Work, Careers, and Social Integration," *International Social Science Journal,* 12 (1960) pp. 543–560.

29 For an account of the relation between demotion and paranoia see Edwin M. Lemert, "Paranoia and the Dynamics of Exclusion," *Sociometry,* 25 (1962), pp. 2–20.

30 In this and the case mentioned above, the demotions were fairly obvious to others familiar with the individuals in their previous status. Not *all* moves are ambiguous; they vary from complete clarity of implication to total obscurity. But the ambiguous ones determine the organization's culture. Even in clear-cut cases like this one, demoted individuals were frequently sent to other locations. A separate study of specific moves is needed, to develop an index of ambiguity and to document the effects of different degrees of ambiguity.

31 This individual was happy because the demotion took him out of a situation that was ruining his health. An often-quoted study of the relation between striving and ulcers is Jurgen Ruesch *et al., Duodenal Ulcer* (Berkeley: University of California Press, 1948). The study shows that patients with ulcers were more likely to be climbers than statics or decliners. Unfortunately, no adequate comparisons were made with a normal population.

32 One such investigation deals with downward mobility and work careers, in an attempt to explain the optimism of the downwardly mobile. See Harold L. Wilensky and Hugh Edwards, "The Skidder," *American Sociological Review,* 24 (1959), pp. 215–231. Another important attempt to understand the process whereby success is defined is David C. McClelland, *The Achieving Society* (Princeton, N. J.: D. Van Nostrand Co., Inc., 1961).

19 Some Effects of Close and Punitive Styles of Supervision*

by ROBERT C. DAY and ROBERT L. HAMBLIN

Introduction

Close supervision was originally isolated and studied as a style or dimension of

Reprinted from "Some Effects of Close and Punitive Styles of Supervision," American Journal of Sociology, *69 (March, 1964), pp. 499–510, by permission of the authors and The University of Chicago Press.*

supervision by teams of researchers connected with the Survey Research Center at the University of Michigan and led by Daniel Katz.[1] In an early study of female workers in a large metropolitan insurance firm, Morse reported that workers subjected to a close supervision style were less satisfied with the supervisor's ability to handle people, less satisfied with the reasonableness of her expectations, and generally less satisfied with the rules she enforced.[2] These findings suggest a specific hypothesis that aggressive feelings are instigated by close supervision. Katz and Kahn reported finding this relationship between close supervision and aggressive feelings of workers in a tractor plant.[3] Furthermore, if lowered productivity is taken as a form of retaliatory aggression toward the supervisor, data reported earlier by Katz and his associates[4] are also consistent with this hypothesis. Gouldner produced evidence, from an illuminating study of a gypsum factory, that further supports the close supervision-aggression hypothesis.[5]

In the present study, close supervision is conceptualized as one end of a continuum that describes the degree to which a supervisor specifies the roles of the subordinates and checks up to see that they comply with the specifications. There are two other points of this continuum worth noting, however. The opposite extreme to close supervision might appropriately be termed "anomic supervision," as it would involve no specifications (that is, no expectations or norms) and no checkups. Somewhere in the middle area of this theoretical continuum, the general style of supervision can be postulated; it involves a moderate number of specifications and checkups, at least enough to let the workers know what they are supposed to do. Thus, in close supervision the attempt is to structure completely the workers' behavior and in general supervision to structure it only to the point where the worker does not feel at a loss as to what to do; in anomic supervision no attempt is made at all to structure the behavior. Although it would have been interesting, anomic supervision was not included in the present investigation because of the limits of time.

To account for the relationship between close supervision and aggressive feelings or actual aggression, a softened version of the frustration-aggression hypothesis can be used,[6] since close supervision apparently is frustrating to the subordinate. To the extent that it is frustrating, then, the subordinate should be instigated to aggress against the supervisor as the agent of frustration and, in some cases, perhaps actually to translate his impulses into direct aggression, such as angry words, or indirect aggression, such as a conscious retaliatory slowdown in productivity.

However, an important point to grasp here is that close supervision is not in itself aggression; for to be aggression, a manifest intention in applying it would necessarily be to hurt or injure the subordinate. But as Gouldner has suggested, the manifest intention involved in using the close style of supervision is probably to increase productivity.[7] The supervisor may not even be aware that his close supervision is frustrating, thus producing psychological pain or injury. In terms of intention or awareness, the close style of supervision may be contrasted with a second style, "punitive" supervision, which involves the intentional, conscious use of aggression to gain the compliance of subordinates.

To the extent that a supervisor enforces work specifications or rules by aggressing against those subordinates who depart from or violate the rules, he is using a punitive style of supervision. When the punitive supervisor uses aggression (most often in the form of angry, ego-lacerating reprimands), he is attempting to reinforce the avoidance of behavior that violates work rules. Thus, he is usually aware that his aggression is painful to the subordinate and is in effect saying to him, "I know this hurts, but it is your own doing. If you want to avoid it in the future, follow my rules." Because it is so painful, he is probably aware that his aggression instigates subordinates to counteraggress, but because of his authority to hire, fire, promote, or demote, he evidently also assumes ultimate victory in any aggressive exchange. Furthermore, since the workers are aware of his superior power, he counts upon their not wanting to start an aggressive exchange by counteraggressing.

Yet, unresolved tensions have a way

of being channeled into more subtle forms of indirent aggression that are not easily detected or eliminated, as, for example, when workers channel their aggressive impulses into conscious, retaliatory slowdowns in production. If artfully practiced, this form of aggression can hurt the supervisor badly while making it most difficult for him to fix blame or take active corrective measures. This evidently happened with railroad section-gangs studied by Katz and his associates, who found that foremen of low-producing gangs tended to use a punitive style of supervision.[8]

Thus far, we have postulated that aggression is the overall result of both the close and the punitive styles of supervision because both styles, whether intentionally or not, are painful to subordinates. Specifically, we have mentioned two forms of aggression: angry words and a conscious, retaliatory slowdown in production. But these may not be the only manifestations of aggression that result from the frustrations inherent in the close and punitive styles of supervision. Negative emotions often become displaced and consequently could magnify out of proportion the aggression that sometimes accompanies routine conflicts among workers. Furthermore, these emotions might also be displaced to magnify any incipient dissatisfaction with the work situation itself. Thus, in hypothesizing that both the close and the punitive styles of supervision result in increased aggression, we are actually predicting that they both result in (1) an increase in the amount of verbal aggression toward the supervisor, (2) a decrease in productivity, (3) an increase in verbal aggression toward co-workers, and (4) an increase in dissatisfaction with the work situation. In making our predictions we should note however, that Pepitone and Reichling found that relationshops based on displacement are usually weaker than the others.[9]

Although the close supervision-aggression hypothesis has been generally supported in a number of investigations, evidently the strength of the relationship is quite variable. Again, if lowered productivity is taken as an indication of indirect aggression, the data reported by Katz and his associates in 1950 show that a strong relationshop exists where the close versus general styles are used by second-line supervisors in their relations with section heads, but only a moderate relationship in relations between section heads and their subordinates.[10] Data from a second study in 1951 by Katz and associates indicate no relationship at all between close versus general supervision and worker aggression.[11] These variations seem to indicate that a third variable mediates the relationship between close supervision and aggression. In this instance, the mediator is probably a characteristic of the subordinate that influences the amount of frustration he experiences when he is subjected to close and perhaps punitive supervision. The rationale for suggesting self-esteem as the mediating variable is best understood in the context of Goffman's dramaturgical theory of social behavior.[12]

Using the theoretical metaphor extensively, Goffman views the behavior of persons in social contexts as a sequence of carefully guided performances serving to create a "front" or an impression. In attempting to create and maintain a satisfactory self-image, the individual tries to define the situation in such a way that he is able to guide and control the impressions that others obtain of him in the situation. The individual's concern, then, is to put his act over successfully, to maintain by various techniques a favorable, creditable self-image. Thus, in a bureaucratic situation the workers may be viewed as striving to project a self-image to the supervisor and to co-workers, "and the characteristic issue, the crucial concern, is whether it [the self-image] will be credited or discredited."[13]

From the assumption that the workers are attempting to project a creditable self-image, it follows that the close and punitive styles of supervision would be frustrating for two reasons. First, the styles imply a lack of competence, a lack of skill on the part of the worker. Second, they imply a lack of motivation on his part to do the right thing or, in fact, a kind of malicious motivation to do the wrong thing. Thus, when a subordinate is subjected to either of these two styles of supervision, his self-image may be discredited severely. Furthermore, he may be able to do very little to change the situation so that he can create a more favorable impression.

However, and this is the critical assumption, not all subordinates may be equally concerned with maintaining the front, with presenting a creditable self-image. Specifically, our assumption is that some individuals have such strong, favorable self-images, such high *self-esteem*, that they are relatively *unconcerned* with impression management, whereas other individuals have such ambiguous, ambivalent self-images, such low *self-esteem*, that they are *highly concerned* with impression management, with maintaining a front and thus projecting a creditable self-image. If so, the amount of frustration an individual experiences when subjected to close or punitive supervision should vary inversely with his self-esteem. Furthermore, since the strength of the postulated relationship between either style of supervision and aggression should be a function of the amount of frustration experienced,[14] the strength of the relationship should also be a function of the self-esteem of subordinates. Perhaps a simpler statement is: The association between the two styles of supervision and the various aggression variables should be relatively weak among subordinates who have high self-esteem but relatively strong among those with low self-esteem.

Method

The experimental groups

Twenty-four groups, each consisting of four women recruited from undergraduate classes and dormitories at Washington University, were used in the experiment.

Controls were applied for age (17–19 years) and years of schooling (freshmen and sophomores).

The experimental situation

At an appointed time each group arrived at the laboratory and was ushered into an experimental room designed to simulate reasonably well an industrial work station. Here the subjects were given a pre-experimental questionnaire and then task instructions. After these had been completed, each group worked at the task for a period of forty minutes and then completed a post-experimental questionnaire. The forty-minute experimental session included ten-minute periods with a supervisor (a trained member of the experimental staff) in the room and two intervening five-minute periods during which the supervisor left the room for the expressed purpose of evaluating the workers' production. Her absence, however, was designed to give the subjects a chance to be alone and thereby some freedom to express any aggressive feelings toward the supervisor or the experiment. Her exits and entrances were timed precisely with a stopwatch that she held in her hand and that, in addition to accurate timing, provided a note of precision and authority. As in a factory setting, an impersonal buzzer was used to signal the beginning and end of the work period.

The task consisted of assembling models of molecules using pegs, springs, and various colored balls provided in Sargent Kits, which are often used in university chemistry classes. Drawings of elaborate, complicated molecular structures were provided as "blueprints" for molecule construction. These models seemed to be novel and complex enough to interest and involve the subjects for the required forty-minute work period. The fact that the task was complex and naturally suited for assembly-line procedures contributed to making this a natural situation where various styles of supervision could be used. (In any experiment it is important that the manipulation not be external to the situation and thus relatively obvious to the subjects, who usually are interested in guessing "what they're after." The general assumption is, of course, that subjects cannot systematically fake behavioral effects unless the goals of the experimenters are obvious.) In addition to providing a natural environment for the manipulations, the kits for molecule construction afforded a rather simple but reliable quantitative measure of productivity.[15]

To simulate an industrial setting, the member of the experimental staff who took the role of supervisor was introduced simply with, "This is Miss Bradshaw, your supervisor during the work period." To heighten the impersonality of the situation, subjects were not introduced to the supervisor but were addressed by numbers conspicuously displayed at each of their work stations. In addition, words such as "supervisor," "worker," "blueprint," "material bin," "work efficiency,' "production unit," "subassemblies," and "production line" were used to convey the atmosphere of an industrial situation. However, in order to promote interaction, the situation was designed to be different from the usual production line in one important way: The subjects were stationed around an oval table that permitted each subject to view all co-subjects during the work period.

The experimental design

Technically, the experiment involved a two-by-two factorial design with high-low manipulations of the two independent variables—that is, the close and punitive styles of supervision. Using a table of random numbers, six of the twenty-four groups were assigned to each of the four "cells," as shown in the following figure.

To operationalize the four styles of supervision, two lists of remarks were drawn up for use by the supervisor. To operationalize closeness of supervision, a set of clear, concise instructions (role definitions) was developed. In the general supervision situations, the eight most

	Close Supervision	General Supervision
High Punitive Style	6 Groups	6 Groups
Low Punitive Style	6 Groups	6 Groups

essential of these instructions were used by the supervisor to give a minimum definition of the situation. In the close supervision situations, forty instructions were used; also, certain amounts of obvious hovering and watching as well as repetitions of previous instructions were used as checkup techniques.

To operationalize the punitive style in both the close and general situations, a list of sarcastic, negative, status-deflating remarks was developed for the supervisor to use as punitive sanctions. In the high-punitive situation, she made forty such remarks; in the low-punitive situation, she made none at all.

Two members of the staff who observed verbal aggression by the subjects also counted the supervisor's punitive remarks. The experimenter kept a count of the instructions and checkups, and a system of lights informed the supervisor when she had given the required number of remarks for each situation.

Fourteen practice sessions were required to standardize and internalize the multiple facets of the supervisor's role.[16] All extraneous remarks had to be identified and inhibited, and important nonverbal gestures (facial and body) had to be standardized. She had to learn to recognize and "control" subjects who were skilled at becoming dependent on the supervisor through asking for support. To help the supervisor control and minimize support-giving, observers registered all supportive remarks by the supervisor during this training period. Finally, she had to practice giving instructions that were devoid of aggressive connotations.

Measurement

Self-esteem. The measure of self-esteem used in this experiment was developed by de Charms and Rosenbaum[17] and was based in part on an earlier measure by Janis.[18] The subjects were instructed to choose an answer ranging from "strongly agree" through "strongly disagree" that best characterized their usual reactions. . . .

1. I feel capable of handling myself in most social situations.
2. I seldom fear my actions will cause othes to have a low opinion of me.
3. It doesn't bother me to have to enter a room where other people have already gathered and are talking.
4. In group discussions I usually feel that my opinions are inferior.
5. I don't make a very favorable first impression on people.
6. When confronted by a group of strangers, my first reaction is always one of shyness and inferiority.
7. It is extremely uncomfortable to accidentally go to a formal party in street clothes.
8. I don't spend much time worrying about what people think of me.
9. When in a group, I very rarely express an opinion for fear of being thought ridiculous.
10. I am never at a loss for words when I am introduced to someone.

Agreement with items 1, 2, 3, 8, and 10 and disagreement with items 4, 5, 6, 7, and 9 probably indicate high self-esteem or self-confidence and little concern with the presentation of self, that is, with the management of the image presented to others. On the other hand, opposite responses to these items indicate low self-esteem and low self-confidence and a great deal of concern and anxiety about the presentation of self in everyday situations.

Aggressive feelings. To measure covert aggressive feelings toward the supervisor, that is, those aggressive feelings which did not erupt into overt behavior, the following items were used:

1. How often did you become annoyed with the supervisor?
2. How often did you become irritated with the supervisor?
3. If you were to participate in this group again, how would you feel about having the supervisor replaced?

On the first two items, the subjects were asked to make responses on a six-point scale ranging from "continually" to "never"; for the third item, a seven-point scale was used ranging from "extremely favorable" to "extremely unfavorable." The responses provided an estimate of the frequency with which each subject experienced aggressive feelings toward the supervisor during the work period.

Two sets of items similar to these were used to measure aggressive feelings toward co-workers and dissatisfaction with the task. The first set was identical with the above items except that the term "co-workers" was substituted for "supervisor." The response alternatives were the same except for the third item; here the subjcts were asked to indicate the actual number of co-workers they would prefer to have replaced. In measuring dissatisfaction with the task, only the first two of the above items were used, but they were used twice, first with the term "molecules" and second with the phrase "job in general" substituted for the term "supervisor." Ranging from "continually" to "never," the response alternatives were the same as before.

Overt aggression. As may be recalled, we assumed that overt aggression might be expressed directly as verbal aggression or indirectly as a conscious slowdown in production. Two rather complex measures thus were required.

After two female observers had reached a level of competence where they could reliably code verbal aggression as it occurred during the experimental-work period, they independently entered marks on forms each time a subject (*a*) antagonistically criticized the supervisor or used indirect sarcasm with definite negative content in reference to the supervisor;

(b) antagonistically criticized or used sarcasm about her co-worker; or (c) antagonistically criticized or joked about the task or the experimental situation. In general, the observers were asked to perceive and evaluate each remark simultaneously along two dimensions: objective content and affective content. All remarks that were negative in objective meaning were counted as verbal aggression regardless of affective content. Remarks that were not objectively negative but tended to carry negative affective connotations were more difficult to categorize reliably. However, eighty-five per cent agreement of two observers was obtained throughout the experiment on items, not just cell totals.

The production-line arrangement of work required to encourage interdependence in interaction among subjects virtually precluded the possibility of taking accurate or even meaningful measures of each subject's production rate. Consequently, a measure based on the group's total production was used. This was calculated as the sum of the model components (the colored balls, pegs, and springs) completed per forty-minute work period, minus errors and omissions.

Factor analysis. Data from each of the scales administered in the pre-and post-experimental questionnaires were factor-analyzed using the principal-axis method. The obtained factor weights were used, together with standardized scores for each of the subjects, to obtain indexes for each of the above-mentioned dimensions.[19]

Results

* * *

The basic hypotheses tested with group data

* * *

...[The data indicate] that close supervision produced a significant and large increment in aggressive feelings toward the supervisor. The data also indicate a moderate and near-significant increment in aggressive feelings toward co-workers.

On the other hand, close supervision was not significantly related to dissatisfaction with the task, to verbal aggression against the supervisor or co-workers, or to verbal dissatisfaction with the task. Finally, the data indicate that close supervision results in a significant and rather substantial decrease in productivity.

...[The findings] also indicate that the punitive style of supervision resulted in a large, significant increment in aggressive feelings toward the supervisor. But, in this case the relationships between punitive supervision and aggressive feelings toward co-workers or dissatisfaction with the task are both small and insignificant, as are the relationships between punitiveness and verbal aggression toward co-workers or verbal dissatisfaction with the task. Unlike close supervision, however, punitive supervision resulted in a large, significant increase in verbal aggression toward the supervisor. Finally, it is evident that punitive supervision also resulted in a relatively large decrease in productivity—a decrease which, because of a small N, is of borderline significance.

Thus far the data have not supported all of the basic hypotheses. The results with respect to direct verbal aggression and the displacement of aggressive feelings toward co-workers and the task were variable. Consequently, the more detailed analysis will be limited to two dependent variables: aggressive feelings toward the supervisor and productivity.

Hypotheses involving self-esteem and analysis in terms of individual scores

* * *

The findings indicate a significant interaction between closeness of supervision and self-esteem with respect to feelings of aggression toward the supervisor, but not with respect to productivity. In Table 1, the means indicate that this significant interaction is precisely the one that was predicted. The relationship between close supervision and aggressive feelings toward the supervisor is much stronger among subjects with low than among subjects with high self-esteem. In fact, the difference between the means for subjects with high self-esteem is nil. In other words, the overall relationship observed between closeness of supervision and aggressive

TABLE 1

Means Involved in Significant Interaction between Close Supervision and Self-esteem with Respect to Aggressive Feelings toward Supervisor

Means	*Aggressive Feelings, Supervisor*
General style, low self-esteem	1.54
Close style, low self-esteem	1.74
General style, high self-esteem	1.64
Close style, high self-esteem	1.66

feelings toward the supervisors is due primarily to the subjects with low self-esteem. Yet, at the level of indirect aggression apparently no difference existed, since the intereaction between close supervision and self-esteem with respect to productivity involved very little variance and was insignificant as well. In the close-supervision variations, the subjects with high self-esteem evidently engaged in indirect aggression through lowered productivity as readily as did those with low self-esteem. The difference apparently was in their emotional state; that is, whether or not aggressive feelings, perhaps anger, accompanied their decision to decrease productivity. However, it should be noted that this pattern could be an artifact of the group-productivity scores.

. . . The interactions between punitive supervision and self-esteem with respect to both aggressive feelings and productivity are insignificant. Apparently the experience of being aggressed against in the form of punitive supervision produces aggressive feelings as well as indirect aggression equally in subjects with high and low self-esteem. We can make this assumption with some confidence because the variance involved in the relevant interactions is very low and because we have seen that the measure of self-esteem

is sensitive enough to detect rather precise effects.

Finally, are the effects of the two supervisory styles a simple additive function? If they are, the interactions between close and punitive supervision with respect to any of the aggression variables will be insignificant. . . . The interaction between the close and punitive styles of

TABLE 2

Means Involved in Significant Interactions between Close and Punitive Supervision with Respect to Productivity

Means	*Productivity*	
	No. of Units	*Percentage Reduction*
General style, non-punitive. .	84	100
Close style, non-punitive . . .	63	75
General style, punitive	65	77
Close style, punitive	56	67

supervision with respect to aggressive feelings toward the supervisor only approaches significance at the ten per cent level; however, the interaction with respect to productivity is significant, even though a modest amount of variance is involved. This result, of course, implies something more than a simple additive effect with respect to productivity. Apparently the effects of punitive and close supervision with respect to productivity are less than would be expected on the basis of the effects of close supervision alone and punitive supervision alone. As can be noted in Table 2, close supervision by itself reduces productivity by 25 per cent and punitive supervision reduces it by 23 per cent. Together they do not reduce it by 48 per cent as would be expected if the effects were a simple additive function, but only by 33 per cent. Since the decrease in productivity, indicating as it does an increase in aggression, is less than might be anticipated, we will refer to the phenomenon apparent in this interaction as the dampened-increment effect.

This dampened-increment effect might have occurred for one of two reasons.

First, productivity in the experimental situation might have been very difficult to reduce below some minimal level regardless of aggressive feelings or impulses to reduce it still further. Second, the aggressive feelings themselves might not have been additive. In other words, double frustration may not lead to double aggressive feelings but to something much less than double. . . . The data are consistent with this latter interpretation. The scores indicating aggressive feelings toward the supervisor are increased (from .73) 41 points by close supervision alone and 42 points by punitive supervision alone. Together, however, they increase the score only 54 points, as compared with an increment of 83 points that would be predicted if the effects were not dampened. These data, showing as they do a dampened-increment effect, are remarkably consistent with the data in the previous paragraph which showed a similar effect with respect to productivity.

Discussion

Overall, the results present an interesting pattern that is laden with implications. The lack of support for a number of the hypotheses matters very little, as these involved displacement which usually vitiates the strength of aggressive phenomena. But the interesting thing is that in the close-supervision situations a certain amount of displacement evidently did occur. The subjects by and large expressed more than usual aggressive feelings against one another as co-workers. It is this tendency to displace, plus the absence of verbal aggression toward the supervisor, which distinguishes the close from the punitive supervision situations. In the latter, the tendency to displace aggressive feelings was conspicuously absent and verbal aggression toward the supervisor conspicuously present. Why should such a difference obtain?

A number of explanations are possible, but the one that suggests itself involves the generic distinction between close and punitive supervision made in the theoretical section—that of intention. Our argument there was that with close supervision the *intention* is simply to increase production; the resulting psychological pain is unanticipated, unintentional, and possibly even an unknown consequence. Therefore, close supervision was characterized as frustrating rather than aggressive. On the other hand, with punitive supervision, the pain-producing activities are used intentionally because the pain presumably reinforces the desired avoidance responses. Since activities used with the intention of producing pain or injury are by definition aggression, we pointed out that punitive supervision is a form of aggression. Thus, at a more generic level, the close supervision-aggression hypotheses tested here are simply variants of the basic frustration-aggression hypothesis, whereas the punitive supervision-aggression hypotheses are basically aggression-aggression hypotheses. Phrased this way, these hypotheses may appear to be circular, but they are not. What really is meant is: "To the extent that A frustrates B, B will be instigated to aggress against A," and "To the extent that A aggresses against B, B will be instigated to aggress against A." In other words, genuine causal relationships are involved in the hypotheses because the hypotheses involve an exchange between two individuals.

If this distinction is valid, then the difference in response patterns to close and punitive supervision may actually represent a more generic difference in response patterns to frustration and aggression. Evidently, when A either frustrates B or aggresses against B, the unvarying result is the instigation of aggressive feelings in B. Furthermore, if an indirect avenue of aggression is available, such as decreasing productivity, then in either case B will use this indirect aggression against A. However, a basic difference evidently arises at the level of direct verbal aggression. Although they recognized that the pain they felt was not intended, those subjects who were frustrated by the close-supervision practices had a difficult time expressing their aggressive feelings directly at the verbal level, whereas those subjects who felt the aggression inherent in punitive supervision, perhaps because they recognized it as intentional, retaliated openly in kind. Apparently because the latter subjects were able to verbalize their aggressive feelings directly, they were not led into displacing the feelings as were the subjects who experienced the frustrations of close supervision.

Before concluding, we must pay tribute to the women who were subjects in this investigation. Although their behavior was not predicted precisely, it was not entirely unpredictable, as we sometimes feared it would be. They probably reacted to the various styles of supervision in much the same way as men would have reacted; most differences probably would be a matter of degree. But, our empirical impression is that women suppress their tendencies to overt aggression, particularly verbal aggression, more than do men. Rather than express their negative feelings in words, they tend to express them more in nervous laughter or alternatively to withdraw more than do men. In other words, if the experiment were duplicated using men, we think any change in results would be with respect to verbal aggression: Verbal aggression would be much more frequent in the punitive situation, and a significant relationship might obtain between close supervision and verbal aggression.

---

* This research was supported in part by a contract with the Office of Naval Research Nonr 816 (11), and the computer analysis was supported in part by a grant from the National Science Foundation, No. G-22296. The authors also wish to thank Professor Alvin W. Gouldner for his encouragement, suggestions, and criticisms.

1 D. Katz and R. L. Kahn, "Some Recent Findings in Human-Relations Research in Industry," in G. E. Swanson, T. M. Newcomb, and E. L. Hartley, eds., *Readings in Social Psychology*, 2d ed. (New York: Holt Rinehart & Winston, Inc., 1952), pp. 650–656; D. Katz and R. L. Kahn, "Leadership Practices in Relation to Productivity and Morale," in D. Cartwright and A. Zander, eds., *Group Dynamics*, 2d ed. (Evanston, Ill.: Row, Peterson & Company, 1960), pp. 554–570; D. Katz, N. Maccoby, G. Gurin, and Lucretia G. Floor, *Productivity, Supervision and Morale among Railroad Workers* (Ann Arbor: Survey Research Center, University of Michigan, 1951); and D. Katz, N. Maccoby, and Nancy C. Morse, *Productivity, Supervision and Morale in an Office Situation,* Part 1 (Ann Arbor: Survey Research Center, University of Michigan, 1950).

2 Nancy C. Morse, *Satisfactions in the White Collar Job* (Ann Arbor: Survey Research Center, University of Michigan, 1953).

3 Katz and Kahn, "Leadership Practice," *op. cit.*

4 Katz and Kahn, "Some Recent Findings," *op. cit.*

5 A. W. Gouldner, *Patterns of Industrial Bureaucracy* (New York: Free Press of Glencoe, Inc., 1954).

6 N. E. Miller, "I. The Frustration-Aggression Hypothesis." *Psychological Review,* 48 (1941), pp. 337–342.

7 Gouldner, *op. cit.*

8 Katz, Maccoby, Gurin, and Floor, *op. cit.*

9 A. Pepitone and G. Reichling, "Group Cohesiveness and the Expression of Hostility," *Human Relations,* 8 (1955), pp. 327–37.

10 Katz, Maccoby, and Morse, *op. cit.*

11 Katz, Maccoby, Gurin, and Floor, *op. cit.*

12 We wish to express our appreciation to Alvin W. Gouldner for suggesting Goffman's theory as the conceptual context in which to discuss self-esteem as a mediating variable (E. Goffman, *The Presentation of Self in Everyday Life* [Garden City, N.Y.: Doubleday & Co., Inc., 1959]).

13 *Ibid.,* p. 253.

14 Miller, *op. cit.*

15 Several considerations went into the decision to set up a production line. First, it was desirable to standardize and keep constant the overall sequence of operations for all groups. To this end, subjects were given definite subtasks to perform: that is, the groups did not determine their own division or non-division of labor. Second, it was undesirable either for the final combinations of operations to be so inefficient or slow that tension would be generated by the task itself, or for each worker to be allowed to proceed to construct whole models by herself in relative isolation, with no interdependence with the others. Although the latter procedure would have maximized productivity in the time allotted to the task, intersubject conflict would have been virtually absent even in high-tension situations. Consequently, although the sequence of operations chosen was

efficient enough to keep frustrations at a minimum, it included enough interdependence among subjects to make some conflict inevitable.

[16] The supervisor's role demanded a person who could combine a certain ability to act with emotional stability, maturity, and general interpersonal insightfulness. The role was taken by a recent graduate in nursing who had a major in psychiatric nursing and whose past experience in therapeutic role-playing with mental patients and hospital-ward supervision constituted an excellent background for the job.

[17] R. de Charms and M. E. Rosenbaum, "Status Variables and Matching Behavior," *Journal of Personality*, 28 (1960), pp. 492–502.

[18] I. L. Janis, "Personality Correlates of Susceptibility to Persuasion," *Journal of Personality*, 22 (1954), pp. 504–518.

[19] These procedures are outlined in detail in M. J. Hagood and D. O. Price, *Statistics for Sociologists* (New York: Holt, Rinehart & Winston, Inc. 1952), pp. 526–530.

part five

PERSONALITY, OCCUPATION, AND ORGANIZATION

Much has been said in recent years about pressures for conformity brought about by the growth of large organization. Surprisingly, there are few rigorous studies which attempt to confirm or refute the "organization-man" notions. Correspondingly, there has been even less attention devoted to the question of how men's personalities mold the organizations and economies in which they work.

The latter problem is tackled by David C. McClelland in "Business Drive and National Achievement." McClelland develops the interesting theory that it is men with great desires to achieve who push and pull organizations into profit and economies into rapid growth. The first problem mentioned about—conformity in organizations—is analyzed in Robert K. Merton's article "Bureaucratic Structure and Personality." Merton holds that organizations emphasize calculability and reliability of behavior, which in turn produce pressures upon workers to conform. Merton further suggests that often employees conform to such an extent that they forget the purposes or goals to be reached by following rules. Instead workers follow rules for their own sake. (For further discussion of these ideas see March and Simon's article in Part Two.)

Chris Argyris continues this stream of thought but develops a more sociopsychological basis for his arguments. He assumes that men are socialized to be mature, creative, self-regulating individuals but are encouraged to behave like immature children in modern organization.

The "Red Executive" presents a surprising comparison for his American counterpart. David Granick directs his interest to major assumptions which Westerners hold about red leaders and compares the Russian and American executives.

Our final paper in this section examines the frustrations and positive characteristics of lower participants in automated production firms. Intensive interviews that were conducted by Walker and Guest with assembly-line workers give us much insight into personality structures of blue-collar workers.

20 Business Drive and National Achievement

by DAVID C. McCLELLAND

What accounts for the rise in civilization? Not external resources (i.e., markets, minerals, trade routes, or factories), but the entrepreneurial spirit which exploits those resources—a spirit found most often among businessmen.

Who is ultimately responsible for the pace of economic growth in poor countries today?—not the economic planners or the politicians but the executives whose drive (or lack of it) will determine whether the goals of the planners are fulfilled.

Why is Russia developing so rapidly that, if it continues its present rate of growth, it will catch up economically with the most advanced country in the world, the United States, in twenty-five or thirty years?—not, as Russia claims, because of the superiority of its communist system, but because, by hook or by crook, it has managed to develop a stronger spirit of entrepreneurship among executives than we have today in the United States.

How can foreign aid be most efficiently used to help poor countries develop rapidly?—not by simply handing money over to their politicians or budget makers, but by using it in ways that will select, encourage, and develop those of their business executives who have a vigorous entrepreneurial spirit or a strong drive for achievement. In other words: *Invest in a man, not just in a plan.*

What may be astonishing about some of these remarks is that they come from a college professor and not from the

National Association of Manufacturers. They are not the defensive drum rattlings of an embattled capitalist, but are my conclusions, based on nearly fifteen years of research, as a strictly academic psychologist, into the human motive that appears to be largely responsible for economic growth—research which has recently been summarized in my book, entitled *The Achieving Society.*[1]

Since I am an egghead from way back, nothing surprises me more than finding myself rescuing the businessman from the academic trash heap, dusting him off, and trying to give him the intellectual respectability that he has had a hard time maintaining for the last fifty years of so. For the fact is that the businessman has taken a beating, not just from the Marxists, who pictured him as a greedy capitalist, and the social critics, who held him responsible for the Great Depression of the 1930's, but even from himself, deep in his heart.

One of the queerest ironies of history, as John Kenneth Galbraith points out in *The Affluent Society,*[2] is that in a sense Marx won his case with his sworn enemies, the capitalists. Marx loudly asserted that they were selfish and interested only in profits. In the end many agreed. They accepted the Marxist materialistic view of history. The modern businessman, says Galbraith, "suspects that the moral crusade of reformers, do-gooders, liberal politicians, and public servants, all their noble protestations notwithstanding, are based ultimately on self-interest. 'What,' he inquires, 'is their gimmick?' "[3]

If not only the Marxists, but Western economists and even businessmen them-

Reprinted from "Business Drive and National Achievement" by David C. McClelland. Used by permission of the Harvard Business Review, 40 *(July–August, 1962).*

selves, end up assuming that their main motive is self-interest and a quest for profit, it is small wonder that they have had a hard time holding their heads high in recent years.

But now the research I have done has come to the businessman's rescue by showing that everyone has been wrong, that it is *not* profit per se that makes the businessman tick but a strong desire for achievement, for doing a good job. Profit is simply one measure among several of how well the job has been done, but it is not necessarily the goal itself.

The Achievement Goal

But what exactly does the psychologist mean by the "desire for achievement"? How does he measure it in individuals or in nations? How does he know that it is so important for economic growth? Is it more important for businessmen to have this desire than it is for politicians, bishops, or generals? These are the kinds of questions which are answered at great length and with as much scientific precision as possible in my book. Here we must be content with the general outline of the argument, and develop it particularly as it applies to businessmen.

To begin with, psychologists try to find out what a man spends his time thinking and day-dreaming about when he is not under pressure to think about anything in particular. What do his thoughts turn to when he is by himself or not engaged in a special job? Does he think about his family and friends, about relaxing and watching TV, about getting his superior "off his back"? Or does he spend his time thinking and planning how he can "sell" a particular customer, cut production costs, or invent a better steam trap or toothpaste tube?

If a man spends his time thinking about doing things better, the psychologist says he has a concern for achievement. In other words, he cares about achievement or he would not spend so much time thinking about it. If he spends his time thinking about family and friends, he has

a concern for affiliation; if he speculates about who is boss, he has a concern for power, and so on. What differs in my approach from the one used by many psychologists is that my colleagues and I have not found it too helpful simply to *ask* a person about his motives, interests, and attitudes. Often he himself does not know very clearly what his basic concerns are—even more often he may be ashamed and cover some of them up. So what we do is to try to obtain a sample of his normal waking thoughts by asking him just to tell a few stories about some pictures.

Stories Within Stories

Let us take a look at some typical stories written by American business executives. These men were asked to look briefly at a picture—in this case, a man at a worktable with a small family photograph at one side—and to spend about five minutes writing out a story suggested by the picture. Here is a very characteristic story:

> The engineer is at work on Saturday when it is quiet and he has taken time to do a little daydreaming. He is the father of the two children in the picture—the husband of the woman shown. He has a happy home life and is dreaming about some pleasant outing they have had. He is also looking forward to a repeat of the incident which is now giving him pleasure to thing about. He plans on the following day, Sunday, to use the afternoon to take his family for a short trip.

Obviously, no achievement-related thoughts have come to the author's mind as he thinks about the scene in the picture. Instead, it suggests spending time pleasantly with his family. His thoughts run along *affiliative lines*. He thinks readily about interpersonal relationships and having fun with other people. This, as a matter of fact, is the most characteristic reaction to this particular picture. But now consider another story:

> A successful industrial designer is at his "workbench" toying with a new idea. He

WHAT IS YOUR OWN ACHIEVEMENT MOTIVATION?

We suggest that you take this test, which is explained in detail on these pages.

Look at this picture for ten or fifteen seconds. Now write a brief but imaginative story suggested by the picture and by the following questions:

1. What is happening? Who is the man?

2. What has led up to this situation? That is, what has happened in the past?

3. What is the man thinking? What is wanted? By whom?

4. What will happen? What will be done?

You can get an indication of your own achievement motivation by determining which of the illustrative stories (on pages 186 and 187) your story most resembles.

is "talking it out" with his family in the pictur. Someone in the family dropped a comment about a shortcoming in a household gadget, and the designer has just "seen" a commercial use of the idea. He has picked up ideas from his family before—he is "telling" his family what a good idea it is, and "confidentially" he is going to take them on a big vacation because "their" idea was so good. The idea will be successful, and family pride and mutual admiration will be strengthened.

The author of this story maintains a strong interest in the family and in affiliative relationships but has added an achievement theme. The family actually has helped him innovate—get a new idea that will be successful and obviously help him get ahead. Stories which contain references to good new ideas, such as a new product, an invention, or a unique accomplishment of any sort, are scored as reflecting a concern for achievement in the person who writes them. In sum,

this man's mind tends to run most easily along the lines of accomplishing something or other. Finally, consider a third story:

The man is an engineer at a drafting board. The picture is of his family. He has a problem and is concentrating on it. It is merely an everyday occurrence—a problem which requires thought. How can he get that bridge to take the stress of possible high winds? He wants to arrive at a good solution of the problem by himself. He will discuss the problem with a few other engineers and make a decision which will be a correct one—he has the earmarks of competence.

The man who wrote this story—an assistant to a vice president, as a matter of fact—notices the family photograph, but that is all. His thoughts tend to focus on the problem that the engineer has to solve. In the scant five minutes allowed, he even thinks of a precise problem— how to build a bridge that will take the stress of possible high winds. He notes that the engineer wants to find a good solution by himself, that he goes and gets help from other experts, and that he finally makes a correct decision. These all represent different aspects of a complete achievement sequence—defining the problem, wanting to solve it, thinking of means of solving it, thinking of difficulties that interfere with solving it (either in one's self or in the environment), thinking of people who might help in solving it, and anticipating what would happen if one

there are two ideas in it which are scorable as related to achievement.

Each man usually writes six such stories and gets a score for the whole test. The coding of the stories for "achievement imagery" is so objective that two expert scorers working independently rarely disagree. In fact, the test has recently been programed for a high-speed computer that does the scoring rapidly, with complete objectivity and fairly high accuracy. What the score for an individual repre-

Average in Achievement Scores of Managers and Professionals in three Countries

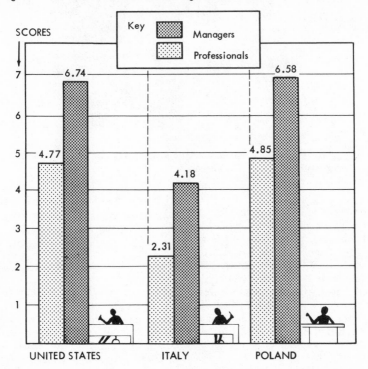

succeeded or failed.

Each of these different ideas about achievement gets a score of + 1 in our scoring system so that the man in the last incident gets a score of + 4 on the scale of concern or need for achievement (conventionally abbreviated to *n* Achievement). Similarly, the first man gets a score of − 1 for his story since it is completely unrelated to achievement, and the second man, a score of + 2 because

sents is the frequency with which he tends to think spontaneously in achievement terms when that is not clearly expected of him (since the instructions for the test urge him to relax and to think freely and rapidly).

Thinking makes it so

What are people good for who think like this all the time? It doesn't take much imagination to guess that they might make particularly good business executives. People who spend a lot of their time thinking about getting ahead, inventing new gadgets, defining problems that need to be solved, considering alternative means of solving them, and calling in experts for help should also be people who in real life *do* a lot of these things or at the very best are readier to do them when the occasion arises.

I recognize, of course, that this is an assumption that requires proof. But, as matters turned out, our research produced strong factual support. Look, for instance, at EXHIBIT 1. It shows that in three countries representing different levels and types of economic development managers or executives scored considerably higher on the average in achievement thinking than did professionals or specialists of comparable education and background. Take the two democratic countries shown there:

1. In the United States the comparison was between matched pairs of unit managers and specialists of the same position level, age, educational background, and length of service in the General Electric Company. The managers spent more of their time in the test writing about achievement than the specialists did.
2. The same was true of middle-level executives from various companies in Italy when contrasted with students of law, medicine, and theology who were roughly of the same intelligence level and social background.

In other words it takes a concern for achievement to be a manager in a foreign country like Italy, for instance, just as it does in the United States. It is worth noting in passing, however, that the level of achievement thinking among Italian managers is significantly lower than it is among American managers—which, as will be shown later, quite probably has something to do with the lower level and rate of economic development in Italy.

What about a communist country? The figures for Poland are interesting, because (1) the level of concern for achievement is about what it is in the United States and (2) even in businesses owned and operated by the state, as in Poland, managers tend to have a higher concern for achievement than do other professionals.

Another even more striking result, not shown in EXHIBIT 1, is the fact that there is *no real difference* between the average *n* Achievement score of managers working for the American government (9.3) and those in American private business generally (8.90). Apparently, a manager working for the Bureau of Ships in the Department of the Navy spends as much time thinking about achievement as his counterpart in Ford or Sears Roebuck; government service does not weaken his entrepreneurial spirit. Whether he is able to be as effective as he might be in private business is another matter, not touched on here.

Careful quantitative studies of the prevalence of achievement concern among various types of executives also yield results in line with what one would expect. Thus, sales managers score higher than other types of managers do.

In general, more successful managers tend to score higher than do less successful managers (except in government service where promotion depends more on seniority). The picture is clear in small companies, where the president tends to score higher than his associates. In large companies, the picture is a little more complicated. Men in the lowest salary brackets (earning less than $20,000 a year) definitely have the lowest average *n* Achievement scores, whereas those in the next bracket up ($20,000 to $25,000 a year) have the highest average *n* Achievement level. Apparently an achievement concern helps one get out of the ranks of the lowest paid into a higher income bracket. But from there on, the trend fades. Men in the highest income brackets have a somewhat lower average concern for achievement and apparently turn their thoughts to less achievement-oriented concerns. Possibly these men are doing well enough to relax a little.

Businessmen and Achievement

Businessmen usually raise either one of two questions at this point:

1. "Where can I get this test for *n* Achievement? It sounds like a good way of picking young executives!"
2. "Why is this concern for achievement specific to being a success as a business manager? What about other types of achievement? Why isn't the entrepreneurial spirit necessary for success as an opera star, a preacher, a great teacher, or a great scientist?"

The answer to the first question, unfortunately, is simple: No practicable, marketable test for assessing achievement concern exists as yet. The method of measurement we have been using is too sensitive, too easily influenced by the social atmosphere surrounding the people who take the test, to give reliable individual results. Under carefully controlled conditions it works adequately to distinguish large groups of people like managers versus professionals, but it is not yet useful for individual selection. What we have here is a theoretical, scientific "breakthrough," not a practicable working device.

The second question is harder to answer, but it takes us further in the direction of understanding exactly what kind of a person it is who spends a lot of his time thinking about achievement. To begin with, the facts are clear: Many important types of professionals (doctors, lawyers, priests, or research scientists) fail to score on the average as high as business executives; yet clearly their work is in every sense as much of an achievement as the businessman's. How come?

Let us consider a particular case for a moment—that of the research scientist. Certainly his work represents an important achievement, for he is the one who often makes the breakthrough on which new technological and economic advances depend. Should he not be thinking about defining a problem, doing a good job of solving it, getting help from experts, etc.?

Yet, when we tested a number of such scientists—including several outstanding Nobel Prize winners—we found, somewhat to our surprise, that they were not unusually high in *n* Achievement but rather tended to be average. Then it occurred to us that having a very high concern for achievement might make a person unsuitable for being a research scientist. Why? Simply because in research a man must often work for what may become very long periods of time without any knowledge of how well he is doing. He may not even know if he is on the right track for as much as five or ten years. But a man with a high need for achievement likes to know quickly whether he is accomplishing anything and quite possibly would become frustrated by the lack of feedback in basic science as to whether he is getting anywhere. He would then more likely move into an area such as management where results are more tangible. On the other hand, the research scientist obviously needs *some* achievement concern, or he is not likely to want to engage in his occupation at all.

Characteristics of achievers

Considerations like these focus attention on what there is about the job of being a business entrepreneur or executive that should make such a job peculiarly appropriate for a man with a high concern for achievement. Or, to put it the other way around, a person with high *n* Achievement has certain characteristics which enable him to work best in certain types of situations that are to his liking. An entrepreneurial job simply provides him with more opportunities for making use of his talents than do other jobs. Through careful empirical research we know a great deal by now about the man with high *n* Achievement, and his characteristics do seem to fit him unusually well for being a business executive. Specifically:

1. *To begin with, he likes situations in which he takes personal responsibility for finding solutions to problems.* The reason is obvious. Otherwise, he could get little personal achievement satisfaction from the successful outcome. No gambler, he does not relish situations where the outcome depends not on his abilities and efforts but on chance or other factors beyond his control. For example:

Some business-school students in one study played a game in which they had to choose between two options, in each of which they had only one chance in three of succeeding. For one option they rolled a die and if it came up, say, a 1 or a 3 (out of six possibilities), they won. For the other option they had to work on a difficult business problem which they know only one out of three people had been able to solve in the time allotted.

Under these conditions, the men with high *n* Achievement regularly chose to work on the business problem, even though they knew the odds of success were statistically the same as for rolling the dice.

To men strong in achievement concern, the idea of winning by chance simply does not produce the same achievement satisfaction as winning by their own personal efforts. Obviously, such a concern for taking personal responsibility is useful in a business executive. He may not be faced very often with the alternative of rolling dice to determine the outcome of a decision, but there are many other ways open to avoid personal responsibility, such as passing the buck, or trying to get someone else (or a committee) to take the responsibility for getting something done.

The famed self-confidence of a good executive (which actually is related to high achievement motivation) is also involved here. He thinks it can be done if *he* takes responsibility, and very often he is right because he has spent so much time thinking about how to do it that he does it better.

2. *Another characteristic of a man with*

a strong achievement concern is his tendency to set moderate achievement goals and to take "calculated risks." Again his strategy is well suited to his needs, for only by taking on moderately difficult tasks is he likely to get the achievement satisfaction he wants. If he takes on an easy or routine problem, he will succeed but get very little satisfaction out of his success. If he takes on an extremely difficult problem, he is unlikely to get any satisfaction because he will not succeed. In between these two extremes, he stands the best chance of maximizing his sense of personal achievement.

The point can be made with the children's game of ringtoss, some variant of which we have tried out at all ages to see how a person with high *n* Achievement approaches it. To illustrate:

The child is told that he scores when he succeeds in throwing a ring over a peg on the floor, but that he can stand anywhere he pleases. Obviously, if he stands next to the peg, he can score a ringer every time; but if he stands a long distance away, he will hardly ever get a ringer.

The curious fact is that the children with high concern for achievement quite consistently stand at moderate distances from the peg where they are most apt to receive achivment satisfaction (or, to be more precise, where the decreasing probility-of-success curve crosses the increasing satisfaction-from-success curve). The ones with low *n* Achievement, on the other hand, distribute the choices of where to stand quite randomly over the entire distance. In other words, people with high *n* Achievement prefer a situation where there is a challenge, where there is some real risk of not succeeding, but not so great a risk that they might not overcome it by their own efforts.

Again, such a characteristic would seem to suit men unusually well for the role of business entrepreneur. The businessman is always in a position of taking calculated risks, of deciding how difficult a given decision will be to carry out. If he is too safe and conservative and refuses to innovate, to invest enough in research or product development or advertising, he is likely to lose out to a more aggressive competitor. On the other hand, if he invests too much or overextends himself, he is also likely to lose out. Clearly, then, the business executive should be a man with a high concern for achievement who is used to setting moderate goals for himself and calculating carefully how much he can do successfully.

Therefore, we waste our time feeling sorry for the entrepreneur whose constant complaints are that he is overworking, that he has more problems than he knows how to deal with, that he is doomed to ulcers because of overwork, and so on. The bald truth is that if he has high n Achievement, he loves all those challenges he complains about. In fact, a careful study might well show that he creates most of them for himself. He may talk about quitting business and living on his investments, but if he did, he might then *really* get ulcers. The state of mind of being a little overextended is precisely the one he seeks, since overcoming difficulties gives him achievement satisfaction. His real problem is that of keeping the difficulties from getting *too* big for him, which explains in part why he talks so much about them because it is a nagging problem for him to keep them at a level he can handle.

3. *The man who has a strong concern for achievement also wants concrete feedback as to how well he is doing.* Otherwise how could he get any satisfaction out of what he had done? And business is almost unique in the amount of feedback it provides in the form of sales, cost, production, and profit figures. It is really no accident that the symbol of the businessman in popular cartoons is a wall chart with a line on it going up or down. The businessman sooner or later knows how well he is doing; salesmen will often know their success from day to day. Furthermore, there is a concreteness in the knowledge of results which is missing from the kind of feedback professionals get.

Take, for example, the teacher as a representative professional. His job is to transmit certain attitudes and certain kinds of information to his students. He does get some degree of feedback as to how well he has done his job, but results are fairly imprecise and hardly concrete. His students, colleagues, and even his college's administration may indicate that they like his teaching, but he still has no real evidence that his students have *learned* anything from him. Many of his students do well on examinations, but he knows from past experience that they will forget most of that in a year or two. If he has high n Achievement and is really concerned about whether he has done his job well, he must be satisfied with sketchy, occasional evidence that his former pupils did absorb some of his ideas and attitudes. More likely, however, he is not a person with high n Achievement and is quite satisfied with receiving from his work the affection and recognition that gratify his other needs.

The case of the true entrepreneur is different. Suppose he is a book publisher. He gets a manuscript and together with his editors decides that it is worth publishing. At time of issuance, everyone is satisfied that he is launching a worthwhile product. But then something devastatingly concrete happens—something far more definite than ever happens to a teacher— namely, those monthly sales figures.

Obviously not everyone likes to work in situations where the feedback is so concrete. It can prove him right, but it also can prove him wrong. Oddly enough, the person with high n Achievement has a compelling interest to know whether he has been right or wrong. He thrives and is happier in this type of situation than he is in the professional situation.

Two further examples from our research may make the point clearer. Boys with high n Achievement tend to be good with their hands, to like working in a shop or with mechanical or electrical gadgets. What characterizes such play again is the concrete feedback it provides as to how well a person is doing. If he wires up an electric circuit and then throws the switch, the light either goes on or it does not. Knowledge of results is direct, immediate, and concrete. Boys with high *n* Achievement like this kind of situation, and although some may go on to become engineers, others often go into business where they can continue getting this kind of concrete feedback.

What money means

In business, this feedback comes in the form of money, in costs and profits that are regularly reported. It is from this simple fact that the confusion between the so-called profit motive and the achievement motive has arisen in the minds of both Marxist and classical economists. For, in the typical case, a concern for profit in a capitalist economy does *not* mean that the businessman is primarily interested in money for its own sake. Rather, this concern is merely the *symptom* of a strong achievement concern, since profitability in a capitalist economy provides the best and simplest measure of success. It provides the same sort of concrete knowledge of achievement that a person with high *n* Achievement seeks all the time. Research findings clearly support this analysis. If you simply offer a person with high *n* Achievement a larger money reward for doing a certain tasks, he doesn't do any better than he did without the prize. In fact, he tends to do a little worse because the money makes him nervous. Not so the person with low *n* Achievement; he works harder when he has a chance of taking some money away from a situation. The money in and of itself means more to him than it does to the person with high *n* Achievement.

Of course, it follows that concrete measures of achievement other than money could be devised by other types of economic systems to satisfy the entrepreneurial spirit. Something like this has apparently happened in communist states like Poland and Russia, where plant managers work under a fairly rigid quota system which demands that they make

their quotas—or else! In the free enterprise system a businessman must make his profit—or else. The psychological effects, so far as the achievement motive is concerned, are apparently pretty much the same. In both systems the manager gets feedback in concrete terms as to how well he is doing. If he has high *n* Achievement, he is more likely to live and survive under such a challenge.

Although these three characteristics of people with a strong concern for achievement—the desire for personal responsibility, the tendency to set moderate achievement goals, and the need for concrete feedback of results—are the most important, there are some other minor characteristics possessed by these people which tend to suit them for an entrepreneurial job. They like to travel, they are willing to give up one bird in the hand to get two in the bush, and they prefer experts to friends as working partners. But to discuss any of these in detail would take us far afield.

Achieving Nations

If the theory underlying the experiments with determining *n* Achievement in individuals is correct, then what is true for groups of individuals might well prove true for nations. Does a high achievement concern herald a nation's rise? Let's take a look at the facts.

Naturally, tests of individual businessmen in particular countries would not prove very much about the influence of achievement concern on the nation's success; however, we figured that by coding popular literature of past and present we could get a rough estimate of the strength of the concern for achievement in a give country at a given time period. So we took samples from various time periods of a wide variety of the most popular imaginative literature we could find—poems, songs, plays—and scored them for *n* Achievement just as we had scored the simple stories written by individuals.

When we plotted the number of achievement ideas per hundred lines sampled in a given time period against economic indexes for the same time period, we got two curves that showed a very interesting relationship to each other. Normally, we found, a high level of concern for achievement is followed some fifty years or so later by a rapid rate of economic growth and prosperity. Such was certainly the case in ancient Greece and in Spain, in the late Middle Ages. Furthermore, in both cases a decline in achievement concern was very soon followed by a decline in economic welfare. The relationship between the two curves is shown most dramatically in Exhibit II, which plots the data for the

literature, a smaller one prior to the growth spurt around 1600 and a large one prior to the Industrial Revolution.

What clearer evidence could one ask for? What people are concerned about determines what they do, and what they do determines the outcome of history!

Present confirms past

In modern nations, too, the picture is very much the same. Children's stories used in public-school textbooks proved to be the most standardized form of popular literature that we could get from a large number of different countries. As a matter of fact, the simple imaginative stories that every country uses to teach its children to read are very similar in

How Achievement Thinking Expressed in English Literature Predicts the
Rate of Industrial Growth 50 Years Later

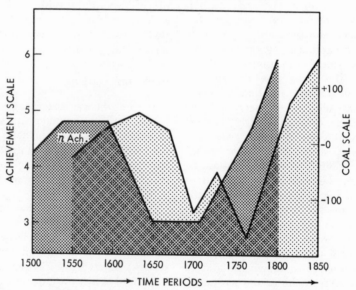

three hundred-year time span from Tudor times to the Industrial Revolution in England:

> There were two waves of economic growth in this time period, one smaller one around 1600 and a much large one around 1800 at the beginning of the Industrial Revolution. Each wave was preceded by a wave of concern for achievement reflected in popular

format to the stories produced by individuals when we test them as described earlier, particularly if one concentrates as we did on second-, third-, and fourth-grade readers, in which normally political influences are quite unimportant. The stories could be coded quite easily by the standard *n* Achievement scoring system.

Growth rates had to be estimated from

the only figures available that could be trusted for such a wide variety of countries —namely, the figures showing electric-power consumption (but there is ample evidence to show that electricity consumed is probably the best single available index of gross national income in modern times).

The n scores, when compared with the subsequent rates of economic growth for various countries, confirm the findings of the historical studies to a surprising extent. The higher the n Achievement level in the children's readers around 1925, the more rapid the subsequent rate of economic growth. (For twenty-two countries, the correlation was actually a substantial .53). Furthermore, the higher the n Achievement level in a country's children's readers around 1950, the more rapid its rate of growth between 1952 and 1958. In fact, of twenty countries above average in n Achievement in 1950, thirteen (or 65 per cent) showed a rapid rate of economic growth in the period from 1952 to 1958; whereas, of nineteen low in n Achievement, only five (or 26 per cent) achieved a rapid rate of growth.

Prediction possibilities

How meaningful are these findings, especially when one realizes the crudity of the data? In a certain sense, the cruder one admits the data to be, the more remarkable the findings appear. After all, the data suggest that one could have got a pretty good line on the economic future of various countries by studying its stories for children in 1925—regardless of a major depression, a world War, and a host of other political and economic factors.

Is it possible that we have stumbled on a way of predicting the future course of history? And from such an almost laughable source—stories for children—rather than the serious pronouncements of statesmen, generals, and economists? How is it possible?

The best interpretation of such findings would appear to run somewhat as follows.

The stories tell us what is on the minds of significant elites in the country, what these influential persons tend to think about most naturally when they are "off guard," so to speak, and not under any particular pressure to think one thing or another. In this sense, the stories are exactly analogous to the ones written for us by individuals. If you ask a man whether he is interested in achievement, the chances are that he will tell you that of course he is. Similarly, if you were to ask a country's leaders whether they wanted their nation to forge ahead, they would find it unpatriotic to say no. But, regardless of what such leaders say in public, the stories in the children's readers of many nations will show whether their peoples' thoughts turn naturally to achievement or to matters other than achievement.

Here is an illustration. Take a simple story theme like one in which some children are building a boat. Such themes are frequently borrowed by one culture from another and appear in several different readers, but the way they are embroidered may be quite different and quite revealing. For example:

1. In Country A, an *achievement*-oriented country, the emphasis is on making the boat, on constructing something that will work and not sink or tip over in a strong wind.
2. In Country B, the emphasis may be on *affiliation,* on the fun that the children have in playing together to sail their boat. Here little may be said about the details of constructing a seaworthy craft and much about the personal interaction of the children.
3. In Country C, the story may center on *power* and describe how the children were organized to produce the boat. One boy might set himself up as a leader, coordinating the work of the other children and telling them what to do.

Apparently, what comes most readily to the minds of these authors—whether concepts of achievement, affiliation, or power—reflects sufficiently well what is on the minds of key people in the country. And not only will these concepts seem natural and pleasing to the readers of these stories but will determine what they spend their time doing in the years to come. Thus, if the stories stress achievement, it means that an entrepreneurial spirit is abroad in the land. It indicates that many key people are thinking in achievement terms even when they do not need to.

In a nation, a strong achievement orientation affects particularly the business or economic sector of the population. And if the entrepreneurial types are strongly motivated to do well, they apparently succeed in getting the economy moving at a faster rate. So the children's stories are a symptom of the quality or "drive" of the entrepreneurial sector of an economy.

Rising and falling nations

With this in mind it is interesting to look at scores for particular countries—if only to make a better guess as to where to invest one's money! A generation ago, the north European countries, particularly Sweden and England, were very high in n Achievement, but both have fallen in the 1950's to well below average. Is it just a coincidence that one hears reports of stagnation or "maturity" in both economies? Are England's present difficulties the fault of outside circumstances, or do these difficulties stem from the fact that its citizens have lost their achievement drive? For some reason, the central European countries—France, Germany, and Russia—were all low in achievement concern in 1925, but by the 1950's all had increased sharply.

The case of Russia is particularly critical for us. How does the United States stand in achievement motivation as compared with Russia? According to a historical study, achievement concern in the United States increased regularly from 1800 to around 1890 but has decreased more or less regularly since, although there is a possibility that the decline has

leveled off in the past thirty years. We are still above average and, in fact, were at approximately the same level as Russia in 1950, although we were probably on the way down while they were certainly on the way up.

From the point of view of this analysis, the argument as to whether a socialist or a free enterprise system is the better way of stimulating an economy has been based on a false premise all along. Americans claimed that the success of their economy resulted, naturally, from the free enterprise system. Then, when the Soviet Union scored successes in outer space and in other fields, the Russians immediately claimed that these great economic and technological achievements stemmed from the superiority of their system.

Both contentions may well be wrong. Economic success and technological development depend on achievement motivation, and the rapid rate of Russian economic growth is due to an increase in her achievement concern just as ours was a generation or so earlier. There are other issues involved in comparing the two social systems, of course, but so far as this particular issue is concerned it has been misunderstood by both sides.

Need for acceptance

There is one final question that must be answered before we move on. Is it possible that achievement motivation will be aroused in *any* nation which comes in contact with modern technology and sees vividly the opportunity for a better life? Cannot achievement motivation be "borrowed" or assimilated from one nation to another? Are there not good illustrations of countries in which need for achievement has risen as they see more and more clearly the possibilities of growing and developing into modern, economically advanced nations? Are we just describing the "revolution of rising expectations" in fancy psychological jargon?

Opportunity is part of the story, of course. It does arouse people to act, but it arouses precisely those who *already* have some need of achievement. The soil must be ready for the seeds, if they are to grow. After all, many countries have been in touch with Western technology for generations—for example, the Islamic nations around the Mediterranean; yet they have been very slow to respond to the possibilities of a better life clearly presented to them all this time.

Consider, for example, a nation like Nigeria, which provides a good illustration of how opportunity and motivation must interact. Nigeria is essentially a federation of three regions, each of which is dominated by a different cultural group. Only one of these groups—the Yoruba—is known to be very high in need of achievement. In fact, long before the Yoruba had much contact with the West, this tribe was noted for its skill and interest in trade and native financial transactions. An indication of the validity of the achievement theory is shown by the fact that the Yoruba tribe, when exposed to new opportunities, produced a much stronger and more successful economic response than did the other tribes—as would be predicted. The regional bank operated by the Yoruba is in a much sounder position, for example, than the other two regional banks in Nigeria.

Opportunity challenges those who are achievement-oriented. Like two other groups high in n Achievement, American Jews and American Catholics between the ages of 35 and 45 (President Kennedy, for example), the Yoruba reacted vigorously to develop economic opportunities as they became available. Exposure to economic and technological opportunities did not produce as vigorous a response from groups lower in n Achievement in Nigeria any more than a similar exposure has done through the years to similar low n Achievement groups in the United States.

What Can We Do?

Is it inevitable that the achievement concern shown by U.S. citizens should continue to decline? Must we fade out in time as all other civilizations have in the past? Not if we understand what is happening and take steps to change it. Not if we move decisively and quickly to influence the sources of achievement concern in individuals and in our nation.

What are those sources? Clearly, they are not race or climate—those traditional external explanations of the superior energies of some nations. For Russia's n Achievement level has increased decisively since 1925, whereas Sweden's and England's have dropped. Certainly there have been no equally decisive changes in the gene pools or the climates of those nations in that time period.

In fact, external factors are usually unimportant, though occasionally they may play a role, as they have in helping to create generally high levels of n Achievement in immigrant countries like the United States, Canada, and Australia. Such nations tended to attract immigrants higher in n Achievement, because:

1. They drew their population initially from countries that were higher in achievement concern than those from which the Latin American countries drew.
2. They provided a haven for many persecuted religious minorities whose achievement concern was very strong.
3. They did not provide as many opportunities for "getting rich quick" as did Mexico and Peru, for example, with their plentiful supplies of gold and silver.

In short, countries like the United States were lucky. The barrier to migration was so formidable that primarily those with high n Achievement climbed it.

Historians have sometimes claimed that it was the great frontier in the United States that provided the challenge and stimulus to development. Nonsense. Great frontiers have existed and still exist in many South American countries without eliciting a similar response. It was the achievement-oriented immigrants to America who regarded the frontier as a challenge to be overcome. It was not the frontier that made them achievement-oriented. Opportunities, like new frontiers, always exist, but it takes a certain kind of person to see them and believe he can exploit them.

Whereas our distance from Europe, our tolerance for religious minorities, our good fortune in drawing immigrants initially from countries high in n Achievement tended to ensure that we got more citizens with high achievement motivation, our later restrictive immigration policies have drastically reduced our chances of continuing to receive such people. These policies continue to give preference to immigrants from the northern European countries, whose achievement drive has dropped significantly, and to restrict immigration from other countries where the n Achievement has been rising sharply. It would be a tragic irony of history if, in an endeavor to protect ourselves, we managed to shut off the supply of that entrepreneurial spirit that made our country great!

Sources of achievement

Where does strong achievement motivation come from? Values, beliefs, ideology —these are the really important sources of a strong concern for achievement in a country. Studies of the family have shown, for instance, that for a boy three factors are important in producing high n Achievement—parents' high standards of achievement, warmth and encouragement, and a father who is not dominating and authoritarian. Here is a typical study that reveals this fact:

A group of boys were blindfolded and asked to stack irregularly shaped blocks on top of each other with their left hands, at home in front of their parents. Separately, the mothers and fathers were asked how high they thought their sons could stack the blocks. Both parents of a boy with high n Achievement estimated that their boys should do better; they expected more of him than did the parents of a boy with low n Achievement. They also encouraged him more and gave him more affection and reward while he was actually doing the task. Finally, the

fathers of boys with high n Achievement directed the behavior of their sons much less when they were actually stacking the blocks: that is, they told them less often to move their hands this way or that, to try harder, to stop jiggling the table, and so forth, than did the fathers of boys with low n Achievement.

Other studies have shown that fathers must be respected by their sons; but after the boy is capable of achieving something for himself, his father must stop directing every step he takes if the boy is to develop a strong concern for achievement.

In a sense, however, these family studies only push the question further back. Where did the parents get their standards? Why do some emphasize achievement and affectionately reward self-reliance? Because, very simply, they themselves believe in achievement for their family or for their political, social, or religious group. For one reason or another they are caught up in some great wave of achievement ideology.

One of the paradoxes of history is that often the achievement concern was not itself initially directed toward business or economics. For instance, the two great waves of achievement concern in the history of England shown in Exhibit II were each associated with waves of Protestant reform or revival, the explicit aims of which were not secular but strictly religious. The Methodists, for example, in the second wave of the English Protestant revival, stressed religious perfection in this life; yet even John Wesley recognized with some puzzlement that devout Methodists tended to get rich, a fact which he considered a handicap in attaining religious perfection.

But now we can understand what happened. The strong concern for Christian perfection in this world tended to produce an achievement orientation in Methodist parents and their sons that turned the boys toward business because, as we have shown above, an achievement concern is most easily satisfied in business. In our day, it is the secular religions of nationalism and communism that have placed the highest emphasis on achievement and tended to create higher levels of *n* Achievement in underdeveloped and communist countries. Communism lays the same claims to superiority as a means of salvation that Christianity once did. However wrong we may feel it to be, we must recognize that it tends to create a strong atmosphere of achievement that has important consequences for economic growth.

---

1 David C. McClelland, *The Achieving Society* (Princeton: D. Van Nostrand Co., Inc., 1961).

2 John Kenneth Galbraith, *The Affluent Society* (Boston: Houghton Mifflin Company, 1958).

3 *Ibid.*, p. 71.

21 Bureaucratic Structure and Personality

by ROBERT K. MERTON

A formal, rationally organized social structure involves clearly defined patterns of activity in which, ideally, every series of actions is functionally related to the purposes of the organization.[1] In such an organization there is integrated a series of offices, of hierarchized statuses, in which inhere a number of obligations and privileges closely defined by limited and specific rules. Each of these offices contains an area of imputed competence and responsibility. Authority, the power control which derives from an acknowledged status, inheres in the office and not in the particular person who performs the official role. Official action ordinarily occurs within the framework of preexisting rules of the organization. The system of prescribed relations between the various offices involves a considerable degree of formality and clearly defined social distance between the occupants of these positions. Formality is manifested by means of a more or less complicated social ritual which symbolizes and supports the pecking order of the various offices. Such formality, which is integrated with the distribution of authority within the system, serves to minimize friction by largely restricting (official) contact to modes which are previously defined by the rules of the organization. Ready calculability of others' behavior and a stable set of mutual expectations is thus built up. Moreover, formality facilitates the interaction of the occupants of offices despite their (possibly hostile) private attitudes toward one another. In this way, the subordinate is protected from the arbitrary action of his superior, since the actions of both are constrained by a mutually recognized set of rules. Specific procedural devices foster objectivity and restrain the "quick passage of impulse into action."[2]

The Structure of Bureaucracy

The ideal type of such formal organization is bureaucracy, and, in many respects, the classical analysis of bureaucracy is that by Max Weber.[3] As Weber indicates, bureaucracy involves a clear-cut division of integrated activities which are regarded as duties inherent in the office. A system of differentiated controls and sanctions is stated in the regulations. The assignment

Reprinted from "Bureaucratic Structure and Personality," by permission of the author and the publisher, Social Forces, *23 (1945), pp. 405–415.*

of roles occurs on the basis of technical qualifications which are ascertained through formalized, impersonal procedures (e.g., examinations). Within the structure of hierarchically arranged authority, the activities of "trained and salaried experts" are governed by general, abstract, and clearly defined rules which preclude the necessity for the issuance of specific instructions for each specific case. The generality of the rules requires the constant use of *categorization*, whereby individual problems and cases are classified on the basis of designated criteria and are treated accordingly. The pure type of bureaucratic official is appointed, either by a superior or through the exercise of impersonal competition; he is not elected. A measure of flexibility in the bureaucracy is attained by electing higher functionaries who presumably express the will of the electorate (e.g., a body of citizens or a board of directors). The election of higher officials is designed to affect the purposes of the organization, but the technical procedures for attaining these ends are carried out by continuing bureaucratic personnel.[4]

Most bureaucratic offices involve the expectation of lifelong tenure, in the absence of disturbing factors which may decrease the size of the organization. Bureaucracy maximizes vocational security.[5] The function of security of tenure, pensions, incremental salaries and regularized procedures for promotion is to ensure the devoted performance of official duties, without regard for extraneous pressures.[6] The chief merit of bureaucracy is its technical efficiency, with a premium placed on precision, speed, expert control, continuity, discretion, and optimal returns on input. The structure is one which approaches the complete elimination of personalized relationships and nonrational considerations (hostility, anxiety, affectual involvements, etc.).

With increasing bureaucratization, it becomes plain to all who would see that man is to a very important degree controlled by his social relations to the instruments of production. This can no longer seem only a tenet of Marxism but a stubborn fact to be acknowledged by all, quite apart from their ideological persuasion. Bureaucratization makes readily visible what was previously dim and obscure. More and more people discover that to work, they must be employed; for to work, one must have tools and equipment. And the tools and equipment are increasingly available only in bureaucracies, private or public. Consequently, one must be employed by the bureaucracies in order to have access to tools in order to work in order to live. It is in this sense that bureaucratization entails separation of individuals from the instruments of production, as in modern capitalistic enterprise or in state communistic enterprise (of the mid-century variety), just as in the post-feudal army, bureaucratization entailed complete separation from the instruments of destruction. Typically, the worker no longer owns his tools nor the soldier his weapons. And in this special sense, more and more people become workers, either blue-collar or white-collar or stiff-shirt. So develops, for example, the new type of scientific worker, as the scientist is "separated" from his technical equipment (after all, the physicist does not ordinarily own his cyclotron). To work at his research, he must be employed by a bureaucracy with laboratory resources.

Bureaucracy is administration which almost completely avoids public discussion of its techniques, although there may occur public discussion of its policies.[7] This secrecy is confined neither to public nor to private bureaucracies. It is held to be necessary to keep valuable information from private economic competitors or from foreign and potentially hostile political groups. And though it is not often so called, espionage among competitors is perhaps as common, if not as intricately organized, in systems of private economic enterprise as in systems of national states. Cost figures, lists of clients, new technical processes, plans for production—all these are typically regarded as essential secrets of private economic bureaucracies that might be revealed if the bases of all decisions and policies had to be publicly defended.

The Dysfunctions of Bureaucracy

In these bold outlines, the positive attainments and functions of bureaucratic organization are emphasized and the internal stresses and strains of such structures are almost wholly neglected. The community at large, however, evidently emphasizes the imperfections of bureaucracy, as is suggested by the fact that the "horrid hybrid," the bureaucrat, has become an epithet, a *Schimpfwort*.

The transition to a study of the negative aspects of bureaucracy is afforded by the application of Veblen's concept of "trained incapacity," Dewey's notion of "occupational psychosis" or Daniel Warnotte's view of "professional deformation." Trained incapacity refers to that state of affairs in which one's abilities function as inadequacies or blind spots. Actions based upon training and skills which have been successfully applied in the past may result in inappropriate responses *under changed conditions*. An inadequate flexibility in the application of skills will, in a changing milieu, result in more or less serious maladjustments.[8] Thus, to adopt a barnyard illustration used in this connection by Burke, chickens may be readily conditioned to interpret the sound of a bell as a signal for food. The same bell may now be used to summon the trained chickens to their doom as they are assembled to suffer decapitation. In general, one adopts measures in keeping with one's past training and, under new conditions that are not recognized as *significantly* different, the very soundness of this training may lead to the adoption of the wrong procedures. Again, in Burke's almost echolalic phrase, "People may be unfitted by being fit in an unfit fitness": their training may become an incapacity.

Dewey's concept of occupational psychosis rests upon much the same observations. As a result of their day-to-day routines, people develop special preferences, antipathies, discriminations, and emphases.[9] (The term psychosis is used by Dewey to denote a "pronounced character of the mind.") These psychoses develop through demands put upon the individual by the particular organization of his occupational role.

The concepts of both Veblen and Dewey refer to a fundamental ambivalence. Any action can be considered in terms of what it attains or what it fails to attain. "A way of seeing is also a way of not seeing—a focus upon object A involves a neglect of object B."[10] In his discussion, Weber is almost exclusively concerned with what the bureaucratic structure attains: precision, reliability, efficiency. This same structure may be examined from another perspective provided by the ambivalence. What are the limitations of the organizations designed to attain these goals?

For reasons which we have already noted, the bureaucratic structure exerts (1) a constant pressure upon the official to be "methodical, prudent, disciplined." If the bureaucracy is to operate successfully, it must (2) attain a high degree of reliability of behavior, (3) an unusual degree of conformity with prescribed patterns of action—hence, the (4) fundamental importance of discipline which may be as highly developed in a religious or economic bureaucracy as in the army. Discipline can be effective only if the ideal (5) patterns are buttressed by strong sentiments which entail devotion to one's duties, (6) a keen sense of the limitation of one's authority and competence, and (7) methodical performance of routine activies. The efficacy of social structure depends ultimately upon infusing group participants with appropriate attitudes and sentiments. As we shall see, there are definite arrangements in the bureaucracy for inculcating and reinforcing these sentiments.

At the moment, it suffices to observe that, in order to ensure discipline (the necessary reliability of response), these sentiments are often more intense than is technically necessary. There is a margin of safety, so to speak, in the pressure exerted by these sentiments upon the bureaucrat to conform to his patterned obligations, in much the same sense that added allowances (precautionary overestimations) are made by the engineer in designing the supports for a bridge. But this very emphasis leads to a transference of the sentiments from the *aims* of the organization onto the particular details of behavior required by the rules. Adherence to the rules, originally conceived as a means, becomes transformed into an end in itself; there occurs the familiar process of *displacement of goals* whereby "an instrumental value becomes a terminal value."[11] Discipline, readily interpreted as conformance with regulations, whatever the situation, is seen not as a measure designed for specific purposes but as an immediate value in the life-organization of the bureaucrat. This emphasis, resulting from the displacement of the original goals, develops into rigidities and an inability to adjust readily. Formalism, even ritualism, ensues with an unchallenged insistence upon punctilious adherence to formalized procedures.[12] This may be exaggerated to the point that primary concern with conformity to the rules interferes with the achievement of the purposes of the organization, in which case we have the familiar phenomenon of the technicism or red tape of the official. An extreme product of this process of displacement of goals is the bureaucratic virtuoso, who never forgets a single rule binding his action and hence is unable to assist many of his clients.[13] A case in point, where strict recognition of the limits of authority and literal adherence to rules produced this result, is the pathetic plight of Bernt Balchen, Admiral Byrd's pilot in the flight over the South Pole.

According to a ruling of the department of labor Bernt Balchen...cannot receive his citizenship papers. Balchen, a native of Norway, declared his intention in 1927. It is held that he has failed to meet the condition of five years' continuous residence in the United States. The Byrd antarctic voyage took him out of the country, although he was on a ship carrying the American flag, was an invaluable member of the American expedition, and in a region to which there is an American claim because of the exploration and occupation of it by Americans, this region being Little America.

The bureau of naturalization explains that it cannot proceed on the assumption that Little America is American soil. That would be *trespass on international questions* where it has no sanction. So far as the bureau is concerned, Balchen was out of the country and *technically* has not complied with the law of naturalization.[14]

Structural Sources of Overconformity

Such inadequacies in orientation which involve trained incapacity clearly derive from structural sources. The process may be briefly recapitulated.

1. An effective bureaucracy demands reliability of response and strict devotion to regulations.
2. Such devotion to the rules leads to their transformation into absolutes; they are no longer conceived as relative to a set of purposes.
3. This interferes with ready adaptation under special conditions not clearly envisaged by those who drew up the general rules.
4. Thus, the very elements which are conductive of efficiency in general produce inefficiency in specific instances.

Full realization of the inadequacy is seldom attained by members of the group who have not divorced themselves from the meanings which the rules have for them. These rules in time become symbolic in cast, rather than strictly utilitarian.

Thus far, we have treated the ingrained

sentiments making for rigorous discipline simply as data, as given. However, definite features of the bureaucratic structure may be seen to contribute to these sentiments. The bureaucrat's official life is planned for him in terms of a graded career, through the organizational devices of promotion by seniority, pensions, incremental salaries, *etc.*, all of which are designed to provide incentives for disciplined action and conformity to the official regulations.[15] The official is tacitly expected to and largely does adapt his thoughts, feelings, and actions to the prospect of this career. But *these very devices* which increase the probability of conformance also lead to an overconcern with strict adherence to regulations which induces timidity, conservatism, and technicism. Displacement of sentiments from goals onto means is fostered by the tremendous symbolic significance of the means (rules).

Another feature of the bureaucratic structure tends to produce much the same result. Functionaries have the sense of a common destiny for all those who work together. They share the same interests, especially since there is relatively little competition in so far as promotion is in terms of seniority. In-group aggression is thus minimized, and this arrangement is therefore conceived to be positively functional for the bureaucracy. But, the *esprit de corps* and informal social organization which typically develops in such situations often leads the personnel to defend their entrenched interests rather than to assist their clientele and elected higher officials. As President Lowell reports, if the bureaucrats believe that their status is not adequately recognized by an incoming elected official, detailed information will be withheld from him, leading him to errors for which he is held responsible. Or, if he seeks to dominate fully, and thus violates the sentiment of self-integrity of the bureaucrats, he may have documents brought to him in such numbers that he cannot manage to sign them

all, let alone read them.[16] This illustrates the defensive informal organization which tends to arise whenever there is an apparent threat to the integrity of the group.[17]

It would be much too facile and partly erroneous to attribute such resistance by bureaucrats simply to vested interests. Vested interests oppose any new order which either eliminates or at least makes uncertain their differential advantage deriving from the current arrangements. This is undoubtedly involved in part in bureaucratic resistance to change, but another process is perhaps more significant. As we have seen, bureaucratic officials affectively identify themselves with their way of life. They have a pride of craft which leads them to resist change in established routines—at least, those changes which are felt to be imposed by others. This nonlogical pride of craft is a familiar pattern found even, to judge from Sutherland's *Professional Thief,* among pickpockets who, despite the risk, delight in mastering the prestige-bearing feat of "beating a left breech" (picking the left front trousers pocket).

In a stimulating paper, Hughes has applied the concepts of "secular" and "sacred" to various types of division of labor; "the sacredness" of caste and *Stande* prerogatives contrasts sharply with the increasing secularism of occupational differentiation in our society.[18] But, as our discussion suggests, there may ensue, in particular vocations and in particular types of organization, the *process of sanctification* (viewed as the counterpart of the process of secularization). This is to say that through sentiment-formation, emotional dependence upon bureaucratic symbols and status, and affective involvement in spheres of competence and authority, there develop prerogatives involving attitudes of moral legitimacy that are established as values in their own right and are no longer viewed as merely technical means for expediting administration. One may note a tendency for certain bureaucratic norms, originally introduced for technical reasons, to become rigidified and sacred, although, as Emile Durkheim would say, they are *laique en apparence*.[19] Durkheim has touched on this general process in his description of the attitudes and values which persist in the organic solidarity of a highly differentiated society.

Primary vs. Secondary Relations

Another feature of the bureaucratic structure, the stress on depersonalization of relationships, also plays its part in the bureaucrat's trained incapacity. The personality pattern of the bureaucrat is nucleated about this norm of impersonality. Both this and the categorizing tendency, which develops from the dominant role of general, abstract rules, tend to produce conflict in the bureaucrat's contacts with the public or clientele. Since functionaries minimize personal relations and resort to categorization, the peculiarities of individual cases are often ignored. But the client who, quite understandably, is convinced of the special features of *his* own problem often objects to such categorical treatment. Stereotyped behavior is not adapted to the exigencies of individual problems. The impersonal treatment of affairs which are at times of great personal significance to the client gives rise to the charge of "arrogance" and "haughtiness" on the part of the bureaucrat. Thus, at the Greenwich Employment Exchange, the unemployed worker who is securing his insurance payment resents what he deems to be "the impersonality and, at times, the apparent abruptness and even harshness of his treatment by the clerks. . . . Some men complain of the superior attitude which the clerks have."[20]

Still another source of conflict with the public derives from the bureaucratic structure. The bureaucrat, in part irrespective of his position within the hierarchy, acts as a representative of the power and prestige of the entire structure. In his official role he is vested with definite authority. This often leads to an actually or apparently domineering attitude, which may only be exaggerated by a discrepancy between his position within the hierarchy and his position with reference to the public.[21] Protest and recourse to other officials on the part of the client are often ineffective or largely precluded by the previously mentioned *esprit de corps* that joins the officials into a more or less solidary ingroup. This source of conflict *may* be minimized in private enterprise since the client can register an effective protest by transferring his trade to another organization within the competitive system. But with the monopolistic nature of the public organization, no such alternative is possible. Moreover, in this case, tension is increased because of a discrepancy between ideology and fact: the governmental personnel are held to be "servants of the people," but in fact they are often superordinate; and release of tension can seldom be afforded by turning to other agencies for the necessary service.[22] This tension is in part attributable to the confusion of the status of bureaucrat and client; the client may consider himself socially superior to the official who is at the moment dominant.[23]

Thus, with respect to the relations between officials and clientele, one structural source of conflict is the pressure for formal and impersonal treatment when individual, personalized consideration is desired by the client. The conflict may be viewed, then, as deriving from the introduction of inappropriate attitudes and relationships. Conflict within the bureaucratic structure arises from the converse situation, namely when personalized relationships are substituted for the structurally required impersonal relationships. This type of conflict may be characterized as follows.

The bureaucracy, as we have seen, is organized as a secondary, formal group. The normal responses involved in this organized network of social expectations are supported by affective attitudes of members of the group. Since the group is oriented toward secondary norms of impersonality, any failure to conform to these norms will arouse antagonism from those who have identified themselves with the legitimacy of these rules. Hence, the substitution of personal for impersonal treatment within the structure is met with widespread disapproval and is characterized by such epithets as graft, favoritism, nepotism, apple-polishing, and so forth. These epithets are clearly manifestations of injured sentiments.[24] The function of such virtually automatic resentment can be clearly seen in terms of the requirements of bureaucratic structure.

Bureaucracy is a secondary-group structure designed to carry on certain activities which cannot be satisfactorily performed on the basis of primary-group criteria.[25] Hence behavior that runs counter to these formalized norms becomes the object of emotionalized disapproval. This constitutes a functionally significant defense set up against tendencies which jeopardize the performance of socially necessary activities. To be sure, these reactions are not rationally determined practices explicitly designed for the fulfillment of this function. Rather, viewed in terms of the individual's interpretation of the situation, such resentment is simply an immediate response opposing the "dishonesty" of those who violate the rules of the game. But this subjective frame of reference notwithstanding, these reactions serve the latent function of maintaining the essential structural elements of bureaucracy by reaffirming the necessity for formalized, secondary relations and by helping to prevent the disintegration of the bureaucratic structure that would occur should these be supplanted by personalized relations. This type of conflict may be generally described as the intrusion of primary-group attitudes when secondary-group attitudes are institutionally demanded, just as the bureaucrat-client conflict often derives from interaction on impersonal terms when personal treatment is individually demanded.[26]

Problems for Research

The trend towards increasing bureaucratization in Western society, which Weber had long since foreseen, is not the sole reason for sociologists to turn their attention to this field. Empirical studies of the interaction of bureaucracy and personality should especially increase our understanding of social structure. A large number of specific questions invite our attention. To what extent are particular personality types selected and modified by the various bureaucracies (private enterprise, public service, the quasi-legal political machine, religious orders)? Inasmuch as ascendancy and submission are held to be traits of personality, despite their variability in different stimulus-situations, do bureaucracies select personalities of particularly submissive or ascendant tendencies? And since various studies have shown that these traits can be modified, does participation in bureaucratic office tend to increase ascendant tendencies? Do various systems of recruitment (e.g., patronage, open competition involving specialized knowledge or general mental capacity, practical experience) select different personality types?[27] Does promotion through seniority lessen competitive anxieties and enhance administrative efficiency? A detailed examination of mechanisms for imbuing the bureaucratic codes with affect would be instructive both sociologically and psychologically. Does the general anonymity of civil service decisions tend to restrict the area of prestige symbols to a narrowly defined inner circle? Is there a tendency for differential association to be especially marked among bureaucrats?

The range of theoretically significant and practically important questions would seem to be limited only by the accessibility of the concrete data. Studies of religious, educational, military, economic, and political bureaucracies dealing with the interdependence of social organization and personality formation should constitute an avenue for fruitful research. On that avenue, the functional analysis of concrete structures may yet build a Solomon's House for sociologists.

---

1 For a development of the concept of "rational organization," see Karl Mannheim, *Mensch und Gesellschaft im Zeitalter des Umbaus* (Leiden: A. W. Sijthoff, 1935), especially 28 ff.

2 H. D. Lasswell, *Politics* (New York: McGraw-Hill Book Company, 1936), pp. 120–121.

3 Max Weber, *Wirtschaft und Gesellschaft* (Tübingen: J. C. B. Mohr, 1922), Pt. III, Ch. 6, pp. 650–678. For a brief summary of Weber's discussion, see Talcott Parsons, *The Structure of Social Action*, especially pp. 560 ff. For a description, which is not a caricature, of the bureaucrat as a personality type, see C. Rabany, "Les types sociaux: le fonctionnaire, "*Revue generale d'administration*, 88 (1907), pp. 5–28.

4 Karl Mannheim, *Ideology and Utopia* (New York: Harcourt, Brace & World, Inc., 1936), 18n., pp. 105 ff. See also Ramsay Muir, *Peers and Bureaucrats* (London: Constable & Co., Ltd., 1910), pp. 12–13.

5 E. G. Cahen-Salvador suggests that the personnel of bureaucracies is largely constituted by those who value security above all else. See his "La situation materielle et morale des fonctionnaires," *Revue politique et parlementaire* (1962), p. 319.

6 H. J. Laski, "Bureaucracy," *Encyclopedia of the Social Sciences*. This article is written primarily from the standpoint of the political scientist rather than that of the sociologist.

7 Weber, *op. cit.*, p. 671.

8 For a stimulating discussion and application of these concepts, see Kenneth Burke, *Permanence and Change* (New York: New Republic, 1935), pp. 50 ff; Daniel Warnotte, "Bureaucratie et Fonctionnarisme," *Revue de l'Institut de Sociologie*, 17 (1937), p. 245.

9 *Ibid.*, pp. 58–59.

10 *Ibid.*, p. 70.

11 This process has often been observed in various connections. Wundt's *heterogony of ends* is a case in point; Max Weber's *Paradoxie der Folgen* is another. See also Robert M. MacIver's observations on the transformation of civilization into culture and H. D. Lasswell's remark that "the human animal distinguishes himself by his infinite capacity for making ends of his means." See Robert K. Merton, "The Unanticipated Consequences of Purposive Action," *American Sociological Review*, 1 (1936), 894–904. In terms of the psychological mechanisms involved, this process has been analyzed most fully by Gordon W. Allport in his discussion of what he calls "the functional autonomy of motives." Allport amends the earlier formulations of R. S. Woodworth, James Tolman, and William Stern and arrives at a statement of the process from the standpoint of individual motivation. He does not consider those phases of the social structure which contribute to the "transformation of motives." The formulation adopted in this paper is thus complementary to Allport's analysis: the one stressing the psychological mechanisms involved, the other considering the constraints of the social structure. The convergence of psychology and sociology toward this central concept suggests that it may well constitute one of the conceptual bridges between the two disciplines. See Gordon W. Allport, *Personality* (New York: Holt, Rinehart & Winston, Inc., 1937), Ch. 7.

12 See E. C. Hughes, "Institutional Office and the Person," *American Journal of Sociology*, 43 (1937), pp. 404–413; E. T. Hiller, "Social Structure in Relation to the Person," *Social Forces*, 16 (1937), p. 34–44.

13 Mannheim, *Ideology and Utopia*, p. 106.

14 Quoted from the *Chicago Tribune* (June 24, 1931), p. 10 by Thurman Arnold, *The Symbols of Government* (New Haven: Yale University Press, 1935), pp. 201–202. (My italics.)

15 Mannheim, *Mensch und Gesellschaft*, pp. 32–33. Mannheim stresses the importance of the "Lebensplan" and the "Amtskarriere." See the comments by Hughes, *op. cit.*, p. 413.

16 A. L. Lowell, *The Government of England* (New York: McGraw Hill Book Company 1908), I, pp. 189 ff.

17 For an instructive description of the development of such a defensive organization in a group of workers, see F. J. Roethlisberger and W. J. Dickson, *Management and the Worker* (Boston: Harvard School of Business Administration, 1934).

18 E. C. Hughes, "Personality Types and the Division of Labor," *American Journal of Sociology*, 33 (1928), pp. 754–768. Much the same distinction is drawn by Leopold von Wiese and Howard Becker, *Systematic Sociology* (New York: John Wiley & Sons, Inc. 1932), pp. 222–225 *passim*.

19 Hughes recognizes one phase of this process of sanctification when he writes that professional training "carries with it as a by-product assimilation of the candidate to a set of professional attitudes and controls, *a professional conscience and solidarity. The profession claims and aims to become a moral unit.*"

Hughes, *op. cit.*, p. 762. (My italics.) In this same connection, William Graham Sumner's concept of *pathos*, as the halo of sentiment which protects a social value from criticism, is particularly relevant, inasmuch as it affords a clue to the mechanism involved in the process of sanctification. See his *Folkways* (New York: Blaisdell Publishing Co., 1940) pp. 180–181.

20 "They treat you like a lump of dirt they do. I see a navvy reach across the counter and shake one of them by the collar the other day. The rest of us felt like cheering. Of course he lost his benefit over it.... But the clerk deserved it for his sassy way.'" E. W. Bakke, *The Unemployed Man* (New Haven: Yale University Press, 1940). pp. 79–80. Note that the domineering attitude was *imputed* by the unemployed client who is in a state of tension due to his loss of status and self-esteem in a society where the ideology is still current that an "able man" can always find a job. That the imputation of arrogance stems largely from the client's state of mind is seen from Bakke's own observation that "the clerks were rushed and had no time for pleasantries, but there was little sign of harshness or a superiority feeling in their treatment of the men." Insofar as there is an objective basis for the imputation of arrogant behavior to bureaucrats, it may possibly be explained by the following juxtaposed statements. "Auch der moderne, sei es öffentliche, sei es private, Beamte erstrebt immer und geniesst meist den Beherrschaten gegenüber eine spezifisch gehobene, 'ständische' soziale Schätzung." Weber, *op. cit.*, p. 652. "In persons in whom the craving for prestige is uppermost, hostility usually takes the form of a desire to humilate othes." Karen Horney, *The Neurotic Personality of Our Time* (New York: W. W. Norton & Company, Inc. 1937), pp. 178–179.

21 In this connection, note the relevance of Koffka's comments on certain features of the pecking order of birds. "If one compares the behavior of the bird at the top of the pecking list, the despot, with that of one very far down, the second or third from the last, then one finds the latter much more cruel to the few others over whom he lords it than the former in his treatment of all members. As soon as one removes from the group all members above the penultimate, his behavior becomes milder and may even become very friendly.... It is not difficult to find analogies to this in human societies, and therefore one side of such behavior must be primarily the effects of the social groupings, and not of individual characteristics." K. Koffka, *Principles of Gestalt Psychology* (New York: Harcourt, Brace & World, Inc., 1935), pp. 668–669.

22 At this point the political machine often becomes functionally significant. As Robert Steffens and others have shown, highly personalized relations and the abrogation of formal rules (red tape) by the machine often satisfy the needs of individual "clients" more fully than the formalized mechanism of governmental bureaucracy.

23 As one of the unemployed men remarked about the clerks at the Greenwich Employment Exchange: "'And the bloody Blokes wouldn't have their jobs if it wasn't for us men out of a job either. That's what gets me about their holding their noses up.'" Bakke, *op. cit.*, p. 80. See also H. D. Lasswell and G. Almond, "Aggressive Behavior by Cilents Towards Public Relief Administrators," *American Political Science Review*, 28 (1934), pp. 643–655.

24 The diagnostic significance of such linguistic indices as epithets has scarcely been explored by the sociologist. Sumner properly observes that epithets produce "summary criticisms" and definitions of social situations. Dollard also notes that "epithets frequently define the central issues in a society," and Sapir has rightly emphasized the importance of context of situations in appraising the significance of epithets. Of equal relevance is Linton's observation that "in case histories the way in which the community felt about a particular episode is, if anything, more important to our study than the actual behavior...." A sociological study of "vocabularies of encomium and opprobrium" should lead to valuable findings.

25 *Cf.* Ellsworth Faris, *The Nature of Human Nature* (New York: McGraw-Hill Book Company, 1937), pp. 41 ff.

26 Community disapproval of many forms of behavior may be analyzed in terms of one or the other of these patterns of substitution of culturally inappropriate types of relationship. Thus, prostitution constitutes a type-case where coitus, a form of intimacy which is institutionally defined as symbolic of the most "sacred" primary-group relationship, is placed within a contractual context, symbolized by the exchange of that most impersonal of all symbols, money. See Kingsley Davis, "The Sociology of Prostitution," *American Sociological Review*, 2 (1937), pp. 744–755.

27 Among recent studies of recruitment to bureaucracy are: Reinhard Bendix, *Higher Civil Servants in American Society* (Boulder: University of Colorado Press, 1949); Dwaine Marwick, *Career Perspectives in a Bureaucratic Setting* (Ann Arbor: University of Michigan Press, 1954); R. K. Kelsall, *Higher Civil Servants in Britain* (London: Routledge and Kegan Paul, 1955); W. L. Warner and J. C. Abegglen, *Occupational Mobility in American Business and Industry* (Minneapolis: University of Minnesota Press, 1955).

22 Individual Actualization in Complex Organizations[*]

by CHRIS ARGYRIS

Recently the writer completed the first phase of a research project having two objectives. The first is to provide knowledge concerning mental health problems in industrial organizations: more specifically, to understand the difficulties the individual faces and the opportunities he has for self-actualization in complex organizations. The second objective is to test parts of a theoretical framework about human problems of complex organizations and is reported in detail elsewhere.[1] The purpose of this paper is to present some recent results which may alter some commonly accepted notions of individual self-actualization in complex organizations.

Although the research to be discussed is being conducted in an industrial organization, the theory and the results are believed to apply to other kinds of complex organizations (for instance, hospitals, schools, banks, government agencies). Therefore, although the terms "management" and "employee" will be used, it is assumed that the results apply to any (genotypically) similar relationship between any administrator and employees.

Theoretical Framework

Since discussions of the theoretical framework and the many studies from which it is evolved are available in other publications[2] only some of the main propositions are defined in order to give the reader an acquaintance with the theoreti-

Reprinted from Mental Hygiene 44 (1960), 226–337 by permission of the author and The National Association for Mental Health, Inc.

cal foundations of the research. The most relevant propositions follow:

Personality is conceptualized as

1. Being an organization of parts in which the parts maintain the whole and the whole maintains the parts;
2. Seeking internal balance (usually called adjustment) and external balance (usually called adaptation);
3. Being propelled by psychological as well as physical energy;
4. Located in the need system; and
5. Expressed through the abilities.
6. The personality organization may be called "the self," which
7. Acts to color all the individual's experiences, therby causing him to live in "private worlds," and which
8. Is capable of defending or maintaining itself against threats of all types.

The development of the human personality can be hypothesized to follow the directions and dimensions outlined in the following model. It is assumed that human beings in our culture:

1. Tend to develop from a state of passivity as infants to a state of increasing activity as adults. (This is what Erikson[3] has called self-initiative and Bronfenbrenner[4] has called self-determination.)
2. Tend to develop from a state of dependence upon others as infants to a state of relative independence as adults. Relative independence is the ability to "stand on one's own two feet" and simultaneously to acknowledge healthy dependencies.[5] It is characterized by the liberation of the individual from his childhood determiners of behavior (for

example, his family) and his development of his own set of behavioral determiners. The mature individual does not tend to react to others (for example, the boss) in terms of patterns learned during childhood.[6]

3. Tend to develop from being capable of behaving only in a few ways as an infant to being capable of behaving in many different ways as an adult.[7]

4. Tend to develop from having erratic, casual, shallow, quickly dropped interests as an infant to having deeper interests as an adult. The mature state is characterized by an endless series of challenges; and the reward comes from doing something for its own sake. The tendency is to analyze and study phenomena in their full-blown wholeness, complexity, and depth.[8]

5. Tend to develop from having a short time-perspective (that is, one in which the present largely determines behavior) as an infant to a much longer time perspective as an adult (that is, one in which the behavior is more affected by the past and the future[9]). Bakke cogently describes the importance of time perspective in the lives of workers and their families and the variety of foresight practices by means of which they seek to secure the future.[10]

6. Tend to develop from being in a subordinate position in the family and society as an infant to aspiring to occupy an equal and/or superordinate position relative to their peers.

7. Tend to develop from a lack of awareness of self as an infant to an awareness of and control over self as an adult. The adult who tends to experience adequate and successful control over his own behavior tends to develop a sense of integrity (Erikson)[11] and feelings of self-worth.[12] Bakke[13] shows that one of the most important needs of workers is to enlarge those areas of their lives in which their own decisions determine the outcome of their efforts.

Most human problems in organizations arise because relatively healthy people in our culture are asked to participate in work situations which coerce them to be dependent, subordinate, submissive, to use few of their more than skin-surface abilities.

There are three major sets of variables which cause the dependence and subordination. The formal organization structure is the first variable (this includes the technology). Directive leadership is the second, and managerial control (budget, incentive systems, quality control, motion and time studies) is the third.

The degree of dependence and subordination that these three variables cause tends to increase as one goes down the chain of command, and the lower echelons of the organization take on the characteristics of mass production.

Healthy human beings (in our culture) tend to find dependence, subordination, and submissiveness frustrating. They would prefer to be relatively independent, to be active, to use many of their deeper abilities; and they aspire to positions equal with or higher than their peers. Frustration leads to regression, aggression, and tension. These in turn lead to conflict (the individual prefers to leave but fears doing so). Moreover, it can be shown that under these conditions, the individual will tend to experience psychological failure and short time perspective.

Individuals will adapt to the frustration, conflict, failure, and short time perspective by creating any one or a combination of following informal activities:

1. Leave the situation (absenteeism and turnover).

2. Climb the organizational ladder.

3. Become defensive (daydream, become aggressive, nurture grievances, regress, project, feel a low sense of self-worth).

4. Become apathetic, disinterested, nonego involved in the organization and its formal goals.

5. Create informal groups to sanction the defense reaction in 3 and 4.

6. Formalize the informal groups in the form of trade unions.
7. De-emphasize in their own minds the importance of self-growth and creativity and emphasize the importance of money and other material rewards.
8. Accept the above described ways of behaving as being proper for their lives outside the organization.

Management will tend to increase the employees' dependence, subordination, submissiveness, which in turn will increase their frustration and sense of failure, which in turn will increase the informal activities. Management will react to the increase in the informal activities by the formal structure, directive leadership, and managerial controls. This closes the circuit and one has a circular process in seemingly perpetual motion.

The Focus of the Study and the Sample

The objective of the research, conducted in a multistory manufacturing plant, is to study the mental health of highly skilled as compared to low-skilled employees. Our hypothesis is that since high-skilled employees tend to have a greater opportunity to express more mature behavior (be creative, use many abilities, be challenged in their work, and so on), they will tend to have a healthier work world. This in turn should lead to the highly skilled employees' behaving in more mature ways (as defined by our model above). For example, the high-skill employees (Department A) should express less indifference, apathy, dependence, and submissiveness than the low-skill employees (Department B). Also the high-skill employees should express greater sense of self-worth, self-satisfaction, and develop more lasting friendships than the low-skill employees.

Thirty-four employees from Department A and ninety employees from Department B constitute the sample. The schedules of the questions used are semi-structured. They outline specific areas which ought to be covered but leave the interviewer free to decide upon the sequence of the questions.[14]

The interviews were held in the plant, on company time. Notes were taken during the interview and recorded immediately at the end of the day. Interviews were held on different days of the week for a period of seven months.[15]

Evidence that the Experimental Conditions Exist for the Employees

The design of the study calls for a priori predictions about employee behavior in Department A and B. The differences, if any are found, are to be attributed to the differential characteristics assumed to exist in the technology of Departments A and B. (For example, A gives employees much more opportunity for varied, creative work than does B.) Before the hypotheses can be tested, however, we must show some evidence that the employees perceive the differences between A and B as we assume they do. The researcher's assumption of differences is based upon management's job-classification structure. It is one thing for management to classify the jobs in Department A as skilled and Department B as nonskilled and to pay the employees according to these classifications; it is quite another for employees to perceive these differences.

Evidence that the employees experience the experimental conditions as the researchers assume can be obtained from a number of sources. Ninety-four per cent of the employees in Department A (high-skilled) report that they have jobs in which they experience "plenty of variety," "as much variety as they can handle or more." Eighty-seven per cent of the employees in Department B report that they have jobs which are "completely routine," "dull," "monotonous," "with little if any variety."

Further evidence is obtained by analyzing the data related to "perceived personal satisfaction" about their jobs. Eighty-five per cent of Department B (low-skilled) report that they obtain "no satisfaction from their work excepting good wages." Eighty-three per cent of the employees in Department A report that they gain "much personal satisfaction because they have challenging and creative work."

A few qualitative examples to illustrate the differential feelings are: Department A: "I think the satisfaction I get is to know that I have done a job well. I like to do a perfect job; I like to feel something's done really good; it's really perfect. When I take a look at a piece that I can tell has been made well, I get a real sense of satisfaction." Department B: 1. "If the work is all right, then I make money, and that's my biggest satisfaction. If I don't...What else is there to be satisfied about? I learned long ago the only thing you can get out of a good job is good pay."

2. "The only reason I work is to make money. No other reason. Some guys (damn few) say they work for pleasure. They must be bats. How the hell am I supposed to get satisfaction from this job? I'd just as soon get out and dig holes, at least I'd be in the fresh air."

A second assumption made by the research design is that the degree of dependence and subordination required of the employees by the leadership and the managerial controls will not vary significantly between Departments A and B. These assumptions must also be verified as representing reality from the employees' point of view.

Seventy-five per cent of the employees in B and 84 per cent in A view the leadership as "excellent because they hardly ever bother us, because they continually try to help us earn good wages and have secure jobs." In discussing the contacts that they have with management, 63 per cent in B and 68 per cent in A view the management as being "friendly," "down-to-earth," "interested in the employees," and "continually striving to make the employees feel they are not simple machines."

Turning to controls, we find that almost no employees in either department describe the budgets as pressuring them. One explanation of this may be that the budget system, only a few months old, has not been in existence long enough to be felt by the employees. Turning to the incentive system, 67 per cent in Department B and 62 per cent in Department A view the piece rates as "being fair," "some rates rough, some easy, but the overall average is fair," and "wish they were slightly higher, but this is not a complaint."

In response to a question on the freedom the employees feel, reflecting on the leadership and the controls together, 83 per cent in Department A report they have "as much, or almost as much, freedom as they desire." Finally, in an overall indication of the degree of pressure the employees feel, 91 per cent in Department B and 100 per cent in Department A say that they "never, or hardly ever, experience pressure."

It seems reasonable to assume that the degree of dependence and subordination required of the employees in Department A and B does not vary significantly between the departments. This says nothing about the amount of dependence and submissiveness perceived by the employees. We are simply saying that whatever the amount is, it is about equal in both departments.

Some Differences Between High-skill And Low-skill Employees

A method has been developed to infer the predispositions that individuals manifest while at work, plus their potency (in the Lewinian sense of the term).[16]

A word about our use of the concept "predisposition." For the sake of consistency and simplicity, the personality aspects upon which we focus are all categorized as "predisposition." A predisposition is defined as a tendency to act in a particular situation. The predispositions are inferred from the interview data. The analyst combs the interview for any themes from which he can infer the desires that the participant wishes to satisfy while at work.[17] An analysis of these data show that statistically the high-skill (HS) employees differ significantly from the low-skill (LS) employees as follows.

These data confirm the hypothesis that the technology has an impact upon the predispositions and activities of human beings. Further analysis, however, raises the question of how significant this impact is if one is focusing on mental health problems.

The Degree of Self-actualization of HS and LS Employees

The answer to this question becomes evident when we note that the self-actualization scores of the LS and HS employees do not differ significantly. Both sets of employees have equally high scores. These scores purport to quantify (in a primitive manner) the degree to which an individual actualizes himself while in the organization.

In other words, even though the LS and HS employees differ significantly in self-actualization, then it must be that in addition to the dissimilar predispositions they must have similar ones which are being expressed. The data confirm this hypothesis. The four predispositions with

TABLE 1.

High-Skill	Statistical Significance*	Low-Skill
1. Express a high sense of self-worth and self-regard related to their technological capabilities.	.001	1. Express a very low sense of self-worth and self-regard.
2. Express need to be active.	.001	2. Express need to be passive.
3. Express need to work with others.	.001	3. Express need to be alone.
4. Express need for variety and challenge in their work world.	.001	4. Express need for routine, non-challenging work.
5. Express need to have some close friendships while at work.	.01	5. Express desire not to make close friendships while at work.
6. Express need to produce quality work.	.001	6. Express need to produce adequate (quantitative) work to make a fair day's pay.
7. Express almost no need to overemphasize the importance of material rewards.	.01	7. Overemphasize the importance of material rewards.
8. Express need to learn more about other kinds of work within the same job family.	.001	8. Express almost no need to learn other kinds of work.
9. Participate in activities outside their workplace judged by the researcher to be creative.	.01	9. Participate in activities outside their workplace judged by the research to be noncreative.

* The probability of obtaining by change a difference as large as that reported is computed by employing statistical procedures appropriate for use with independent proportions. See Quinn McNemar, *Psychological Statistics* (New York, John Wiley & Sons, Inc. 1955), p. 60.

the highest potency are similar for both groups of employees. They are:

	Frequency of choice	
	HS (%)	LS (%)
1. To be left alone by management	97.0	89.0
2. To be noninvolved, indifferent, and apathetic about the formal goals and problems of the organization	96.0	86.0
3. To experience skin-surface interpersonal relationships	96.0	90.0
4. To earn fair wages and to have secure jobs	92.0	89.0

From the first two predispositions we may infer the employees' desire to be left alone by the formal authorities and not to be required to become ego-involved in the objectives of the company. Apparently the employees have withdrawn psychologically from the organization. They may be said to be in a state of apathy.

Apathy also seems to characterize the employees' predispositions with regard to their interpersonal relationships with others. We note that they desire few interactions and those to be mere skin-surface relationships. This apathy toward human relationships (as differentiated from apathy toward nonhuman relationships) may be defined as alienation. Employees who are alienated are therefore defined as those who do not tend to desire the rich interpersonal activity usually assumed by some personality theorists to be a basic characteristic of man.[18] In short, alienated people are willing to separate themselves from human relationships.

From the employees' point of view (especially those on low-skill jobs), alienation may be a sensible way to adapt to their working world. Why, they reason, should they become ego-involved in a world that will not permit them to express mature aspirations and to gain satisfaction of their adult needs?

At this point, the data simply permit us to hypothesize the primitive state of interpersonal relationship inferred to exist in the activities the employees engage in during their nonworking hours.[19] Thus the employee may be hurting his "long-range self" without realizing it.

Here is an important area for research. What precisely are the mental health implications of prolonged experiences of apathy and alienation? Can prolonged apathy and alienation lead to mental illness? If so, by what processes and toward what types of illnesses?

Returning to the data, one may further hypothesize that the alienation (apathy toward others and toward one's self) will tend to lead the employees in both groups to express a low degree of competence in their dealing with "things." These hypotheses are confirmed. LS and HS employees' sense of competence and regard for their competence in interpersonal relationships is low and about the same for both groups. On the other hand, we have seen (Table 2) that only the HS employees report a high degree of competence in their dealing with "things."

TABLE 2.

Frequency distribution of self-actualization scores in high-skilled and low-skilled employees

	HS (%)	LS (%)
0—49.5	...	...
50—54.5	2.9	1.1
55—59.5	2.9	1.1
60—64.5	...	3.3
65—69.5	5.9	8.9
70—74.5	5.9	16.7
75—79.5	8.8	11.1
80—84.5	23.6	16.7
85—89.5	20.6	21.1
90—94.5	14.7	10.0
95—100	8.8	10.0

Some Comments on the "Human Climate" of the Organization

Let us now look briefly at the environmental culture of the organization in which these results are being obtained.

An analysis of the data shows that management believes, and the employees agree, that the organization is not pressure-oriented. (In fact, in the writer's experience, this is the least pressure-oriented plant he has ever studied). The leadership consciously refrains from pressure tactics. As to managerial controls, they are just being established. One of the highest officials remarks that if controls upset people, the controls will go!

The employees in both groups report that they appreciate the lack of pressure. They are very loyal to the organization, produce an amount that is appreciated by all levels of management, have continually voted down a union, and have a long record of low absenteeism, low turnover, and low grievance rates.

Oversimplified Theories of Individual-organizational Health

From the above, it is not difficult to see why both management and employees are quite content with each other and with the organization. Each group feels it is getting what it desires.

On the other hand, the employees report that they desire a world in which

1. They are not required to become ego-involved and made (partially) responsible for the organization's health.
2. They are permitted to be alienated.
3. They are paid well (from their point of view) and guaranteed a secure job.

It must be stressed again that no adequate evidence exists to help the mental health practitioner decide how mentally unhealthy or healthy is this state of affairs. (As far as the writer is aware, not even a reliable and valid concept of mental health exists.) It may be that the situation herein described is not unhealthy for individuals and will not lead to mental health problems. On the other hand, there is enough evidence to hold with equal vigor the hypothesis that, as Fromm implies, alienation can lead us to become a sick society.[20] I tend to believe Fromm has made an important point. However, much research is needed really to test the hypothesis.

The other argument that must be kept in mind is that mental health of the individual is a product of his total life-situation. It may be that an individual can endure a significant amount of deficiency in actualization within the plant and make up for it in activities outside of the plant. What little evidence I have seen seems to suggest that there is a correlation between the in-plant actualization and outside activities. People with low actualization within the plant do not seem to make up for it as judged by the kind of community activities in which they participate.[21] Recent, and as yet unpublished, research by the writer reinforces the above conclusion. For example, most of the employees (low- and high-skill) do not participate in "outside" organizations in the community. However, systematic research is lacking and no definite conclusions may be drawn at this time.

On the other hand, we find that the managers' concept of organizational health is equally obscure if not invalid. Management is using a set of criteria about organizational health which leads the executives to diagnose the health of the organization as high. For example, they see that absenteeism, turnover, grievance rates are low and that the production and loyalty are high, and on the basis of their theory judge that all is well. The problem is that their theory about organizational health is oversimplified and internally inconsistent. It is oversimplified because it does not include the health of the individuals working for the organization. It is inconsistent because it has two inconsistent and independent sets of criteria for organizational health rather than one unified set. For example, management assumes that an organization with low absenteeism, low turnover, low grievance, will also tend to have employees who are productive and who desire to be identified with the company, to participate in all decisions that directly influence them, to worry about making the company more effective, to feel some responsibility for the overall health of the company, and to develop close relationships with management and each other so that such phrases as "one happy family," and "we're a close company," mirror reality.

Our data show that the above theory is not as integrated as management assumes. For example, the plant has a very low rate of absenteeism, turnover, and grievances. The employees are productive. Up to this point, management's theory holds. The same employees, however, also express little identification with the company, little desire to feel some responsibility for its overall health, little desire to win promotions as foremen, little desire to have close friendships with management or with each other. Nor do they express strong needs to belong to cohesive groups.

This does not mean, however, that the plant is not "one happy family." The employees, according to our measures, are very loyal to the organization because they need to be in situations where they are simply asked to produce and not required to become identified with, or deeply involved in, the company. As one employee puts it, "I love this company; it's a wonderful place. They pay excellent wages, give good benefits, and they leave you alone. There's a relaxed friendly feeling here. You don't feel the constant pressure as you do in Company Y. No sir, I wouldn't leave this company even

if someone wanted to pay me more." Thus, strong loyalty is not necessarily built upon an active, interested, healthy employee group. On the contrary, the opportunity to be apathetic, disinterested, noninvolved, could generate strong loyalties within the employees as long as wages and job security remain high.

The most crucial needs HS and LS employees report are wages, job security, job control, noninvolvement, and togetherness, in that order. Does this mean that money is most important? Are we back to the economists' theory of rational man? The answer to the first question is, "Yes," and to the second, "No." If money is important, it is not because man is the inherently rational being pictured by some economists. The employee is still a complex organism with inner strivings to grow, to develop, to have a sense of inner worth. It is precisely because he is not permitted truly to actualize his potential that he makes a decision to "simplify" his personality, making money and other material factors most important. It is as if the employee says to himself, "I want to be a healthy creative human being; I cannot be and still produce what I am required to produce. Therefore, I will say, 'To hell with my total personality,' and place the major emphasis on money."[22]

Such a decision is not a rational one. It is a deep, emotional, human one. Nevertheless, it makes money and job security very important to the employee. If this is valid, then administrators of complex organizations are faced with one of the most difficult human problems ever to challenge them. On the one hand, it becomes easy for both the administrator and the employees to de-emphasize human values and to operate on a *quid pro quo* basis of money, job security, and benefits. As long as a minimum standard of human relationships is maintained, the "rational-man relationship" could well flourish. But, as the data point out, such a theory will produce and reward apathy, indifference, alienation, and noninvolvement.

Relating Individual Health to Organizational Effectiveness

If the above is valid, clearly individual and organizational "health" are so interrelated that it may be impossible to consider one without considering the other. Men like Lewin and Harry Stack Sullivan showed years ago that man cannot be separated from his environment. In studying the problems of industrial mental health, it may be that man may not be separated from the organization. The unit becomes the individual-organization.

In stating this position, are we making a value judgment that it is good for organizations to exist? The answer must be provided on two levels. First, as far as the researcher is concerned, organizational survival is not a matter of value. Organizations must exist for the researcher as do leaves for the botanist, human bodies for the biologist, and birds for the ornithologist. Without organizations, the researcher on organizations would have nothing to study.

Turning to the value problem from the mental health practitioner's point of view, the following may be said. Most students agree that, basically, organizations are created by man to fulfill needs that require the collective efforts of human beings. These needs are essential if man is to survive. Thus, stating that organizations must survive is simply affirming the most basic needs of mankind. It is precisely because human survival and health are crucial that organizational effectiveness is emphasized. Without organizational effectiveness, man could lose his individual health.

This position is openly acknowledged by the employees. Interviews with the employees show quite clearly that they feel responsible for keeping the organization alive. The problem, from a mental health point of view, is that they too have internalized management's inadequate standards of organizational effectiveness. Consequently they, too, feel that low absenteeism, turnover, grievance rates, and high production imply a healthy organization. They report a high degree of satisfaction with their mental health. In fact, our data lead us to predict that over 90 per cent of the employees and 100 per cent of the management in this plant would resist or even reject a mental health program that attempts to emphasize individual health "vs." or "over" the requirements of the organization. The employees report themselves to be "too realistic" to see such a program as in their interest.

Difficult as the situation may sound, there is at least one possible direction to consider. These feelings of responsibility for organizational effectiveness could become the foundations for the building of an effective preventive mental health program in industry. Is it not a sign of some health when an individual is willing to see himself in a realistic perspective in his relationship with his society? To be willing to give of one's self without feeling one is giving up one's self may be an important building block for a healthy society.

The argument is not being made that an overemphasis on organization could not lead to the ideal of an "organization man" who submits his uniqueness and his health to the demands of the organization.... Organizations are tools which help man to survive. They are created by man. Man can change them to facilitate individual growth.

Changing organizations today, however, is a very difficult task and the major barrier is that there exists no theory or empirical knowledge that tells us in which direction changes ought to be made. As mentioned above, the traditional management theories are inadequate. One must conclude from this study that the informal employee system, assumed by many social scientists to be one answer to the problem, does not offer a solution. The informal employee system in this plant sanctions and protects employees apathy, indifference, and alienation.

Herein lies the challenge of the future for preventive mental health. Much thinking needs to be done on developing dimensions of organizational effectiveness.[23] Much research needs to be conducted on how to maximize individual-organization health. In the organization studied only such a theory would appeal to both the employees and the management, who express a deep desire that the plant must survive, even, if necessary, at their psychological "expense."

[1] See Chris Argyris, "Individual Actualization in Complex Organizations," *Mental Hygiene,* 44:2 (April, 1960), 226–237.

[2] *Ibid.*; see also Chris Argyris, *Personality and Organization* (New York: Harper & Row, Publishers, Inc., 1957).

[3] See E. H. Erikson, *Childhood and Society* (New York: W. W. Norton & Company, Inc., 1950); see also R. Kotinsky, *Personality in the Making* (New York: Harper & Row Publishers, Inc., 1952), pp. 8–25.

[4] Urie Bronfenbrenner, "Toward an Integrated Theory of Personality," in Robert R. Blake and Glen B. Ramsey, eds., *Perception* (Chicago: G. P. Putnam's Sons, 1953).

[5] This is similar to Erikson's "sense of autonomy" and Bronfenbrenner's "state of creative interdependence."

[6] Robert W. White, *Lives in Progress* (New York: Dryden Press, 1952).

[7] Lewin and Kounin believe that as the individual develops needs and abilities the boundaries between them become more rigid. This explains why an adult is better able than a child to be frustrated in one activity and still behave constructively in another. See Kurt Lewin, *A Dynamic Theory of Personality* (New York: McGraw-Hill Book Company, 1935); and Jacob S. Kounin, "Intellectual Development and Rigidity," in R. Barker, J. Kounin, and H. R. Wright, eds., *Child Behavior and Development* (New York: McGraw-Hill Book Company, 1943), pp. 179–198.

[8] White, *op. cit.,* pp. 347 ff.

[9] Lewin also cites the billions of dollars that are invested in insurance policies. See Kurt Lewin, "Time Perspective and Morale," in *Resolving Social Conflicts* (New York: Harper & Row, Publishers, Inc., 1958) p. 105.

[10] See E. W. Bakke, *The Unemployed Worker* (New Haven: Yale University Press, 1940).

[11] Erikson, *op. cit.*

[12] Carl R. Rogers, *Client-centered Therapy* (Boston: Houghton Mifflin Company, 1951).

[13] Bakke, *op. cit.,* pp. 29, 247.

[14] For a more detailed discussion see Chris Argyris, *Human Problems in a Large Hospital* (New Haven: Labor and Management Center, Yale University, 1956).

[15] A monograph being written provides detailed discussion of the research methods and analysis of the organization as a social system. This work is tentatively entitled "Theory and Method of Diagnosing Organizational Behavior."

[16] Lewin, *op. cit.*

[17] A predisposition is not assumed to be as basic as the "needs" or "need system" postulated by many psychologists. The psychologist's concept of "need" usually refers to those predispositions (to use our terms for the moment) that are more genotypic (that is, they are manifested in many different types of situations). Our predispositions are limited to the organizational context being studied.

[18] See Lewin, *A Dynamic Theory of Personality;* Erich Fromm, *The Sane Society* (New York: Holt, Rinehart & Winston, Inc., 1955); Harry Stack Sullivan, *Conceptions of Modern Psychiatry* (William Alanson White Psychiatric Foundation, 1947); Rogers, *op. cit.*

[19] Argyris, *Personality and Organization.*

[20] Fromm, *op. cit.,* p. 275.

[21] Argyris, *Personality and Organization.*

[22] Two points worth noting are: It is not only industry which forces the employee to simplify his personality. The family, schools, churches, etc., may all have similar impacts. Second, the employee is willing to simplify his personality up to a point. This does not mean he will accept money to be treated in an inhuman manner.

[23] For some preliminary dimensions of organizational health, see the author's "Organizational Leadership," ONR Conference (March, 1959), in a book to be edited by Luigi Petrullo.

* The writer is indebted to Dr. Raymond Gould of the National Institute of Mental Health for many helpful comments regarding this research project. (Project No. USPHS 3M-9128).

23　The Red Executive

by DAVID GRANICK

It is usually considered sound administrative procedure to avoid, wherever possible, asking permission for dubious activities. In the Soviet Union, visits by tourists to research institutes fall into this category. Thus, when I wished to visit the Research Institute attached to the State Planning Commission, I simply went there without any by-your-leave.

When I arrived, I was greeted with rather more formality than I had experienced during the preceding two weeks in the Soviet Union. A young, efficient-looking guard at the entrance stopped me with a military salute. This reception was a far cry from the sweet-old-lady doorkeeper at most Soviet buildings, who will generally ignore you if you walk by resolutely, acting as though you belonged there and knew exactly where you were going. The guard wanted to know my business; I gave it. He telephoned the office, and a young economist came to escort me upstairs to the office of the assistant director of the institute.

From here on, all proceeded normally. I spoke briefly to the assistant director, told him that I wished to talk with some of the institute's economists, and gave him a list of the problems I wished to ask about. He said that he would make arrangements. (A week later I had a three-hour interview).

These formalities over, my guide and I chatted. He was a bright economist, in his mid-twenties, and surprisingly familiar with American economic writing about the Soviet Union. He asked what various

American scholars were now doing, and who was now teaching what at the different American universities. Except for the fact that we were talking in Russian, the whole visit was much like one I might have had at an American institution housing classified documents.

It was only when we turned to a discussion of American industry that the tone changed. I pointed out to him that there was no good factual evidence for a substantial increase in the degree of monopoly during the past half-century and that, if anything, the weight of the evidence pointed toward a mild decline. He in turn pointed out to me that Marxian economic theory proved the inevitability of an increase in monopoly, and he gave me a quick rundown of the relevant sections of a course in Political Economy I. I was willing to give him points for theory but appealed back to the facts. "The facts be damned," was obviously his feeling; he *knew* the truth of the matter. Finally, he cited some data which was clearly beside the point. We left it at that.

I have thought of this conversation many times since. This young Soviet economist had a fairly simple view of America. He accepted a theory which predicted trends of development, and if facts conflicted with it—then the worse for the facts.

Now this intellectual position is not quite as nonsensical as it sounds. "Facts" often have the discomforting characteristic of later turning out to be not true at all. The history of the natural sciences and of invention is full of cases of men who ignored the "facts"—followed their theories or hunches—and proved to be right. All the same, it would seem that the odds are against you when you ignore whatever weak collection of "facts" do exist.

Soviet social science has certainly suffered from its certitude in a priori knowledge of America. But Russian Marxists are not the only ones to accept a simple image of a foreign society, drawn from a theoretic concept of what seems reasonable. Americans also have been known, on occasion, to suffer from the same disease.

Soviet society is a complex one. Russia is a big country. One can find evidence for "the things everyone knows" about Russia—and plenty of counterexamples also. In this chapter, I shall try to show some of the variety.

"Everyone knows that Russian managers have no authority, and all decisions are made at the top."

For the American tourist, it is a major undertaking to get into a Russian factory. The Soviet agency Intourist—which is supposed to handle all of the official contacts between the tourist and Soviet institutions—is primarily organized for arranging museum visits, buying theater tickets, etc., and in most towns is quite at a loss in going beyond this.

When I had been in Moscow for several days and had not received any answer to my request to see factories, I decided that direct action was in order. Moscow is full of kiosks where for a price varying between three and seven cents one can get addresses, telephone numbers, and directions. I asked for the address of a well-known machine-tool plant, took an Intourist car to the plant gate, and told the driver not to wait. He drove off readily, and I was on my own.

"Red Proletariat," an old Moscow plant, is a collection of fairly small multistory buildings. The main building faced on the street, and I walked in. From the entranceway, I could see some of the shop operators working; but in between was a guard checking passes. I decided to try to bull my way through and got in line behind a couple of Russians who seemed to be new workers.

When I reached the guard, I asked for the chief engineer of the plant—a man comparable to an American plant superintendent. The guard treated my question as routine and sent me around to the office which provides passes. This was in a separate building located further within the plant grounds, but apparently there was no objection to a stranger walking around alone in the factory area.

The office for distributing passes was a crowded one. There were some women, who seemed to be new workers, and several men, apparently agents from other plants or organizations, who were waiting to carry on their business in the plant. The phone in the waiting room was in frequent use for intraplant calls.

When my turn in line came, I told who I was and whom I wanted to see. Consternation. Did I want a job? Was I sent there on business by some other Russian organization? Where were my papers? Sure enough, just as I had claimed, I had a foreign passport.

At this point the clerk called over a guard who seemed in charge and with relief turned my case over to him. The guard retired with my passport into a far corner of the room and examined it with suspicion. When he reached the point of carefully examining all visa stamps from countries other than Russia, it was clear that he was simply stalling until he could think of something to do with me.

Meanwhile, some of my fellow benchwarmers in the waiting room joined in. If I wanted to see the chief engineer, why didn't I call him? Here was the phone; they knew his extension and supplied it. It seemed a better idea than depending on the guard, but I felt committed to the ways of officialdom.

Finally, the guard came back with a new address for me. He could not give me a pass; but if I would go to the

Regional Economic Council, they could supply one. The Council had a special sector for Foreign Relations, and I was their problem.

This was a new angle for getting into plants, one which Intourist had never mentioned, so back I went to the center of town. At the Sector for Foreign Relations I was greeted with open arms. What would I like to see? I named four plants. Were those the only ones? Weren't there any more? I gave ten more names. I asked to see one of the officials in the Regional Economic Council. Fine! They would arrange things. I should call back in two days.

I called back. Embarrassment. Yes, I could see the official in the Council (I did), but the factories were a different proposition. They had called each of the plants I had mentioned, and in each case were turned down. The managers were busy, and none could spare the three to four hours which would normally be involved. There was nothing to be done; the plant managers had the last word.

Later, I tried again through another, and presumably more impressive, staff organization. Again promises, and again a veto from the plant level.

Here, apparently, was a normal line-staff relationship. The staff sectors of higher bodies could intercede, but the decision was a line one on the local level.

In another situation, however, plant managers were much less independent. In the Moscow City Council organization, I talked with the man in charge of all industry under the City Council. After our interview, he too promised to arrange a plant visit.

This time, when I called back, the appointment was on. I was to come to the Moscow City Council and go out from there to the plant. When I arrived, the director of the factory I was to visit was waiting for me. Apparently, he had been unceremoniously summoned to meet me downtown and personally escort me

to his plant. It was quite clear that in this case, with a line official making the arrangements, the plant director was not asked for his consent.

"Everyone knows that Russia is a land of secrecy and watchfulness, where security-consciousness-plus reigns supreme."

Buildings which house institutions of any type—universities, courts, administrative bodies—all have doorkeepers whose job it is to learn your business before you may enter. No one, Russian or foreigner, is allowed to enter even such an innocuous institution as a university without a special pass. This is bad enough, but for the foreigner there are further provisions. If you order a car through Intourist, you must say where you are going, and the information is entered into a bound volume as a semipermanent record. The theory as to security is rigid indeed.

The practice, however, is a good bit more pliant. Only once was I ever kept from entering a building for lack of a pass; this was at the New Moscow University, a tourist haven. Yet when I told this fact to my Moscow guide, she seemed honestly surprised that I had never been stopped before. At the University of Kiev, the university president is apparently a stickler for regulations. Three or four times a year, according to a student there, he personally stands at the university entrance to check on student passes. But since half of the students will have left their passes in their rooms, classwork is pretty thoroughly disrupted on these mornings.

In Moscow, Leningrad, and Kiev I wandered freely through buildings housing the City and Regional Economic administrative bodies. When I had appointments there, my hosts would sometimes escort me part way out of the building when we were through, but usually they were quite happy to return to work when I protested that I could find my own way out.

Even the regulation requiring Intourist to know where you are going by car is only loosely enforced. It is quite acceptable to say that you'll be "driving around the city." Furthermore, Intourist is only interested in your first stop; they have no record of any additional ones. Finally, there is nothing to prevent the foreigner from walking or taking a bus, streetcar, or cab and completely ignoring Intourist.

Communist Party buildings and meetings are said to have far stricter security provisions than those I encountered. Even here, however, theory and practices seem widely separate. A Ukrainian secretary of a Young Communist League student group claimed she never carries her membership card, even to show at large meetings where she is not personally known, and yet has never been kept out of a meeting for this reason.

"Everyone knows that the standard of living of the Russian man-on-the-street is practically nonexistent."

Housing is the strongest case for this. In Kiev, where new apartment houses were still going up at great speed in 1958, space per family even in the new buildings was extremely tight. Apartments were being built with one to three rooms, plus bathroom and small kitchen. It was just as well that few refrigerators are available in the Soviet Union, for a family which owned one could never fit it into one of these "compact" kitchens. But the most striking feature to an American is the size of family required to qualify for one of these apartments. An apartment of three rooms is intended for seven to eight people, two rooms for five or six people, and any smaller family is expected to fit into one room. These rooms seemed medium-sized—about 165 square feet apiece.

Soviet official statistics for 1956 show that Kiev was just average for Soviet cities, with 83 square feet of housing space per capita—including halls, kitchens, bathrooms, and closets.

A Moscow court case which I attended illustrated in comic form the consequent situations. It was a civil case, brought by a woman against her former husband who was still officially registered as living in her apartment. He had actually not been there for several years, for he was living elsewhere in Moscow with a second wife. But since he was still officially registered in his first wife's apartment, he had the legal right to return whenever he wished. The woman wanted his name expunged from the register.

The husband put forth a fascinating defense. His second wife's apartment was crowded, he said. It was a single room of 130 square feet and he, his wife, their baby, and his mother-in-law were all living there. His second wife refused to allow him to be registered as officially living in this apartment for who knew what might happen in the future? They might separate, or—apparently a greater risk—he might bring into the apartment his child by his first wife; for this child was still registered on his passport. But, the husband insisted to the court, he had to be registered as living somewhere. It was the law. Where should he go? To the moon?

The court granted the first wife's request for removing his name from the apartment's register. Although the judge and the spectators found the case a bit on the farcical side, I felt a sneaking sympathy for the second wife, who wished to be absolutely certain that a fifth person would not legally be jammed into her single room.

This is one side of the Russian living standard. But there is the other side, symbolized by the mystery which bothered me all through my stay in Russia: the case of the missing children.

Walk down the streets of the big cities in the summertime; look in the parks; go to the housing developments; no kids. Only a handful can be seen of all those between infancy and fourteen to sixteen years old. Where are the children?

Off at camp, was the answer I was given for the older ones. For the younger ones, their nurseries and kindergartens simply moved lock, stock, and barrel out to the country. The kids were on vacation.

A Moscow factory operated a Pioneer camp for the children of its own workers. The factory had a total labor force of 400, and the camp had room for 360 school-age children at a time. The director said that children went either for one month or for the entire summer, depending on the parents' wishes. According to the director, most parents were not charged anything for the camp. The maximum charge is 90 rubles per month per child ($9 at the tourist exchange rate) compared to a cost of operation of 600 rubles per month per child; the subsidy was contributed equally from factory and trade-union funds.

I could not believe that most of Russia's children really got away from the big cities during the summer. But if not, where were they? I was forced to conclude that the story I was told seemed to be borne out. Later, I checked official Soviet statistics for the entire urban population of the country. Estimated from the data for 1955 (the latest year available) showed that 60 per cent of all the seven- to thirteen-year-olds went away during the summer in some organized group fashion, and over one fourth of the total went to camp. The 60-per-cent figure does not include those many children who simply went to the country with their families.

This is the difficulty with comparing living standards in different countries. Minimum housing by American standards is the height of luxury in Russia.

But summer camp, a major expense for those American parents who can afford it, is commonplace and virtually free of charge for Russian urban dwellers.

"Everyone knows that Soviet working conditions are terrible—a throwback to the nineteenth century."

At the Moscow airport, waiting for the plane to Kharkov, I chatted with two American engineers. They had recently visited the Kharkov Tractor Plant, which was first built in the early 1930's and is still one of the major factories in the Soviet Union. Their main impression was one of dismay at the lack of safety precautions. Dangerous conditions extended even to such matters as slippery floors in the work areas.

In the various plants I visited, slippery floors were not a problem. But one could not help being impressed by the relative absence of safety devices on presses and cutting-machine tools. This was despite the fact that, in each town, I was clearly taken to see one of the more efficient plants.

The American iron and steel delegation, also visiting Russia that summer, was told that there were about 720 lost-time accidents during 1957 in the Magnitogorsk steel works. These accidents included four fatalities and six cases of severe disability. This accident rate is about twenty-three times as high as that of the American steel industry.

The "Hammer and Sickle" combine motor plant in Kharkov is an old plant in name only, for it was almost completely destroyed during the war. I was shown around the machine shop, the foundry, the forging-pressing shop, and the main assembly building, all of which have been built since the war. It is a plant with new buildings, an old reputation, and a skilled work force, and thus should be highly favored as industrial factories go.

Despite these advantages, there seemed

to be only one toilet for each large building. Water fountains existed, but they were so scarce that I noticed only one on my tour. Nothing resembling Coke machines existed; there was no traveling canteen; the coffee break was an unknown institution. In the "workers' state," worker amenities seemed to have a low priority indeed.

At present, instead of a coffee break, a physical-training break is being tried. In early 1959, Moscow News reported that over 400,000 workers in Moscow factories were involved in this organized exercise. Salutary results for industrial safety have been claimed.

Yet, to show the other side of things, I spoke to an American who had sold agricultural equipment to the Russians, and he recalled a discussion of a particular machine. The Russians agreed that his machine was both cheaper and more efficient than a competitor's—but still it was unacceptable. It was too noisy and made the operator too dirty; better to have a less efficient machine which provided superior working conditions.

The chief engineer of a Leningrad plant, discussing mechanization which he had introduced, insisted that one important criterion for judging a given mechanization proposal was its effect on the amount of worker strain in plant operations. Now it may or may not be true that this criterion has been operationally important, but certainly worker conditions are *thought of* by Russian managements when they are planning changes—whether they actually do much about them or not. Even this is more than was true of some nineteenth-century managements.

"Everyone knows that the Russian economy is operated as a tightly coordinated, planned system."

All major decisions are made with the State Planning Commission, the nerve center of the economy. Investment programs are decided upon—and decisions as to these are linked with plans for output growth in each of the main sectors of manufacturing, trade, and agriculture. Plans are laid as to the number of workers to be employed by each sector. Schedules are worked out for the use of materials. In 1958, the State Planning Commission itself approved the allocation to users of 760 different types of materials, fuels, and equipment.

These decisions, in turn, get siphoned down to the level of the individual plant. A director receives a yearly program for his factory which tells him how much it to produce, what his product-mix is to be, how many workers he can hire, and how much he should pay them. He receives allocation orders for the materials and fuels he needs, and there is little he can buy without these orders. Management's job is to product the planned output—and more if possible—with the inputs given to it.

Moreover, the factory's inputs and outputs are stated both in physical terms (X tons of steel as inputs, and Y number of trucks as output) and in rubles. The director buys and sells at prices set by the government. He is expected to earn a profit and even has a "plan" for how much this is to be. (The government, as owner, then absorbs virtually all of this profit into the state budget.) Here is a system of planning with a vengeance.

Under these circumstances, industry should be little concerned with the marketing of goods or the buying of materials, for these activities are programmed ahead of time. The Moscow City Council, for example, has roughly 250,000 industrial employees under its control. In this large operation, only about 2 per cent of the total number is involved in buying and selling goods for the various industrial plants. (This 2-per cent figure, of course, excludes both warehousing workers and all retail salesmen.) This ratio seems low by American standards.

At the same time, the Soviet planning system leaves plenty of room for bargaining on the local level. Let us take, for example, the management of a shoe plant. The factory director will be told the total number of shoes to produce, and this total will be broken down into three subgroups for men, women, and children. In addition, he will be given a single ruble figure for the value of his total planned shoe output. But the particular types of shoes he produce will be up to him.

This arrangement leaves the director a good deal more leeway than appears on the surface. He is given a certain labor force, a specific amount of equipment, and a fixed volume of materials with which to work. It is up to him to try to negotiate the sort of product-mix of shoes which will be easiest to produce with his resources. True, he cannot produce only cheap shoes; for although this would make it easy to fulfill his quota for the number of shoes, their total value would be less than called for by his plan. But there are other, slightly more subtle, methods of juggling his production.

If the director can get away with producing only a few styles of shoes, he will have long production runs and be able to cut costs. If he can bias his production toward small-size shoes and away from large ones, he can save on leather inputs. Finally, although the state sets the prices for his shoes, different styles will yield him different profit mark-ups. The director can try to specialize in those styles which offer the highest profit.

How far the director can go in all this depends on his bargaining position. In the past, this position has been good, indeed. Always less has been produced than the customers would buy. Thus, wholesalers have been fairly easy to deal with; since they could sell anything, why antagonize the producer in a sellers' market? Only the final customer complained bitterly about the results of this system.

In recent years the sellers' market has eased off somewhat. Much greater stocks of goods seem available now than in the past, particularly of items like shoes

which are sold to individual consumers. The wholesalers or retail stores which continue to buy "shoes," without worrying about sizes and styles, are likely to find too many shoes remaining on their shelves—and their own sales plans will remain unfulfilled. As the sellers' market has eased, the wholesalers' backs have stiffened. The bargaining positions have changed. But the bargaining remains; the "plans" only set the framework within which it occurs.

Where negotiations are important, where state organizations can shop around, the man with the salesman's personality comes into his own. But in the Soviet Union's sellers' market he does not gravitate into sales but into purchasing. It is here that he operates with his expense account, his personal contacts, his joviality. His bonuses are a substitute for commissions. He has even been known to operate as a "five-percenter."

"Everyone knows that Soviet managerial recruitment is a highly organized affair."

Recruitment begins on the educational level. Generally speaking, the starting line for the race to Soviet industrial management ranks is today located squarely at the point of graduation from an engineering or business administration institute. But the number of freshmen entering these institutes is considerably below the number of applicants. It is the schools that choose their students—although it is true that their choice is limited to those who voluntarily apply to them.

When the student graduates, the American West Point system applies. The top student chooses his job out of those openings available to graduates; then the next chooses; and so forth down to the low men on the totem pole, who take what is left. But all must accept the jobs offered and stay there for two to three years. Recruitment of new candidates for the management team is organized in this fashion.

What happens after the three years? In a formal sense, the man is free to go where he chooses. But all industry is state-owned, and working one's way ahead within it is like trying to advance inside a single American company. The young manager cannot go off and join the competition.

Although there are a few exceptions, managers generally cannot move up even to the plant-director level without first becoming Communist Party members. In joining the Party, however, a new and fundamental obligation is undertaken. The Party member must take any position to which he is sent; his services are exclusively at the service of the Party. This tradition is a carry-over of the pre-Revolutionary concept of the Russian Communist Party: that only professional revolutionaries are fit for membership. The Communist Party maintains various personnel bureaus to determine the slots into which its members should be placed.

Thus the ambitious manager joins the Communist Party, but in doing so loses all freedom of movement. He may even be sent into some entirely different field of activity. During a campaign to improve agriculture, the Moscow shop superintendent of a machine-tool plant may suddenly learn that he is now to become a Ukrainian collective-farm chairman.

This is the overall view. But let us look at the recruitment picture as it appears from interviews with Soviet managers.

I asked the director of the Moscow Electric Meter Plant how he came to be appointed. He said that he was asked in and offered the job by the representatives of the organization which owned the plant; namely, the Moscow City Council. Thereupon he resigned his post as chief engineer of a factory under the control of an industrial ministry which was quite unconnected with the Moscow City Council. Although he was a member of the Communist Party, he claimed that the Party played no active role in this change of job. It was effected only by

the decision of the Moscow City Council organization to offer him a post and by his own decision to accept this chance for advancement. Here was a type of recruitment which seems quite unorganized—one organization simply pirating away the best management men from wherever it could find them.

The chief engineer of this plant, also a Party member, was hired four years ago when his predecessor went elsewhere to take a better job. He also had been hired away from an industrial ministry, and the director told me the story of how it was decided to make him an offer.

The Moscow Council's industrial staff first nominated the winning candidate and then asked the director for his opinion. Since the chief engineer's former plant was in the same part of town as the electric-meter plant, the director knew the candidate and okayed his selection. According to the director, he would have been allowed a veto power in this choice of his chief assistant. After the director had approved, the job offer was made.

How does managerial recruitment look from the viewpoint of the man in charge of industry at the Moscow City Council? Recruitment of recent college graduates is completely organized, he said. The Council sends its requests to the Ministry of Higher Education, and recent graduates are sent to it for a two- to three-year period. Here the Council has little choice.

For higher posts, an effort is first made to recruit from inside the organizations under the Council. "Promotion from within" is the policy. But when no good candidate is available here, the personnel department looks elsewhere. How does it go about looking? I asked. Informally, was the answer. It may advertise in the popular newspaper *Evening Moscow;* those who know of the opening will tell their friends elsewhere, and these can apply directly. No formal channels exist for such recruitment.

I asked whether management people feel free to accept an offer, since this means leaving their existing organization. This is no problem, I was assured. An offer of a better position elsewhere is considered a valid reason for resigning a post; nor is the resignation a blot on a man's record. Managerial mobility between plants and even between organizational jurisdictions is common enough; a man is expected to take the best position available.

In all this, no word about the Communist Party. Does this really mean that the Party plays no role in the changing of jobs of Party members? My guess is that, where the Party has no special plans for a particular member, his job can be left to negotiations between him and the hiring organization. Why should the Party interfere in most cases? The Party cannot take an active role in everything. But when the Party organization does care to take a hand, its word is decisive.

"Everyone knows that Russian managers are competitors for power with the Communist Party Officials."

Everywhere in Soviet society there stands the Communist Party: the counterpart of the holder of legitimate power. At the topmost rung of society there is the Council of Ministers—and opposite it is the Praesidium of the Central Committee of the Communist Party. In the plant there is the director—and the secretary of the plant committee of the Party.

To quote Stalin, in words which still remain the very heart of Soviet orthodoxy: "The Party is the core of power. The Party directive has the force of law." But the Party directive does not by itself create law; it only defines its direction and purpose. "Party directives are only the kernel of law, just as the Party is the kernel of state power."

This orthodoxy is a solid foundation for permanent built-in conflict. The director of a factory is "responsible" for its operations. But although the words of authority are the director's, the spirit is that of the plant committee of the Party. Among its other duties, the Party plant committee must assure itself that the factory administration makes the proper decisions and carries them out correctly. Moreover, the plant committee means in particular one man: the secretary of the Party committee.

The conflict would be resolved if the Party secretary really ran the plant, with the director taking his orders. But things are not that simple. When a director follows the instructions of his Party committee and his actions later prove to be wrong in the eyes of the government representatives supervising the plant, the director is personally held at fault. He cannot slough off responsibility. At the same time, if things go badly in the plant, the higher Party authorities will hold the Party secretary to account. Thus, willy-nilly, the two must form a team.

Here, then, we have a problem in small-group behavior. There may be cooperation with equality, but clearly a simpler—if often less satisfactory—relationship is for either the director or the Party secretary to dominate. But if the relationship is to be that of domination and subordination, who will dominate? The answer is not given by the situation, which is unstructured; generally speaking, it will be the stronger personality with the greater personal prestige. But if they cannot work together in any fashion, one or both will be removed by higher-ups.

This structure builds competition for power directly into the management systems. But still, we can ask, is this competition really between Party and management or just between individuals? After all, the managers normally are also Party members.

One way of getting at this issue is to ask whether individuals almost always remain within the ranks of either Party or management officialdom without crossing over to the other camp. If they do cross over, if this year's manager may well be a Party official next year, then it is difficult to interpret the conflict as Party-management struggle.

I have tried to query Soviet managers about this. Do people switch back and forth between the management and Communist Party hierarchy, I asked, or do they tend to stay in one or the other? When I put the question directly, all agreed that there was little crossing over. But it was clear from the answers of these same people to other questions that they wished to emphasize the tendency of people to remain in the same job. This desire certainly may have biased their answers.

There is another way to get at this same question. Who are the Party secretaries and organizers, the functionaries on the plant level? I tried this form of the question on one high official in a regional economic council who had just been insisting to me that the industrial and Party hierarchies did not intermingle. Oh, he said, a Party organizer in a factory *must* be an engineer! How else could he know what technical problems to look out for in the work of the factory? By "engineer," he elaborated, he did not mean a recent graduate; he meant someone who had not only a degree but also experience as an engineer in one or more plants.

In interpreting this answer—which, it is fairly clear, represents some degree of exaggeration—one must remember the role of the engineer in Soviet plants. A typical starting job for him is as assistant foreman. Management ranks above the foreman level seem mainly staffed with engineers. A man chosen as Party secretary in an important plant would be moving into a tough administrative post, and he would be expected to have had responsible administrative experience. It seems a fair guess that engineers chosen for Party posts have not served their apprenticeships in design or in methods departments but in management positions.

Clearly, movement also sometimes runs from Party to management ranks. Thus, the United States iron and steel delegation in 1958 reported that the director of the major steel plant in Chelyabinsk had a few years earlier been Party secretary of that area.

Furthermore, when we think of the Party secretaries, we must remember that many hold these posts as leisure-time activities. In smaller plants, the secretary will be a full-time factory employee, just like the president of a small union local in American industry.

In one such plant with a labor force of four hundred, I was told that the current Communist Party secretary was in charge of planning and scheduling for the factory and had a business-school education. Moreover, he had not come to the plant as Party secretary but had originally been hired in the dispatching office. Some time after he had become head of planning—a key management post within the plant—he was also elected Party secretary. It is hard to believe that when he and the plant director differ, whether it occurs when both are wearing their management hats or in the evening when they are acting as members of the Communist Party plant committee, either interprets the clash as a management vs. Party fight.

"Everyone knows that since there is no free enterprise in Russian industry, incentives for management are very weak."

The Soviet Union is a country in which the manager has no possibility of starting his own business and gaining future financial independence in this way. He cannot share in his firm's profits through becoming a partner or by stock options. He has no path to wealth through capital gains and stock purchases of growth companies.

Even when he has plenty of money, there are things he would badly like to have but which are simply not for sale. He cannot rent a larger or better-built apartment by looking in higher-rent areas; there are no free enterprise builders ready to put up luxury apartments to meet the rental market. He can build his own house and then own it outright. But he cannot build on the scale he wishes and can afford; building materials are scarce, and allocation orders are required for them. Thus, money cannot be transformed into better housing —for the profit incentive of the builders is missing.

It is not so easy for the manager to pass on his advantages to his children. Think, for example, of education. Tuition is free for all—right through postgraduate training. But partly as a result of this, there is a tremendous press of students at the college level. The father's ability to meet a high tuition bill offers his children no advantage in the severe competition for entrance into the freshman class. The major work incentive of being able to pass on his advantages to his children is lost to the Soviet manager. The children must stand on their own feet.

But, of course, the Soviet manager has financial incentives of his own. These are far from negligible.

Take salary and bonuses. In one Leningrad plant of the food industry which I visited, earnings of average workers were 700–800 rubles monthly. At the same time, the monthly salary of the plant director was 3000 rubles, and he earned monthly bonuses averaging 1500–1600 rubles. In Moscow, the head of all construction work under the City Council, building twelve million square feet of housing a year, receives a monthly salary of 4000 rubles. He was singled out to me as a man who regularly earns "high bonuses"; in construction, the top bonus permissible is equal to the basic salary. So here was a man with an income of probably 7000–8000 rubles. This is perhaps nine to ten times the monthly earnings of the average worker in his organization.

It seems reasonable to think of directors of plants with a total labor force of 500–1500 employees as receiving something on the order of five to six times the earnings of the average worker. To see this in American terms, the average wage earned by an American worker employed all year in manufacturing in 1957 was $4300. An American plant director would have to earn $22,000 a year in order to attain the same position relative to the average American worker as the Russian director holds compared with the Russian worker. One small-scale 1957 study of American firms showed that, in actual fact, the top policy-making executive in firms of under 1000 employees earned an annual average of $28,000 in salary and bonus.

Moreover, we have not considered the tax angles. The top income tax rate in the Soviet Union is only 13 per cent. Take a Russian director with three children: his tax will be about 12 per cent of his income. Our American manager earning $22,000 a year, also with three children, would pay some 17 to 19 per cent in tax.

Yet, before we go overboard, let us remember what the Soviet manager earns in absolute terms. Our Leningrad director, earning 4500 rubles a month, is still only receiving an annual gross of $5400 at the tourist exchange rate of 10 rubles to 1 dollar. This is just 25 per cent more than the wages of the average American factory worker.

Let us come back to the manager's problem in educating his children. Have we really painted the whole picture when we said that his money and position give him no advantage here?

One obvious consideration comes to mind. Personal favors play their role in any society. A plant manager is more likely to be able to exercise some influence—especially in marginal cases—than is a loom operator. It is, of course, impossible to know how important a role is played by influence. We hear or read the occasional complaint about it. But, by and large, college admissions officers do not discuss the matter.

Another consideration, curiously enough,

is purely financial. Soviet college students receive free tuition, but the problem of living expenses is still a real one. Where do they get the money for this?

The regular day student does not work on the side during the academic year. It is unclear whether school authorities would forbid him to do so if the situation arose, but apparently no student tries. Studying is considered a full-time occupation.

Soviet colleges do, however, give cash stipends to their students. But to qualify, one needs about a "B" average. Higher stipends are given to those with all "A's." The pressure is on.

Now this means that the academic standard set for stipends is about that equivalent to Dean's List in an American college. True, since admissions standards are much higher than in most American colleges, only about 20 per cent of Soviet college students fall below this level. But this marginal group must get financial help from home if it is to study. It is here that a manager's income can be a real help to his children—a mixed satisfaction.

"Everyone knows that a Russian manager's job is a risky one. The pay may be good, but life expectancy is short."

The Russian manager works within a fine mesh of rules, procedures, and detailed targets for all aspects of his operations. If he breaks these rules, he is not simply violating company policy. He is committing a criminal offense under Soviet law; for it is sacred Soviet dogma that "The Plan is Law." Yet, if the manager is to operate at all, he must cut red tape. It seems a fair generalization that all Soviet managers are, *ipso facto*, criminals according to Soviet law.

Clearly, this does not mean that they are all regularly hauled into court. Yet the past record in this regard has not been good.

Many Soviet managers of the 1920's and early 1930's were people who had gained their experience before the Revolution. This meant that, in Communist Party eyes, they were tainted by their bourgeois past. Always they were suspect of desiring a return to the old regime, and the accusation of sabotage came easily to the fore. Machinery breakdowns—common in a period of vast industrial expansion with an unskilled labor force—were likely to be followed by court proceedings or, even worse, by secret-police hearings.

By the mid-thirties, these managers had largely disappeared. A new generation of long-time Communists had taken their places. But the great purges of 1936–38 cleared out this group as well. Their jobs made them centers of attention, antagonism, and envy—and this was dangerous indeed in this period of storm.

There were possibilities of this purge reoccurring during the years at the end of Stalin's life and during the political infighting among his successors. But the fact is that it did not take place. It seems clear that the labor camps were virtually emptied of political prisoners and have not been refilled. There are no indications that changes of top personalities in the Soviet Union have strongly affected the fate of managements at the plant level or even at somewhat higher strata. Soviet managerial life has not again been caught up in the turmoil of the thirties. Even the legal situation has eased somewhat, with managers recently being freed from criminal responsibility for some of their production failures. The unsuccessful manager today is not likely to be faced with anything worse than demotion.

All the same, it cannot be comfortable for the Soviet manager to have constantly to pursue—in the normal course of duty —activities which are criminally punishable. Yet at this point, it is worth glancing at the American scene for perspective.

Back in 1949, Professor Edwin H. Sutherland in his book *White Collar Crime* examined the legal history of seventy of our two hundred largest nonfinancial and nonutility corporations. He traced the records for the number of convictions of these corporations and their subsidiaries during the corporate lifetime —which averaged forty-five years. Most convictions seem to have occurred during the fifteen-year period after 1934.

Of the seventy corporations examined, 60 per cent had convictions entered against them in criminal court. For this 60 per cent, the average number of convictions was four apiece.

This record would seem to indicate that Russian managers are not alone in finding that one cost of doing business is the violation of some laws. Moreover, just as the American business community general-ly looks upon these as "technical" rather than "real" crimes, the same seems to be true of the Soviet business community.

Thus, one Russian manager boldly stated—and not just in private conversation but in a signed article in a newspaper with national coverage—that the zealous plant director must be willing to juggle his books so as to cover necessary expenditures from grants made for other purposes. It was clear that he considered complete obedience to the rules and laws governing Soviet industry as the sure sign of a ne'er-do-well manager.

24 The Man on the Assembly Line

By CHARLES R. WALKER and ROBERT H. GUEST

There are a lot of good things about my job. The pay is good. I've got seniority. The working conditions are pretty good for my type of work. But that's not the whole story ...You can't beat the machine. They have you clocked to a fraction of a second. My job is engineered and the jigs and fixtures are all set out according to specifications. The foreman is an all right guy, but he gets pushed, so he pushes us. The guy on the line has no one to push. You can't fight that iron horse.—*Worker on an assembly line, interviewed by the authors.*

Machines alone do not give us mass production. Mass production is achieved by both machines *and* men. And although we have gone a long way toward perfecting our mechanical operations, we have not successfully written into our equation whatever complex factors represent man, the human element.—*Henry Ford II, in a talk before the American Society of Mechanical Engineers, shortly after he was made President of the Ford Motor Company.*

Reprinted from "The Man on the Assembly Line," by permission of the authors and the publisher, Harvard Business Review, *30 (May —June, 1952), pp. 71–83.*

The principal social and psychological problems connected with mass production and human nature have been stated many times and in many different forms. Their importance in an age of advancing technology is hardly in dispute. The question has become rather: What shall we do about them?

Here are a few of the common problems. Since individuals react very differently to industrial occupations, what are the personality characteristics of those who adjust quickly to—and appear to thrive on—mechanically paced and repetitive jobs? What, on the other hand, are the personality characteristics of those who suffer mentally and physically on such jobs—and who therefore tend to perform them badly? Can the adjustment problem, in other words, be solved by selection? Or is the modern work environment simply *wrong* for the normal human being?

Or to take an engineering and management approach: In the present state of the mechanical arts, what part of a worker's skill and power can the engineer build into a machine? What must he leave out? Precisely how and to what extent in the most mechanized sectors of our economy does the human equation still affect quantity and quality?

Or again, granted that the principles of mass production such as breakdown of jobs into their simplest constituent parts are sound and vital to efficient manufacture, have we yet found how to combine these principles with equally well authenticated principles of human behavior?

Or taking still another approach, if a man spends a third of his life in direct contact with a mass-production environment, why should we not consider important (to him and to society) the hours of living time he spends inside the factory —as important and valuable, for example, as the product he produces which is consumed outside the factory? We talk of a high standard of living, but frequently we mean a high standard of consumption. Man consumes in his leisure yet fulfills himself not only in his leisure but in his work. Is our mass-production work environment making such fulfillment more difficult?

A short way to sum up these and a great many more questions is: To what degree can—or should—men be "adjusted" to the new environment of machines, and to what degree is it possible to adjust or rebuild that environment to fit the needs and personalities of men?

Need for Systematic Study

Despite the tremendous contribution of mass-production methods to the productiveness of the economic system under which we live, and notwithstanding the fact that editors, philosophers, and propagandists have long speculated and written about the beneficent or injurious effects of highly mechanized jobs on human behavior, there has been singularly little systematic effort to discover "whatever complex factors represent man, the human element" in the mass-production

method as such. The relatively small number of studies which have been made of assembly-line and other types of repetitive work have been mostly laboratory experiments, not explorations of experience in actual industrial plants.

A notable exception is the series of monographs which for some 25 years have been published from time to time under the auspices of the British Medical Council on the effects of mechanization and the repetitive job on productivity and *mental* fatigue. Even these, however, have only touched occasionally on the subject of assembly lines and have never at all— to the best of our knowledge—dealt specifically with that advanced sector of a mass-production economy, the final assembly line of a plant making a large, complex product like automobiles.

Survey of automobile assembly plant

For these reasons the authors undertook two years ago an exploratory survey of a modern automobile assembly plant.[1] This is intended as the first of a series of studies designed to define more clearly the several "human equations" involved in assembly work, to prepare and sharpen tools of research, and to look for proximate and empirical answers to the more acute practical problems posed for men and management.

In this article we shall emphasize how an assembly line looks and feels to the men who work on it, rather than its importance to the engineers who designed it, the executives who manage it, or the public who buys its product.

In order to preserve the anonymity of those who freely supplied information— managers, workers, and union leaders— the plant in question has been called Plant X. Over a period of months 180 workers were interviewed in their homes about all phases of their life on "the line." These workers constituted a substantial— and representative—sample of the total number of productive workers in the plant.

Nearly 90 per cent of the men working

at Plant X came from jobs where the pace of work was not machine-governed in a strict sense and from jobs over 72 per cent of which were not repetitive. In short, the area from which they were recruited had few mass-production factories. One might say, then, that these men were like the majority of workers who in the past 30 years have made the transition from occupations characteristic of the first industrial revolution to work environments characteristic of a mass-production era. Their attitudes should be all the more revealing.

Most people, in thinking about an assembly line and the workers on it, focus only on the effect of the line on what a man does hour by hour, even minute by minute, with his mind and his muscles. Any serious study of the human effects of the mass-production method, however, must extend its field of vision. For the method not only impinges directly on a man's immediate or intrinsic job but molds much of the character of the in-plant society of which he is a part, including both his relations with his fellow workers and his relations with management. Accordingly we shall discuss the impact of the mass-production method not only directly but indirectly on human nature.

Definition of mass-production method

But what is the "mass-production method?" We must have a definition if our discussion and our findings are to be understandable.

Although the methods of mass production or, more accurately and specifically for our purposes, the methods of *progressive manufacture* have been defined and discussed in different ways by different writers, it is agreed by nearly everyone that these methods derive from at least two fundamental and related ideas: (a) standardization and (b) interchangeability of parts.

Given these basic ideas, plus the accurate machining methods which make them applicable to manufacture, Ford was able to work out and apply the three

following additional "principles" of progressive manufacture: (c) the orderly progression of the product through the shop in a series of planned operations arranged so that the right part always arrives at the right place at the right time; (d) the mechanical delivery of these parts and of the product as it is assembled to and from the operators; and (e) a breakdown of operations into their simple constituent motions.[2]

Let us look now at how these principles translate themselves into job characteristics from the standpoint not of the engineer but of the man on the assembly line. In the first place, most automobile assembly jobs are *mechanically paced* (especially those on the main line). In the second place, since the engineer has broken the jobs down into simple and separate elements and assigned only a few to each man, they are clearly *repetitive.* Among other characteristics of most jobs are these: They have a low skill requirement, permit work on only a fraction of the product, severely limit social interaction, and predetermine for nearly every worker any use he may make of tools and methods.

Taken together, automobile assembly-line jobs exemplify all these characteristics, but not every job exemplifies all of them. Put another way, in spite of many common characteristics, automobile assembly jobs are far from being equal— either as to the quantity or quality of job content or as to the satisfaction or dissatisfaction which workers derive from them. They differ both in the number of the several assembly-line characteristics they exemplify and in the degree of impact of any one characteristic. An understanding of this point must mark the beginning of any serious inquiry into the relation of human behavior to assembly-line work.

Attitude toward jobs

But that is enough of making distinctions. Now let the men on the assembly line tell us themselves about their jobs and tell us also what they like and what they do not like about them. Here are six jobs by way of illustration: two on the main moving line, one off the main line but on a moving conveyor, one off the main line and not on a moving conveyor, one repair job on the line, and one utility job on the line. These six will illustrate at least the principal differences in human impact of mass-production assembly-line jobs. (It should be remembered, however, that these six are not representative of the distribution of jobs in the whole plant, where one-half the jobs are on the *main moving assembly line.* Specifically, the distribution of jobs in our sample was as follows: main assembly line, 86; subassembly on moving belt, 28; subassembly not on moving belt, 38; repairmen, 14; utility men, 11; and other, 3.)

On the main moving line

Here is the way the assembler of the baffle windbreaker in the trim department describes his job:

"As the body shell moves along the line, I start putting on a baffle windbreaker (two fenders fit on it) by putting in four screws. Then I put nine clips at the bottom which hold the chrome molding strip to the body. On another type of car there is a piece of rubber which fits on the hood latch on the side and keeps the hood from rattling. I drill the holes in the rubber and metal and fit two screws in. Also I put four clips on the rubber in the rear fender. On another type of body, I put the clips on the bottom molding, and in the trunk space I put two bolts which hold the spare-tire clamp. I repeat these things all the time on the same types of car."

How does this man's job measure up in terms of some of the characteristics we have mentioned, particularly pace and repetitiveness?

To begin with, the job is on the main line, and the worker rides along on the conveyor, completing his cycle of operations in less than two minutes while the conveyer is moving over a distance of about 30 feet. He then walks to his starting point and begins over again. In short,

his pace is directly determined by the moving belt. On the other hand, he is sometimes able to work back up the line and so secure a breather for himself.

The job is clearly repetitive, but there is some element of variety since between five and ten operations are required to complete the job cycle. There are also different models to be worked on. Comparing the repetitiveness of this job with that of other assembly jobs, it is somewhere in the middle range—far less repetitive than a single-operation job and far more repetitive than the job of a repairman.

Similarly, in the matter of skill it is in the middle as assembly-line jobs go. Because of the number of parts handled, learning time is slightly longer than that for many assembly jobs. The worker reported that it took him a month to do the job properly. As for the expenditure of physical energy, it is a light job.

Also on the main moving line

Or consider the job of the worker who installs toe plates and who performs operations typical of short-cycle, on-the-main-line jobs:

I put in the two different toe plates. They cover the holes where the brake and clutch pedals are. I am inside the car and have to be down on the seat to do my work. On one kind of car I put in the shift lever while another man puts in the toe plates.

While doing his job this man rides along in the car and must complete the job before he is carried too far. After finishing his work cycle he returns to his station, climbs into another car, and begins another installation. Thus his pace is strictly governed by the moving line. This particular worker told the interviewer that he did not mind the pace.

Such a job which demands but two operations in a two-minute cycle is highly repetitive. Only slight variety is introduced when the man installs a shift lever instead of a toe plate on certain cars.

The job demands very little skill and has a learning period of just two days.

Although the worker gets in and out of cars 20 or 30 times an hour, his expenditure of physical energy on the actual assembly operation is slight.

Off the main line but on a moving conveyor

The job of a seat-spring builder is typical of those off the main line but on a moving belt:

I work on a small conveyor which goes around in a circle. We call it a merry-go-round. I make up zig-zag springs for front seats. Every couple of feet on the conveyor there is a form for the pieces that make up the seat springs. As that form goes by me, I clip several pieces together, using a clip gun. I then put the pieces back on the form, and it goes on around to where other men clip more pieces together. By the time the form has gone around the whole line, the pieces are ready to be set in a frame, where they are made into a complete seat spring. That's further down the main seat cushion line. The only operation I do is work the clip gun. It takes just a couple of seconds to shoot six or eight clips onto the spring, and I do it as I walk a few steps. Then I start right over again.

This job is clearly paced by a moving conveyor quite as much as if it were on the main line. A comment by the worker regarding his previous job emphasized the point: "I liked the piecework system on my old job. If I wanted to stop for a few minutes, I could. You can't do that here."

As for variety, there is none. The job is highly repetitive, consisting of one set of operations repeated every few seconds on a part which is standard for all models.

The skill requirement is minimum. This worker gave two days as his learning time, with a few days more "in order to do it like I do it now."

As for physical energy, the job would probably be rated as light since the worker guides an automatic hand gun. But there is considerable fatigue because the worker performs the operation standing up.

The worker's overall estimate of the job is typical. As to what he liked about the job, he mentioned good pay, steady work, and good working hours—in that order of priority. As to what he disliked, he said that he could not set his own pace, that he did not have interesting work, and that his job was physically tiring.

Off the main line but not on a moving conveyor

We turn to a blower-defroster assembler, who works off the main line and not on a moving belt:

I work at a bench on blower defrosters. The blowers come in two parts. I take one part and attach the blower motor to it. I then connect the fan to the motor shaft. Then I take the other half on the air pipe and put two parts together with fourteen screws. I test the motor to see if it works, and if it does, I put in a fifteenth screw which grounds it to the pipe. The materials are brought to me and put in a pile by a stock-chaser. After I finish, I put each assembled blower on one of six shelves.

Here is an example of a job where pace is only indirectly determined by the main line. The worker must keep his shelves stocked with a supply of blower defrosters, but he has some choice of pace in doing so. He may work fast and "build up a bank," then slow down and take a breather. Or he may choose to work quite steadily. The demands of the stock-chaser who brings him materials and takes away the finished assembly are the determinants of his work pace rather than the moving conveyor.

There is not much variety since there are only three operations; however, a slight variation is introduced through differences in models. The worker called his job completely repetitive but said he did not mind it.

His job operations require a minimum of skill: "I learned it in a couple of hours, though it took me about a week to get up speed." He does not move around, and the materials he handles are light, so very little physical energy is demanded.

Summing up his job, this worker gave good bosses, good pay, and good working conditions as his first three reasons for liking the job. He mentioned only one thing he disliked: "I cannot do different things."

Repairman

Here is a job description by a repairman in the car-conditioning section of the chassis department:

I work in a pit underneath the final line. The cars move along over the pit. On the previous assembly operations, the inspectors for the under parts of the car have indicated where parts were missing or damaged or not properly attached. There are any number of things which can be wrong, and they are usually different for each car. Sometimes we have a run of the same thing which we have to work on until they get at the bug earlier in assembly operations. The shock absorbers may be bad, gas line in wrong, brake lines or spring attachments off. I fix whatever I see checked by the inspector. The others in the pit do the same thing. I just work down the line until I get it cleared up. Sometimes I have to work down a long way on one thing. Other times it's just a simple problem on a number of different things.

This worker is on the main line, but this pace is not strictly governed by the moving conveyor. "We don't feel the pressure of the line since we don't have to do just one thing in a given area and length of time."

The variety the job offers is derived from the nature of the work. "There are any number of things which can be wrong, and they are usually different for each car. . . . There is something different all the time."

As for skill, the job as repairman requires manual skill and mechanical experience. A garage repairman's job would be a good preparation. (The man whose job description is given here had, in fact, worked as a repairman in a garage before coming to Plant X.)

The job varies between light and medium-heavy work, with the expenditure of physical energy called for changing appreciably from job to job and from day to day.

The worker's personal satisfaction with his job was clear. He gave as three reasons for liking the job: "I can set my own pace, I have good working conditions, and I have steady work." He also commented favorably on being able to "use my brains," "do different things," and "choose how the job is to be done."

Utility man

A utility man in the chassis department describes his job as follows:

I work on the whole length of that part of the chassis line beginning with motor drop up to where the wheels are mounted. My job is to fill in wherever I am needed. A man might be absent or away from the job or may need help on the job.

We start where the motor is lowered onto the frame (motor mount). The clutch assembly is installed and hooked up. Then the exhaust system is attached and the bolts tightened. The clutch-assembly bolts and the motor-mount bolts are also tightened. In the next area on the line the brake chambers are filled and bled.

Off to the side, the subassembly men put the steering column together. The steering post and the Pittman arm-assembly are put in. Further down the line, men put in air cleaners and inject hydraulic fluid for the transmission.

Next, the brakes are tested and the clutch linkage hooked up. The bumper brackets are put on; a serial number is attached next; and then the bumper brackets are tightened up. Finally, the chassis is sprayed, mounted on wheels, and moved on toward body drop. All in all, about twenty-eight men work on these jobs, each man with his own special operation. I go on each of these jobs, depending on where I am needed most. It is different each day. Some of the jobs are hard to learn, so when I take over one on which I haven't had much experience, it's hard to keep up. I have been learning how to do the work ever since I've been in the plant. I can never learn everything because new changes are always being made.

The pace of this utility man's work, since it is on the main line, is as strictly governed as that of any assembly worker. In certain ways he may feel the pressure more acutely than some of those for whom he substitutes, since he has less practice on any single job than its regular holder.

To compensate him, however, there is plenty of variety, for, as he points out, he shifts about among twenty-eight different jobs. Notice how in describing his many tasks this utility man gives a very clear account of a whole segment of assembly operations in the chassis department.

Notice, too, the character of a utility man's skill. It is the sum of many little skills of many repetitive jobs. The learning time is six months to a year. The worker said: "Sometimes I walk up and down checking the line. I ask questions of the different men. I rarely stay on the same job more than a couple of days." That his job is not easy is suggested by an additional comment:

> Some days you feel like learning, other days you don't. On jobs that take time to learn, you get disgusted because it's hard to keep up. A utility man, when on a job, has more trouble keeping up than the regular man.

This man mentioned good pay, steady work, and good bosses as the three main reasons for liking his job, in that order. Other items bearing on the immediate job which he liked were "having interesting work, having to use my brains, doing many different things," as in the case of the repairman, and also "talking with others." He had only one complaint about the job: that it was "physically tiring."

Summary of attitudes toward jobs

In all of this classification of the automobile assembly workers' jobs, we have clearly been concerned not with an engineering analysis but with factors which have an effect on satisfaction or dissatisfaction with the immediate job. Mechanical pace, repetitiveness, minimum skill requirement, and the other factors were all found reflected in attitudes and feelings.

These examples underline some of the commonest facts and feelings which are part of the daily experience of the productive worker in an assembly plant. To recall a few:

1. Contrary to popular belief, all jobs on an assembly line are not alike, either in skill, variety, learning time, or the degree of satisfaction or dissatisfaction which they offer the average wage earner.
2. There are definite ways on certain jobs to get a break or a breather, such as "working back up the line," or "bank building."
3. There is a general, though not a unanimous, desire to move from highly paced jobs to jobs "which are less highly paced, and "off the line."
4. It is evident from the statements of the six workers—which for illustrative purposes we have selected from 180—that other factors such as good pay, a good foreman, and a secure job must be considered in appraising the total index of a worker's satisfaction or dissatisfaction.

Major Reactions of Workers

Looking over the range of factors connected with their immediate jobs by all the men interviewed, we see that the two which were given greatest prominence were (a) mechanical pacing and (b) repetitiveness.

To mechanical pacing

We asked no direct attitude questions on the first and central characteristic of any automobile assembly plant—the moving conveyor—but nearly every worker expressed his opinions about it when describing his job, when talking about the company, or at some other point in the interview. These free-association comments on pace as governed by the moving conveyor showed that: (1) A large majority of the workers regarded the moving line or belt as an undesirable feature of the job. (2) A small minority expressed themselves as enjoying the excitement of the moving line.

Following are typical comments of workers who were highly critical of the line:

The bad thing about assembly lines is that the line keeps moving. If you have a little trouble with a job, you can't take the time to do it right.

On the line you're geared to the line. You don't dare stop. If you get behind, you have a hard time catching up.

The line speed is too great. More men wouldn't help much. They'd just expect more work out of an individual. There's an awful lot of tension.

I don't like rushing all the time...I don't mind doing a good day's work, but I don't like to run through it.

The work isn't hard; it's the never-ending pace. ...The guys yell "hurrah" whenever the line breaks down...You can hear it all over the plant.

In contrast, a minority liked the challenge and excitement of keeping up with the line:

I do my job well. I get some satisfaction from keeping up with a rapid-fire job. On day when the cars come off slowly, I sometimes get bored.

I get satisfaction from doing my job right and keeping up with the line.

It makes you feel good...when the line is going like hell and you step in and catch up with it.

To repetitiveness

Turning now to the job characteristic, repetitiveness, our findings are that: (1) A majority of the workers were critical of the repetitive character of their jobs. (2) A minority preferred the repetitive character of their work or were indifferent to it. (3) A large number of workers compared on-the-line jobs unfavorably with off-the-line jobs, because off-the-line jobs offered more variety.

We found we were able to correlate the number of operations a man performed (which can serve as a rough measure of repetitiveness) with expressions of interest or lack of interest in his job. The number of operations performed on any given job was determined not by direct questioning but by analysis of the job descriptions.

The workers, however, were asked directly: "Would you say your job was very interesting, fairly interesting, not at all interesting?" The correlation with number of operations was as follows:

Operations Performed	Very or Fairly Interesting	Not Very or Not At All Interesting
1	19	38
2–5	28	36
5 or more	41	18

In the column of workers giving a positive rating to "interest," the number of workers increases as the number of operations increases. In other words, there is a tendency for interest in work to vary directly with the number of operations performed.

Following are typical comments of those men who were critical of the repetitive nature of their jobs:

I dislike repetition. One of the main things wrong with this job is that there is no figuring for yourself, no chance to use your brain. It's a grind doing the same thing over and over. There is no skill necessary.

I'd rather work for a small company any day. They're interested in doing good work, and they are willing to allot enough time for it. The assembly line is no place to work, I can tell you. There is nothing more discouraging than having a barrel beside you with 10,000 bolts in it and using them all up. Then you get a barrel with another 10,000 bolts, and you know every one of those 10,000 bolts has to be picked up and put in exactly the same place as the last 10,000 bolts.

I'd like to do different things on this job. I get bored. It's the same thing all the time. Cars always coming down the line endlessly every time I look up.

I would like to perform different operations, but I do the same thing all the time. I always know what I'm going to do when I come in. There's nothing to look forward to like there was on my old job.

The monotony is what I don't like. It's pretty noisy, but you get used to that. I'd never get used to the monotony. I dislike the plant for this reason.

It's not a matter of pace. It's the monotony. It's not good for you to get so bored. I do the same thing day after day; just an everlasting grind.

The job gets so sickening—day in and day out plugging in ignition wires. I get through with one motor, turn around, and there's another motor staring me in the face.

A minority of workers who declared that they were indifferent to or preferred doing the same thing over and over again commented as follows:

I keep doing the same thing all the time, but it dosen't make any difference to me.

Repeating the same thing you can catch up and keep ahead of yourself. I like the routine. You can get in the swing of it.

We do the same thing all the time, but I don't mind it really.

I like doing the same thing all the time. I'd rather stay right where I am. When I come in in the morning, I like to know exactly what I'll be doing.

I like to repeat the same thing, and every car is different anyway. So my job is interesting enough.

Explanation of why this minority group either preferred or was indifferent to the factor of repetitiveness in contrast to the majority of workers in our sample would appear to lie in the pattern of their individual personalities. An investigation of the psychological characteristics of men who react this way is clearly suggested. We sought but found no other unique characteristics in the group as regards education, age, or any of the other categories of information we used.

Effect of Human Equation

In the introductory paragraphs of this article we reviewed some of the typical questions on which it was hoped research into the human equation of assembly-line work might throw light, including some of special interest to both the production manager and the engineer: What part of a worker's skill and power can the engineer build into a machine? What must he leave out? Precisely how and to what extent in the most mechanized sectors of our economy does the human equation still affect quantity and quality?

Influence of workers on quality

So far as assembly lines go, there is still a widespread belief on the part of *outsiders* that the machine has completely taken over and that on mechanized conveyor-line jobs the individual has no influence on quality. There is also a belief widely held by *insiders* (employers and production managers) that, even though the quality of individual performance on a mechanized job may still be important for the final product, the average worker no longer cares or gets satisfaction from doing a good job.

In Plant X, both beliefs were shown to be unfounded.

As many as seventy-nine men in the sample of 180 felt that it was difficult to sustain the kind of quality performance which was expected of them or which they themselves wanted to sustain. To most of the seventy-nine, *this was a discouraging and negative feature of the job.*

About half the workers felt it was possible to do the kind of quality job expected of them. Few of these workers, however, had jobs which were strictly line-paced. Rather they included mostly repairmen, utility men, workers on off-line jobs, or men on the line who had longer time cycles or greater freedom to move up and down the line. Typical comments among this group were:

No time limit is set on my job, so I can do it right. I get satisfaction out of really fixing a job. I can usually get this, but sometimes the company doesn't want the cars fixed as well as I'd like to.

I get satisfaction and quality because I have time to complete my job right.

I never let a car go by with my number on in unless it is done right. Maybe some of the men on the line don't get quality.

You can take time to get quality. It's not like on the line when you have to rush so much And I get satisfaction. It makes me feel good when I put out a good day's work and get no kickbacks.

The effects of poor-quality work on job satisfaction were reflected in many of the comments of men on conveyor-paced jobs:

The cars come too fast for quality. It's quantity instead of quality. I'm doing the best I can, but could do a neater job slower.

On an assembly line you just do it once; if it's wrong, you have no time to fix it. I get no satisfaction from my work. All I do is think about all the things that went through wrong that should have been fixed. My old job was nothing like this.

I try to do quality work, but I'm too rushed. This keeps me from getting pleasure from the work. They say 'haste makes waste,' and they're getting plenty of both.

I'd rather do less work and do it right. How can you get quality when they don't give you time? The 'quality' signs they have mean nothing.

These comments tend to show that the characteristics or components of the assembly man's immediate job do have a significant bearing upon the quality of the product and that mass production restricts rather than eliminates the "human factor" as a determinant of quality for any given part of for the total product. Most workers were conscious of this fact. For a substantial number, inability to put out quality was a source of irritation, whereas putting out quality was a source of job satisfaction.

Constructive Measures by Management

Are there any measures that management can take to modify on-the-job conditions of work in the interest of greater efficiency and of increased satisfaction for the individual operator?

One answer to this question may be sought in the elements of satisfaction or of compensation which some workers already found in their jobs. To begin with, it should be remembered that there was a minority of workers who preferred or were indifferent to repetitiveness and mechanical pacing. Presumably by improved methods of recruiting and selection this minority could be increased. Then there were a number of men who found their immediate jobs on and off the line satisfying—actually all the repairmen and utility men interviewed with one exception. The only measures needed here are protective—to make sure that the content of these jobs is not diluted.

This still leaves the majority of the production workers. Here the clue to constructive action lies in the fact that many of them reacted favorably to particular features of their jobs:

1. Social interaction breaking the monotony
2. Enough operations on their particular jobs to give variety
3. Opportunity to work back up the line and get a breather
4. Opportunity to build up a bank and get a breather
5. Opportunity to alternate one set of operations with another set of a substantially different character
6. Opportunity to alternate jobs with other workers within the same section
7. A long time cycle encompassing a larger number of operations than usual and those of a more interesting character

A practical directive for management would appear to be exploration of the possibility of extending these and other desirable features so that more assembly men could share in them. The degree of that extension would necessarily vary with the special circumstances—physical and organizational—of individual plants and with the ingenuity of management; but there would be few plants where something could not be done in this direction.

Detailed discussion of such measures is beyond the scope of this article, but the tenor of our thinking may be indicated by reference to two of the seven features to which Plant X workers reacted favorably.

Job rotation

Take Number 6—alternation of jobs between workers, a technique often called "rotation." At Plant X we were struck with the unusually high degree of job satisfaction expressed by the members of one work group under a particular foreman. With the permission and encouragement of their foreman, the men were working under a system of job rotation. It was to this system that the members of the group ascribed their relatively high job satisfaction. And to the same system the section foreman owed in part a smoothly running and efficient work unit. Top plant management is now encouraging a more widespread application of this practice.

In connection with any system of job rotation the question immediately comes to mind: Since it requires some effort to learn several jobs instead of one, will not the worker—unless he is exceptional—object? Many managers seem to find it difficult to get workers to change jobs frequently.

The best answer to this question about worker resistance is the pragmatic one. In certain sectors on the line at Plant X rotation *is* working. Moreover, in other industries and on other types of assembly lines the practice of rotation is steadily gaining ground. For most people, learning to do something new is hard work, and it is only undertaken when an adequate reward is held out. For a considerable number of assembly-line workers, the rewards of variety and of possessing a repertory of skills will be sufficient.

Of course, some resistance to an experiment in rotation is to be expected. The key to the situation lies, we suggest, in the word "experiment." Where rotation has been successfully installed on other types of assembly lines, it has

usually been started as an experiment, with management guaranteeing to the work group or to any single individual a return to stationary assignments if desired—and rarely have the workers wished to return.

Another question is: Will the work be done as well or as fast under job rotation? The answer for the Plant X section that practices it is an affirmative one. For other work groups in other industries with which the authors are familiar, the answer has also been "yes." Of course there are work situations where job rotation appears either altogether impractical or less efficient. But always the real test is in the overall and long-term performance of the group. Gains in quality and a drop in turnover or absenteeism may balance some decrease in output, if it occurs.

Job enlargement

Or consider Number 7—a long-time cycle encompassing a larger number of operations than usual and those of a more interesting character, sometimes called "job enlargement." Here is a concept and a practice that has proved successful in decreasing monotony without impairing efficiency in certain sectors of other industries. We here suggest that it be introduced experimentally into automobile assembly work.

Job enlargement is simply the recombining of two or more separate jobs into one. Certain plant managers in other industries have been finding that a law of diminishing returns applies to the subdivision of jobs and that a recombination of certain fractured parts has increased efficiency. This points toward a lengthening of time cycles. Job enlargement in the sense in which we suggest it does not mean turning automobile assembly back into the hands of master mechanics with one worker assigned to the assembly of one car. It does mean paying greater attention to psychological and social variables in the determination of time cycles and, by the same token, paying more attention to the *content* of individual jobs.

To one unfamiliar with assembly-line work experience, the difference between a job with five operations and a job with ten, or between a job taking two minutes to perform and a job taking four minutes, might seem a matter far too trivial to concern anyone. Our data have shown that this is not true. Management has a vital interest in such matters; the proper assignment of time cycles throughout an assembly plant will make an important difference in the efficiency of the plant. As for the worker, one of the most striking findings of this study is the psychological importance of even minute changes in his immediate job experience.

At the risk of oversimplification, the point may be summarized this way: Other things being equal, the difference between a satisfied and a dissatisfied worker may rest on whether he has a ten-operation or a five-operation job.

Relationship among workers

Another place to look for possibilities of improvement is in the area of indirect influences—the impact of mass-production methods on the plant's social structure. Ever since the early studies of Elton Mayo, it has been widely accepted that the character of the "work group" frequently exercises a decisive influence on a worker's efficiency—not to mention on his satisfaction on the job. How did the technology of the automobile assembly line affect the grouping of men at Plant X?

Most workers are located along the "main line" according to the particular manpower requirements of each segment

Social Interaction Pattern of Typical Main Assembly Line Worker—Polisher Paint Department.

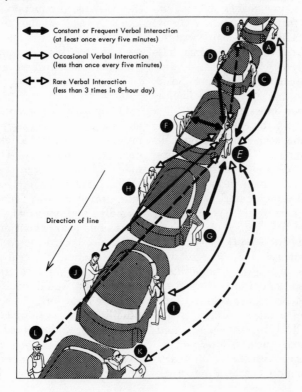

of the assembly process. Each operator works in a limited area completing his own operations independently of others as the car is carried by the conveyor down the line. A particular individual may talk with the men immediately around him, but these men cannot be said to comprise a bona fide work group in the usual sense of the term. Take as an illustration the polishing line. Exhibit I shows in diagrammatic form an actual interaction pattern of a left-front-door polisher, Worker E.

The ten men from A to J comprise a work group of which Worker E is a part, and he has some social contact with all the other nine. His really close contacts, however, are only with C, D, F, and G. Note that these four workers comprise a group—*but only from E's point of view.* As to the social-relationship pattern of G, his immediate group would consist of E, F, H, and I; it would not include C and D, who were clearly members of E's group. Further variations occur, for example, when a line makes a bend or loop and brings men in different sections closer together. Thus each man, because of the nature of conveyor operations, has a slightly different circle of associates from that of the man next to him. So it goes along the entire stretch of a line, a line well over two miles long.

In our interviews these men exhibited little of what the sociologist would call "in-group awareness." Rarely, for example, did they talk about "our team" or "our group" or "the men in our outfit." Instead, the following remark was typical: "I've been here over a year, and I hardly know the first names of the men in the section where I work."

In sharp contrast, however, to the majority of line workers, a minority—principally off-line operators—worked on bona fide teams or crews; that is, they were members of a close working group, were functionally interdependent, and frequently assisted their fellows or exchanged operations with them. On charting the interaction pattern of such

groups it was found that the frequency of conversational exchange was high and constant for nearly all members of the group. Of greater significance, the group exhibited a marked *esprit-de-corps* not found among the bulk of line operators.

It is clear that the present technology of an automobile assembly line limits social interaction and does not lend itself to the arrangement of men in bona fide teams or crews. It is suggested, however, that in the design of *new* plants and at periods of retooling or of layout revisions an effort be made to maximize the opportunities for social interaction and for team relationships.

Relations With Management

Still another area of social relationships —that of worker to supervisor—is crucial to an intelligent understanding of social organization.

The formal organizational structure of the various production departments in Plant X was similar to that found in many plants. In interviews with workers we came to know the quality of relationship between workers and supervisors.

Foremen

Qualitative comments by the men about their foremen suggested a relatively informal and friendly relationship on the part of the majority. The average foreman had from fifteen to twenty-five men under him, and talking between worker and foreman was generally frequent, friendly, and informal. The sort of remarks one hears about any good foreman were also heard here, as for example: "Our foreman is a real good guy. We're lucky. If he got into trouble, the whole department would back him right up."

There were criticisms of foremen, but usually these were not directed at the individual. Rather they were aimed at the "line" and the role the foreman had to play with reference to the line. As one man said: "After all, the foreman has to be a pusher, and nobody likes to be pushed. He's got to hold his job. If he doesn't push, somebody else will get his job."

Often men exonerated foremen for "pushing" since they recognized that the compulsion of line production was not the fault of the foremen. One man put it this way: "I guess you'd say the foreman gets along with the men. But they don't need a foreman. *The line is the foreman.* You have to keep up with the line."

Higher supervisors

An interesting finding which came out of the study was the relationship, or lack of it, between workers and management above the foreman level. The one hundred eighty men in our sample were asked to indicate contacts with supervisors in their department at the general-foreman and department-head levels. Only fifty-nine reported that they talked with their general foreman as often as once a week; fifteen put it at one to three times a month; and eighty-eight said less than once a month. Contact between workers and upper departmental supervisors was even less, with 70 per cent saying they spoke with their department heads less than once a month. (Departments ranged in size from two hundred to four hundred.)

It is significant in this connection that in a steel fabricating plant which we recently studied the workers talked far more frequently with supervisors above the foreman level. There the nature of the process and the high degree of worker skills made for a closer relationship. It was an everyday experience to find a superintendent in charge of four hundred men talking with an individual worker or group of workers. He did this because the technical and skilled judgment of the individual worker was important in the production process.

On the automobile assembly line, on the other hand, because of the high degree of mechanization and fractional assembly there appears to be less need for supervisors to discuss production matters with individual workers. Management relies on the judgment of the engineer, not the worker. Thus the basic factor which determines the rate and quality of worker-supervisor interaction is the technology of mass production.

Impact on Wage Structure

Not the least important secondary effect of the mass-production method has been its impact on the wage structure. A leveling of workers' skills has inevitably resulted in a narrowing of differentials between wage grades, in contrast to industries where the latest mass-production methods have not been applied. For example, in the steel fabricating plant which we investigated—a seamless-tube mill—the differential between the rates of the lowest- and of the highest-paid workers was over a dollar an hour. At Plant X, however, the differential between the lowest-paid and the highest-paid was around ten cents for the major categories of production workers, and over half the workers in the production departments received exactly the same hourly wage.

It is obvious that changes in skill levels and in wage categories affect what the wage administrator calls the "system of job progression." Before the application of mass-production methods most industries had many well-defined steps in their ladders of promotion. Mass-production methods, although often raising the general level of wages and bringing other benefits, have knocked out a good many rungs in these promotion ladders. To turn again to the steel mill for contrast: There were as many as seven or eight steps from laborer to roller, each one associated with progressively higher wages, skills, and prestige.

This system of promotion, with its connotations of growth, incentive, and progress, has been weakened or virtually eliminated on the assembly line. Almost any assembly worker can—and some do

—say: "There are hundreds of jobs like mine, not much better, not much worse. The differences are so slight—or seem so slight to management—that I am interchangeable." Consequently, to escape a resulting sense of anonymity as much, perhaps, as to escape monotony, the average worker at Plant X does not aspire to climb into another slightly better production job but rather into a utility man's job or a repairman's job or out of production altogether, where he can be recognized and where also he can recognize himself—as an individual.

Most of the benefits of the mass-production method are obvious and have often been celebrated. If we are to continue to enjoy them and to expand and refine the method, we should understand more fully its impact on the traditional organization of industry. Surely the problems as well as the promises of mass production are worthy of study.

Conclusion

It is obviously impossible in a single article to do more than sketch some of the problem areas in the broad field of relations between mass production and human nature. Concerning the direct impact of the method on the individual we made a few empirical suggestions and tried to point out at least one direction in which management might seek practical solutions.

But what can be said about the *indirect* impact of mass production on human nature through the character of work groups, the wage structure, and the promotion system? In a negative sense, at least, all these phenomena appear to be related: At Plant X they tended to increase the workers' sense of anonymity within the production enterprise of which they were functional parts. In fact, one way to express the net result of these several influences might be to say that little sense of membership in a common work community existed. (Our evidence showed that to some extent membership in the

union gave the worker the feeling of personal identity and "belonging" which neither the shop nor relations with management supplied.)

It seems to us significant that the average worker appeared to be oppressed by this sense of anonymity *in spite of the fact that he declared himself well satisfied with his rate of pay and the security of his job.* The answer to this problem in the most general terms would appear to be a program designed to re-create the sense *and also* the reality of a bona fide work community. And for such a program to be successful we believe that both union and management would have to agree on the measures to be taken.

A comment by a man on the line will suggest the nature of the problem more clearly than many paragraphs of exposition:

> There is a different feeling in this plant. It's much bigger than people around here have ever seen. It's just like the kid who goes up to a grown-up man and starts talking to him. There doesn't seem to be a friendly feeling. At the plant I used to work in there was a different feeling. Everyone spoke to everyone else.... Nobody goes to other departments in this plant. The understanding could be better—happier and much easier. Here a man is just so much horsepower.

Perhaps the human needs in Plant X are merely an expression in more explicit terms of the needs of our industrial civilization. The problem of reintegrating the several faculties of man into a significant unity presents itself in many fields—in industry, science, and government, to name but three—in an age of overspecialization.

It is striking that throughout the survey of Plant X both union and management agreed with the authors that the more basic problems to be explored were not those connected with a particular plant, industry, or corporation. Rather they were problems related to technological and organizational trends common to modern industry. Both agreed that modern American civilization as we know it rests upon mass-production principles quite as much as upon the natural resources of the United States. The attitude of both, therefore, was a simple and heartening one: *Since these problems exist, let us get all the facts we can. In time we shall be able to solve them.*

As Saint-Exupéry, the French aviator and author, wrote:

The Machine is not an end. . . . It is a tool . . . like the plough.

If we believe that it degrades Man, it is possibly because we lack the perspective for judging the end results of transformations as rapid as those to which we have been subjected. What are two hundred years in the history of the Machine when compared with two hundred thousand years in the history of Man? We have scarcely estab-

lished ourselves in this country of mines and of central electricity. It is as if we had hardly begun to live in the new house that we have not yet finished building. Everything has changed so rapidly around us: human relations, conditions of work, customs. . . . Every step in our progress has driven us a little further from our acquired habits, and we are in truth pioneers who have not yet established the foundations of our new country.[3]

---

[1] The full details of this survey are. . .published in *The Man on the Assembly Line* (Cambridge: Harvard University Press (1952).

[2] This is a rephrased and slightly more explicit statement of the three principles of mass production as set down in "Mass Production" by Henry Ford in the *Encyclopedia Britannica,* 14th Ed., 15, pp. 38–39.

[3] Antoine de Saint-Exupéry, *Terre des Hommes* (Paris, Gallimard, 1939), p. 58.

part six OCCUPATIONS AND PROFESSIONS

Our attention is directed in this final section to diversity in the style of "work life" which surrounds different occupations and professions. In the lead paper, "Confessions of a Block-Buster," Alfred Balk examines fascinating methods of selling real estate by appealing to customers' fears of minority groups.

The current and future position of labor unions in our occupational and economic structure is discussed by Albert A. Blum in "Labor at the Crossroads." Are labor unions dying out? Are they becoming conservative, bureaucratic units? Have the intellectuals abandoned the union ranks? Blum attempts to answer these questions.

An occupation with which we all have experience, although mostly on a superficial basis, is that of the cabdriver. Have you ever thought about what it would be like to be a "cabbie"? How do cabdrivers view their customers? Fred Davis presents an interesting review of these questions in "The Cabdriver and His Fare."

The fourth article portrays the intricate complexities of the "executive life." Whyte discusses in "How Hard Do Executives Work," the motivations which propel executives to work sixty hours a week. He examines the sacrifices and gains which accompany the stress-laden tasks of the managerial profession.

The final article in this section represents an excellent analysis of changes which have confronted individuals in supervisory roles in organizations. Technology, size of organizations, cultural patterns and other characteristics of work situations have lessened the sphere of discretion which foremen have traditionally been allowed to exercise. The supervisor is faced with many responsibilities, but has less authority to complete his duties.

25 Confessions of a Block-Buster

by NORRIS VITCHEK as told to ALFRED BALK

* * *

Not long ago in an all-white block on Chicago's West Side, a "For Sale" sign appeared in front of a modest frame bungalow. Immediately a wave of fear swept across the block. A Negro family already was living several blocks away. Not far from that was the western edge of Chicago's "Black Belt." Every year its border had been moving closer, enclosing blocks like this one along the way. Suppose the bungalow came into possession of a Negro? What would happen to the rest of the block?

All the residents were plainly worried. Among them were a widow, who had been living alone and had no assets but her home and the parents of four young children, who feared what "change" might mean to the youngsters' safety. "Relax," said the bungalow owner. "I'm selling this through a white real estate man. I won't even talk to a Negro."

Imagine their shock, then, when the "For Sale" sign came down and the new owners moved in—Negroes. And consider the impact of what happened next. Three more buildings, which were already owned by property speculators, "turned" immediately. Other Negro families arrived to look at homes in the block. Real estate men, both white and Negro, swarmed in.

Almost overnight the family with four children sold out at a sizable loss. So did six other home-owners in quick succession. "We'll stay," a few owners said. "We're broad-minded." But the situation

was out of control. Finally the last of the whites left—whether or not they could afford to move. Like hundreds of others who have been similarly blitzed, they never really knew what had hit them.

I knew. I triggered the whole sequence of events by buying the bungalow and quickly selling it to a Negro. I am a block-buster. Another and perhaps slightly less odious name for my craft is real estate speculator.

Cornering a Share of the Harvest

I specialize in locating blocks which I consider ripe for racial change. Then I "bust" them by buying properties from the white owners and selling them to Negroes—with the intent of breaking down the rest of the block for colored occupancy. Sometimes the groundwork —the initial block-busting—has already been done by some other speculator by the time I arrive on the scene. In that case all I have to do is to work on the remaining whites and reap my share of the harvest.

I make my money—quite a lot of it, incidentally—in three ways:

1. By beating down the prices I pay the white owners by stimulating their fear of what is to come
2. By selling to the eager Negroes at inflated prices
3. By financing these purchases at what amounts to a very high rate of interest.

I'll have more to say about these techniques later.

Block-busting is a relatively new business—only ten to fifteen years old ac-

Reprinted from the Saturday Evening Post, 235, 27 (July 14, 21, 1962), 15–19 by Permission of Alfred Balk and The Curtis Publishing Company.

tually—but already it is a crowded field. Block-busters also operate in Washington, D.C., Baltimore, Philadelphia, New York City, Boston, Cleveland, Detroit, St. Louis, and other cities and in some of their suburbs. Chicago alone has more than one hundred of us. Because few Negroes can command the necessary financing to enter this occupation, most of us are white, as I am. Over the past ten years we have helped "change" an average of two to three blocks a week in Chicago. Even now, with the overall housing market rather quiet, we bust a new block in Chicago every four to eight days.

With the nation's Negro population exploding and continuing to concentrate in urban areas, the demand simply never lets up. More than half the citizenry of Washington, D.C., is Negro, Philadelphia is one fourth Negro. In Chicago the Negro population, now one fourth of our citizenry, has nearly doubled in the past ten years and probably will double again in the next thirty, rising to 1,700,000 persons, or half the city's present population. Even its suburbs, now mostly white, are expected to contain nearly 700,000 Negroes by 1990.

Average Citizens, Average Prejudices

If you are an average white citizen, with average prejudices, you may regard all this as the ruin of metropolitan neighborhoods. I think of it merely as more business for what already is a growth industry. My attitude stems from the fact that few white neighborhoods welcome Negroes who can afford to buy there; yet the need for homes for Negroes keeps growing. I assist in the solution of this problem. My function, which might be called a service industry, is to drive the whites from a block whether or not they want to go, then move in the Negroes.

You might think it would be difficult to bust a block, especially your block. It isn't really. In most blocks someone almost always is being transferred, want-

ing a larger or smaller house, or moving away for his health. If I offer enough money I can buy any building I want—if not directly, then through a front. It doesn't matter whether Negroes now live nearby. The shock effect of the block-busting, plus my ready financing, can cave in enough of the block to make my efforts successful.

But I prefer blocks near others where Negroes live—especially old, middle-class blocks with a mixture of frame homes and walk-up apartments. Whites already there have been conditioned to insecurity by the inexorable march of the color line in their direction. This makes these blocks setups for the quick turnover, large volume, and the large profits I like. The case of a South Side block I busted is typical.

Twenty-five years ago when most of the block's residents moved in and Chicago's population was only 8 per cent Negro, none of the whites imagined that they might be "endangered." All this racial business was somebody else's problem. Then one day reality began to dawn on them. All-white streets along which they drove to the Loop suddenly "turned." Fairly distant stores and theaters they had patronized, friends' homes they had visited, or churches they had attended were being swallowed.

"We'll organize," some residents said. "We'll keep the niggers out." But other speculators and I already were buying in adjacent blocks and holding them until we thought the area was ready to be turned for maximum profit.

You can't appreciate the psychological effect of such a color-line march unless you have seen it. First, Negro students begin enrolling in neighborhood schools. Then, churches and businesses in the area quit fixing up facilities as they normally might. Parks which have been all white suddenly become all Negro. A home-owner applies to his bank for a home-improvement loan and is turned down. "Too close to the color line," he is told.

Small businesses begin to close. New

whites, if they move into the area at all, are apt to be of lower class than before, and they are tenants, not owners. Because lending institutions always blacklist an area for regular mortgages when change appears imminent, whites can't buy there if they want to.

So it went in my typical South Side block. But the residents still thought they were safe because everyone had agreed not to sell to Negroes. Hence they weren't too disturbed when a bluff, friendly accountant who was retiring and moving to Florida announced to neighbors that he was listing his three-flat building for sale. As weeks passed, however, and no buyer was found, their suspense grew, and the owner became desperate. "We're stuck," he told his wife. "We told everyone we wouldn't sell them out. But we have to."

Up to this point only a few Negro real estate men rather tentatively had rung doorbells in the block. Now we speculators and brokers, both white and Negro, really went to work. One paid several Negroes with noisy cars to begin driving up and down the street a few times a day. He also paid a Negro mother who drew aid-to-dependent-children payment to walk the block regularly with her youngsters. Another arranged to have phone calls made in the block for such people as "Johnnie Mac." Sometimes calls would consist only of a whisper, a drunken laugh or a warning—such as, "They're coming!"

I didn't participate in these vicious tactics. Few large speculators do. If I operated so crudely, frankly I wouldn't have consented to write this report, even under the fictitious name in the by-line. I just use psychology.

I began my work in this case by sending a postcard to everyone in the block and others in adjacent blocks. The cards said, "I will pay cash for your building." That was all except my phone number. The word "cash" was the key. It assured home owners they could get out quickly and reminded them that their neighbors could too. Then a canvasser and I headed

for the block to repeat the offer in person.

Best Price for First Building

My first stop was at the home of the retired accountant who owned the three-flat building. "How much are you asking for your building?" I asked him.

"Twenty-two thousand," he said.

"Well," I said, "you might get that if you wait. But you know what is happening in the neighborhood. If you want a quick cash deal, I'll give you $18,000." But, knowing that we speculators often pay proportionately more for the first building on a block to go, he would come down only $1,000 in price. At that point I got a break. My canvasser, who had been talking with other owners, rang the doorbell and called me onto the porch to tell me something.

"His neighbor in the one-story brick just sold for $14,000," he told me.

"Sorry," I told the accountant. "Negroes will be moving in next door. $18,000 is tops." His quick call to the neighbor confirmed my canvasser's report, and he accepted my offer on the spot.

The moment I make a deal, I always place a "Sold by" sign in front of the building. A few such signs—the gaudier the better—show that events are moving. So does the ringing of door bells. And with thirty other real estate men working a block, including regular dealers as well as speculators, those bells ring often.

Changing the rest of this block, as in most other blocks, was easy. After posting my signs, I merely sent a man down one side of the street and went up the other punching doorbells.

When a delivery driver who had two young daughters in school said he "probably would leave for the good of the kids" but wanted to think about it, my man discussed the pros and cons in a friendly way. "If you take my quick deal," he concluded, "you'll have no worries about the kids. You can give them a nice yard and have them in a good suburban school next week." The man and his wife, obviously troubled, decided my canvasser was right. They sold at a $2,000 loss.

To an elderly couple who hesitated, saying their home and neighborhood were the only ones they had known throughout their marriage and they would "stay around and see what our new neighbors are like," my man said, "I know what waiting has meant to people like you in worry and strain. Waiting never makes it easier. If you take my cash deal while I still can offer it, you can begin looking for a new retirement home tomorrow." They sold too.

First "Break" Can Bring Trouble

"No thanks," several owners told my canvasser. "My own real estate man is finding me a Negro buyer."

Some owners on every block consider this. If they can close a deal directly with a Negro, usually it is for a price close to the property's value—thus benefiting both. But most whites are reluctant to bargain with a Negro over so large a sum. They know that, in the sixty to ninety days before the closing date, he is more likely than a speculator to have to cancel the deal, despite having earnest money down. Many times, although the owner has listed his property with a neighborhood agent, the real estate man ends up by arranging a deal with me— with the seller not only accepting a depressed price but also having to pay a broker's commission.

And so day by day, week by week, month by month, the block collapses further, until the last white family moves away.

Now, admittedly, although somebody would perform this economic function if I did not, these dealings are not always pleasant. In the first place, the Negro able to buy property usually doesn't want trouble. Yet, being the first to "break" an all-white block, or even second or third, can and often does bring trouble.

For example, there was the case of a Negro salesman who had just been promoted to a supervisory position in his firm. He came to a speculator seeking an income property into which he could move with his family. The speculator told him about a three-flat building he had just bought from whites. "The place we're renting is bad," the Negro said, "but we don't want any trouble. Has the block been busted?" The speculator owned another building there, but the block hadn't been busted in the sense that Negroes already were living there. However, knowing the three-flat building would be a good investment for the Negro and that he should be able to carry it financially, the speculator told him OK.

In the first few days after the Negro moved in, a bottle was thrown through the front window, his wife was insulted by several whites who lived in the block, and his two children were harassed on their way home from school.

Few Negroes or whites on Chicago's West Side have forgotten the riots involving thousands, three summers ago, after a speculator's sale of a building to Negroes on West Jackson Boulevard. Luckily only the building got hurt. And, fortunately, any incidents connected with the move-ins I handle are so minor in comparison to what Negroes have experienced that they soon are forgotten.

"You've Sold Out Your Own Race"

Actually, block-busting probably is tougher on the whites than the Negroes. Nobody who has lived in a neighborhood for years, seen his children grow up there, remodeled his home exactly to his liking, and become accustomed to nearby school, church, and shopping facilities likes to be uprooted. This is particularly true if it happens so suddenly that he has no new neighborhood in mind, if he has to accept less living space and a higher-interest mortgage than he previously had, and if he must sell his property at a loss.

Several elderly persons have died because of the anguish and upheaval involved.

As a result of my business dealings, I have been cursed, called "nigger-lover," "vulture," and "panic peddler," had doors slammed in my face and even been chased by an irate woman with a broom. "You're communist and un-American!" one owner shouted at me. "You've sold out your own race!" others have yelled.

It is hard to forget, too, how even long-time neighbors and friends may become jealous, suspicious, and antagonistic toward one another. After one middle-aged couple had built a suburban home and sold their former home to a speculator —and the speculator had "turned" it— several former neighbors hired a sound truck and drove to the couple's new home. They cruised the block, shouting, "Be sure and meet your new neighbors, the Joneses. They sold out their old block to Negroes."

Once a block has been busted, some white owners simply stare, almost dumfounded, as we draw up sale papers for them. Others break down and cry. Some say, "It's OK to show the place to Negroes before we move, but we don't want to be in the house to watch it when you do."

But no matter how emotional or awkward some situations may be, there is one compensation for it all—money. Some brokers or investors make a good return only on some deals. I make it on every deal in the three ways I mentioned earlier.

You may believe your home is worth $15,000, for example. If I bust your block, I will expect to buy it for $12,000 cash. The odds are that eventually you will sell for that price, if not to me then to another speculator. If you and your white neighbors did not run, you probably would gain rather than lose. More than four-fifths of the white neighborhoods into which Negroes move hold their own or enjoy an increase in value, according to a five-year Fund for the Republic study of ten thousand transactions in northern interracial neighborhoods. But the myth that "Negroes lower property values" persists—so whites run, and we block-busters clean up. Within a few days comes profit No. 2: I advertise and sell it to a Negro, not for $15,000, but for $18,000. Financing the deal myself, I will accept $500 to $1,500 down, with remainder on contract. The easy-payment plan, I believe it is called—that is, $150 to $200 a month until the contract is fulfilled. When is that? This is profit No. 3, the big one. The contract is fulfilled when I have been paid principal and interest totaling $36,000.

These terms, I am told, force Negroes to overcrowd and overuse their buildings by renting out part of them or to skimp on maintenance, starting the neighborhood on the way to blight. (In most Negro neighborhoods in Chicago the population density is five times that of white areas.) The contract burden, I am also told, forces Negro mothers to work, despite the presence of youngsters at home, compels fathers to take two jobs, and can lead to numerous other problems because of the financial strain and anxiety.

Even so, the number of Negro buyers who default on their payments is small. When it does happen in my own business, it is no loss to me, since I retain title to property until contracts are completed. I keep all the payments made until that time, evict the owners, and either rent the building or resell it on about the same terms.

The Urban League of Chicago says we speculators make nearly $1,000,000 a month in our city in "abnormal" profit from Negroes who buy former white property on contract. This could be. I know that I make four times the profit I could for the same amount of effort in all-white real estate. If anybody who is well established in this business in Chicago doesn't earn $100,000 a year, he is loafing.

"A dirty business," you say? One that whites should fight?

White people in dozens of neighbor-hoods have tried fighting. They have pressured neighborhood banks and sav-ings-and-loan associations to quit black-listing their areas, resulting in token con-cessions. They have held block meetings to warn home-owners not to deal with those of us who advertise "Quick Cash Sales" in newspapers or the classified phone directory, have passed out leaflets listing speculators' names and have rip-ped up "Sold by" signs which were of a larger size or were posted longer than city ordinance allows. They even won a fraud-and-misrepresentation case against two block-busting brokers in Chicago, thanks to several blunders which no estab-lished operator would have made. De-spite all such resistance, once a block has been busted, only rarely has its complete breakdown been halted. Too many forces are working for us speculators.

Ordaining the "Cave-in" Method

The Chicago Real Estate Board, an organization of the city's most promis-ing realtors, all but ordained the "cave-in" method in a policy laid down in 1917. "It is desired in the interest of all that each block shall be filled solidly (with Negroes) and that further expansion shall be confined to contiguous blocks......"

The board, which is all white, no longer makes a copy of this statement available in its office, but the policy has never been rescinded or repudiated. None of the board's 1,700 members violates it. No member, if he deals with Negroes at all, is likely to arrange for a sale to them in a white neighborhood that is not next to a "Negro block." Once a neighbor-hood begins changing, none will show homes there to whites.

Lending institutions' "no-Negro" or "no-integrated-area" loan policies further perpetuate the trend, restricting Negroes to blocks we bust and forcing them to rely mainly on our contract sales for financing.

The City council and Mayor Richard J. Daley, who, like his two immediate predecessors, comes from the all-white Bridgeport area of the city, also help. They regularly table every request for open-occupancy ordinances, which by opening up any neighborhood to Negroes who could afford to buy there would take the pressure off the few collapsing ones which are open.

The police put down violence promptly in any blocks which are busted in a "permissible" area. Yet, if a Negro leap-frogged into a home beyond this zone, the protests somehow always get out of hand. In one case, a policeman guard-ing a Negro's new home was seen show-ing several youths how to make a Molotov-cocktail incendiary bomb.

Some churches accept all this, often serving as rallying points for whites try-ing to "hold the line." One parish even has acted as an agent in the purchase of twenty-two buildings which normal turnover otherwise might have placed in the hands of speculators. When change begins, most churches then simply close up shop and sell most or all of their property.

Relentless March of the Color Line

Neighborhood-improvement associations actually are usually "all-white" im-provement associations. One, the Back of the Yards Neighborhood Council, has kept its area all white. But it began in the 1930's and has a unique authoritarian control extending through stores, banks, churches, and industry in its stockyards neighborhood. Every other neighborhood, including one in which retail business-men raised a war chest of $100,000, had "gone" when the color line reached it. And associations which opposed me be-fore any breakthroughs end up happy to cooperate—if I will only "go slow" and not change blocks until association offi-cials say they are "ready." I usually do this to keep their goodwill.

Newspapers, too, help prepare the way. Their only stories in this field usually concern the "panic" aspects. If they print stories about Negroes, it's only in connection with crime or welfare problems of population increases, not with Negro church activity or business and educational success or other aspects of normal life in good Negro neighborhoods.

The Board of Education contributes by writing off a school once it begins to change racially, consigning it to overcrowding, double shifts, and supervision by the least experienced and lowest-paid teachers—and by giving it the lowest proportion of counselors.

Then there are my financial sources, which are among the most reputable in the city. My credit is good in almost any bank or savings-and-loan association in town. It also is good with insurance companies, including several Negro firms. Merely by placing an ad in a daily newspaper, I can raise cash by selling my contract paper at a discount to some of the most reputable doctors, dentists, lawyers, and other business and professional men in town.

With forces such as these on my side, why should I feel guilty? Am I really the basic cause of whites' fleeing? Do I depress their property values and inflate prices for Negroes? When a Negro has been turned away from a bank, do I "trap" him into accepting a contract sale?

And what alternative can you provide for my function? Would you try to influence your bank or savings-and-loan association to begin lending to Negroes? Would you help remove the pressure on "busted" areas by welcoming a Negro family into your block? Do you even care that my business operates as it does? Whatever my faults and whatever the social stigma I endure, I don't believe I am hypocritical about all this. Can you honestly say the same?

26   Labor at the Crossroads

by ALBERT A. BLUM

Not only does the labor movement have to withstand the buffeting of Boulwarism, the grimaces of Goldwater, the litigation under the Landrum-Griffin Act, and the huffing and puffing of Hoffa; but, as if this were not enough, Meany and his associates have to face the fulminations of writers who fear for labor's future. The charge these critics level against organized labor is that *the trade union movement is in the midst of a crisis and is doing little about it.* They describe the

ills; they suggest some cures; but they doubt that the patient will listen to them.

Although many labor leaders ignore their critics, others strike back. In fact, George Meany at the last AFL-CIO convention devoted a large share of his introductory speech to lambasting the critics. Others, from the Secretary of Labor down, interjected in their talks phrases poking fun at or denouncing these creators of "myths and fallacies" as Meany called them.

The defenders of organized labor condemn its detractors as being eggheads or intellectuals, left-wingers, cynics, ignorant, out-of-date, or filled with a sense of guilt for having left the labor move-

Reprinted from "Labor at the Crossroads," by permission of the author and the publisher, Harvard Business Review, *42 (July-August, 1964), pp. 6–20.*

ment. Perhaps the unionists' anger is increased since these criticisms come from the left or center, from those who the union movement might expect would act as friends.

As for the critics—the authors such as Paul Jacobs,[1] B. J. Widick,[2] Sidney Lens,[3] Solomon Barkin,[4] Paul E. Sultan,[5] and the contributors to the book Solomon Barkin and I edited (*The Crisis in the American Trade-Union Movement*[6])— they generally believe they are acting as friends. What are these authors writing that evokes such bitterness among labor leaders and causes them to feel that "if these are our friends, what must our enemies be saying?"

Talk vs. Action

There is one thing several of the critics agree on. They grudgingly admire James Hoffa as being symptomatic both of what is the worst and of what is the best in the labor movement.

Jacobs, Widick, and Lens, all pay close attention to the tough trade-union leader and admire him for his guts because he will stand up and be counted and *do* something. They disparage other trade-union leaders (even Walter Reuther, with whom they frequently compare Hoffa) as social critics with feet of clay who talk much and do little. Hoffa talks but also acts.

Further, they even admire some of his actions. He recognized the need for structural changes toward more centralized control within his union and pushed for it—even though many of the ideas stemmed from Trotskyites in Minneapolis. And he, Hoffa, is conscious of the need for membership contact. He goes out and meets the Teamsters. He talks with them and in their language. This may be the Tammany Hall approach to democracy—that of the ward politician who provides largess as a semblance of democracy rather than its reality. Never-

theless, these authors feel that this is more than many trade-union presidents do. The latter sit in their marble palaces in Washington and talk about union democracy without practicing it.

Thus Hoffa comes out rather well in several of these books. This tough, working-class "stiff" has guts, flexibility, and membership contact—traits that these writers wish other union leaders would emulate. In addition, the writers hope that Hoffa and other heads of labor will free themselves from the "big-business union" straitjacket that binds most of them.

These critics also argue that the members of unions and others in society are becoming alienated from organized labor. They feel that the collective bargaining process is failing and that labor is losing its political influence just when it should be expanding its political activity. Finally, they point out that unions are not growing. These are severe indictments (each author says them differently, omits one or more of them, or adds others) and surely are worthy of more consideration than labor leaders (and business leaders) are giving them.

Barren Democracy

One problem, however, that does concern all the critics is the lack of membership participation in the labor movement. Jacobs' concern with lack of participation and union democracy pervades many sections of his volume. Thus he critically examines the role played by A. J. Hayes, the Machinists' head, in handling his opposition. Hayes, who is also the head of the AFL-CIO Ethical Practices Committee, may be ethical, but he brooks no opposition. Hayes believes that those of his members who resist his decisions should resolve their disputes internally within his union's halls. Jacobs disagrees —"since unions are recognized and protected by public law, some 'rights of members' are indeed properly a matter of public concern."[7]

But Jacobs is intelligently alert to another problem—namely, that democratic unions do not necessarily favor policies that are for the common good. He points to the labor organization that many observers have called the archetype of union democracy—the International Typographical Union—and notes that certain of this union's policies, such as favoring featherbedding practices, are not socially useful. He believes this may be due to the fact that some unions are relatively isolated from community pressures and therefore view their selfish standards as those of the society.

The difficult problem of increasing membership participation in unions is made even more pronounced, says Jacobs, by the tendency of workers to conceive of their labor organizations as purely service agencies, though they have become far more than that. "In reality the unions have become part of the machinery of American industrial life, sharing in important areas of managerial decision-making."[8]

And as a result unions, like their business counterparts, develop bureaucracies and organization men. The desire on the part of leaders of unions, industry, and the government for "harmony in labor-management relations" has resulted in all three groups trying to squelch any vital opposition within the labor movement.

The bureaucracy and lack of democracy in the union movement disturbs the other writers too—particularly when it goes beyond the local union level. Emanuel Stein, in fact, feels somewhat hopeless since members fail to participate "not because of member apathy, nor because of the ambition or cupidity of the leaders, but simply because the size of the union and the complexity of its functions make such participation substantially impossible."[9] In lieu of such participation, therefore, he believes it

essential that the workers' civil liberties be protected.

Loss of Rights

But how are the civil liberties of those who differ from their labor leaders protected? Badly, if at all, responds Paul Sultan. Sultan analyzes in fascinating detail some of the basic principles of a number of trade unionists who have bitterly attacked labor leaders and, as a result, have received harsh retribution from their leaders. Sultan joins those "individualists who have not been able to comprehend why unions, designed to protect the worker against impersonal market forces, should themselves emerge as impersonal and detached sources of power."[10]

What Sultan portrays is a labor movement that rarely will permit its members to offer any basic criticisms of its policies, one that has become as paternalistic as some firms, and one that believes, as many parents do about their children, that union members should be seen but not heard. To Sultan, the tragedy is not only that the members have lost their rights, but also that the union leaders have failed to understand that the dissenters may be saying something worth hearing. Their different ideas might help labor break the bureaucratic mold it has formed for itself and consequently be better able to meet the new challenges of American society. To Sultan's plea the other writers would generally offer a fervid "Amen."

Negroes Neglected

One challenge of our society—the place of the Negro—has not been adequately met by unions. Today, the Negro is separating from organized labor. He has become disenchanted with unions, proclaim most of the critics, because unions have not led in fighting for and providing equal rights. Jacobs points out that what the Negro wants is not the benevolence which labor has offered but equal rights—and not tomorrow but today!

Labor leaders protest that all they can do is to educate their members who, after all, still reflect the mores of their communities. But Jacobs argues that unions are supposed to lead in the community. In any case, unless they are in the forefront of the civil rights fight (and this is unlikely, given the independence of the unions that make up the AFL-CIO), all that will remain of a strong Negro-labor relationship will be an "uneasy alliance."

Both Widick and Lens pronounce similar judgments—that while the CIO unions once fought for Negro rights (at least at the workplace), the fire is now gone and it may be the Negroes' turn to light a fire under unions.

Intellectual Sterility

The growing separation of the Negro from the union movement is related to another split that disturbs the critics—this one between the intellectuals and the labor movement. Widick suggests many reasons why the intellectual, once so sympathetic to unionism, today is bored, if not angry, with it.

Labor is no longer the underdog; its goals are narrow and often selfish. It has become more like the organization it was created to fight—the corporation. It is hostile to any criticism and has contempt for and misuses its own staff intellectuals. (Labor's credo for its staff intellectuals is, according to Widick, a cynical "policy is the best honesty.") It suffers from a lack of support for worthwhile research, a stimulating labor press, and a vital and meaningful worker education program. And, finally, it now basically fails to lock horns with challenging ideas. "Is it a wonder," Widick asks, "that the union movement in the 1960's is such a desert of original thought, with no attraction

for intellectuals and no serious significance in the ideological life of the nation?"[11]

Maurice F. Neufeld critically assays the historical relationships between intellectuals and the labor movement. He concludes that any real joining together of both groups could only have been short-run, since the labor movement has more narrow goals than the intellectual, who is usually more concerned with the overall social welfare of the nation.[12]

Widick, Jacobs, and Lens believe, however, that the labor movement should become more concerned with the social welfare of the whole society. Because labor is not concerned, the unions are becoming increasingly alienated from their own members and from those groups in society that formerly worked with them—the Negro and the intellectual.

Challenges to Bargaining

To add to labor's dilemma, the method it has used with great success to achieve its more narrow economic goals is starting to decline in importance—namely, collective bargaining. In "Old Before Its Time: Collective Bargaining at Twenty-Eight" (an essay included in his book), Jacobs concludes that the collective bargaining system is "collapsing," because it cannot really solve the problems faced today by unions and managements or by those outside the collective bargaining system. He points to the railroad and the airline disputes as examples of situations wherein collective bargaining cannot succeed because jobs, and even unions, are likely to be negotiated out of existence. Automation and the unneeded workers that follow in its wake cannot be handled by negotiations solely between unions and companies; government also must play an important role.

And how is collective bargaining going to help the unemployed, the poor, and, for that matter, those who are steadily moving out from under the umbrella of blue-collar unionism into the unprotected white-collar area? Without members, Jacobs points out, labor's collective bargaining power is meaningless. And even for those who still have membership cards, the cards have less and less meaning. The worker wants his job protected. Unionism, through bargaining, is mainly concerned with collective action and thus cannot often solve adequately the individual's specific problem. But more importantly, collective bargaining is incapable, according to Jacobs, of dealing "with the economic conditions that are making unemployment a permanent way of life for millions."[13]

What, then, does Jacobs offer as alternatives to unions? To help provoke imagination and energy among labor leaders, he suggests competition: the splitting up of the merged unions so that they can again compete for members and for ideas. More government involvement is inevitable. Continuous bargaining between contracts—a tendency now developing—might replace the crisis bargaining that has until now been the pattern.

Jacobs concludes that labor will have to use its economic muscle less and its political muscle more; for "the place of unions in the structure of industrial justice will continue to grow smaller unless unions return to the political function that once was primary with them."[14] (*When* politics was the primary function of labor, the author does not say.) Unions must become intimately involved in the political process (as they are in Israel, Scandinavia, and England), because their economic technique, collective bargaining, is becoming obsolete.

Widick, too, is critical of the bargaining process. He entitled one of his chapters "The End of Free Collective Bargaining?" The question mark, he fears, should really be an exclamation point. He notes what other critics have pointed out—namely, that what purports to be collective bargaining often really amounts to little more than big labor and big business cooperating to raise prices for the public. The price rises are often unjustified, says Widick, by the increased labor costs involved.

But his main concern is that the government is intervening too much. He criticizes unions for believing that government assistance has built up their strength. Actually, inept management has done far more than the government to strengthen unionism. Instead of reflecting what the union members want, labor leaders and the government are more concerned with industrial peace and with the political repercussions of the settlements. Labor, government, and management each enters into collective bargaining convinced it knows what is good for the workers and rarely, if ever, tries to find out what, in fact, the workers want. Widick wants labor to find out and act accordingly.

But Professor Melvin Rothbaum points out that, even if there were a consensus of views between labor's rank and file and its leaders, there would still be many problems that collective bargaining could not solve—for example, unemployment. Government fiscal and monetary policy is an essential ingredient in the solution to this problem. Collective bargaining may at best be only the spice. Moreover, certain demands can have conflicting effects. Raise wages, and jobs may be reduced; shorten hours, and firms may also lessen employment by increasing efficiency. Thus, collective bargaining may only have limited utility—a utility which has been lessened by the impact of automation.[15]

Automation's Blows

"The Greatest Threat" Widick calls automation. He argues that because of recent technological changes (a) the strains and tensions among factory workers are increasing, not diminishing; (b) unemployment is rising; (c) the nature of the work force has changed; and (d) the labor movement has not met these challenges.

Jacobs, in his essay on technological change in the printing and airline industries and the resulting featherbedding, notes that unions have taken some action to cushion its impact—but not enough. He feels that we need new standards for assessing the effects of technology on society. If the effects of a new change are socially harmful, then the labor movement (among others) should attempt to limit its use, just as the petroleum industry limits the amounts of crude oil pumped from the fields. Jacobs concludes:

> If we do not develop standards beyond the single one of efficiency for judging technological change, if we do not create new jobs by devising new theories of industrial justice for the technological dilemmas of the twentieth century, only two alternatives may be open in the twenty-first century: Either there will be so few jobs available that only an elite will be allowed to work while the remainder of society consumes, or the practice of 'unwork' will need to spread."[16]

Whether the trouble is automation or other factors, the writers voice discontent with the collective bargaining process as it operates today. But after all, as Jacobs points out, negotiations are of value mainly to those who belong to unions. Yet one of the main criticisms launched against labor (which is offered as proof that there is indeed a crisis within the labor movement) is that organized labor since 1945 has not grown appreciably in proportion to the labor force and, since 1956, has in fact declined.

Union Atrophy

Though all the writers touch on it, the most important study of why unions have not grown can be found in a pamphlet published by the Center for the Study of Democratic Institutions, authored by Solomon Barkin—who, as one commentator put it, was the "dean of the intellectuals within the labor movement," before he recently resigned.

To Barkin, a labor movement that does not grow tends to stagnate and atrophy. He describes the many factors external to the labor movement that hinder union expansion: employer opposition, unsympathetic labor legislation and administration, state right-to-work laws, lack of social discontent, and "the sullied image of unions."

He then describes the negative attitudes of specific groups: employer resistance, such as in southern textiles; lack of union interest in organizing new groups, such as workers in residential construction or in small towns; and worker apathy among women, nonmanual, Negro, and service workers.

He also examines internal union impediments to expansion: the lack of centralized coordination of organizational drives by the AFL-CIO headquarters; apathy of local members and officers; inadequate missionary spirit among organizers; use of obsolete organizing techniques at the same time that management is employing more sophisticated methods; and interunion rivalry (a point that differs from Jacobs' view).

But Barkin is not satisfied with portraying the failures. Although he believes labor faces a crisis at a time when the public wrongly still thinks of trade unions as "Goliaths of power," Barkin still has hope. He tries to spell out methods by which labor can grow and rejuvenate itself; for new members will help bring about the rejuvenation Barkin so ardently desires. Moreover, Barkin is committed to the need for unionism as an important factor in safeguarding individual freedom, as an essential part of American democracy. He consequently suggests new approaches to the labor movement, along these specific lines:

1. "The image of the movement must transcend that of the constituent unions."[17] (Barkin wants the AFL-CIO headquarters to mean something as once the old CIO did. To achieve

this, the national federation must have more power.)

2. "The basic purposes of the movement must be emphatically reasserted."[18] (Barkin feels that labor must serve as a social critic, an economic leveler, a stimulator to management, and a focal point of social idealism.)

3. "The movement must put specific programs into effect."[19] (Barkin suggests that unions fight poverty, support growth of the national economy, make sure the free market operates in the public interest, pressure management and unions to follow responsible economic policies such as research and development, educate society as to the values of collective action, adhere to democratic principles, foster full employment, enhance individual freedom in life outside work, and be catholic in its concerns.)

4. "The structure of the labor movement needs revision."[20] (More centralized power is one proposal Barkin offers.)

5. "There is no area where the shift in power and initiative is more urgent than in the field of organization."[21] (More union cooperation, better personnel in organizational work, and improved union educational programs are all part of Barkin's answer.)

Crusade for Justice

We must "again see a revival of the Messianic spirit of former years,"[22] declares Barkin. The former years mean the 1930's to Barkin—and Jacobs, Widick, and Lens would all echo this somewhat romantic refrain. Moreover, Barkin argues that labor should be a social critic and fight the good fight for social unionism. This too is what Jacobs, Widick, and Lens believe—namely, that much of the fault in modern unionism is that unions which had as their purpose the remolding of society (or should have had, according to these critics) have instead been re-molded by society. Organized labor sought to change business; instead business changed it. Now labor operates more and more like a corporation and less and less like a union that claims special treatment because its goals are to serve mankind and "to fight against injustice."

This is what Sidney Lens wants labor to do—fight injustice again. To achieve this, he favors labor's starting a political party or at least moving in that direction. Because he wants the rank and file to become more involved, since "business unionism can be checked only to the extent that the rank and file is involved,"[23] he suggests that more power be given to the city central bodies and to local labor unions (side by side with the local labor political clubs). "The centralized structure" of national unions "is a halter around labor's neck."[24] The programs of these unions should foster an expansion of a social welfare state. And Lens concludes that "the only means by which labor can make a new step forward is through new crusades that infuse idealism, more idealism, and still more idealism."[25]

Widick, too, is sympathetic to forming a labor party and hopes that the possible victory of the Labour Party in England may become infectious in the United States. Widick is committed to the idea that unions should no longer be guided by business philosophy, but instead should act as a "nonprofit, do-good movement." To expand, unions must try to "do good" and to secure a greater share of society's benefits for its members and for the deprived members of the community. Though he may differ in detail, Jacobs also wants labor committed to politics, to social welfare changes—and less to the old goals of business unionism.

And thus the critics end their attack. They feel that for one brief moment unions were on the right track—during the early days of the CIO. But now, some thirty years later, they sadly report that labor has stalled; in fact, it may be moving backwards. Each of these critics wants it to shift gears and move forward again. They call to mind the question that President Kennedy asked when some union spokesmen were leaving his office: "And where is the pressure from the left?" Several of these books attempt to provide this pressure, even if the labor movement will not.

Points of Agreement

What conclusions can we draw from these critics?

First, they vary in their diagnosis of details: the importance of centralization and the effects of democracy in unionism, to name just two. But more important, they agree on the essentials:

1. The lack of imaginative leadership
2. The paucity of fresh ideas
3. The need for a switch from business to social unionism with an increased concern for politics
4. The weakness of collective bargaining
5. The related dilemmas raised by automation
6. The alienation of the Negro, the intellectual, and union members in general from the labor movement.

Secondly, their dreams concerning the labor movement have not been fulfilled. They want it to be a source of social idealism, a movement that will take the lead in creating a society that will provide more social welfare legislation and government involvement in economic life (this does not prevent some of them from objecting to government involvement in collective bargaining).

Since the labor movement has failed to achieve these goals and to achieve them in the manner the critics want, they are disillusioned. (Labor's detractors on the right would argue just the reverse. They feel that what is wrong with unions is that they do fight for, and often secure, the passage of social legislation.) A pessimistic feeling permeates all of the critics' books, an assurance that labor will do

nothing about the crisis it faces and, in fact, will deny there is a crisis and attack those who claim there is one.

One does not have to agree with all of the claims made by the authors surveyed. Some are clearly correct: labor has not grown; collective bargaining cannot solve many of the problems facing workers and society today (even though one can argue with Jacobs over whether it is obsolete); labor has lost the support of many who once backed it; its leadership is old; its structure remains virtually unchanged; and its proposals frequently are uninspired.

And what can management learn from reading these books? It can, of course, note that corporations are rarely mentioned, except as the group which unions once fought but which they are not fighting strenuously any longer. Some of the writers are convinced that business has, in a sense, won the struggle. Business transformed unions into something akin to itself—in structure and in philosophy. Through sophisticated personnel policies, business won the support of many employees and, as a result, also thwarted unions.

False Lure

Many executives may read these commentators' moans about labor's crisis and believe this is their great opportunity. Despite the conviction of some of the authors that industrial relations conflict is disappearing, many executives do not believe this is the case.

But if, in fact, unions *are* in the midst of a growing crisis, if, in fact, they *are* growing potentially weaker, then some managers will read this as an invitation to fight the unions, to try to beat them back, to practice hard bargaining, to drive them out of the plant, and thus to write an epitaph for labor. If, in short, management believes that a labor movement in crisis is the time for it to try to destroy organized labor and the protections that unions have sought for their members through contracts and legislation, then management will have learned as little from those who criticize company industrial relations policies of the 1920's and 1930's as labor is learning from its critics in the 1960's.

Widick put it well when he claimed that "the longtime stupidity of management has given unions their power and maintains viable union organization."[26] If the lesson these authors teach management is that this is the time to fight labor, then they may indeed have helped unions —no matter how inadvertently; for perhaps one of the great hopes of a revitalized labor movement in America is a hostile and uncompromising management that believes it knows what is best for its employees and will not really listen to its employees' own spokesmen.

This may force organized labor and its leadership again to become hostile and uncompromising. It may force unions to fight for the loyalty of their members— and, in the face of potential loss of power, to launch a real drive for new members. It may even force labor to think through new answers to the problems it now faces. In fact, such management policies may bring new leaders to the fore; drive some of the groups, now alienated, into backing organized labor again; and prompt some organized groups of employees that are not unions (such as engineer and teacher associations) to begin to act like unions.

Thus, the epilogue to these books may yet be written by business executives. It would be called, "The Decline of the Labor Movement and What Management Did to Force a Resurrection."

Looking Back*

Is labor still at the crossroads? Unions have not grown, as a percentage of the labor force, since I wrote the article. Marked growth in labor unionism normally is associated with workers being discontented about something—job security, wages, comparisons with other workers, unfair management practices, and so forth. Where unionism has been expanding and showing real vitality is in those areas where there is such discontent —school teachers, to name one example— and/or where management has been facilitating unionism, such as in the federal and local government agencies. The relatively high level of our economy has made it difficult for unions to expand for two reasons: First, many of the workers are not discontented or interested; second, the leadership is also not particularly troubled, and new ideas have not been forthcoming from the labor movement concerning how to identify and use the discontent that does exist.[1] It may be that the recent changes in the leadership in a number of unions may provoke some new ideas or, on the other hand, the revolts may, in fact, only have been palace revolutions. We shall have to wait and see, particularly since the age of a number of other trade-union leaders means that they will have to step down too.

On the part of management, prosperity has caused most industrialists to hesitate to "rock the boat" by actively fighting the unions that do exist. What their attitude will be if there is a downturn in the economy may be another matter.

Clearly, whether the labor movement is or is not in a crisis depends upon one's definition of a crisis. Unions may not have grown during the past few years, but they still do relatively well for their members and have also created pressure for legislation that organized labor feels will help those who are unorganized. Thus, we will just have to wait until tomorrow to discover whether today's labor movement is, in fact, at the crossroads.

---

[1] Paul Jacobs, *The State of the Unions* (New York: Atheneum Publishers, 1963).

[2] B. J. Widick, *Labor Today* (Boston: Houghton Mifflin Company, 1964).

[3] Sidney Lens, *The Crisis of American La-*

bor (New York: A. S. Barnes & Co., Inc., 1961).

4 Solomon Barkin, *The Decline of the Labor Movement and What Can Be Done About It* (Santa Barbara, California: Center for the Study of Democratic Institutions, 1961).

5 Paul E. Sultan, *The Disenchanted Unionist* (New York: Harper & Row, Publishers, Inc., 1963).

6 *The Annals of the American Academy of Political and Social Science,* 350 (November 1963), hereafter cited as *The Annals.*

7 Jacobs, *op. cit.,* p. 110.

8 *Ibid.,* p. 150.

9 Emanuel Stein, "The Dilemma of Union Democracy," *The Annals,* p. 54.

10 Sultan, *op. cit.,* p. viii.

11 Widick, *op. cit.,* p. 111.

12 Maurice F. Neufeld, "The Historical Relationship of Liberals and Intellectuals to Organized Labor in the United States," *The Annals,* p. 115.

13 Jacobs, *op. cit.,* p. 291.

14 *Ibid.,* p. 292.

15 Melvin Rothbaum, "Economic Dilemmas of Collective Bargaining," *The Annals,* p. 95.

16 Jacobs, *op. cit.,* p. 255.

17 Barkin, *op. cit.,* p. 68.

18 *Ibid.,* p. 69.

19 *Ibid.,* p. 19.

20 *Ibid.,* p. 72.

21 *Ibid.,* p. 73.

22 *Ibid.,* p. 74.

23 Lens, *op. cit.,* p. 302.

24 *Ibid.*

25 *Ibid.,* p. 308.

26 Widick, *op. cit.* p. 55.

* Prepared by the author for this volume.

1 See my "The Prospects for Office Employee Unionism," *Proceedings* (Industrial Relations Research Association, 1963), pp. 182–93.

27 The Cabdriver and His Fare: Facets of a Fleeting Relationship*

by FRED DAVIS

* * *

Even in an urban and highly secularized society such as ours, most service relationships, be they between a professional and his client or a menial and his patron, are characterized by certain constraints on too crass a rendering and consuming of the service.[1] That is to say, in the transaction, numerous interests besides that of simply effecting an economic exchange are customarily attended to and dealt with. The moral reputation of the parties,[2] their respective social standing, and the skill and art with which the service is performed[3] are but a few of the

Reprinted from "The Cabdriver and His Fare," American Journal of Sociology, 65 *(September, 1959), pp. 158–165. By permission of the author and the University of Chicago Press.*

noninstrumental values that are usually incorporated into the whole act.

Tenuous though such constraints may become at times—particularly in large cities where anonymous roles, only segmentally related, occur in great profusion —it is at once evident that, for them to exist at all, something approximating a community must be present. Practitioners and clients must be sufficiently in communication for any untoward behavior to stand a reasonable chance of becoming known, remarked upon, remembered, and, in extreme cases, made public. And, whereas the exercise of sanctions does not necessarily depend on a community network[4] that is closely integrated (or one in which there is a total identity of values and interests), it does depend on there being some continuity and stability in the relationships that make up the network, so that, at minimum, participants may in the natural course of events be able to identify actions and actors to one another.[5]

It is mainly, though not wholly, from this vantage point that big-city cab-driving as an occupation is here discussed, particularly the relationship between cabdriver and fare and its consequences for the occupational culture.[6] Approximating in certain respects a provincial's caricature of the broad arc of social relations in the metropolis, this relationship affords an extreme instance of the weakening and attenuation of many of the constraints customary in other client-and-patron-oriented services in our society. As such, its analysis can perhaps point up by implication certain of the rarely considered preconditions for practitioner-client relations found in other, more firmly structured, services and professions.

In a large city like Chicago the hiring of a cab by a passenger may be conceived of in much the same way as the random collision of particles in an atomic field. True, there are some sectors of the field in which particles come into more frequent collision than others, for example, downtown, at railroad depots, and at the larger neighborhood shopping centers. But this kind of differential activity within the field as a whole provides little basis for predicting the coupling of any two specific particles.

To a much more pronounced degree than is the case in other client-and-patron-oriented services, the occupation of cabdriver provides its practitioners with few, if any, regularities by which to come upon, build up, and maintain a steady clientele. The doctor has his patients, the schoolteacher her pupils, the janitor his tenants, the waitress her regular diners; and in each case server and served remain generally in some continuing or renewable relationship. By contrast, the cabdriver's day consists of a long series of brief contacts with unrelated persons of whom he has no foreknowledge, just as they have none of him, and whom he is not likely to encounter again.

Furthermore, by virtue of the differential spatial, social, and organizational arrangements of the community, it is also likely that the clients of these other practitioners will, in some manner at least, know one another and be related to one another in ways that often transcend the simple circumstance of sharing the same services: they may also be friends, kin, neighbors, or colleagues. For this reason the clientele of most practitioners is something more than an aggregate of discrete individuals; it is, as well, a rudimentary social universe and forum to which the practitioner must address himself in other than purely individual terms.[7]

The cabdriver, by comparison, has no such clientele. He has no fixed business address, and his contacts with passengers are highly random and singular. To a striking degree he is a practitioner without reputation, because those who ride in his cab do not comprise, except perhaps in the most abstract sense, anything approximating a social group. They neither know nor come into contact with one another in other walks of life, and, even if by chance some do, they are unaware of their ever having shared the services of the same anonymous cab-driver. Even were the driver deliberately to set out to build up a small nucleus of steady and favored passengers, the time-space logistics of his job would quickly bring such a scheme to nought. Unable to plot his location in advance or to distribute time according to a schedule, he depends on remaining open to all comers wherever he finds himself. Much more so than other classes of service personnel, cabdrivers are both the fortuitous victims and the beneficiaries of random and highly impersonal market contingencies.

This set of circumstances—fleeting, one-time contact with a heterogeneous aggregate of clients, unknown to one another—exerts an interesting influence on the role of cabdriver.

Unable, either directly through choice or indirectly through location, to select clients, the cabdriver is deprived of even minimal controls. His trade therefore exposes him to a variety of hazards and exigencies which few others, excepting policemen, encounter as frequently; for example: stick-ups, belligerent drunks, women in labor, psychopaths, counterfeiters, and fare-jumpers. Unlike the policeman's, however, his control over them is more fragile.

Nor, incidentally, is the cabdriver's social status or level of occupational skill of much help in inducing constraint in fares. Patently, his status is low, in large part precisely because, unlike the professional and other practitioners commanding prestige, he can hardly be distinguished from his clients in task-relevant competence. Not only is the operation of a motor car a widely possessed skill, but a large proportion of fares have, for example, a very good idea of the best routes to their destination, the rules and practices of the road, and the charges for a trip. Though they are rarely as adept or sophisticated in these matters as the cabdriver, the discrepancy is so small that many think they know the driver's job as well as he does. Periodically, a cabdriver will boldly challenge a difficult and critical passenger to take over the wheel himself. Others, wishing to impress on the fare that theirs is a real service requiring special talent and skill, will resort to darting nimbly in and out of traffic, making neatly executed U-turns, and leaping smartly ahead of other cars when the traffic light changes.

Goffman[8] speaks of a category of persons who in some social encounters are treated as if they were not present, whereas in fact they may be indispensable for sustaining the performance. He terms these "nonpersons" and gives as an example a servant at a social gathering. Although cabdrivers are not consistently approached in this way by fares, it happens often enough for it to become a significant theme of their work. Examples

are legion. Maresca[9] tells of the chorus girl who made a complete change from street clothing into stage costume as he drove her to her theater. More prosaic instances include the man and wife who, managing to suppress their anger while on the street, launch into a bitter quarrel the moment they are inside the cab; or the well-groomed young couple who after a few minutes roll over on the back seat to begin petting; or the businessman who loudly discusses details of a questionable business deal. Here the driver is expected to, and usually does, act as if he were merely an extension of the automobile he operates. In actuality, of course, he is acutely aware of what goes on in his cab, and although his being treated as a nonperson implies a degraded status, it also affords him a splendid vantage point from which to witness a rich variety of human schemes and entanglements.

The fleeting nature of the cabdriver's contact with the passenger at the same time also makes for his being approached as someone to whom intimacies can be revealed and opinions forthrightly expressed with little fear of rebuttal, retaliation, or disparagement. And though this status as an accessible person is the product of little more than the turning inside-out of his nonperson status—which situation implies neither equality nor respect for his opinion—it nevertheless does afford him glimpses of the private lives of individuals which few in our society, apart from psychiatrists and clergy, are privileged to note as often or in such great variety. It is probably not a mistaken everyday generalization that big-city cabdrivers, on their part, feel less compunction about discussing their own private lives, asking probing questions, and "sounding off" on a great many topics and issues than do others who regularly meet the public, but less fleetingly.[10]

In cabdriving, therefore, propriety, deference, and "face" are, in the nature of the case, weaker than is the case in most other service relationships. This absence contributes to a heightened pre-occupation with and focusing on the purely instrumental aspect of the relationship, which for the driver is the payment he receives for his services. This perhaps would be less blatantly the case were it not for the gratuity or tip. For the non-cab-owning company driver, the sum collected in tips amounts roughly to 40 per cent of his earnings. Considering, for example, that in Chicago in the late forties a hard-working cabdriver, who worked for ten hours a day, six days a week, would on the average take home approximately seventy-five dollars a week including tips, the importance of tipping can readily be appreciated. For the family man who drives, tips usually represent the difference between a subsistence and a living wage. Also, tips are, apart from taxes, money "in the clear," in that the driver does not have to divide them with the company as he does his metered collections.[11] Sum for sum, therefore, tips represent greater gain for him than do metered charges.

It would probably be incorrect to hold that pecuniary considerations are the sole ones involved in the cabdriver's attitude toward the tip. Yet, in such tip-sensitive occupations as cabdriving, waitering, and bellhopping, to suggest[12] that the tip's primary significance is its symbolic value as a token of affection or appreciation for a service well performed would be even wider of the mark. Vindictive caricatures abound among cabdrivers, as they do among waiters, waitresses, and bellhops, of the "polite gentleman" or "kind lady" who with profuse thanks and flawless grace departs from the scene having "stiffed" (failed to tip) them. In occupations where the tip constitutes so large a fraction of the person's earnings, the cash nexus, although admittedly not the only basis upon which patrons are judged, is so important as the relegate other considerations to a secondary place. Will the fare tip or will he "stiff"? How much will he tip? The answers remain in nearly every instance problematic to the end.

Not only is there no sure way of predicting the outcome, but in a culture where the practice of tipping is neither as widespread nor as standardized as in many Continental countries, for example, the driver cannot in many cases even make a guess.

No regular scheme of work can easily tolerate so high a degree of ambiguity and uncertainty in a key contingency. Invariably, attempts are made to fashion ways and means of greater predictability and control; or, failing that, of devising formulas and imagery to bring order and reason in otherwise inscrutable and capricious events. In the course of a long history a rich body of stereotypes, beliefs, and practices[13] has grown up whose function is that of reducing uncertainty, increasing calculability, and providing coherent explanations.

A basic dichotomy running through the cabdriver's concept of his client world is of regular cab-users and of non-cab-users, the latter referred to as "jerks," "slobs," "yokels," "public-transportation types," and a host of other derogatory terms. The former class, though viewed as quite heterogeneous within itself, includes all who customarily choose cabs in preference to other forms of local transportation, are conversant with the cab-passenger role, and, most of all, accept, if only begrudgingly, the practice of tipping. By comparison, the class of non-cab-users includes that vast aggregate of persons who resort to cabs only in emergencies or on special occasions and are prone too often to view the hiring of a cab as simply a more expensive mode of transportation.

Take, for example, the familiar street scene following a sudden downpour or unexpected breakdown in bus service when a group of individuals cluster about a bus stop, several of whom dart from the curb now and then in hope of hailing a cab. Such persons are almost by definition non-cab-users, or they would not be found at a bus stop in the rain; nor would they be keeping an eye out for a possible bus. A potential fare in this predicament is to the cabdriver a foul-weather friend, and drivers are on occasion known to hurtle by in spiteful glee, leaving the supplicant standing.

He who hires a cab only on special occasions, frequently to impress others or, perhaps, himself alone, is another familiar kind of non-cab-user. Writing of his experiences as a London cabdriver, Hodge relates a by no means uncommon encounter:

> But tonight is different. Perhaps the Pools have come up for once. Anyhow, he's got money. He signals me with exaggerated casualness from the cinema entrance.... She steps in daintily, the perfect lady, particularly where she puts her feet. As soon as she's safely inside, he whispers the address .. and adds, as one man of the world to another, "No hurry, driver." Then he dives in with such utter *savoir faire, comme il faut,* and what not, that he trips over the mat and lands face first on the back seat.[14]

Perhaps the most obvious kind of non-user is the person who, after hailing a cab, will ask the driver some such question as, "How much will it cost to take me to 500 Elm Street?" By this simple inquiry this person stands revealed as one who takes a narrow view of cab travel and from whom not much, if anything, can be expected by way of tip. On the other hand, regular cab users demonstrate in a variety of ways that for them this is a customary and familiar mode of travel. The manner in which they hail a cab, when and how they announce their destination, the ease with which they enter and exit, how they sit—these, and more, though difficult to describe in precise detail, comprise the *gestalt*.

There exists among drivers an extensive typology of cab-users, the attributes imputed to each type having a certain predictive value, particularly as regards tipping. Some of the more common and sharply delineated types are:

The Sport.—The cabdriver's image of this type combines in one person those attributes of character which he views as ideal. Although the Sport's vocation may be any one of many, his status derives more from his extravocational activities, e.g., at the racetrack, prizefights, ball games, popular restaurants, and bars. He is the perennial "young man on the town." Gentlemanly without being aloof, interested without becoming familiar, he also is, of course, never petty. Most of all, his tips are generous, and even on very short rides he will seldom tip less than a quarter. A favorite success story among cabdrivers describes at length and in fine detail the handsome treatment accorded the driver on an all-night tour with a Sport.[15]

The Blowhard.—The Blowhard is a false Sport. Although often wearing the outer mantle of the Sport, he lacks the real Sport's casualness, assured manners, and comfortable style. Given to loquaciousness, he boasts and indiscriminately fabricates tales of track winnings, sexual exploits, and the important people he knows. Often holding out the promise of much by way of tip, he seldom lives up to his words.

The Businessman.—These are the staple of the cab trade, particularly for drivers who work by day. Not only are they the most frequently encountered; their habits and preferences are more uniform than those of any other type: the brisk efficiency with which they engage a cab, their purposefulness, and their disinclination to partake of small talk. Though not often big tippers, they are thought fair. Thus they serve as something of a standard by which the generosity or stinginess of others is judged.

The Lady Shopper.—Although almost as numerous as businessmen, Lady Shoppers are not nearly as well thought of by cabdrivers. The stereotype is a middle-aged woman, fashionably though unattractively dressed, sitting somewhat stiffly at the edge of her seat and wearing a fixed glare which bespeaks her conviction that she is being "taken for a ride." Her major delinquency, however, is undertipping; her preferred coin is a dime, no more or less, regardless of how long or arduous the trip. A forever repeated story is of the annoyed driver, who, after a grueling trip with a Lady Shopper, hands the coin back, telling her, "Lady, keep your lousy dime. You need it more than I do."[16]

Live Ones[17]—Live Ones are a special category of fare usually encountered by the cabdriver who works by night. They are, as a rule, out-of-town conventioneers or other revelers who tour about in small groups in search of licentious forms of entertainment: cabarets, burlesques, strip-tease bars, pick-up joints, etc. As often as not, they have already had a good deal to drink when the cabdriver meets them, and, being out-of-towners, they frequently turn to him for recommendations on where to go. In the late forties an arrangement existed in Chicago whereby some of the more popular Near North Side and West Madison Street "clip joints" rewarded cabdrivers for "steering" Live Ones to their establishments. Some places paid fifty cents "a head"; others a dollar "for the load." As do the many others who regularly cater to Live Ones—e.g., waitresses, bartenders, female bar companions (B-girls), nightclub hosts and hostesses, entertainers, prostitutes—cabdrivers often view them as fair game. And while their opportunities for pecuniary exploitation are fewer and more limited than those open, for example, to B-girls and nightclub proprietors, many drivers feel less inhibited about padding charges and finagling extras from Live Ones than they do from other fares. Often extravagant in their tips because of high spirits and drink, Live Ones are also frequently careless and forget to tip altogether. Knowing that Live Ones are out to "blow their money" anyway, many drivers believe they are justified in seeing to it that they are not deprived of a small portion.

Although the cab culture's typology of fares stems in a large part from the attempt to order experience, reduce uncertainty, and further calculability of the tip, it is questionable, of course, as to how accurate or efficient it is. For, as has often been remarked, stereotypes and typologies have a way of imparting a symmetry and regularity to behavior that are, at best, only crudely approximated in reality. Too often it happens, for example, that a fare tabbed as a Sport turns out to be a Stiff (nontipper), that a Blowhard matches his words with a generous tip, or that a Lady Shopper will give fifteen or even twenty cents. The persistence of the typology therefore has perhaps as much to do with the cabdriver's a posteriori reconstructions and rationalizations of fare behavior as it does with the typology's predictive efficiency.

To protect and ensure themselves against an unfavorable outcome of tipping, many drivers will, depending upon circumstances, employ diverse tactics and stratagems (some more premeditated than others) to increase the amount to tip or to compensate for its loss should it not be forthcoming. Certain of these are listed below. It should be understood, however, that in the ordinary instance the driver makes no attempt to manipulate the fare, believing resignedly that in the long run such means bear too little fruit for the effort and risk.

Making Change.—Depending on the tariff and the amount handed him, the driver can fumble about in his pockets for change or make change in such denominations as often to embarrass a fare into giving a larger tip than he had intended. The efficacy of this tactic depends naturally on the determination and staying power of the fare, qualities which many fares are averse to demonstrate, particularly when it comes to small change.

The Hard-luck Story.—This is usually reserved for young persons and others who, for whatever reason, evidence an insecure posture vis-à-vis the driver. Typically, the hard-luck story consists of a catalogue of economic woes, e.g., long and hard hours of work, poor pay, insulting and unappreciative passengers, etc. In "confiding" these to the fare, the driver pretends to esteem him as an exceptionally sympathetic and intelligent person who, unlike "the others," can appreciate his circumstances and act accordingly. Most drivers, however, view the hard-luck story as an unsavory form of extortion, beneath their dignity. Furthermore, although it may work in some cases, its potential for alienating tips is probably as great as its success at extracting them.

Fictitious Charges.—The resort to fictitious and fraudulent charges occurs most commonly in those cases in which the driver feels that he has good reason to believe that the fare will, either through malice or ignorance, not tip and when the fare impresses him as being enough of a non-cab-user as not to know when improper charges are being levied. Once, when I complained to a veteran cabdriver about having been 'stiffed" by a young couple, newly arrived in Chicago, to whom I had extended such extra services as carrying luggage and opening doors, I was told: "Wise up kid! When you pick up one of these yokels at the Dearborn Station carrying a lot of cheap straw luggage on him, you can bet ninety-nine times out of a hundred that he isn't going to tip you. Not that he's a mean guy or anything, but where he comes from, they never heard to tipping. What I do with a yokel like that is to take him to where he's going, show him what the fare is on the meter, and tell him that it costs fifteen cents extra for each piece of luggage. Now, he doesn't know that there's no charge for hand luggage, but that way I'm sure of getting my tip out of him."

The "psychological" approach.—Possibly attributing more art to their trade than is the case, some drivers are of the opinion that a cab ride can be tailored to fit a passenger in much the same way as can a suit of clothes. One cabdriver, boasting of his success at getting tips, explained: "In this business you've got to use psychology. You've got to make the ride fit the person. Now, take a businessman. He's in a hurry to get someplace and he doesn't want a lot of bullshit and crapping around. With him you've got to keep moving. Do some fancy cutting in and out, give the cab a bit of a jerk when you take off from a light. Not reckless,

mind you, but plenty of zip. He likes that.[18] With old people, it's just the opposite. They're more afraid than anyone of getting hurt or killed in a cab. Take it easy with them. Creep along, open doors for them, help them in and out, be real folksy. Call them 'Sir' and 'M'am' and they'll soon be calling you 'young man.' They're suckers for this stuff, and they'll loosen up their pocketbooks a little bit."

In the last analysis, neither the driver's typology of fares nor his stratagems further to any marked degree his control of the tip. Paradoxically, were these routinely successful in achieving predictability and control, they would at the same time divest the act of tipping of its most distinguishing characteristics—of its uncertainty, variability, and of the element of revelation in its consummation. It is these —essentially the problematic in human intercourse[19]—which distinguish the tip from the fixed service charge. And though another form of remuneration might in the end provide the cabdriver with a better wage and a more secure livelihood, the abrogation of tipping would also lessen the intellectual play which uncertainty stimulates and without which cabdriving would be for many nothing more than unrelieved drudgery.

That the practice of tipping, however, expressly befits only certain kinds of service relationships and may under slightly altered circumstances easily degenerate into corruption or extortion is demonstrated, ironically enough, by the predicament of some cabdrivers themselves. To give an example: In the garage out of which I worked, nearly everyone connected with maintenance and assignment of cabs expected tips from drivers for performing many of the routine tasks associated with their jobs, such as filling a tank with gas, changing a tire, or adjusting a carburetor. Although they resented it, drivers had little recourse but to tip. Otherwise, they would acquire reputations as "stiffs" and "cheapskates," be kept waiting interminably for repairs, and find that faulty and careless work had been done on their vehicles. Particularly with the dispatcher did the perversion of the tipping system reach extortionate proportions. His power derived from the assignment of cabs; to protect themselves from being assigned "pots" (cabs that would break down in the middle of the day), drivers tipped him fifty cents at the beginning of every week. Since nearly every driver tipped the dispatcher and since there were more drivers than good cabs, a certain number of drivers would still be assigned "pots." Some, wishing to ensure doubly against this, would then raise the bribe to a dollar and a half a week, causing the others to follow suit in a vicious spiral. If little else, this shows how the tip—as distinguished from the gift, honorarium, inducement, or bribe—depends for its expressive validity on there not being a too close, long sustained, or consequential relationship between the parties to a service transaction.

Among service relationships in our society, that between the big-city cabdriver and his fare is, due to the way in which they come into contact with each other, especially subject to structural weakness. The relationship is random, fleeting, unrenewable, and largely devoid of socially integrative features that in other client- and patron-oriented services help sustain a wider range of constraints and controls between the parties to the transaction. (Much the same might be said of such service occupations as waitress, bellhop and hotel doorman, the chief difference being, however, that these operate from a spatially fixed establishment, which in itself permits of greater identifiability, renewability, and hence constraint in one's relationship to them.) As a result, the tendency of the relationship is to gravitate sharply and in relatively overt fashion toward those few issues having to do with the basic instrumental terms of the exchange. The very fact of tipping, its economic centrality, and the cab culture's preoccupation with mastering its many vagaries reflect in large part the regulative imbalance inherent in the relationship.

By inference, this analysis raises anew questions of how to account for the many

more formidable and apparently more binding practitioner-client constraints found in other personal service fields, in particular the professions. To such matters as career socialization, colleague groups, socially legitimated skill monopolies, and professional secrecy there might be added a certain safe modicum of continuity, stability, and homogeneity of clientele.[20] For, given too great and random a circulation of clients among practitioners, as might occur for example under certain bureaucratic schemes for providing universal and comprehensive medical service, the danger is that informal social-control networks would not come into being in the community, and, as in big-city cabdriving, relations between servers and served would become reputationless, anonymous, and narrowly calculative.

* This article is based largely on notes and observations made by me over a six-month period in 1948 when I worked as a cabdriver for one of the larger taxicab firms in Chicago. I am greatly indebted to Erving Goffman, Everett C. Hughes, and Howard S. Becker for their comments and criticisms.

1 Talcott Parsons, *The Social System* (New York: Free Press of Glencoe, Inc., 1951), pp. 48–56.
2 Erving Goffman, *The Presentation of Self in Everyday Life* (Edinburgh: University of Edinburgh Social Science Research Centre, 1956), pp. 160–162.
3 Everett C. Hughes, *Men and Their Work* (New York: Free Press of Glencoe, Inc., 1958), pp. 88–101.
4 Because it better delineates the boundaries and linkages of informal sanctioning groups found in large cities, the term "network" is used here to qualify the more global concept of "community." See Elizabeth Bott, *Family and Social Network* (London: Tavistock, 1957), pp. 58–61.
5 Robert K. Merton, "The Role Set: Problems in Sociological Theory," *British Journal of Sociology*, 8 (June, 1957), p. 114.
6 Parallel studies of this aspect of occupational culture are: Hughes, *op. cit.*, pp. 42–55; Howard S. Becker, "The Professional Dance Musician and his Audience," *American Journal of Sociology*, 57 (September, 1951), pp. 136–44; Ray Gold, "Janitors versus Tenants: A Status-Income Dilemma," *American Journal of Sociology*, 57 (March, 1952), pp. 486–493.
7 Merton, *op. cit.*, pp. 110–112.
8 Goffman, *op. cit.* p. 95.

[9] James V. Maresca, *My Flag Is Down* (New York: E. P. Dutton & Co., Inc., 1945). Essentially the same incident is related by an unidentified cabdriver on the documentary recording of Tony Schwartz, *The New York Taxi Driver* (Columbia Records, ML5309, 1959).

[10] Cf. Schwartz, *op. cit.* In fact, these characteristic qualities, with a work-adapted, bittersweet admixture of cynicism and sentimentality, comprise the core of the personality widely imputed to cabdrivers by the riding public. Cf. Hughes, *op. cit.*, pp. 23–41.

[11] In Chicago in 1948 the company driver's share of the metered sum was $42\frac{1}{2}$ per cent. Since that time the proportion has been increased slightly.

[12] Cf. William F. Whyte, *Human Relations in the Restaurant Industry* (New York: McGraw-Hill Book Company, 1948), p. 100.

[13] Cf. here and in the section to follow the pertinent remarks of Hughes on "guilty knowledge" developed by those in a service occupation with reference to their clientele. Hughes, *op. cit.*, pp. 81–82.

[14] Herbert Hodge, "I Drive a Taxi," *Fact,* 22 (January, 1939), pp. 28–29.

[15] As in the past, the Sport still serves as something of a hero figure in our culture, particularly among the working classes. A type midway between the Playboy and the Bohemian, his unique appeal rests perhaps on the ease and assurance with which he is pictured as moving between and among social strata, untainted by upper-class snobbishness, middle-class conventionality and lower-class vulgarity. In *The Great Gatsby,* Fitzgerald gives us a penetrative exposition of the myth of the Sport and its undoing at the hands of the class system.

[16] The sterotype of women as poor tippers is widely shared by other tip-sensitive occupations. Cf. Frances Donovan, *The Woman Who Waits* (Boston: Richard G. Badger, 1920).

[17] The term "Live Ones" is employed in a variety of pursuits as apparently diverse as retail selling, nightclub entertainment, traveling fairs, and panhandling. Generally, it designates persons who are "easy touches," eager to succumb to the oftentimes semifraudulent proposals of the operator. Cf. W. Jack Peterson and Milton A. Maxwell, "The Skid Row Wino," *Social Problems,* 5 (Spring, 1958), p. 312.

[18] Cf. Hodge, *op. cit.*, p. 17.

[19] Cf. Donovan, *op. cit.*, p. 262.

[20] William J. Goode, "Community Within a Community: The Professions," *American Sociological Review,* 22 (April, 1957), pp. 198–200; and Eliot Freidson, "Varieties of Professional Practice," draft version of unpublished paper, 1959.

28   How Hard Do Executives Work?

by WILLIAM H. WHYTE, JR.

There is an interesting fiction these days that goes something like this: executives are at last getting sensible about work. The worker long ago cut down his work week to forty hours or less, and now the executive is doing the same. Why shouldn't he? Taxes, as top executives themselves so frequently say, have taken away the incentive to overwork. Furthermore, the argument goes, the trend to "multiple management" makes the extra hours unnecessary anyway. Indeed, it

makes them downright undesirable; since results come from many people working together in harmony, the effective executive is the rested man free from tensions— the man who prizes his leisure and encourages his subordinates to do the same.

The facts? A study of executives' working habits—and executives' attitudes toward them—made by *Fortune* shows that:

1. Executives are working as hard as they ever did. It is difficult to see how they could possibly work harder.
2. Despite all grumbling by executives, high income taxes have had remark-

ably little effect on executives' drive.

3. Executives are subject to more tensions than ever before. Although the swing to "human relations" and committee management has eliminated many of the old work pressures, it has substituted plenty of new ones.

For the corporation man the balanced life is as elusive as ever, possibly even more so. With some businessmen—the entrepreneur, in particular—life is still unrepressed. The corporation man, however, faces something of a dilemma.

If there is one thing that characterizes executives, it is a keen sense of self—a desire to control one's environment rather than be controlled by it. Only in degree have their drives changed from those that always characterized leaders, and beneath the modulated exterior of today's executives there often burns an ego as powerful as any that drove a nineteenth-century buccaneer.

As the corporation becomes more and more bureaucratized, however, the executive is called upon to act out something of a denial that he is really the kind of man he is. Today the executive must appear to enjoy listening sympathetically to subordinates and team-playing around the conference table. It is not enough that he work hard now, he has to be a "damn good fellow" to boot. And that, as we shall see, is a large part of the rub.

At this point, a distinction is in order. For purposes of this article, "executives" are defined as corporation men who have reached or passed the vice presidential level or as those in middle management who have demonstrated that they are among those likely to get to the top levels.

Just as the corporation man differs from the entrepreneur, so the "executive" differs from management man in general. In preparing this report five cross sections of management men, from recruits at the bottom to presidents at the top, were studied. While differences are sometimes subtle, it is clear that the lower the group,

the more hopeful are men of escaping the tensions and long hours of the executive life. Possibly this may foreshadow a real change in the way corporation people will work twenty years from now. It is equally possible, however, that the differences may identify those who have the making of top executives and those who have not.

The pressures and the hours that beset the executive depend somewhat on whether the company is static or dynamic. Some companies, indeed some whole industries, are supposed to have a great number of unlined faces in them. On the whole, however, the cross section reveals few significant differences. Regionally, executives often fancy strong variations; in each area one hears that, because of the *esprit* unique to the region, executives are more devoted to their work, more selfless, etc., than elsewhere. It is hard, however, to find supporting evidence. Despite the alleged weakness of West Coast executives for the good life, for example, they appear to work as hard as anybody else.

In most places the average executive office-week runs between forty-five and forty-eight hours. Most executives arrive at the office between 8:00 and 9:00 A.M. and leave about 5:30 or 6:00 P.M. At this point the executive is past the halfway mark; the work night has begun. On the average he will work four nights out of five. One night he will be booked for business entertaining—more, probably, if he's a president. Another night he will probably spend at the office or in a lengthy conference somewhere else.

On two other nights he goes home, not to a sanctuary so much as to a branch office. Only a minority of executives have equipped their dens with dictating machines and calculators and such, but the majority devote at least two nights a week to business reading.

And then the telephone. Many executives simply cannot resist it. "I do a lot of spot checking by phone from home," says an Atlanta executive. "I'd rather do that at night than in the daytime. I have more time, and besides most people have their guard down then." Those on the receiving end don't seem to mind the intrusion. "It's a good time to gas things over," says a Chicago executive. "Sometimes it's not so good, though, particularly when you've won a battle with the kids as to which television program to turn on and then they have to sit and watch your program while you talk business. But on the whole, I don't really mind it."

Perhaps the most significant change in executive work—and the cause of a good deal of the extra work—is the fact that it involves more and more contacts with more and more individuals. Physically, executives used to inhabit a fairly limited world; today the sheer number of human relationships that executives are engaged in over a month's time has reached enormous proportions. The question, in short, is not simply how much executives work; it is how they find time to work.

Now that "committee management" has become so much the rule, the average executive spends roughly six of his eight office hours talking with other executives in meetings and conferences; and he would be considered an "odd bird" indeed if he went out to lunch by himself. The other two hours are not spent in solitary contemplation; they are no more than the sum of a few minutes here and there between meetings and the ringing of the telephone. The executive, as one puts it, is never alone. Never physically, at any rate.

In many instances the team-play has grown so frenetic that executives look on the office day as something of an interruption in their actual work. This not only explains the amount of after-hours work, it also explains the tendency of many executives to get to work in the morning earlier than anyone else. "I found this out the few times I was working weekends," explains an executive. "I found I could get so much done when nobody else was around the office that I figured the best way to keep my workweek under control was to get to the office

before the rat race starts. Honestly, in one hour when nobody's around I can get as much work done, real work, as I can during the rest of the day."

Putting all the commitments together, we get a workweek something like this: forty-five to forty-eight hours of daytime work; one night working late at the office, two nights working at home, one night entertaining—all in all, some fifty-seven to sixty hours. And this evidently is a minimum; come convention time, a trip, a company emergency, and the week can easily go to seventy or eighty hours.

Public pronouncements of many corporations suggest that they fear this kind of speedup will debilitate their executives. In practice, however, the corporation does about everything it can to encourage the speedup. Executives questioned were unanimous that their superiors approved highly of the fifty-five-hour week and liked the sixty-hour week even better. One company, for example, has a pool of Dictaphones to loan executives—the better for them to do homework. In other companies the five-day week is pure fiction; and executives are quick to learn that, if they drop around at the office Saturdays to tidy things up, it won't be held against them. In almost all companies, furthermore, executives are encouraged to do extensive reading of business periodicals; but although the subscription price may be on the house, the reading time isn't. In many offices executives would never dream of doing the reading during the day—thus signifying that they are "not busy enough." Into the briefcase goes the reading.

Executives admit that they in turn impose the same kind of pressure upon their subordinates. Some lean toward praising men pointedly for extra work, others prefer to set impossible goals or to use an unusually eager man as a "rate-busting" example to the others. "What it boils down to," explains one executive, "is this: You promote the guy who takes his problems home with him."

In theory, executives shouldn't be working hard at all. According to folklore, what has made American business dynamic is the lure of enormous cash incentives for businessmen to surpass themselves. But now the harder a man works, the smaller become his extra cash rewards. Is it not reasonable to argue—as businessmen so frequently do—that taxes have inhibited executive motivation?

The cross section of executives were asked this question: Would you be working harder now if your taxes were less? The majority sheepishly said no, they would not. How, some added, *could* they be working harder?

Although executives are not the slightest bit happy over high taxes, they make clear that to them the key thing about a salary is not its absolute but its *relative* size. This, taxes do not affect. The part of the pay stub that shows income before taxes may be cause for hollow laughter, but it is still the part that is critical; and the man who makes $35,000 a year finds little consolation in the thought that his $37,000-a-year rival nets only $892 more than he does.

Salaries, of course, are more than merely an index of success, being also useful for the purchase of food, clothing, shelter, and sundries. But once a certain level has been reached, the competitive aspect of salaries becomes as important as the purchasing aspect. Some of the corporation executives interviewed had sizable independent incomes, yet these men were just as keenly interested in the relative size of their salaries as anyone else. They worked, furthermore, just as hard as others and sometimes, under the baleful gaze of the steely-eyed old gentleman in the picture on the wall, a good bit harder.

Why, then, do they work so hard? The executives' motivations, it appears, essentially are what they have always been. Here are the drives most often identified by executives in justifying the amount of work they do:

Self-expression. In talking about why he works, the executive does not speak first of pressures from the organization; very rarely does he even mention his family as a goal. He speaks of himself— and the demon within him. "People are like springs," explains one company president. "The energy you have in you has to come out one way or another. I would really get in bad shape if I didn't work." "It's like baseball," another executive puts it. "A good player never stops to think of his contract when he comes to the plate. He drives for the fences." Analogies are endless—even concert pianists are alluded to—but the theme is always self-expression.

Sense of contribution. Executives see the expression of the ego as inseparable from service to others. Characteristically, the executive can generate a great sense of excitement about his particular field of work, the frontiers of the job, the saga of the industry, and the like. Although a good bit of hot air is sometimes generated in the process, the fact remains that the executive who cannot identify his drives with the commonweal is likely to be a tormented one.

In this sense management men are fortunate. On the whole they are not much preoccupied with such questions as "Is management a profession?" They are so confident that their status as a group is excellent, so confident that what they do is vital, that they don't debilitate their drive by worrying about their collective prestige. Besides, they don't have the time.

Responsibility. The weight of responsibility can be killing; nevertheless, it is apparent from the way executives talk of it that they wouldn't be happy unless they felt the weight. "If you're in charge of an organization," goes a typical comment, "you never forget that if you fail, it's not your failure alone but a loss to lots of others."

Prestige. Because of the increasingly democratic class structure of the American office, many management aspirants have the mistaken idea that status and "all that sort of stuff" is an extremely minor incentive for executives. In actual fact executives love it, and they have no pious reluctance to admit the fact. "When I walk out of the building," the head of one of America's largest corporations recently told a friend, "a lot of people turn and stare at me and whisper that there goes Mr. Big. My friends think this probably annoys and embarrasses me. Frankly, I thoroughly enjoy it. Why shouldn't I?"

Fear. The growing emphasis on security has convinced some executives that fear is no longer an important incentive. "Men used to work with a strong feeling of fear," says a company president, with just a trace of nostalgia. "They put in terrible hours and were afraid to ask for a day off. Most of that has been eliminated. Now, I don't say it's a bad thing, this change; it's not good to have people fearful and apprehensive. But, well...we have a complacency today, a sense of security we didn't used to have."

But is not preoccupation with security a form of fear? As middle-management executives point out, worries about security now take different forms, but people worry just the same. It's nice to know that today there are built-in restrictions about being sacked; but one effect of this is to allow the executive to fret all the more over the possibility of being pigeon-holed. The office geniality, furthermore, only makes the task of estimating one's own standing in this respect more difficult. "You get into a certain bracket," goes a typical explanation, "and you start getting a scare that somebody else is going to get what you want. But who is he? You can't tell—it's a game of checkers. So you take on a protective coloring to look like the lower brackets. You're afraid of slipping and being surpassed."

The best defense, the executive knows, is to surpass somebody else. Since he also knows that every other executive thinks likewise, he can never feel really secure. "I like to take my vacation in three-or four-day stretches, instead of the full three weeks," one executive says. "Now why do I do that? For my health? You go away for three weeks and you find when you come back that they've rearranged your entire job. Someone has to carry on while you are gone and they are in your files and when you get back the boss will ask you questions about your job on account of what others did while you were away. I don't blame them, mind you. I'd do exactly the same thing."

One of the most revealing clues to executives' motivation is their attitude on "overwork." Of executives questioned, 90 per cent said they did not work too hard. But the answers were not simply "no." They were "Absolutely not." "It's ridiculous to think I overwork!" "Of course not."

Why the protestation? The executives' reaction to a follow-up question is significant. Did other people—their wives, their doctors, their friends—think they worked too hard? In most cases the executives paused and then, somewhat sadly, said yes, others did think they worked too hard. It was a shame, they explained, because actually they really didn't work too hard. The trouble lay in the other people: *They just didn't understand.*

To the executive there is between work and the other aspects of one's life a unity he can never fully explain, least of all to his wife. How can you overwork, executives ask, if your work is your life? "Overwork, as I see it," says one company president, "is simply work that you don't like. But I dearly love this work. You live only one time and you might as well do something you like."

Do they really *want* leisure? When executives talk of such extracurricular functions as entertaining, civic work, and reading, they betray a curiously split attitude. They profess to deplore the impulse that bedevils them into thinking about work after hours. Yet, as their self-diagnoses demonstrate, they would not have it otherwise.[1]

A steel executive: "Instead of relaxing

at night with a mystery story, you keep at it until eleven o'clock and finally you say to yourself, 'The devil with it. I'm going to have a highball or two and go to bed.' But I sit there stewing until twelve-thirty or one. As a result I'm very uncompanionable at breakfast. My wife says I just sit there and dream, and maybe she's right. But I get a kick out of keeping well informed about business."

Even those who resolutely refuse to take a briefcase home confess that they cannot shut off the business stream of consciousness. "I don't carry a thing home with me," says an automobile executive. "When I leave here—except for the two or three nights a week when I attend meetings—I keep my after-office time for myself and my family... After dinner, though, I nearly always go for a long walk, with my dog. Guess you'd call them 'meditation walks,' and I take them rain or shine."

"It's gotten so bad with me," says a New England president, "that I have had to make myself stop working at home evenings. I can't read the shortest report without my mind going into action to plan what to do next. I've found this stimulated my mind so much that I just couldn't go to sleep at a reasonable hour. What I really wish is that there were more hours in the business day."

Executives are well aware that this absorption means less time with their wives and children. Younger executives, in particular, accuse themselves; they are not, they say, the fathers they should be, and they often mention some long-planned project to do something with the little boy, like building a boat. But, they add ruefully, they probably never will. "I sort of look forward to the day when my kids are grown up," says one sales manager. "Then I won't have to have such a guilty conscience about neglecting them."

Executives' attitudes toward entertaining show the same overwhelming preoccupation with work. They do so much of it

that one might wonder whether most of it is not mere play thinly disguised as work —a way of enjoying the good life without paying for it. To a degree it is; in his first years with the company the management man finds the expense account a heady contrast to life in the ranch house at 7111 Crestmere Drive.

But not for very long. "For the first five years or so it's wonderful to play the big shot when you are out on the road," explains one Chicago executive, "but after a while you realize that all you are doing is lousing up your regular standard of living. You forget there are balconies in theaters."

All this does not mean that executives as they go up come to dislike entertaining; they merely grow more choosy. Increasingly, play that is play and no more irritates them. What they enjoy is the kind of after-hours socializing that has some relevance to their business—the kind, as they so often put it, where you can't tell whether it's work or play.

Clutching at straws in the wind, younger men think they can see a trend toward unalloyed play. In many companies, for example, there is a great deal of talk that sure-the-brass-works-hard-but-brother-they-play-hard-too—usually documented by tales of fast country-club living, extra-long weekends for plain good fellowship at the lodge, and the like. In other companies top executives have set up glorified health clinics in the form of company-sponsored lodges or desert oases —where, ostensibly, they go off to brainwash themselves of business thoughts.

Question: but what do they talk about when they get there?

Civic work, theoretically, should be a good change of pace from regular business. One of the most surprising disclosures in this survey, however, is the attitude corporation executives privately express about community activity. They don't particularly like it. When they engage in it they do so more out of a sense of obligation, or on order from their company, than for any inward satisfaction they expect from the participation. Older executives are often heavily involved in good works, but the involvement, many confess, is more entrapment than free choice. "I had looked forward to taking it easy," says one sixty-five-year-old executive, "but the trouble is that as soon as you get more free time the word gets around. Then they put the finger on you."

Rightly or wrongly, most executives consider civic work a diffusion of their energies, and only when they see a clear relation between civic work and their careers do they perform it with enthusiasm. Significantly, the businessmen who plunge into civic work with gusto usually are the bankers and merchants and others for whom it is virtually part of their job.

Culture? Executives do tend to have broader tastes in music, reading, and the like than their less successful contemporaries. But that, as executives themselves concede, isn't saying very much. Most of those questioned were conscious that they didn't read enough good books about something besides business, and some executives went out of their way to berate themselves on that score.

But where, the executive asks, can he find time? Much as he might like to read more history or take in more plays, he looks on this as too marginal, too little relevant to his career to warrant making the time. His judgment is debatable on this point, but that is another story; the fact is that he doesn't see much relationship, and thus, as with the long-deferred project to build a boat with the boys, he will keep on planning that reading he hopes to get around to. One of these days.

Hobbies? Even here, the executive applies the yardstick of business relevance. While some executives are genuinely absorbed in a hobby for the sheer creative "bang" of it, for a larger number the pursuit carries strong therapeutic overtones. For them the hobby is not a joy in itself but simply a means of restoring themselves between rounds. To this end some executives go through an almost compulsive ritual—like watering the flowers at a regular weekend time whether or not it has just rained. To borrow an old phrase, they are never less at leisure than when they are at leisure.

The existing picture, in sum, is of men so completely involved in their work that they cannot distinguish between work and play, and they are glad they can't. Will this, however, be the pattern in the years ahead? After the current generation of middle management passes on, there will be nobody left with memories of the Depression. This, plus the still growing bureaucratization of the corporation could quite possibly lead to a softening of the drives that spur today's executives.

This cross section of executives does indicate a difference in attitudes by age levels. On four questions involving potential tensions and conflicts, younger executives showed themselves measurably more hopeful of enjoying the balanced life than the older ones. They were more in favor of group judgment and management by conference; they were more inclined to company loyalty—that is, to accept with equanimity control of their destiny by the organization; they thought modest ambitions healthy; and on the key question of whether or not the executive life was likely to enforce more conformity and tensions in the years ahead, they were optimistic.

What is the correct interpretation? One possibility is that the very fact that the younger men cherish these goals will help make them a reality. The other is simpler: the young men believe what they do because they haven't had time to learn better.

If the latter is the true explanation, as appears plausible, the differences in attitude between age groups take on another significance; for if they are not portents of trends, then they very well may be fresh clues to an old question. As the following comparisons of viewpoint between older and younger men may suggest, when management people discuss the conflict between work and the organization they say a great deal about what makes an executive.

Committee management. By and large, younger men not only feel it makes work easier, they often endow this suppression of individual ego with virtually religious overtones. What about the sheer waste of time often involved? The suffering of fools gladly? "Any man who feels frustrated by these things," one young man says, "is not really an executive. These things are the heart of his job." Most younger men aren't quite so evangelistic, but on the basic thought they agree: The group way is the best way.

They might also add, on less philosophical grounds, that it is certainly the best way for a young man "on the make." What better way to short-circuit the chain of command? Through the conference the neophyte exposes himself to his superiors and, given minimum committeemanship skills, by an adroit question here and a modest suggestion there, he can gain a degree of attention that several years of solitary work never could attract.

Very quickly, however, the man who is going up begins to see the many ways in which multiple management makes his work more difficult. Down deep he has always had a strong preference for his own judgment, and the more he surpasses his contemporaries the more confirmed he becomes in his preference. He is, to be sure, a skilled team player—he wouldn't have risen if he hadn't been. But what he once thought of as good communication he now is apt to describe as creeping paralysis.

"You're always selling," an executive complains. "Everything you do is subject to review by all sorts of people. So you have to spend as much time getting allies as you do on your project—you've got to keep making peace with people at all levels. Sometimes I go home worn to a frazzle just over this." The complaint is

characteristic; when one's job is tangled so inextricably with the work of others, executives point out, the sense of individual creativity, the satisfaction of being able to deliver a tied-up package of achivment, is hard to come by. According to one facile characterization, the good executive is the man who can so "organize" his job that there are no worries left dangling at five or five-thirty. Seasoned executives laugh hollowly. How can you organize a job when you can't control it?

Company loyalty. Whom, really, does the executive work for? The company? Or himself? Younger executives tend to think that there is no difference: i.e., that there is such complete compatibility between the individual and the organization that one should be thoroughly a "company man." "It figures," says one young trainee, "if you do a good job, that's good for the company and it's just intelligent self-interest for them to do right by you." In loftier terms many management thinkers argue much the same thing: They submit that now that life has become so complicated and so rootless, mental health lies in sublimating oneself within one encompassing, benevolent organization—and the corporation, with its increasing willingness to envelop the executive's whole life with benefits, is ideal in this respect.

The true executive, however, resists. The continuity that he seeks in his life is work that satisfies his drives, and thus, unless he is the top man who is doing the enveloping, he remains always a potential rebel. On the question of whether or not the executive should keep his eye open for opportunities elsewhere, two-thirds of the older group thought he should, vs. only one-third of the younger. The threat is not an idle one; turnover figures demonstrate that, despite the rapid growth of entrapping benefits, more executives are switching companies than ever before.

The successful executive has a high capacity for loyalty; like the junior, he *wants* to identify himself with the company. He also, however, takes care to make frequent readings of the loyalty coming from the other direction. He can grow as misty-eyed as the next man at the banquet honoring the Grand Old Man and the Unique Spirit of the company, but the mist will clear away rapidly if the spirit is not accompanied by the opportunity he feels is due.

Mere cupidity has little to do with it. The crux is the man's basic feeling about his environment. The run-of-mill management man tends to accept things as they come. With the man likely to get to the top of the organization, however, the very qualities that make the ascent likely are those which lead him to buck the system. He does not want to be "done right by."

Conformity. Although the executive tries to dominate his environment, he is at the same time realistically aware that it will exact a great deal of conformity from him. Younger executives are also well aware that organization work demands a measure of conformity—indeed, a good half of their time is devoted to finding the right pattern to conform to. But the younger executive is also apt to believe that the conforming is simply a phase—a kind of purgatory that one must suffer before he becomes progressively more independent. "Take this business of entertaining," one young assistant plant manager explains. "You have to go through all that stuff for ten years, maybe, but then you can chuck it. It's like running for the President of the United States; you do a lot of things then that you don't have to do when you get to be President."

Executives know better. "A help-wanted ad we ran recently," one executive explains, "asked for engineers who would 'conform to our work patterns.' Somebody slipped on that one. He actually came out and said what's really wanted around here." And it does not get better, others add, as one goes up. More and more, the executive must act according to the role he was cast for—the calm eyes that never stray from the other's

gaze, the easy control in which laughter is natural but never forced—the whole demeanor which tells everyone that here certainly is a man without neuroses and inner rumblings. Yet, again, the drive, the fierce desire for control over one's destiny, cannot help but produce the kind of inner conflicts that the demeanor would deny. "The ideal," one president recently told a group of young men, "is to be an individualist privately and a conformist publicly—if you can pull it off."

Understandably, presidents appear considerably more at ease in their role than the men just below them. Yet those who aspire to the top job have few illusions that if they make it suddenly all will be easy. Even were there not one rung higher —a board chairman, perhaps a not-too-friendly board of directors—those beneath have their own way of demanding conformity. The executive can now ill afford the luxury of an inadvertent frown; for it will be transmitted all down the line and, eventually, as things go in offices these days, come back and smite him. With "authoritarian" one of the dirtiest things a management man can say about a superior, today's model boss is, above all, permissive. "You have to *ask* a guy now," goes a characteristic complaint. "You can't tell him. It would be a lot easier than this damn sitting and talking, but if you did, well, nobody would co-operate and the thing wouldn't get done right." All of which makes for more, and harder, work. Democracy, as executives can observe, is a lot more fun when you're going up than when you get there.

Ambition. To hear some management aspirants talk, one might assume that older men who complain ambition is dying are correct. Popular, particularly on campuses, is speculation on the desirability of finding a "plateau." What with taxes the way they are, this line of thought goes, the smart man is the man who aims for a slot in the corporation that's rewarding but is somehow removed from the fierce competition that means overwork.

But ambition still burns; only the terms

have changed. When the young man enters the organization, he sees above him a hierarchy so towering that he doesn't let himself dream of scaling its summit. He much prefers the idea of settling in a comfortable little Eden somewhere further down. There are, he reasons, so many good jobs beneath the top now; furthermore, his ego might need a defense, and just in case things don't work out as he would like, he has a nice rationalization to fall back on.

If he starts going ahead of his contemporaries, however, as time goes on the possibility of a top job becomes more and more provocative. After all, he's got this far pretty quick. Perhaps...Maybe... And *why not*? The apple has fallen into the garden.

The question of what changes a man into an executive, and when, can never be fully answered. But there does seem to be a fork in the road, a subtle shift in a man's attitude toward work and its costs, and it is when this subjective change takes place that he really becomes an executive. Until then he has resisted the idea that sacrifices are ahead. The tensions ahead will be no greater. Be loyal to the company, and it will be loyal to you. The good executive is the man who leads a "well-rounded" life. Tell them what you really think and they'll respect you for it. Nobody gives a damn about rank here. We're different. A man who gets ulcers probably shouldn't be in business. It certainly won't happen to me.

The crossing of the line can happen at thirty, maybe ten years later, and some men never know just when the moment of self-realization comes. But after it comes the man will never be the same. At once exhilarated and apprehensive, he has a sense that he is irretrievably committed.

No longer does he cheerily say that hard work never hurt any man and that neuroses, after all, don't come from work but from worry. (Significantly, whereas 60 per cent of the middle-management men interviewed expected tensions to diminish, not one of the upper group

did.) What he wants to do, the executive knows, is what will worry him; and the worries he will have to face alone. His home life will be shorter, and in the midst of the crowd at the office he will be more and more isolated—no longer intimate with those he has passed and not quite accepted by the elders he has joined. Is it worth it all? By conceding the costs, he has already made the decision. This, he knows now, is how it has to be. He is an executive.

But the compensations are his life. Like a monk receiving orders, he sees the sacrifices ahead as a sort of dedication. He feels himself one of a band of men engaged in a great adventure; and when he speaks of making more jobs, of helping people find more satisfaction in their work, of the new frontiers in industry, or of better things for better living, he is not simply rationalizing. Unlike the European businessman, he believes in it.

As long as he feels part of his momentum, the balanced life will remain as elusive as ever. Quite possibly there will be more tensions ahead; for the difference between what the executive is and the role the bureaucratic life calls for may widen further. The costs will be great; yet those who see them as unmitigated neurosis must ask what would happen if executives became so well adapted that they didn't fret and stew.

For the time being, it is not likely to come to pass. Executives still will talk of being more sensible, of getting around to those books, of cutting out this ridiculous night work—and they will keep on doing what they have been doing.

There is too much work to be done.

---

* The Findings of this study are based on interviews, supplemented by questionnaires, with 221 management men. In the "executive" category were (1) fifty-two company presidents (average age, fifty-five); (2) twenty-three vice presidents (average age, fifty-three); (3) fifty-three middle-management men who have marked themselves or have been marked by the company as "comers" (average age, thirty-seven). For comparison two groups below the

"executive" category were also studied: (4) thirty-three men working their way up from lower to middle management (average age, thirty); (5) sixty college graduates in their first two years as corporation trainees.

1 Labor leaders, when they discuss personal work problems, talk just like executives. "My wife tells me I work too hard," says a vice president of a large union. "I do work hard, I'll admit—usually seventy to eighty hours. But I love everything about it. I feel I'm part of a crusade, making the world a better place to live in."

29 Supervisor: Evolution of an Organizational Role

by DELBERT C. MILLER

The title "supervisor" is a generic term covering more than four hundred different names in the United States Census classification of occupational titles,[1] including such titles as traffic supervisor, mine pit boss, buck swamper, corral man, boom master, gang leader, and route supervisor. Sometimes the term supervisor has been used to refer to all persons who direct the work of others.[2] This broad usage occurs in trying to identify all members of an organization who bear a management responsibility, as when training officers seek to emphasize the human-relations and administrative responsibilities which are functions shared by all "supervisors." A broad definition encompassing all first-line, middle, and top management does bring to focus the common elements in managerial functions and ideology. It is as useful for social scientists who wish to identify similar patterns as it is for top managers who wish to inculcate loyalty and secure increased effectiveness in their entire managerial and supervisory staff.

In spite of all efforts to give it such broad meaning, the title still carries the traditional meaning of first-line supervisor. "The supervisor" in this chapter will refer to the person who is supposed to do the actual job of supervising employees. The employees may be professionals or unskilled workers. They may be engaged in producing goods or services. The supervisor is held directly responsible for these employees and must direct them in face-to-face contact. The reader who is used to looking at organization charts must not be confused by the alternate use of the terms foreman and supervisor. There has long been a blue-collar and white-collar segregation which has maintained a prestige differential between the supervisor of production as contrasted with the supervisor of service or commercial activities. For our purposes, "supervisor" will include such persons as foremen, office supervisors, university department heads, school principals, head nurses, and research-laboratory group chiefs.

From Leadership and Productivity *by Robert Dubin, George C. Homans, Floyd C. Mann, Delbert C. Miller. Published by Chandler Publishing Company, San Francisco. Copyright 1965 by Chandler Publishing Company. Reprinted by permission.*

The Foreman as the Historic Supervisor

The foreman has been called both the most important and the least important member of management. In a mass-production society his leadership is vital to the process of supplying material wants. There are over one million foremen in the United States today.[3] To millions of workers, he is the immediate boss—the one who really counts in assigning work and in creating the social climate of their work group. To an earlier generation who saw him as a feared but respected figure, he was the colorful Bull of the Woods. To the social scientist, the foreman's position is a significant index to the internal forces of organization which are becoming general to all supervisory positions.

The position of foreman has felt the brunt of both mass-production technological advances and organizational changes emerging in large-scale bureaucracies. The performance of the foreman and that of his workers is measurable. Industrial production is more measurable than other types of labor. The units produced, the cost of items, and the quantity of scrap can all be counted. The measurement of performance increases the foreman's insecurity. The fact that his position may be short-circuited makes the position even more insecure. If the foreman just had to report to his boss, he could cover up and report only favorable things—as, it seems, everyone else does. However, many staff people can report the foreman's activities to his boss and higher management. The union can and does go over his head. So do inspection, cost-control, engineering, and other staff departments. Down to the foreman comes the question, "Why didn't you inform us?" Down come commands to cooperate with staff people. Down come new people and new studies of his workers' performance. A foreman's life is not a happy one.

The foreman in the historical perspective of the last half century has been compelled to make five major accommodations. These are the (1) ideological accommodation, (2) engineering accommodation, (3) personnel accommodation, (4) organizational-systems accommodation, and (5) labor-relations accommodation.

Ideological accommodation

The newly assigned foreman of fifty years ago was often a man who had won his place by a demonstration of hard work and skilled competence. He was a man who had worked many years on the bench. His advancement to the position of foreman was won by promotion within the ranks. Often he was merely told to "take charge." He knew what this meant because he had worked for other foremen, and he followed their example. The ideological commitment to represent management was a stern requirement in the days when labor unions were regarded as conspiracies. The foreman's responsibilities for production and discipline required a strong-willed man. Even today, the commitment represents a marked adjustment in work and social role. As one foreman commented:

> You can't treat the men as equals. They take advantage of good treatment. When I used to be a man on the line, I knew the way I'd like to be treated if I were to be happy on the job. When I got to be foreman, I started to treat my men in the same way—in other words, the way I'd like to be treated—but you just can't do it. You can't change overnight what's been going on for fifteen years; and these men have just been spoiled by not having too good supervisors in the past. They can always quit if they don't like the job.[4]

The new foreman must weigh his behavior in terms of its effect on his men's respect and on his ability to secure discipline and cooperation. He must neither commit the sin of officiousness nor the folly of fraternity. If he has his beer with the men after work, he must be judicious. When his wife visits with other wives of the men in her husband's department, she must learn that she is now the foreman's wife and what she says about people in the plant will be repeated with authority. Most managements urge their new foremen and their wives to identify with a new social circle of foremen and their wives. The old social ties are to be cut slowly but surely, with informal friendships replaced by more formal contacts. On the job, the logics of cost and efficiency become guides to supervisory behavior and when thoroughly inculcated mark the transition of the worker to foreman. His main function is to ensure that the production or service schedules established for him are actually fulfilled. While performing this job, our foreman of fifty years ago handled such contributory functions as hiring, transferring, and firing men, training new people, planning the production schedule, finding ways of improving machines and production, dealing with complaints, absences, and lateness, inspecting the product, and working to improve quality. He would commonly step into the line or up to the bench to work on production or repair a machine tool. In the evening he might call at the home or at the hospital and chat with a worker who was ill. These functions were almost autonomous. The foreman was in charge, and he made the decisions. He was a skilled worker, clothed with some latitude of decision-making authority.

Engineering accommodation

The first major development to alter the foreman's job was the growth of engineering departments. Engineering became both a research-development and an engineering-improvement division. The foreman was given instructions as to what machines he was to have, how they were to be placed, how he was to operate them, and how they were to be cared for. He was told he must go by the blueprints even when his judgment told him that there was a better way to proceed. Sometimes he could have his say, but usually the engineers had their way. When time-and-motion engineers were sent into the shop, the foreman was asked to give the men a "pep talk" about cooperation while the engineers set production quotas and the amount of time the worker could have in the toilet. When piece-rate incen-

tives were introduced, foremen were asked to push their groups into line with the pace-setters.

The inventor of techniques of time-and-motion study, Frederick J. Taylor, once testified what this role had meant when he was the foreman of a work group operating his system:

> I was a young man in years, but I give you my word I was great deal older than I am now, what with the worry, meanness, and contemptibleness of the whole damn thing. It is a horrid life for any man to live, not to be able to look any workman in the face all day long without seeing hostility there, and feeling that every man around you is your virtual enemy. These men were a nice lot of fellows, and many of them were my friends outside the works. This life was a miserable one, and I made up my mind to either get out of the business entirely and go into some other line of work or to find some remedy for this unbearable condition.[5]

To this day the foreman's most bitter rival is the engineer. He sees himself pitting his hard-earned plant knowledge of technical skill against the college-textbook knowledge of the engineers. The foreman likes to catch engineers suggesting some foolish or less efficient method which they have devised in ignorance of better traditional techniques. It is usually an uneven contest, and the foreman must make the accommodation.

Personnel accommodation

When a personnel department is established, it usually begins as an employment office. Prospective employees are screened, and although office supervisors often make the decision as to whom they shall hire, the plant foreman is usually told to put to work the new employees whom the personnel department has hired. It is explained to the foreman that this arrangement is in his best interests. Personnel can select the best-qualified persons through testing and interviewing programs. This procedure saves the foreman time to concentrate on his production responsibilities. Top management approves with secret satisfaction, since the foreman can no longer pad the payroll with his own favorites. There was a time when a foreman could recruit a work force composed of sons, immediate relatives, and neighborhood friends. In this manner he built a personal loyalty which was not always in management's interest.

What was done with employment was subsequently done with every other personnel function of the foreman such as placement, training, transferring, making merit increases, and firing. In some cases the foreman could recommend and his word might carry weight. In other cases, like training, he might find his function removed by the establishment of a plant training school operated by the personnel department. He was told that all these things were done to help him. To the engineering helpers was added the corps of personnel helpers. Perhaps what hurt most was the new edict that he could recommend firing from his department but not from the company. One foreman described his reaction to this loss of function as follows:

I had this troublemaker. He was a solid gold bricker. He couldn't cut the buck on any job. I tried everything, but he was lazy and he was a loudmouth. I caught him in the toilet after being away from his machine for over an hour. I told him he was through and to go upstairs and pick up his check. And damn, do you know what those college boys up in personnel did? He gives them some bull about being sick and weakly, and the next day he is sitting at a bench in the department next to mine. He says to me, "Well, wise guy, you don't count for nothin' around here. Every time I see you I'm going to call you Mr. Nothin.'"

If the foreman complained to personnel, he was told that new facts were brought to light by the "exit interview" and that improvement in personnel relations necessitated more foreman training. Personnel was already planning a new course especially for foremen, and management was behind it one hundred per cent. To most foremen, this was the signal that they were in for another stretch in the charm school where they would be taught to be kind to their employees.

Organizational-systems accommodation

Organizational systems are the procedures and techniques worked out by such departments as production-planning and control, quality-control, finance and accounting, organizational-planning, and others. These departments all have their eyes on the plant floor where the money is made. Almost all changes proposed by management and staffs are aimed at the foreman and his workers, threatening the security or status of the foreman. The systems departments pose some of the greatest threats. Out of them pour new ideas and new production-scheduling techniques. The existence of such systems not only demanded of the foreman an accommodation to the changes required but also required him to act as a buffer between the staff personnel and the workers. Men in white collars started filtering through the shop and often badgered employees. First it was an inspector, then an expediter, after that it was men or women from any of the above departments. Sometimes counselors from the personnel department came around and asked if there were any problems that anyone had. The foreman could claim that all of these intrusions were making it difficult to meet production quotas; but the "helpers" kept coming, and he was forced to live with them. Paperwork became so heavy that the foreman began to complain that he couldn't get out on the floor. Clerks were assigned to him, but the management controls mounted. Management controls came to be regarded as a fundamental process in management. The foreman became involved in such control mechanisms as organization policies, rate of production, inventory, job specifications, planning, quality of production, product specifications, wages and salaries, costs, manpower, production methods, expenditures, public relations, and supervisory time.

He might take solace in the fact that everyone in management was getting much of this same treatment. But he was expected to get out production, spend time in contact with his people, and still make out reports with strict punctuality. A small fragment of one day's activity for a foreman in an assembly department is described as follows:

> The foreman was hurrying between two of the dozen workbenches in his department when the head of the plant maintenance department stopped him and thrust a jig into his hands.
> *Foreman:* Is this done?
> *Maintenance man:* What are we supposed to do with it?
> *Foreman:* We want a plastic base on that to insulate it.
> *Maintenance man:* We don't need the whole jig. Just give us the specifications.
> *Foreman:* And we need two more up like that.
> *Maintenance man: (taking back the jig).* Why didn't you say so? We will have to copy it. Do you have any pointers?
> The foreman went to a nearby cabinet and looked through some boxes. While he was looking, the maintenance man was paged on the plant-wide call system. The maintenance man was phoning nearby when the foreman turned around. A product engineer joined the foreman and began talking earnestly. The maintenance man hung up the phone and waited impatiently for the engineer to finish. They started a three-way discussion. Another engineer from the experimental section called the foreman away to get some partly finished instruments. The maintenance man left; the first engineer waited impatiently; Before the foreman could get the requested instruments, an employee stopped him to ask about some paperwork. An industrial engineer joined the product engineer, and they talked briefly until the foreman returned. The experimental-section engineer left, and the remaining two men turned to ask the foreman a series of technical questions. A girl

from the production line called him away to answer another question, and a foreman from another department came up to ask him for personnel to do some special packing.[6]

Note how the foreman has become exposed to strong pressures from several directions and how each pressure affects his capacity to handle the others. The organizational systems bring a tangle of interacting events with the foreman in the middle.

Labor-relations accommodation

The labor-relations accommodation came last and perhaps cut more heavily into the foreman's sense of independence than any one of the others. It was bad enough when the pressures were all management pressures from outside the department. Many foremen learned how to weaken and sometimes even nullify these pressures upon them. Unionization, however, meant that pressures from his subordinates were added. These came from stewards permanently stationed in his department. The elected steward would receive the greatest seniority and an opportunity to move freely among the workers soliciting grievances and complaints. These grievances and complaints represented potential trouble from higher management or higher union officials. Management's labor-relations head usually warned foremen of dire consequences which might come from the most innocent actions.

> Be careful what you say to a worker or the NLRB may get you for prejudicial remarks about unionization.
> Be careful what you do in firing a worker or the arbitrator will rule against you.
> Be careful on how you assign overtime or the steward will catch you on the seniority clause.
> Be careful on you transfers. The contract is strict on the proper procedure and pay.
> Just be careful—you could cause a strike by worsening our labor relations.
> In fact, if there is the slightest doubt in your mind, let us handle the problem.

The labor-relations climate can produce a work atmosphere full of foreboding and conspiratorial secrecy. The foreman is told to watch his lead men. "They are not in management and you can't trust them. They will be carrying anything they can find out into the union hall."

The steward is told to read his contract forward and backward and not let the foreman get away with anything. A steward relates how a foreman is dependent on the workers and the process they use to intimidate him:

A short time ago we had a lot of trouble with a certain foreman. He was an ex-committeeman by the way. He started out all right, was a good boy, but the guys took advantage of him. So he had to get back at them. He was making them toe the line ...no quitting early, work from whistle to whistle, no setting down, no horseplay, this and that. I told the committeeman there, "You do the same thing. Every time he does any work, even if he picks up a box, write a grievance, violation of paragraph 66, violation of paragraph 32, violation of paragraph so and so." The first thing you know grievances started mounting—finally had a pile like that.

Things got so bad that they called a meeting of the top committee. I told them that the guys naturally jump at a foreman when he gets that way. This foreman was removed from that department. He was moved to our department, and it's his last chance. If he doesn't make good in this department out he goes. So I went to the guy and told him, "It's your last chance here and you know it. You cooperate with us and we'll cooperate with you. If you don't we'll put the screws on you and out you go." Things are working out pretty good so far.[7]

The attitude of the foreman toward the union may be hostile or friendly, depending on his past experiences with it. If he has been a union man, he may not resent union restrictions on his activities. If he considers his job a step up the management ladder, he may resent the union's restrictions. In any case, it is another organization which limits his freedom of action.

The foreman's dilemma

These accommodations required of foremen represent historic changes in role demands. The foreman of today, in contrast with his predecessors, has lost functions in the engineering, personnel, and organizational areas of his concern. But with every loss in function he has acquired new obligations. He must know more about production, personnel, engineering, organizational procedures, and labor relations. His obligations have increased, his authority has diminished. He lives poised between the two worlds of management and labor. Donald Wray called the foremen the "marginal men of industry."[8] Fritz Roethlisberger called them "masters and victims of double talk."[9]

The foreman's work position is the only one in the entire structure that daily deals with *both* management and labor firsthand. His *difficulties arise not so much out of lack of authority as out of the relative impossibility of reconciling two rather incompatible ideologies or systems of sentiment.* Such a sharp cleavage does not appear among the upper levels because there is essential ideological agreement *within the management* hierarchy.

Management and worker ideologies whipsaw the foreman. The foreman's boss and all levels above him are imbued with the "logic of cost and efficiency": that is, their concern is to make profit by applying rational, economic principles to production. Consequently, they view the work plant as an impersonal economic machine which makes money. The workers are also units to be considered in this process of moneymaking. Although managers do not regard relations among themselves impersonally, they do think of problems on the plant floor as impersonal, financial ones.

The foreman's boss, the superintendent, has assimilated this ideology of cost and efficiency and tries to imbue it in his foreman. The latter, however, has to deal with workers who usually do not share management's conception of their role as cost items. Workers do not consider themselves as machines to be moved about and used according to the best logic of efficiency. They have emotional stakes in their work and want to be considered accordingly. Management is sometimes aware of this fact on its own level but often is not so on the worker's level. The superintendent's view of the men below the foremen is impersonal.

The foreman, like any worker in the structure, does not want to incur the disapproval of his boss openly by violating norms of efficient economic behavior; yet he must deal with the workers as people. He must meet situations which clear economic thinking cannot predict. He knows that he cannot disregard workers' sentiments about jobs, rates, profits, and procedures. He knows "it is impossible to uphold strictly the logic of efficiency without sometimes demoralizing the group." If he informs the superintendent of all the workers' resentments to management ideology, his boss will berate him for having so much dissension in his section. If he does not report these matters, his boss discovers them through other channels. Either alternative is dangerous.

The first-line supervisor as a general type

The discussion has centered around the foreman in production operations, but the inference has been made that the internal-organization forces now bearing upon the foreman are impinging on all supervisors in commercial, governmental, and educational institutions. The first-line supervisor can thus be considered a general type and the foreman's position as in the cultural lead. It may be hypothesized that any variations from this lead type are due solely to time lags in the historic process of organizational change. Meanwhile, variations in organizational size, structure, technology, and the like create temporary differences. We know now that technology knows no bounds and that mass production has techniques for organizing men as well as for producing goods and devices.[10] Neither technology nor mass production is any respecter of any institution, be it family, school, church, or traditional supervision pattern.

Elton Mayo pointed out that all supervisors and managers share three major functions. These are the technical, administrative, and human-relations functions. Floyd Mann and his associates have sought to get research evaluations of foremen and office supervisors, their central concern being with the technical, administrative, and human-relations functions of supervisors.[11] In the past five decades most attention has been directed toward the administrative and human-relations functions. A higher educational level is being demanded in supervisory posts. Some companies insist on the college graduate for the foreman's position and pay salaries between $8,000 and $12,000. It has been suggested that most supervisors, when they can shift their attention from the pressure of immediate assignments, hold the following human-relations goals:

1. To raise the level of human motivation
2. To increase the readiness of subordinates to accept change
3. To improve the quality of all decisions
4. To develop teamwork and morale
5. To further the individual development of employees.[12]

All supervisors are being "helped" today in the pursuit of their tasks—personnel departments help screen some of the applicants, training departments attempt to provide training on the administrative and human-relations functions, staff experts help explain the new machines and equipment from computers to visual aids. Special functionaries worry about organizational effectiveness, and the test specialists devise measurement techniques. Morale surveys, supervisory reviews, and exit interviewing are common techniques in large organizations.

The lines of command grow longer, and supervisors find themselves ever further alienated by communication and authority differentials between the top and the bottom rungs of management. No one is quite sure whether the supervisor is doing the job he should be doing. His paperwork is increasing, but almost everyone is agreed that it should be reduced. His conference time is increasing, but it is agreed that he should have more direct individual contact with members of his department. He is expected to get around more and find out what other departments are doing, but he cannot get away from his desk because of the pressure of reports. Top management cannot understand why is he unable to report more quickly, and his subordinates think he is spending too much time on desk work.

Max Weber's and Parkinson's predictions are coming to fruition. Weber predicted that as an organization grew in size it would engage a growing number of technical specialists who would set an increasing number of controls in motion. Parkinson claimed that administrative-staff growth would surpass the rate of growth in production personnel. These two forces of growth threaten the first-line supervisor with ever more controls and more reports. He becomes more of a manager than supervisor, and in some organizations like International Business Machines he is called a manager.

1 Bureau of the Census, *1960 Classified Index of Occupations and Industries* (Washington, D.C.: U.S. Department of Commerce), pp. 39–45, 73–75.

2 "Training Within Industry," *Job Relations Training* (Washington, D.C.: War Manpower Commission, June 1, 1944).

3 Bureau of the Census, *Current Population Reports,* Labor Force, Series P-57, No. 200 (Washington, D.C.: March 1959), p. 16.

4 F. J. Jasinski, "Human Relations Training: The Missing Link," *Personnel* (May 1956), p. 514.

5 Testimony of F. J. Taylor before Special Committee of the House of Representatives in 1912 to investigate Taylor and other systems of shop management.

6 David N. Ulrich, Donald R. Booz, and Paul R. Lawrence, *Management Behavior and Foreman Attitude* (Cambridge: Harvard Graduate School of Business Administration, 1950), pp. 30–31.

7 Delbert C. Miller and William H. Form, *Industrial Sociology,* Rev. ed. (New York: Harper & Row, Publishers, Inc., 1963), pp. 401–402.

8 Donald E. Wray, "Marginal Men of Industry: The Foremen," *American Journal of Sociology,* 54 (January, 1949), pp. 298–301.

9 Fritz J. Roethlisberger "The Foreman: Master and Victim of Double Talk," *Harvard Business Review* (Spring, 1945).

10 See Peter F. Drucker, *The New Society* (New York: Harper & Row, Publishers, Inc., 1949).

11 Floyd C. Mann and L. Richard Hoffman, *Automation and the Worker* (New York: Holt, Rinehart & Winston, Inc., 1960).

12 Robert Tannenbaum, Irving R. Weschler, and Fred Massarik, *Leadership and Organization* (New York: McGraw-Hill Book Company, 1961), p. 78.

* * *